New Developments in
Systemic Linguistics

Open Linguistics Series

The *Open Linguistic Series*, to which this book makes a significant contribution, is 'open' in two senses. First, it provides an open forum for works associated with any school of linguistics or with none. Linguistics has now emerged from a period in which many (but never all) of the most lively minds in the subject seemed to assume that transformational-generative grammar—or at least something fairly closely derived from it—would provide the main theoretical framework for linguistics for the forseeable future. In Kuhn's terms, linguistics had appeared to some to have reached the 'paradigm' stage. Reality today is very different. More and more scholars are working to improve and expand theories that were formerly scorned for not accepting as central the particular set of concerns highlighted in the Chomskyan approach—such as Halliday's systemic theory (as exemplified in this book) Lamb's stratificational model and Pike's tagmemics—while others are developing new theories. The series is open to all approaches, then—including work in the generativist-formalist tradition.

The second sense in which the series is 'open' is that it encourages works that open out 'core' linguistics in various ways: to encompass discourse and the description of natural texts; to explore the relationship between linguistics and its neighbouring disciplines such as psychology, sociology, philosophy, artificial intelligence, and cultural and literary studies; and to apply it in fields such as education and language pathology.

The series, then, is committed to the concept of an insightful interplay between theory and use. This book makes a significant contribution to the series in that it is the first to be devoted to one of the most fruitful of current linguistic theories: systemic linguistics.

Open Linguistics Series Editor
Robin F. Fawcett, University of Wales Institute of Science and Technology

Modal Expressions in English, Michael R. Perkins
Text and Tagmeme, Kenneth L. Pike and Evelyn G. Pike
The Semiotics of Culture and Language, eds: Robin P. Fawcett, M. A. K. Halliday, Sydney M. Lamb and Adam Makkai
Into the Mother Tongue: A Case Study in Early Language Develoment, Clare Painter
Language and the Nuclear Arms Debate: Nukespeak Today, ed.: Paul Chilton
Functional Approaches to Writing: Research Perspectives, ed.: Barbara Couture
The Structure of Social Interaction: A Systemic Approach to the Semiotics of Service Encounters, Eija Ventola
Grammar in the Construction of Texts, ed.: James Monaghan
On Meaning, A. J. Griemas, trans. by Paul Perron and Frank Collins
Biological Metaphor and Claddistic Classification: An Interdisciplinary Approach, eds.: Henry M. Hoenigswald and Linda F. Wiener

NEW DEVELOPMENTS IN SYSTEMIC LINGUISTICS

Volume 1: THEORY AND DESCRIPTION

Edited by
M. A. K. Halliday and Robin P. Fawcett

 Frances Pinter (Publishers),
London and New York

First published in Great Britain in 1987 by
Frances Pinter (Publishers) Limited
25 Floral Street, London WC2E 9DS

Printed in Great Britain

British Library Cataloguing in Publication Data
New developments in systemic linguistics.—
　(Open linguistics)
　Vol. 1: Theory and description
　1. Systemic grammar
　I. Halliday, M. A. K.　II. Fawcett, Robin P.
　III. Series
　410　P149
ISBN 0-86187-636-9

Typeset by Joshua Associates Limited, Oxford
Printed by SRP Ltd, Exeter

Contents

VOLUME 1 THEORY AND DESCRIPTION

Foreword   ix

Introduction   1
M. A. K. Halliday and Robin P. Fawcett

   0.1 The problem of how to make progress in linguistics—
      and keep your friends   1
   0.2 The other 'new developments'   5
   0.3 Conclusions   9

Part I Theory

  1 The meaning of features in systemic linguistics   14
  James R. Martin

   1.1 Systemic linguistics as an item and paradigm model   14
   1.2 The formal meaning of features   16
   1.3 The formal meaning of features and relational network
      linguistics   26
   1.4 The non-formal meaning of features   30
   1.5 Socio-semantic networks   34
   1.6 Speech functions and MOOD   35
   1.7 Conclusions   37

Part II Discourse

  2 Is teacher an unanalysed concept?   41
  Margaret Berry

   2.1 Introduction   41
   2.2 Some facts about classroom discourse   42
   2.3 The need for an explanation   43
   2.4 The type of explanation that could be offered   44
   2.5 Some facts about doctor–patient interviews and
      committee talk   46
   2.6 Some hypotheses that could account for the facts   48
   2.7 A further set of hypotheses   50

2.8 Future work to test the hypotheses 53
2.9 Conclusion 61

3 Sociosemantic networks and discourse structure 64
Geoffrey J. Turner

3.1 Introduction 64
3.2 The question of 'semantic structures' 64
3.3 Complementary emphases? 66
3.4 Discourse: layers of structure 67
3.5 Speech functions and discourse functions 69
3.6 Berry's proposals 78
3.7 Locating the Birmingham work and the sociosemantic
work 88
3.8 Conclusion 90

Part III Meta-functions

4 Meta-functions: aspects of their development, status and use
in systemic linguistics 94
Michael Gregory

4.1 The development of the concept of meta-functions 94
4.2 Two positions on meta-functions: M. A. K. Halliday
and R. P. Fawcett 97
4.3 J. R. Martin's proposed approach to register and meta-
functions 100

5 The logical and textual functions 107
Jeffrey Ellis

5.0 Introduction 107
5.1 The logical function 107
5.2 The textual function 114
5.3 Relations between the two functions 122

Part IV System networks in the lexico-grammar

6 The semantics of clause and verb for relational processes
in English 130
Robin P. Fawcett

6.1 Basic problems 130
6.2 Some primary choices in the relational process network 136
6.3 Further primary choices 143
6.4 From elegance to usability: some more delicate choices 162
6.5 Summary and conclusions 174

7 The grammarian's dream: lexis as most delicate grammar 184
Ruqaiya Hasan

7.1 The lexico-grammatical stratum 184

7.2 The lexico-grammar of acquisition: *gather*, *collect*,
     accumulate   187
7.3 The lexico-grammar of deprivation 1: *scatter*, *divide*,
     distribute   197
7.4 The lexico-grammar of deprivation 2: *strew*, *spill*, *share*   202
7.5 The continuity of grammar and lexis   206

8 Communicative function and semantics   212
   Christopher S. Butler

   8.1 Aims and scope   212
   8.2 Three approaches to indirect speech acts   212
   8.3 Communicative function as semantic   213
   8.4 The middle path   217
   8.5 The 'surface meaning' approach   220
   8.6 Beyond the semantics   222
   8.7 Conclusion   226

9 Continuative and inceptive adjuncts in English   230
   David J. Young

   9.0 Introduction   230
   9.1 The meaning of the items   231
   9.2 Suppletion: negative and interrogative clauses   232
   9.3 Aspect   239
   9.4 Conjunctive adjuncts   243

Part V The daughter dependency grammar version of the theory

10 Daughter dependency theory and systemic grammar   246
    R. A. Hudson

    10.1 Similarities between DDT and systemic grammar   246
    10.2 The role of features   247
    10.3 Sister dependencies   249
    10.4 Function labels   253
    10.5 System networks and classification rules   255

11 Voice neutrality and functional roles in the English clause: a
    contribution to daughter-dependency grammar   258
    J. Taglicht

    11.0 Introduction   258
    11.1 Functional roles in daughter dependency grammar   258
    11.2 Voice neutrality in English   259
    11.3 The feature [−personal] as a key to voice neutrality   260
    11.4 Raising and voice neutrality   264
    11.5 The functions of raised elements in the matrix clause   265
    11.6 Conclusion   267
          Appendix   269

Part VI Phonology

12 Aspects of word phonology   272
   V. Prakasam

   12.0 Introduction   272
   12.1 Phonetic features   272
   12.2 The basic component   273
   12.3 Efficacy of the functionalist approach   277
   12.4 Lexical registration   282
   12.5 Morphological function of 'sounds'   284
   12.6 Summary   285

Index to Volume 1   289

Foreword

This book is the first of two volumes. Together, they aim to give a picture of the major developments in systemic linguistics since those represented in Halliday and Martin's invaluable *Readings in Systemic Linguistics* (1981).

This first volume is the more theoretical. But the theory that it discusses is always theory that arises out of the description of the actual textual data of languages, and that leads back to further description—thus completing the cycle of the 'renewal of connection', which J. R. Firth wisely advised us to remember to make. One might even propose as a guiding principle: 'No theory without description, and no description without a theory'—the theory, of course, often turning out to be inadequate. It is this cycle of 'theory–description–theory' that is implied in the subtitle of 'theory and description'.

As it happens, many of the contributors to this first volume are among the better known names in systemic linguistics. But this should not be taken as implying that these scholars constitute some sort of priesthood of theoreticians; there are in fact quite a number of well-known systemicists who have NOT contributed a chapter to this volume—including, you may notice, Michael Halliday. I would argue strongly that EVERYONE who uses systemic ideas is potentially a 'systemic theoretician' (see Fawcett (in press)).

But there is a second type of 'renewal of connection', and it occurs when one tries to APPLY a piece of the description of a language—and so inevitably a piece of linguistic theory—to solving some problem that is extrinsic to linguistics. It would in fact be quite impossible to divide systemic linguists into the 'theoreticians' and the 'users of theory'. The fact is that all those who might be thought of as the 'theoreticians' of the school are deeply involved in 'applications' of various kinds; certainly this is true of all the contributors to this volume. But the very notion of developing a theory and then applying it is—or should be—a nonsense. The fact is that theories develop most creatively when descriptions of languages that 'realize' them are tested in applications of various sorts—and, very often, the theories are stretched by the exercise and in due course reworked. It might therefore have been more appropriate (though it would possibly have been less well understood by linguists at large) if we had given the second volume some such subtitle as 'the theory–description–use–theory cycle'. However, you will, I am sure, see what is intended.

The contributors to the second volume include some of the well-known names of systemic linguistics, but also many that may be less well known to theory-and-description-oriented 'systemics-watchers'. Many of these 'new' names are in fact fast becoming well known in their own fields, and their inclusion here reflects both the continuing flow of new scholars who are finding it helpful to use a systemic functional framework for understanding language, and the way in which it is being used in an ever-widening range of areas of application.

The two volumes together, then, combine to give a good picture of current activity in systemic linguistics.

Robin P. Fawcett
Penarth, *April 1987*

BIBLIOGRAPHY

Benson, J. and Greaves, W. S. (eds) (in press), *Systemic Functional Approaches to Discourse: Selected Papers from the Twelfth International Systemic Workshop*, Norwood, N.J., Ablex.
Fawcett, R. P. (in press), 'What makes a "good" system network good?: four pairs of concepts for such evaluations', in Benson and Greaves (eds) (in press).
Halliday, M. A. K. and Martin, J. R. (1981) (eds), *Readings in Systemic Linguistics*, London, Batsford.

Introduction

M. A. K. Halliday
University of Sydney

Robin D. Fawcett
University of Wales Institute of Science and Technology

0.1 THE PROBLEM OF HOW TO MAKE PROGRESS IN LINGUISTICS—AND KEEP YOUR FRIENDS

A title fairly frequently used for books of this type is *Current issues in . . .*, followed by whatever the name of the theory or the subject is. But we have preferred the perhaps less dramatic wording *New developments in . . . .* The choice was deliberate. 'Issues' are often seen as matters that divide people, so that the 'current issues' approach to discussing any phenomenon tends to reflect relationships of an adversarial kind.

It is not so long ago that the adversarial approach was the overwhelmingly dominant model of how to 'make progress' in linguistics. One scholar would propose one model for some area of language, often for some quite limited area of syntax; another scholar would then write a paper offering a battery of reasons why the first model should not be accepted as 'correct'. (The idea of 'correctness' is of course remarkable in itself, in what is essentially a process of exploration.) The assumption was that, if any of the reasons (however trivial, it sometimes seemed) found favour, the proponent of the first view was defeated, and his/her model was therefore to be rejected. It was 'trial by intellectual combat', using the weapons of 'logical' argument, and the major activity of linguists became that of attacking other linguists—with Chomsky as the biggest prize of all.

At first sight this quasi-Popperian approach has about it an intellectually attractive rigour. But it is not, in reality, how progress is made in linguistics or in any other science. Indeed, an excess of rigour may lead to rigor—that is, to rigor mortis. Today, very little indeed of the enormously complex theoretical and descriptive apparatus that was constructed in the brief period of the transformational-generative school's hegemony remains standing. Whatever the merits or demerits of the basic Chomskyan assumptions about the goals and methods of linguistics and the nature of language, the school's discourse practices certainly had many demerits, and probably contributed, in part, to the theory's demise. The aspect of the TG genre of intellectual discussion that is most unsatisfactory is that it leaves little room for the second scholar to take a positive line—to suggest, perhaps, that s/he finds much (or at least some!) common ground with the first approach, and that s/he might not have thought of the ideas being presented without the stimulus of the first scholar's work.

In practice, we make most of our progress not by attacking each other, but by BUILDING cooperatively on each other's ideas—by standing on each other's shoulders, in the well-used metaphor. We do this through a multiplicity of individual efforts that amount in effect to a kind of very loosely organized team work. We present our proposals for modelling language to our fellow explorers, orally or in writing, in a discourse in which evidence and counter-evidence is offered and ideas are exchanged, adopted, adapted and occasion-ally completely rejected—and there is no reason why this discussion should not be FRIENDLY. Intermingled with this social interaction come more individualistic phases, when we may perhaps develop a model further on our own, and try it out in text generation, text analysis, or in various applications in research or practice, sometimes with the help of our students. It is in this sort of way that we are likely to make genuine progress—rather than by trampling each other into the verbal mud (or, for the more genteel, scoring clever put-down points off each other). Indeed, in the long run it probably does not pay to put in the verbal boot too often; it can too easily become a substitute for reasoning. The better course is surely to make a straightforward statement of one's case—which may often usefully include an honest attempt to summarize the pros and cons of other possible approaches, and perhaps a discussion of the new approach's applicability for some specific purpose—and then simply to let other scholars consider the alternatives offered, and make up their own minds as to which is more helpful.

How does this discussion relate to the present volume? One of the current preoccupations of systemic linguistics, as became very clear in the round-table discussion at the Twelfth International Systemic Workshop at Ann Arbor, Michigan in 1985, is precisely with developing more appropriate styles of discussion—better generic structures, as it were, for our conference presentations, for our papers in journals and books such as this, and for our informal person-to-person discussions. These matters relate directly to the first of the 'new developments in systemic linguistics' to which we would like to draw attention: an increasing concern with methodology—and 'metho-dology' must include, as an important component, the way we talk to each other about our ideas. In one way or another, the expression of this concern can be found in many of the contributions to this book—sometimes overtly, as most prominently in Berry's chapter, and sometimes covertly. Other chapters which contribute interestingly to the question of how to relate one's own proposals to those of other linguists include those by Martin, Turner, Gregory, Ellis, Fawcett, Hasan, Butler and Taglicht.

Berry 1980 expressed the conviction that systemic linguistics needs a more hard-nosed approach to argumentation. Indeed, her chapter in this volume is a demonstration of one method of bringing a systematic approach to the development of our models, based on the ideas of the philosopher of science, Popper. Her meticulous spelling out of every step of her method of investigation will be welcomed by many as a guide to certain aspects of systemic methodology in general (e.g. her explanation of why the systems in her network are ordered in dependency as they are) and of her particular methodology for the task in hand. It is of course an IDEALIZED methodology; it is a procedure that few experienced practising linguists will ever in fact follow to the letter. Yet it is, in general terms, the line of approach that ANY linguist whose ideas are going to stand up MUST use. Berry may well be being unduly critical of many of her fellow systemicists, in so far as she seems to be implying that most of those other than herself do not use the same basic approach to developing their models of language. In fact most systemic linguists probably use similar procedures, at least in broad outline—though they certainly do not always make each step of their exploration explicit in their writings, so that they may appear to cut corners. And for some it may be a largely intuitive process. All practising linguists, then, will be grateful for this useful reminder of this type of research method.

But it should be pointed out that this Popperian style of research is not the ONLY way in which progress is made; there is a need too for the speculative new idea, for the vaguely perceived insight which, if published, may spark off further fruitful thinking in others, and ultimately lead to the development of a very different model from the earlier one. We can see this process at work in systemic theory in the major development from Scale and Category Grammar to Systemic Functional Grammar; the early intimations of the new model were little more than footnotes. Often the major steps of progress do NOT come from painstaking methodology—important though this is in its place—but from what has been called 'the creative imagination' (Barnes 1967). And for some people the creative imagination can work directly upon semi-consciously stored linguistic 'facts', resulting from years of analysing texts and thinking about language, in such a way as to produce models, or outline drafts of models, which despite their inexplicitness give a powerful sense of insight. This is not to claim that such insights do not, when confronted with further data, normally require modification—and it is before, during and after this explicit process of confrontation that the methodology described by Berry comes into its own. We would not wish to specify, however, that papers or books or individual chapters of a book such as this should consist of only one of these sorts of contribution, and this volume in fact contains both.[1]

This line of thought suggests that, while one legitimate method of working may be, as Berry advocates, to produce a tightly predictive (i.e. generative) grammar for a small set of data, an equally legitimate approach is to produce a looser, less predictive model based on a very much larger and so statistically more reliable set of data, which may in its early stages be so loose as to defy formalization—and then over a period of time progressively to tighten up the model and adjust it in the light of further data, as it is applied in the analysis or generation of text. It is mainly in this way, in practice, that systemic linguistics has developed, rather than through concentrating on a limited area of language such as syntax and developing falsifiable hypotheses that relate to it alone. The pattern can perhaps be described as one where a new insight for the overall model is followed by a period of testing, adjustment and a relative tightening up of the model; to be followed in turn by various applications (a very important stage); then possibly new insights and a reinterpretation of the existing model; and further testing and tightening up. The result of this long, slow process is that we are now in the position where quite large portions of systemic descriptions of language, both of clauses and their constituents and of discourse grammars, are at or close to the point where they are sufficiently explicit to be expressible as computer programs. Moreover it can be argued that it is precisely BECAUSE of this holistic, text-based approach (as opposed to what we might term the 'initially limited data' approach) that systemic linguistics has had fewer of the journeys down blind alleys that have characterized much of the work in the Chomskyan school. Neither approach, therefore, can in fact claim to be the ONLY legitimate one, and the two offer alternative routes to the ultimate goal of developing maximally predictive models.

Berry's chapter, then, not only makes a substantive contribution to the problem of how to relate social roles to discourse structure, but it also performs a useful service in raising questions about systemic methodology. And it contains, as well as a 'hard-nosed' approach to methodology, her appreciation of the work of others, even when what she is offering is intended to supersede it. Her chapter, like others, shows that it is possible at the same time to attend to the 'interactional' function of language, and so to look after one's relationship with one's colleagues, as one uses the 'heuristic' function to explore new matters.

Where, then, do we stand in relation to the main strands in thinking in the philosophy of science, as discussed by Berry 1980? Very broadly, we stand in the historical tradition of Francis Bacon—though with the important modification that any adequate methodology must give appropriate space for the working of the creative imagination as described, very informally, above. Magee (1973: 56) summarizes the stages thus: '1 observation and experiment; 2 inductive generalisation; 3 hypothesis; 4 attempted verification of hypothesis; 5 proof or disproof; 6 knowledge.' We see the approach of Popper (e.g. 1976) and Lakatos (e.g. 1970), which is so strongly recommended in Berry 1980, as a useful corrective to the over-optimism of expecting to 'prove' conclusively that something is so and to the over-absoluteness of the term 'knowledge', and much of their approach is relevant to the model-testing stage of our overall framework.[2] But if we were forced to chose between the Popper–Lakatos line and some other modern philosopher of science, we would have to side with Feyerabend (1975: 10) who says that 'the only principle that does not inhibit progress is: anything goes'. In systemic linguistics these days quite a lot is 'going', as this book and its companion volume demonstrate.

To summarize: we believe that there is no simple answer to the question 'How do we make progress in linguistics?'. Progress comes in a variety of ways—and certainly through the 'normal science' (to use Kuhn's term) of the systematic testing of hypotheses that arise in the framework of some model, as well as through the leaps, which may be small as well as large, of the creative imagination. Yet Berry may well be right, in the sense that systemic linguistics needs a higher proportion of publicly available so-called 'normal science' at this stage in its development—if only to make our approach to understanding the nature of language more accessible to others.

0.2 THE OTHER 'NEW DEVELOPMENTS'

The first 'new development', then, has been the growth of concern among systemic linguists with methodology. There have been many other new developments in systemic theory and description since those reflected in Halliday and Martin's 1981 seminal book, *Readings in Systemic Linguistics*. Many of them find a place in this book; some provide the motivation for the book's structure, while others occur at scattered points throughout the book. One or two, regrettably, are represented by no more than a passing remark; we shall return to these in due course. It is perhaps worth highlighting the following eight additional new developments.

The first is one that corresponds to a major development in linguistics at large in the 1970s and that is continuing strongly into the 1980s: the emphasis on text and DISCOURSE. Systemic linguistics has always emphasized strongly the use of its descriptions in textual analysis, and early work on INTONATION (Halliday 1963, 1967; Elmenoufy 1969), on STYLISTICS (Halliday 1964) on COLLOCATION (Halliday 1966; Sinclair 1966) and COHESION (Hasan 1968; developed in Halliday and Hasan 1976 and widely elsewhere) might give grounds for claiming that systemic linguistics—along with the Prague school—had already laid the groundwork for much of the fashionable emphasis in the 1970s on 'text linguistics'. But the important body of work at Birmingham, of which two major landmarks are Sinclair and Coulthard 1975, and Coulthard and Montgomery 1981, opened up a new vein of research in the structure of 'exchanges'. Some of the central papers are Halliday 1984, Burton 1981, Berry 1981a, b and c, Butler 1985b, and Martin 1985. (See also Fawcett, van der Mije and van Wissen in Volume 2.) The study of the larger discourse unit of the 'genre' (Hasan 1978; Ventola 1979; Martin 1985) has also been approached in systemic linguistics and, while it does not receive attention in the present volume, it does in volume 2, in Ventola's chapter. The present volume does, however, clearly illustrate the systemic interest in exchange structure in the chapters by Berry and Turner; see also Ellis on text and the textual component. Berry and Turner each propose an interesting extension of systemic theory, both building out from the view of exchange structure as presented by Berry (1981a, b and c). Berry breaks new ground— and in so doing opens up an important new research programme—in proposing explicit rules for relating SOCIAL ROLES such as 'teacher' to their 'realization' in specific EXCHANGE STRUCTURES—not, you will notice, directly in lexico-grammar. This addition to the framework suggested in Halliday's *Language as Social Semiotic* (1978) may prove a useful advance in our efforts to be more explicit in relating language to society, and her chapter is thus a small, early step to filling out and testing that outline model. Turner, on the other hand, takes the concept of SOCIO-SEMANTIC system networks, as developed by Halliday (1973) and himself (Turner 1973), and suggests a way of relating them to a modified version of Berry's proposals for exchanges. (For a recent discussion of socio-semantic networks, see Butler 1985a: 58–62 and 81–2).

The next few 'new developments' concern the area of language that has till recently been regarded unequivocally as the central area of linguistics: the lexico-grammar of the 'sentence' (clause-complex, clause, and their lower-ranking constituent units). The second development has been the concern to find the answer to the question: 'What are the necessary and sufficient CONDITIONS FOR INCLUDING A FEATURE IN A SYSTEM NETWORK?' This is the central topic of Martin's chapter, and it is part of a wider concern to make descriptions as consistent and powerful as possible. This concern with the motivation of features is certainly one that is widely shared and of long standing among systemicists. In 1973, for example, Fawcett wrote that 'semantic features (i.e. features in the transitivity, mood and theme etc. networks) must have some correlate in formal or intonational structure' (1973b/81: 157), and he has consistently maintained this principle ever since; see section 6.1 of his chapter. Halliday too has always required that, except under certain specifiable conditions, all systems have some realizational 'output'. Very similarly (though in relation to a different component of the overall model of language) Berry, at the start of section 2.7 of her chapter, states that she will include in her network 'ONLY THOSE which ... are NECESSARY ... for predicting the occurrence/non-occurrence of forms of discourse' (i.e. aspects of instances of discourse structures). Berry suggests that this 'aspect of my work may surprise other systemicists'; but we find this itself a little surprising, in that most systemicists would probably take a similar line. Is it really true of systemicists in general, as Berry goes on to suggest, that 'often, as systemicists, we clutter up our networks with features that we think just might perhaps conceivably be useful for some undisclosed purpose in the future ...'? (This is a different issue from that of the constraints on theory, where Halliday's concern with 'open-ness' leads him to favour a model that is both 'elastic' and 'extravagant', rather than one tailor-made to a particular interpretation of certain previously delimited 'facts'.) Martin, in his chapter, takes the view that the criteria for setting up systemic features have not been adequately stated, and he in fact redraws some of Halliday's early networks in the light of the conclusions reached. The same topic is discussed briefly by both Berry and Fawcett (see also Fawcett in press for a discussion of the concepts necessary to establish criteria for 'good' system networks.)

The third development has been a growing discussion about the status and number of the FUNCTIONAL COMPONENTS, or META-FUNCTIONS, and the two chapters by Gregory and Ellis bear directly on this question. Gregory suggests that the relationship between the different numbers of meta-functions distinguished by Halliday and Fawcett may be one akin to the system network notion of 'delicacy'. (This is the approach adopted in a recently published introductory systemic textbook (Morley 1985).) Gregory then discusses the meta-functions in relation to certain of Martin's proposals. Ellis provides the fullest discussion yet of the 'logical' meta-function, and relates it interestingly to the textual. It would perhaps be fair to say that, with the increase of work on making systemic functional grammars fully explicit, and so implementable in computers, there has been a growing awareness that the major role of the concept of the meta-functions, seen as groupings of system networks, is as a vital tool in presenting a SUMMARY OF THE BASIC PRINCIPLES of the relevant system networks—which of course has its formal expression in the SIMULTANEITY of the major system networks. The notion of meta-functions is therefore most valuable in practice as an EXPOSITORY aid—both for oneself, in teaching students, and in introducing colleagues to systemic theory. At the same time, however, it must be said that Halliday's concept of three major meta-functions has found a new area of application: Berry's 'multi-layered' approach to discourse is modelled upon the concept (as Turner's chapter brings out clearly), though it is not fully clear how far this is simply a useful starting point, and how far a feature of the model essential to its relationship to 'Level C' (as defined below).

A fourth development has been a continuing discussion about LEVELS. Into this is tied the question of whether it is necessary (or if not absolutely necessary, desirable) to have a stratum of SYSTEM NETWORKS at each level, or whether the final level is generated by realization rules/statements from the penultimate one (which may or may not make use of 'starting structures', as used in Fawcett 1980). If we leave aside the level of linguistic organization traditionally known as segmental phonology that is discussed in systemic terms in Prakasam's chapter, and if we do the same for the 'level' (or in some approaches 'component') of discourse, the question still remains of how many levels of system networks are necessary and/or desirable. Many, but not all, systemic linguists make a broad assumption that language is most insightfully modelled as a series of system networks at different levels, such that each has 'preselection rules/statements' that predetermine the features to be chosen in the networks on the level below, selected from the following:

A   A situation-specific 'sociosemantics' (e.g. Halliday 1973: 72f.) which may or may not be at the same 'level' as a 'discourse semantics' (see Turner's chapter), and which may be an alternative to or which might possibly preselect from B.

B   A 'pure' and generalized semantics, applicable in all situations, less closely form-related than C below (referred to programmatically in various places by Halliday (e.g. 1985: xx) and Butler (e.g. 1985a: 82), but so far unsupported by more than brief sketches of descriptions (e.g. Halliday 1984: 13).

C   The level where we find the well-known system networks of transitivity, mood, theme, etc.—Halliday's level of 'lexico-grammar', characterized as functional rather than formal, and sometimes also described by systemicists as 'semantics' (see Fawcett, *passim*, and Butler 1985a: 63).

D   A 'purely formal' level, as Hudson's systemic work increasingly became (see the chapters by Hudson and Taglicht).

In some possible configurations, C is the lowest level, and in some the lowest is D. Whichever of the two is the lowest level must be the source of the selection expression of features from which the syntactic structures of lexical items and intonation are realized, through realization statements/rules. Possible configurations of levels include (where '>' means 'predetermines options in'):

$$A > B > C; \quad A > B > D; \quad B > C; \quad B > D; \quad C; \quad D.$$

So far the only systemic models of language worked out in any significant degree of complexity consist of C alone (the majority, e.g. Halliday's initial version of the Nigel grammar and its subsequent extension by Mathiessen, and the chapters by Fawcett, Hasan and Young), or D alone (Hudson's 'purely syntactic' grammars, e.g. Hudson 1976, Taglicht's chapter). The chapters by Martin, Fawcett and Butler in particular discuss the question of levels in this sense, and a number of others refer to this problem in passing, or in order to relate it to discourse.

Tied closely in with the question of the number of levels has been a fifth development; a steady increase in the number of systemic linguists committed not just to providing a DESCRIPTIVE tool whose value might be verified informally through its usefulness in the analysis of texts, but a commitment to making models of language that are fully EXPLICIT (i.e. GENERATIVE). Chapters that exemplify this development include those by Berry, Fawcett, Hasan, Young, and Taglicht.

The sixth new development is the revived interest in PHONOLOGY other than intonation (intonation having been a continuing interest in systematic linguistics); there are two such chapters in Benson and Greaves 1985b by Catford and Mock, as well as Prakasam's chapter in this volume. In it he discusses a number of the issues involved in developing a systemic phonology, and he points out that while he himself has provided detailed systemic studies of Telugu phonology (Prakasam 1972, 1976 and, most recently, Chapters 1 and 2 of Prakasam 1985), 'the need for a similar serious systemic study of the English sound-system is clear'. A book of systemic writings on phonology is currently in preparation, edited by Davies and Mock.

The last two 'new developments' are not concerned with specific components of the model, but general approaches. The seventh development, then, has been the steadily growing acceptance among systemic linguists that, even though systemic theory is associated in the minds of most linguists with a SOCIOLOGICAL approach to language, it is an equally promising candidate as a COGNITIVE model of language. Indeed, those who take this view might well argue that it is in part BECAUSE of its social orientation that it provides a good basis for a cognitive model. The first systemic writers to use this perspective were Winograd 1972 and Fawcett 1973a, 1973b/81. It could be argued that all systemic contributions to work in artificial intelligence and computational linguistics—such as that of Mann and Mathiessen, Fawcett and Bateman— are by definition 'cognitive' (see Butler's useful summary of such work in Butler 1985a, and the chapters in Volume 2 by Bateman and Mathiessen). Similarly it could be said of ANY of the chapters in this book, including those by the most avowedly sociolinguistic or systemic linguists, that they contribute to an understanding of what must occur in the communicating human mind. (There is, of course, a deeper issue here, embodied in the whole concept of 'cognitive' interpretations, but that lies beyond our present scope.)

The final development to which we wish to direct attention is the emergence of a number of models of language which seem to assume most if not all of what we would take to be the basic systemic principles—and yet which appear to be seen by their proponents as something other than simply a type of systemic grammar. This view of their nature is marked by the association, sometimes only partly seriously, of a new name with the model. The first and best established is Hudson's DAUGHTER DEPENDENCY GRAMMAR. It is outlined in his chapter, exemplified for a complex area of the grammar of English in the chapter by Taglicht, and described most fully in Hudson 1976. Butler 1985b exemplifies the application of the principles developed for DDG syntax in the discourse component. Once again, Butler (1985a: 114–23) provides a valuable summary of this work. (We should point out that Hudson himself has since moved on to a much modified version called 'word grammar', in which there is virtually no connection with systemic linguistics; see Butler 1985a: 123–5.) The second systemic offspring is COMMUNICATION LINGUISTICS, as developed by Gregory and his colleagues Asp and Malcolm at York University, Toronto. Gregory refers to this in passing in his chapter, and a fuller outline is provided in Gregory 1985, with a sample analysis in Malcolm 1985. The suggestion is that the new model is a blend of systemic, stratificational and tagmemic insights. Finally, a group around Martin at Sydney are developing a more richly stratified approach to language in which great emphasis is placed upon revised and expanded register networks, and the concept of 'genre' is given a stratum of its own. A stage in the development of this model is exemplified in Martin 1985, and Ventola's chapter in Volume 2 shows the model at work in the description of a text, under the half-joking name of SYSTEMIOTICS (or SYSTEMIC SEMIOTICS). Perhaps its most challenging claim is the elevation of the concept of 'genre' to a role such that it 'predetermines' options in register, and so in the rest of language. (See also Ventola 1987.) Both Gregory and Martin are preparing fuller accounts of their models for publication in the *Open Linguistics Series*. How far these various models are significantly different from SYSTEMIC FUNCTIONAL LINGUISTICS is a question that can only be answered with the passage of time, and a careful testing and evaluation of the more mature versions of the alternative approaches, as these emerge. There is a value, we would suggest, in continuing to emphasize what we have in common as well as the insights that these various possible extensions to the overall model may in time be shown to have.

0.3 CONCLUSIONS

The growth of systemic linguistics in the last decade has been one of the significant features of linguistics in this period. The growing number of publications in the theory, of which as we have seen Butler 1985a provides a generally helpful overview, are only one indication of this.

One of the most attractive aspects of the systemic approach to linguistics is the way in which it allows those who work within its overall framework to grow, through contributing new ideas (some no doubt more likely to stand the test of time than others)—and this in turn enables the theory itself to grow.

At the same time, the areas in which it is being found useful as an 'applicable' model are growing too—some through steady expansion, such as literary stylistics, and some as the addition of new areas of application, such as the systemic contributions to Chilton's *The Language of the Nuclear Arms Debate: Nukespeak Today*, and areas such as speech therapy, as in Gotteri's contribution to Volume 2.

We hope you will find resources of both theory and description in this book which are of use for various purposes of application—and also in developing your own account of the very complex phenomena that we refer to collectively as 'language'.

NOTES

1. Because her methodology is so explicit, let us take as an example Berry's own study in this volume. Clearly, the framework she assumes suggests genuinely insightful relationships between situation and language, and the findings described here are extremely promising. But it is nonetheless possible to raise queries about the methodology that Berry herself employs. How can she be sure, one might ask, that the three particular 'facts' of discourse that she has selected as those to be explained, from the many that she could have chosen, are the ones that should decide the main patterns of the network? (She gives no reasons for selecting this particular trio.) In a wider model which sought to account for more 'facts', it just might emerge that other aspects of the data are equally or more central. (Berry does of course make it clear that she is prepared for this eventuality, and would if necessary start again from scratch.)

2. Berry (1980: 3) suggests that 'most systemic linguists do not attempt to begin with observation and experiment', and that 'most systemic linguists neglect . . . the setting up of explicit hypotheses and the testing of these'. We have to say that in our experience this is simply not so. First, the record of the contributions to systemic descriptions of English and many other languages that arise from observation of naturally occurring texts is widely recognized (cf. Butler 1985a: 164). Second, the fact is that linguists perform experiments all the time; typically these are not the time-consuming, semi-public, formally recorded laboratory experiments that we usually associate with the concept of an 'experiment', but 'thought experiments' which are typically momentary, private and unrecorded (but no less rigorous for that). Every judgement that a text is situationally inappropriate or ungrammatical is such an experiment, designed to test a hypothesis; so is every instance of running through a paradigm in search of a counter-example. However, it may well be the case that systemicists should do more to make explicit that they do in fact follow these basic scientific procedures.

BIBLIOGRAPHY

Barnes, K. C. (1967), *The Creative Imagination*, London, Friends Home Service.
Bazell, C. E., Catford, J. C. and Halliday, M. A. K. (eds) (1966), *In Memory of J. R. Firth*, London, Longman.
Benson, J. D. and Greaves, W. S. (eds) (1985a), *Systemic Perspectives on Discourse: Vol. 1 Selected Theoretical Papers from the Ninth International Systemic Workshop*, Norwood, N.J., Ablex.
—— and —— (eds) (1985b), *Systemic Perspectives on Discourse: Vol. 2 Selected Applied Papers from the Ninth International Systemic Workshop*, Norwood, N.J., Ablex.
Bernstein, B. (ed.) (1973), *Class, Codes and Control: Vol. 2 Applied Studies Towards a Sociology of Language*, London, Routledge & Kegan Paul.
Berry, M. (1980), 'They're all out of step except our Johnny: a discussion of motivation (or the lack of it) in systemic linguistics', University of Nottingham (mimeo.).
—— (1981a), 'Polarity, ellipticity elicitation and propositional development, their relevance to the well-formedness of an exchange', *Nottingham Linguistic Circular*, 10, no. 1, 36–63.
—— (1981b), 'Systemic linguistics and discourse analysis: a multi-layered approach to exchange structure', in Coulthard and Montgomery (eds) (1981: 120–45).
—— (1981c), 'Towards layers of exchange structure for directive exchanges', in *Network*, 2, 23–32.
Burton, D. (1981), 'Analyzing spoken discourse', in Coulthard and Montgomery (eds) (1981: 61–81).
Butler, C. S. (1985a), *Systemic linguistics: theory and application*, London, Batsford.
—— (1985b), 'Discourse systems and structures and their place within an overall systemic model', in Benson and Greaves (eds) (1985a: 213–28).
Chilton, P. (ed.) (1985), *Language and the Nuclear Arms Debate: Nukespeak Today*, London, Frances Pinter.
Coulthard, M. and Montgomery, M. (eds) (1981), *Studies in Discourse Analysis*, London, Routledge and Kegan Paul.
Davey, A. (1978), *Discourse Production: A Computer Model of Some Aspects of a Speaker*, Edinburgh, Edinburgh University Press.
Dressler, W. U. (ed.) (1978), *Current Trends in Textlinguistics*, Berlin and New York, de Gruyter.
Duthie, A. (ed.) (1964), *English Studies Today: Third Series*, Edinburgh, Edinburgh University Press.
Elmenoufy, A. (1969), *A Study of the Role of Intonation in the Grammar of English*, unpublished Ph.D. thesis, University of London.
Fawcett, R. P. (1973a), 'Systemic functional grammar in a cognitive model of language', University College London (mimeo).
—— (1973b/81), 'Generating a sentence in systemic functional grammar', University College London (mimeo), reprinted in Halliday and Martin (eds) (1981).
—— (1980), *Cognitive Linguistics and Social Interaction: Towards an Integrated Model of a Systemic Functional Grammar and the Other Components of an Interacting Mind*, Heidelberg, Julius Groos Verlag and Exeter University.
Fawcett, R. P., Halliday, M. A. K., Lamb, S. M. and Makkai, A. (eds) (1984a), *The Semiotics of Culture and Language: Vol. 1 Language as Social Semiotic*, London, Frances Pinter.
——, ——, —— and —— (eds) (1984b), *The Semiotics of Culture and Language: Vol. 2 Language and Other Semiotic Systems of Culture*, London, Frances Pinter.

Fawcett, R. P., van der Mije, A. and van Wissen, C. (forthcoming), 'Towards a systemic flowchart model for local discourse structure', in Fawcett and Young (forthcoming).

Fawcett, R. P. and Young, D. J. (eds) (forthcoming), *New Developments in Systematic Linguistics: vol. 2 Theory and Application*, London, Frances Pinter.

Feyerabend, P. (1975), *Against Method*, London, Verso.

Freeman, D. C. (ed.) (1970), *Linguistics and Literary Style*, New York, Holt, Rinehart and Winston.

Gotteri, N. (forthcoming), 'Systemic linguistics in language pathology', in Fawcett and Young (eds) (forthcoming).

Gregory, M. (1985), 'Towards "Communication Linguistics": a framework', in Benson and Greaves (eds) (1985a: 119–34).

Halliday, M. A. K. (1963), 'Intonation and English Grammar', in *Trans. Phil. Soc.*, 143–69.

—— (1964), 'Descriptive linguistics in literary studies', in Duthie (1964: 25–39), reprinted in Freeman (ed.) (1970: 57–72).

—— (1966), 'Lexis as a linguistic level', in Bazell *et al.* (eds) (1966: 148–62).

—— (1967), *Intonation and Grammar in British English*, The Hague, Mouton.

—— (1970), *A Course in Spoken English: Intonation*, London, Oxford University Press.

—— (1973), *Explorations in the Functions of Language*, London, Edward Arnold.

—— (1978), *Language as Social Semiotic: The Social Interpretation of Language and Meaning*, London, Edward Arnold.

—— (1984), 'Language as code and language as behaviour: a systemic-functional interpretation of the nature of ontogenesis of dialogue', in Fawcett *et al.* (eds) (1984: 3–35).

—— (1985), *An Introduction to Functional Grammar*, London, Edward Arnold.

Halliday, M. A. K. and Hasan, R. (1976), *Cohesion in English*, London, Longman.

Halliday, M. A. K. and Martin, J. R. (1981) (eds), *Readings in Systemic Linguistics*, London, Batsford.

Hasan, R. (1968), *Grammatical Cohesion in Spoken and Written English: Part One*, Programme in Linguistics and English Teaching Paper 7, London, Longman.

—— (1978), 'Text in the systemic functional model', in Dressler (ed.) (1978: 228–46).

Hudson, R. A. (1976), *Arguments for a Non-Transformational Grammar*, Chicago, Chicago University Press.

Lakatos, I. (1970), 'Falsification and the scientific methodology of research programmes', in Lakatos and Musgrave (eds) (1970).

Lakatos, I. and Musgrave, A. (eds) (1970), *Criticisms and the Growth of Knowledge*, London, Cambridge University Press.

Magee, B. (1973), *Popper*, Glasgow, Fontana.

Malcolm, K. (1985), 'Communication linguistics: a sample analysis', in Benson and Greaves (eds) (1985b: 136–51).

Martin, J. R. (1985), 'Process and text: two aspects of human semiosis', in Benson and and Greaves (eds) (1985a: 248–74).

Morley, G. D. (1985), *An Introduction to Systemic Grammar*, London, Macmillan.

Popper, K. (1976), *Unended Quest: An Intellectual Biography*, Glasgow, Fontana.

Prakasam, V. (1972), *A Systemic Treatment of Certain Aspects of Telugu Phonology*, Ph.D. thesis, University of York.

—— (1976), 'A functional view of phonological features', *Acta Linguistica Hungaricae*, 26 (−2), 77–88.

—— (1985), *The Linguistic Spectrum*, Patalia, India, Punjabi University.

Sinclair, J. McH. (1966), 'Beginning the study of lexis', in Bazell *et al.* (eds) (1966: 410–30).

Sinclair, J. McH. and Coulthard, R. M. (1975), *Towards an Analysis of Discourse: The English Used by Teachers and Pupils*, London, Oxford University Press.

Turner, G. (1973), 'Social class and children's language of control at age 5 and age 7', in Bernstein (1973: 135–207).

Ventola, E. (1979), 'The structure of casual conversation in English', *Journal of Pragmatics*, 3, 267–98.

—— (1987), *The Structure of Social Interaction: A Systemic Approach to the Semiotics of Service Encounters*, London, Frances Pinter.

Winograd, T. (1972), *Understanding Natural Language*, Edinburgh, Edinburgh University Press.

Part I
Theory

1 The meaning of features in systemic linguistics

James R. Martin
University of Sydney

This chapter is concerned with the ways in which paradigmatic relations are formalized in systemic descriptions of natural language. Central to this discussion will be the use of FEATURES in SYSTEM NETWORKS. A number of criteria will be established for motivating features and certain notational conventions will be proposed which mark features according to the type of meaning they encode.

1.1 SYSTEMIC LINGUISTICS AS AN ITEM AND PARADIGM MODEL

Hockett's classic article, 'Two models of grammatical description' (1954), outlined the two types of model which underlie most Bloomfieldian research, contrasting the ITEM AND ARRANGEMENT with the ITEM AND PROCESS approach. These two models, albeit soon to be formalized in a generative way by Lamb and Chomsky respectively, have continued to provide the basis for a large number of descriptions since that time. Significantly, Hockett remarks at the beginning of his article that one important descriptive tradition, the WORD AND PARADIGM model, would not be considered. It is this third model, more appropriately designated an ITEM AND PARADIGM model by Hudson (1973), which in fact is related to systemic linguistics in much the same way as the item and arrangement model gave birth to stratificational grammar and the item and process model to transformational grammar.

As is the case with many of the descriptive techniques used by linguists today, the first explicit formulation of an item and paradigm description is found in the work of Harris. In his 'A componential analysis of a Hebrew paradigm' (1948), Harris tackles the problem of describing portmanteau items lacking a constituency of their own. His distributional approach effected a componential analysis of a paradigm of the Hebrew verb. Harris's COMPONENTS would be referred to as FEATURES in systemic linguistics. In effect these 'components' or 'features' are the names placed on rows and columns in paradigms.

The results of Harris's analysis are presented systemically in Figure 1.1. Harris would of course have eschewed the names given to features in this

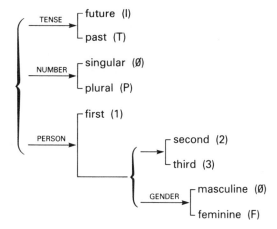

Figure 1.1 A systemic representation of Harris's analysis

network as an incursion of meaning into the analysis. His symbols for the components, in some cases not as abstract as one might expect, are given in brackets after the features to which they correspond. Figure 1.1 classifies the morphemes considered according to TENSE, NUMBER, PERSON and GENDER. The verbs Harris considers are either [future] or [past], either [singular] or [plural], either [first] or not, and if not, then either [second] or [third] and either [masculine] or [feminine]. (Note that features from system networks are by convention shown in running text by square brackets.) In Figure 1.2 the

feature bundles	Hebrew morpheme	English gloss
[past, singular, first]	-ti	'I did'
[past, singular, second, masculine]	-ta	'you did'
[past, singular, second, feminine]	-t	'you did'
[past, singular, third, masculine]	Ø	'he did'
[past, singular, third, feminine]	-a	'she did'
[past, plural, first]	-nu	'we did'
[past, plural, second, masculine]	-tem	'you did'
[past, plural, second, feminine]	-ten	'you did'
[past, plural, third, masculine]	-u	'they did'
[past, plural, third, feminine]	-u	'they did'
[future, singular, first]	a-	'I will'
[future, singular, second, masculine]	t-	'you will'
[future, singular, second, feminine]	t . . . i	'you will'
[future, singular, third, masculine]	y-	'he will'
[future, singular, third, feminine]	t-	'she will'
[future, plural, first]	n-	'we will'
[future, plural, second, masculine]	t . . . u	'you will'
[future, plural, second, feminine]	t . . . na	'you will'
[future, plural, third, masculine]	y . . . u	'they will'
[future, plural, third, feminine]	t . . . na	'they will'

Figure 1.2 The exponence of the network in Figure 1.1

items which realize the bundles of features generated by the network in Figure 1.1 are presented along with English glosses. Harris's article demonstrates that paradigmatic relations in language can be described with the same kind of distributional rigour as syntagmatic ones. Unfortunately, not all linguists have been as careful about motivating features in their descriptions.

1.2 THE FORMAL MEANING OF FEATURES

It is clear that if systemic grammars are to function as explicit generative models, then system networks must include at least those features necessary for generating well-formed structures in a given language. So one can begin exploring the meaning of features in systemic linguistics by establishing criteria which motivate these features in a given network. In other words, one is asking how the presence of features in a network designed to generate well-formed structures can be justified.

For reasons discussed below it is necessary to distinguish TERMINAL from NON-TERMINAL features. To begin, attention will be focused on non-terminal features. The most DELICATE features in the networks used as examples are neutral with respect to terminality unless they are specified as terminal: that is, the example networks are not necessarily exhaustive in delicacy unless so described.

The argumentation developed here is easiest to follow if a three term system like that in Figure 1.3 is presented, and attention is given to specifying those conditions under which a systemicist is justified in rewriting this system as the network in Figure 1.4, which contains two systems and an additional feature [x]. The transformational-looking arrow between figures is intended to capture a systemicist's generalizing inclinations.

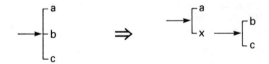

Figure 1.3   **Figure 1.4**

One of the central concerns in motivating a feature is that it have some REFLEX IN FORM (cf. Fawcett 1973/81: 157 and 1980: 101); that is, that it have some generative consequences when systems are related to syntagmatic patterns through REALIZATION RULES. Exactly how this 'renewal of connection', to use Firth's phrase, is effected varies according to the type of realization rule employed. Realization rules are of four general types (cf. Huddleston 1981 and Henrici 1981).

1. Rules which relate features on one RANK or STRATUM to features on another rank or stratum, i.e. DAUGHTER DEPENDENCY RULES, if between ranks on the

same stratum (cf. Hudson 1976). For example, [receptive] clauses require a [passive] verbal group (cf. Halliday 1967).

2. Rules which relate features of one constituent to features of one of its structural sisters, i.e. SISTER DEPENDENCY RULES (cf. Hudson 1976). For example, [factive] verbs can take a [fact] complement.

3. Rules by which features are realized through the insertion of GRAMMATICAL FUNCTIONS or ELEMENTS OF STRUCTURE, i.e. FUNCTION ASSIGNMENT RULES in Hudson 1971 or another type of daughter dependency rule in Halliday 1969; Hudson 1971; Berry 1977. For example, the clause feature [indicative] is realized by the insertion of the function Subject (cf. Halliday 1969).

4. Rules which sequence and conflate functions, bundles of features, or elements of structure, i.e. SEQUENCING RULES (cf. Hudson 1971 and 1976). For example, the clause feature [declarative] concatenates the functions Subject and Finite as Subject^Finite (cf. Halliday 1969).

Initially, then, a feature may be defined as having some reflex in form if it is mentioned in any of these four general types of realization rule.

We shall assume that features [a], [b] and [c] in Figure 1.3 each have a reflex in form, but in order to motivate [x], it must be additionally true that:

(i) [b] and [c] each PRESELECT the same feature in a subsequently entered network;

or (ii) [b] and [c] are mentioned disjunctively in a sister dependency rule;

or (iii) [b] and [c] each specify the insertion of the same constituent;

or (iv) [b] and [c] are mentioned disjunctively in a sequencing rule.

Conditions (i)–(iv) are represented in Figures 1.5, 1.6, 1.7 and 1.8 respectively. Should any of these conditions hold, feature [x] could be inserted to generalize the CONSTITUTIONAL or DISTRIBUTIONAL consequences [b] and [c] share. In effect, this generalization does not simplify the grammar as a whole. Disjunctions are avoided in the realization rules, but an extra feature and system are added to the network. This shift in descriptive responsibility is characteristic of systemic description where system networks form the creative and generalizing heart of the grammar.

$$[b] \longrightarrow [w] \qquad\qquad [b] \vee [c] \longrightarrow [w]$$

$$[c] \longrightarrow [w]$$

Figure 1.5: A Daughter dependency **Figure 1.6: A** Sister dependency rule
rule

$$[b] \searrow +Jm \qquad\qquad [b] \vee [c] \longrightarrow [w]$$

$$[c] \searrow +Jm$$

Figure 1.7: A Function insertion rule   **Figure 1.8: A** Sequencing rule

Criterion A in Figures 1.5–1.8 summarizes the motivation for features discussed above.

A. *A feature is motivated if it has some reflex in form*

It is criterion A which justifies writing the MOOD network for English as Figure 1.10 rather than Figure 1.9. The features [declarative] and [interrogative] in Figure 1.9 both specify the insertion of the function Subject, so the feature [indicative] can be inserted into Figure 1.10 to capture this generalization.

Features in systemic descriptions are realized either through STRUCTURES or LEXICAL ITEMS. The phrase 'reflex in form' is intended to embrace both types of formal exponence and must be interpreted accordingly.

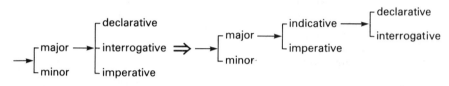

Figure 1.9   **Figure 1.10**

Hudson 1976 suggests that it is not enough for a feature to have a distributional or a constitutional reflex in form, but that only features having both types of reflex in form are justified. Constraining networks in this way makes necessary sister dependency rules which are not used in other versions of systemic grammar. Hudson's proposal entails a large shift in weak generative power away from system networks and into the realization rules. These ideas warrant serious consideration but will not be discussed further here. It is important to note in passing that the ways in which features are motivated in systemic descriptions have very significant ramifications for the shape of systemic grammars as a whole.

Criterion A motivates features with respect to their structural output in a systemic generative model. Next, a number of network internal motivations for features will be considered.

If both [b] and [c] act as an entry condition for some system containing the features [e] and [f], as in Figure 1.11, then it is possible to make a generalization in terms of the networks itself. In effect, the choice of [b] or [c] is simultaneous with the selection of [e] or [f]. In order to avoid presenting these

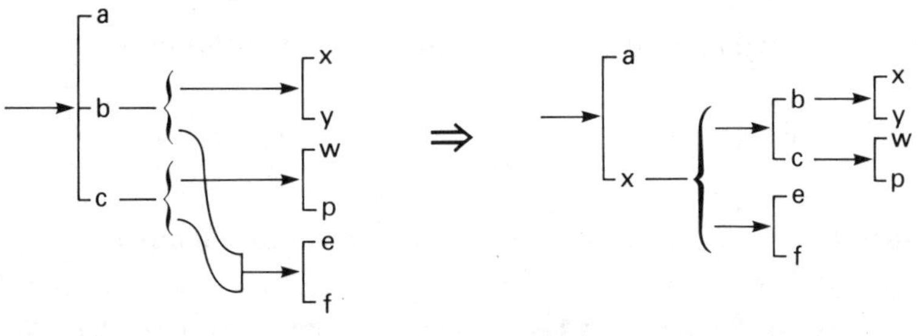

Figure 1.11   **Figure 1.12**

choices at different stages in delicacy, feature [x] can be inserted as an entry condition for the selection of either [b] or [c] and either [e] or [f] as in Figure 1.12. This sort of generalization is typical of systemic descriptions, and was incorporated in the systemic representation of Harris's analysis in Figure 1.1 above (cf. Fawcett, forthcoming, section 6). So a second criterion can be proposed.

B. *A feature is motivated if it acts as an entry condition for simultaneous systems*

Features will be described here as appearing in a CONJUNCTIVE ENVIRONMENT when both may be selected in a single derivation and as in a DISJUNCTIVE ENVIRONMENT when only one can be so selected. In Figure 1.13, features [b] and [c] can be interpreted as appearing in either a disjunctive or a conjunctive environment. By adding the features [x] and [y] as in Figure 1.14, a weak generalization can be incorporated in the grammar through a left-facing 'or' bracket. Because they in one sense neutralize less delicate options, such brackets are viewed with suspicion by some systemicists. Their absence from a network is at least a measure of its elegance. Hudson 1976 claims they are unnecessary in a grammar including sister dependency rules. However uneasy these brackets make systemicists feel, they are not always easy to avoid (cf. Fawcett, forthcoming, section 5; and Fawcett 1980: 144–5). Thus a further criterion is proposed.

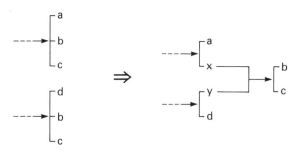

Figure 1.13   **Figure 1.14**

C. *A feature is motivated if it acts as part of a disjunctive entry condition for a more delicate system*

The need for a further criterion is illustrated in Figure 1.15. Here [x] and [y] appear in a conjunctive environment. If both are selected, they form a

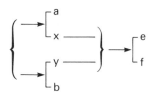

Figure 1.15

compound entry condition to the system containing [e] and [f]. So criterion D is proposed.

D. *A feature is motivated if it acts as part of a conjunctive entry condition to a more delicate system*

Paradigms in natural language are not always symmetrical. In light of this systemicists have employed a number of MARKEDNESS CONVENTIONS which condition networks internally and prevent them from generating bundles of features which have no realization. This markedness is indicated through the indexing of features in order to express what are effectively types of preselection within, rather than between, networks. Three types of markedness obtain in conjunctive environments: POSITIVE, NEGATIVE and CONDITIONAL.

An early example of NEGATIVE marking is found in Huddleston and Uren 1969. Figure 1.16 represents the kind of conditioning they placed on networks when discussing MOOD in French. Feature [f] can be selected only if [c] is not. Figure 1.16 generates the following bundles of features: [a, d], [a, e], [a, f], [b, d], [b, e], [b, f], [c, d], [c, e]; the bundle [c, f] is excluded.

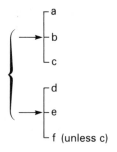

Figure 1.16 Negative marking (1)

Negative marking has not been used by other systemicists. This may be because it is unnecessary when the systems involved are binary ones. Positive marking, as developed by Halliday, could be used to re-express Figure 1.17 as Figure 1.18. The asterisk indicates that [d] is unmarked with respect to all environments—that is, if [a], then always [d]. POSITIVE marking can be illustrated with respect to the systems of nasality and voicing as they apply to plosive phonemes in English. There are no voiceless nasals in English, so the paradigm in Figure 1.19 has an empty box. This pattern can be expressed

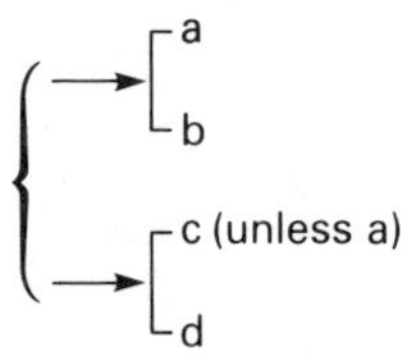

Figure 1.17 Negative marking (2) 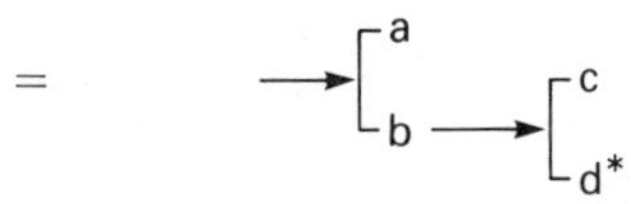   **Figure 1.18** Positive marking (1)

	nasal	non-nasal
voiced	/m,n,ŋ/	/b,d,g/
voiceless	—	/p,t,k/

Figure 1.19 Nasality and voice for English plosives

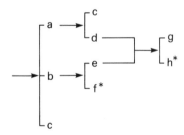

Figure 1.20 Negative marking (3)   **Figure 1.21** Positive marking (2)

systemically using either negative marking as in Figure 1.20 or positive marking as in Figure 1.21.

It is sometimes that case that there is more than a single tangential term in the superordinate systems associated with positive marking of this kind. This happens whenever there is a complex entry condition to a system, involving either disjunction or conjunction. In such cases, the tangential terms (i.e. [a] in Figure 1.18 or [voiceless] in Figure 1.19) may be in a different markedness relation to the starred feature. It thus becomes necessary to indicate which of the tangential terms is involved. This is achieved through paired symbols and is illustrated in Figure 1.22. This network states that [h] is unmarked with

Figure 1.22 Positive marking with paired symbols

respect to [f]; in other words, if [f], then always [h]. Paired symbols are read off from left to right in delicacy: if 'the less delicate of the pair', then 'the more delicate'. A mnemonically clearer notation would involve the use of an 'if/then'-derived I/T notation. Figures 1.21 and 1.22 would be expressed as, using the notation of, Figures 1.23 and 1.24. The Is and Ts would have to be indexed (e.g. I1/T1, I2/T2, etc.) to clarify networks with more than one such markedness relation involved. For this notation to be equivalent to Halliday's positive marking it would have to be constrained so that Is can only be attached to tangential features in systems superordinate to features marked

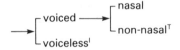

Figure 1.23 I/T version of Figure 1.21

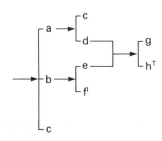

Figure 1.24 I/T version of Figure 1.22

with T. Were the I and T attached to simultaneous features, or were T less delicate than I, this would indicate an increase in the generative power of system networks. For this reason, some caution should be exercised before introducing the I/T notation for reasons of readability.

CONDITIONAL marking of simultaneous features is used by Hudson 1973 and is illustrated in Figure 1.25. Here the features involved are simultaneous, and [f] can be selected as long as [c] is too. Hudson's notation for this is presented in Figure 1.26, and the I/T alternative in Figure 1.27.

Figure 1.25 Conditional marking

Figure 1.26 Hudson's version of Figure 1.25

Figure 1.27 The I/T version of Figure 1.25

Given these marking conventions, one can imagine cases like those in Figures 1.28, 1.30 and 1.32 where, respectively: [f] can be selected unless [b] or [c] are; [f] is unmarked with respect to both [b] and [c]; and [f] can be selected as long as [b] or [c] are. Feature [x] could then be inserted to generalize this network internal conditioning as in Figures 1.29, 1.32 and 1.33.

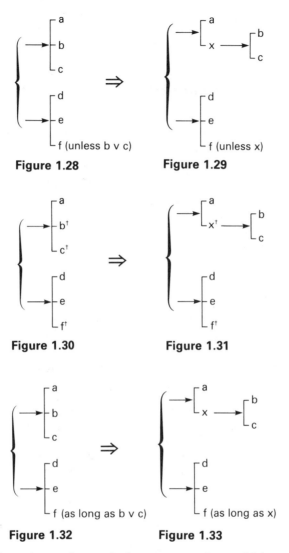

Figure 1.28   **Figure 1.29**

Figure 1.30   **Figure 1.31**

Figure 1.32   **Figure 1.33**

Up to this point, only markedness conventions which are NETWORK INTERNAL have been considered. There is one type of marking, however, which interacts with realization rules. Hudson 1974 has employed an asterisk beside a feature to indicate that it must be selected unless another feature in the system has been preselected by some realization rule. This type of marking will be referred to as DERIVATIONAL marking. In Figure 1.34, [c] must be selected unless [d] is preselected by such a rule. In Figure 1.35, either [b] or [c] may be selected unless [a] is preselected. So feature [x] can be inserted as in Figure 1.36 to capture this generalization. As long as systemicists continue to employ these four markedness conventions, a further criterion is necessary.

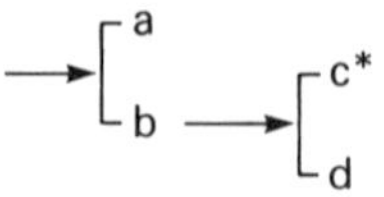

Figure 1.34 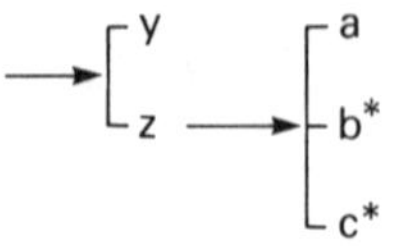   **Figure 1.35** 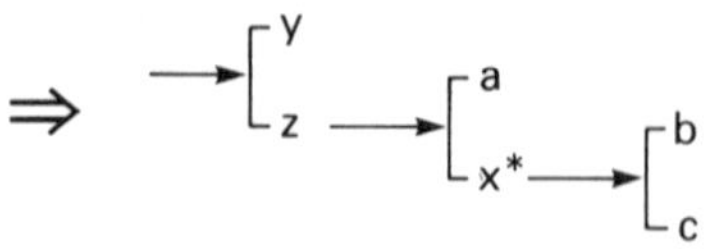   **Figure 1.36**

E. *A feature is motivated if it is associated with a positive, negative, conditional, or
derivational markedness convention*

As indicated above, special consideration must be given to terminal features
in light of criteria A through E. For example, given that features [a], [b] and [c]
in Figure 1.37 are motivated by A through E but [d] is not, one cannot simply
remove [d] from the description and be left with a well-formed system. As yet
systemicists have not provided an interpretation for Figure 1.38 (see, however,
the discussion of GATES below).

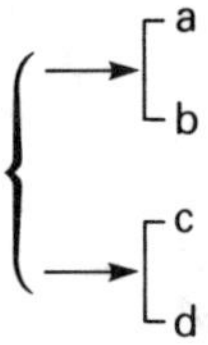

Figure 1.37 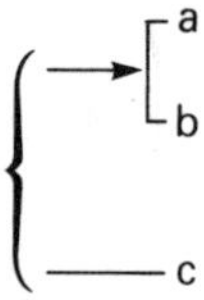   **Figure 1.38**

Similarly, terminal features in a disjunctive environment cannot simply be
removed when unmotivated by A through E. Assuming that [a], [b] and [c]
are so motivated in Figure 1.39, it is not possible to eliminate [d] and conflate
[c] with [y], since the choice of not [a] or [b] or [c] would be lost. Figure 1.40
formalizes a different paradigm than Figure 1.37 (cf. Fawcett's discussion of
zero realization, 1980: 112). Accordingly, a sixth criterion is proposed.

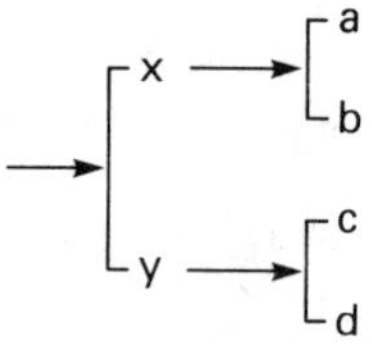

Figure 1.39 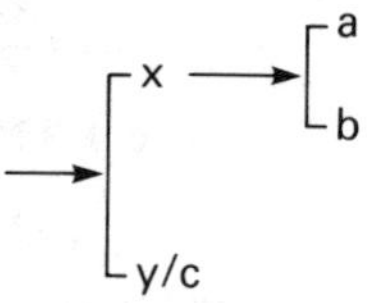   **Figure 1.40**

F. *A terminal feature unmotivated by A through F is justified if all other terms in its
system are so motivated*

In the past, systemicists have approached the problem of motivating networks
in terms of justifying systems rather than the features they contain. The

strongest published position appears in Hudson (1970: 226): '. . . that for every grammatical system there should be at least one formal property which is possible in items with one of the features, but not in items with the other.' If 'having a formal property' is interpreted as 'having a reflex in form', then Hudson's criterion justifies rewriting Figure 1.3 as Figure 1.4 in every case, whether [x] is independently motivated in any way or not, since all items having [a] will possess some formal property which those having [x] do not have.

Such a position makes it possible to take a given network and rewrite it as two networks. In one, configurations like that in Figure 1.3 are maintained, i.e. features unmotivated by A through F are removed. In the other, such configurations are expanded as in Figure 1.4. This latter network could contain nearly twice as many systems as the former and yet be saying the same thing about the linguistic patterns it describes. This ACCORDION GAMBIT makes system networks notoriously difficult to interpret since features motivated by A through F are mixed up with features not so motivated in an unprincipled way. Justifying systems when only one of their terms is motivated by A through F is an indefinitely weaker position than motivating individual features, and has no place in an explicit generative model.

Implicit in Hudson's position is the assumption that every system may be binary. This assumption may prove far less tenable if features themselves are individually motivated. An important related concern involves the expression of system networks as a list of SUB-CATEGORIZATION RULES (cf. Hudson 1976). Note that the network in Figure 1.41 cannot be written as a well-formed sub-categorization rule. The rule in Figure 1.42 is not well formed and must be written as Figure 1.43. But in network terms this involves rewriting Figure 1.41 as Figure 1.44.

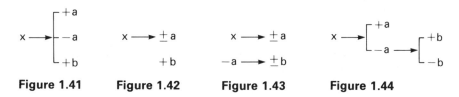

Figure 1.41   **Figure 1.42**   **Figure 1.43**   **Figure 1.44**

As Anderson 1969 has pointed out, the decision to express networks as sub-categorization rules entails that all systems are binary. Expressing networks as sub-categorization rules would thus involve adding a number of features and systems to grammars whose features are individually motivated by criteria A through F. In this sense system networks and sub-categorization rules differ in weak generative power and make different empirical claims about the nature of paradigmatic relations in language. It remains to be seen whether languages in fact contain systems with more than two features motivated by A through F.

Criteria A through F have been developed in this section from the point of view of motivating features in systemic descriptions. Another way of looking at

A through F is to describe them as specifying the FORMAL MEANING of features. Thus any feature justified by A though F can be said to encode formal meaning.

1.3 THE FORMAL MEANING OF FEATURES AND RELATIONAL NETWORK LINGUISTICS

The linguistic theory which takes most seriously the Hjemslevian conception of language as a network of relationships is stratificational linguistics (Lamb 1966). Through the use of network notation and a commitment to realizational as opposed to mutational descriptive strategies (Lamb 1974; Henrici 1981), stratificational and systemic theory share two critical perspectives on the representation of linguistic patterns. But a number of significant differences distinguish the two models. For one thing, stratificationalists have not formally recognized the concepts of RANK and META-FUNCTION, so that more than three strata are involved in many versions of the model (Lamb 1971). Also, since structures are generated and levels related by means of networks rather than realization rules, stratificational networks include ORDERED OR brackets to handle conditioned realization and ORDERED AND brackets for syntagmatic sequencing. And, perhaps most significantly, stratificational linguistics does not separate paradigmatic from syntagmatic relations as levels in its descriptions.

Aside from ordered notes, the most striking difference between a system network and stratificationalist's relational network is the absence of features from the latter. Lamb has argued that naming linguistic relationships, which is in fact what features encoding formal meaning do, has the danger of leading linguists to talk of these relationships as things. Thus a question arises as to why system networks contain features at all.

Taking first those features motivated by criterion A, it is clear that features which have a reflex in form are present in networks so that they can be referred to in realization rules. There is no way of eliminating them from networks other than rewriting a system network and its realization rules into relational network grammar.

Features motivated by criteria B though F, however, do not seem quite so essential in a systemic generative model. Features justified by B, C and D are present for purely network internal considerations. It is not at all difficult to reformulate Figures 1.45, 1.47 and 1.49 as Figures 1.46, 1.48 and 1.50, replacing features motivated solely by B, C and D with wiring.

NEGATIVE, POSITIVE and CONDITIONAL marking all effect paradigmatic conditioning within a network. The notation described above for signalling this conditioning can be replaced with wiring provided that the logic of the wiring is applied to individual features as well as to systems. The negative marking in Figure 1.51 could be re-expressed as Figure 1.52 were this allowed; similarly Figure 1.54 could re-express the positive marking of Figure 1.53 and Figure 1.56 the conditional marking of Figure 1.55. To date, in published work, systemicists have not assigned an interpretation to networks

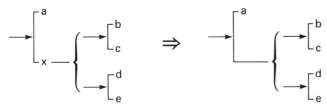

Figure 1.45

Figure 1.46 Figure 1.45 with a criterion B feature wired away

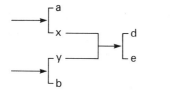

Figure 1.47

Figure 1.48 Figure 1.47 with a criterion C featured wired away

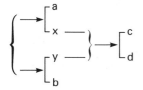 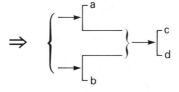

Figure 1.49

Figure 1.50 Figure 1.49 with a criterion D feature wired away

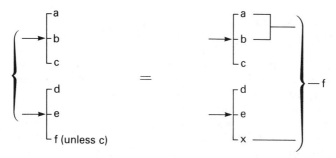

Figure 1.51 Negative indexing

Figure 1.52 Figure 1.51 with a gate wiring away negative indexing

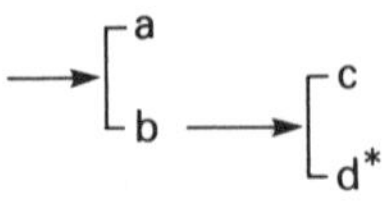

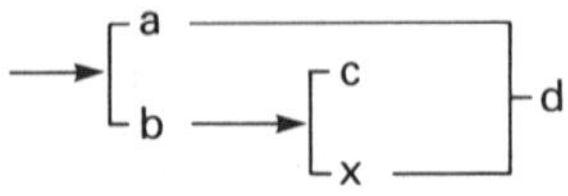

Figure 1.53 Positive indexing

Figure 1.54 Figure 1.53 with a gate wiring away positive indexing

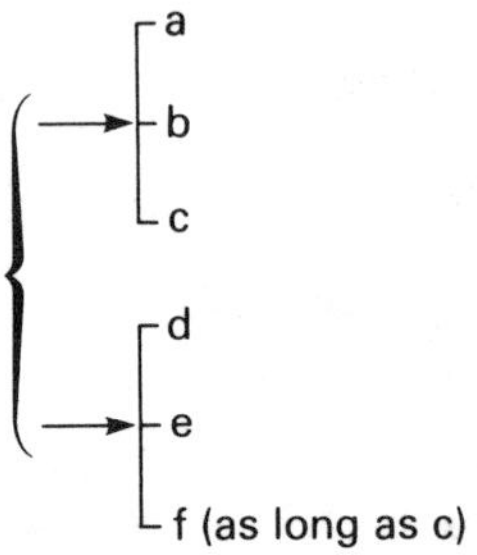

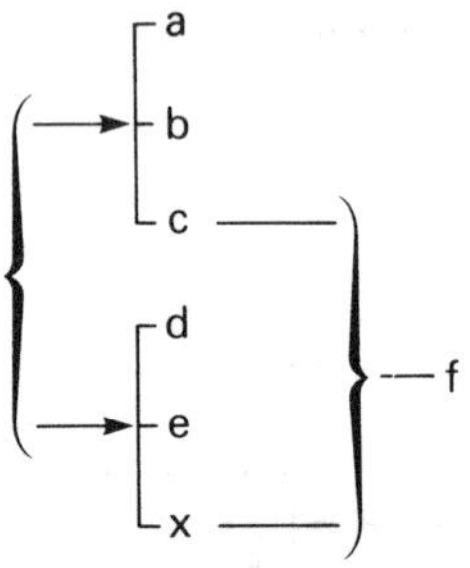

Figure 1.55 Conditional indexing

Figure 1.56 Figure 1.55 with a gate wiring away conditional indexing

of this kind. However, the research on text generation under the direction of W. C. Mann at the Information Sciences Institute has involved the development of such a notation. There, systems consisting of a single feature are referred to as GATES (Mann and Matthiessen 1985: 54; Mann 1985: 67).

The feature [x] which has been added to Figures 1.52, 1.54 and 1.56 to effect this wiring could itself be replaced with wiring since it functions solely as part of a disjunctive or conjunctive entry condition. The gated feature itself could be replaced with wiring if it similarly functions solely as an entry condition for more delicate systems; if it is a terminal feature, it could be replaced with a terminal wire (discussed below) if it has no realization of its own. It thus appears that gates could be used to wire away features whose sole justification is their participation in a markedness relation of the kinds described above.

DERIVATIONAL marking interacts with realization rules, and so features motivated by this convention, like those justified by criterion A, cannot be wired away within a systemic framework.

Features motivated by criterion F could be replaced with a TERMINAL WIRE which would serve to keep the option open in the network as adequately as a feature. Figure 1.59 is equivalent to Figure 1.58 given that [x], [y], [a], [b] and [c] are motivated by A through E but [d] is not.

A note on recursive systems is appropriate here. In Halliday's (1976) description of the English verbal group, TENSE is analysed as a recursive system with the terms [past], [present] and [future]. Halliday's notation for this recursive selection is found in Figure 1.59. The features [go] and [//] can be wired away as in Figure 1.60 since their only function is to make tense

Figure 1.57

Figure 1.58 Figure 1.57 with an unmotivated terminal feature wired away

Figure 1.59 A recursion system

Figure 1.60 Figure 1.59 with a recursion feature wired away

selection recursive. This comparison of relational network and systemic notation points out a number of ways in which system networks can be simplified. Without increasing the weak generative power of system networks, features motivated by criteria B, C, D and F can be replaced with wiring. By introducing gates, the indexing associated with markedness can be eliminated; the features involved can then be wired away if their sole function in the network was their involvement in a markedness relation. It is doubtful, however, whether using gates in this way would do much to improve the readability of system networks, or to clarify the reasons why they have the shape they do.

As was outlined in section 1.2, as far as the formal meaning of features is concerned, features are included in system networks for a number of different reasons. This makes it rather difficult to interpret the formal meaning of features in any one description since so many different factors are involved. The purpose of eliminating certain kinds of features from system networks is simply to make them easier to read and interpret. The wires replacing features motivated by B, C, D and F encode explicitly all the formal meaning of the features they replace. Indexical marking conventions could be maintained for those features motivated by E. And the formal meaning of other features would be that they have some reflex in form. Such networks are both graphically plausible and practicable, as is clear from the work of Winograd 1972, who implicitly adopted these conventions. Linguists comparing Winograd's approach to the graphic formalization of paradigmatic relations with that of other systemicists may find his networks refreshingly easy to interpret. (However, Fawcett (1980: 117) suggests that to wire away features whose sole motivation is that they are entry conditions may actually reduce the readability of a network.)

1.4 THE NON-FORMAL MEANING OF FEATURES

In general, the network descriptions developed by systemicists contain more features than those justified by criteria A through F. In part, this is the result of systemicists' insistence on setting up a system when only one of its terms is motivated. But another important factor is the use of features to encode semantic distinctions whose realization is mediated in turn by more delicate features encoding formal meaning.

Halliday's unpublished description of DEIXIS (1968) in English serves to illustrate this point. (For an alternative formulation, see Kress 1976: 132.) His network is presented in Figure 1.61 along with the deictics through which its features are realized. In Figure 1.62 this network is simplified by means of 'and' and left-facing 'or' brackets. In Figure 1.63 the features in Figure 1.62 are listed and the kind of formal meaning they encode is noted.

Figure 1.63 reveals that two of the features in Halliday's DEIXIS network, [total] and [possessive], are unmotivated by criteria A through F. The formal meaning of the network in Figures 1.61 and 1.62 would be unaffected if these features were removed. Systems 1 and 2 and systems 7 and 11 could be conflated into three term systems in Figures 1.64 and 1.65 respectively.

Since the features [total] and [possessive] in Halliday's DEIXIS network are not encoding formal meaning, the question arises as to what kind of meaning they encode. It appears that both features have been included in order to capture semantic generalizations about the features through which they are realized. The deictics *all*, *both*, *each*, *every*, *neither*, *no*, *either* and *any* refer to the whole of the set of objects to which the nominal group including them applies. The deictics *whose*, *which* (e.g. *boy*)'*s* (e.g. (*John*)'*s* and *my*, *your*, *our*, etc. involve possession. So while the features [total] and [possessive] are not formally motivated in Halliday's description, they do encode NON-FORMAL MEANING which contributes to the analysis. A glance at other features in the DEIXIS network indicates that they too encode non-formal meaning. It is not possible to evaluate the description fully until this fact is taken into account. But the important point here, as far as this chapter is concerned, is that features can be used to encode formal or non-formal meaning or both in systemic linguistics.

In principle it is legitimate to motivate features either formally in terms of criteria A through F or non-formally in light of the semantic generalizations they involve. In practice, however, the presence of features encoding formal or non-formal meaning in a given network makes system networks difficult to interpret. There are two types of solution to this problem.

One solution is primarily notational. Features motivated by criteria A or E would be written in lower case letters (i.e. [feature]). Features motivated by

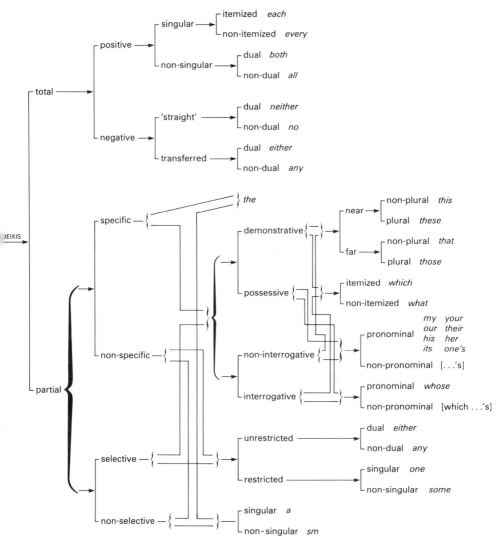

Figure 1.61 Halliday's DEIXIS network (1968)

criteria B, C, D or F would be replaced with wires. Non-formally motivated features would be written in upper case letters (i.e. [FEATURE]). As noted above, it is possible that a feature encode both formal and non-formal meaning. Features motivated by A through F which encode non-formal meaning as well could begin with a capital letter and continue in lower case (i.e. [Feature]). Upper-case letters have been used in the past by systemicists for the names of systems (e.g. TRANSITIVITY; MOOD). The names of grammatical functions have been written with an initial capital (e.g. Agent; Subject).

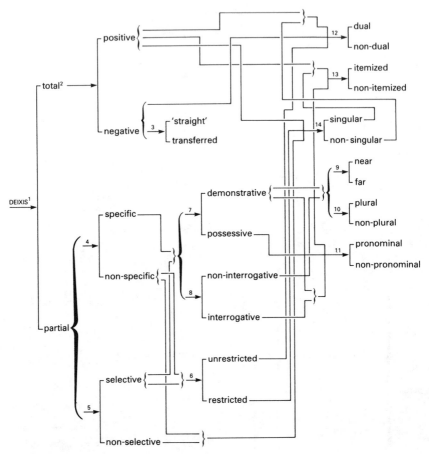

Figure 1.62 A simplified DEIXIS network

This should not prove confusing since the names of systems are written above the arrows leading to systems as in Figure 1.1 above and grammatical functions appear only in realization statements. By enclosing features in square brackets in written text, difficulties need not arise. These notational conventions would make the linguistic content of system networks much more accessible.

The second solution is to place formally motivated features in one network and non-formally motivated features in another. The semantic general-izations non-formally motivated features make about formally motivated ones would be specific through realization statements, whereby non-formally motivated features preselect formally motivated ones. This is in effect to propose stratification on the basis of how features are justified in systemic descriptions.

Features:	Criteria: A	B	C	D	E	F
total						
partial		x				
positive			x	x		
negative		x				
'straight'	x					
transferred	x					
specific	x			x		
non-specific				x		
selective				x		
non-selective				x		
restricted			x			
unrestricted			x			
demonstrative				x		
possessive						
near	x					
far	x					
plural	x					
non-plural	x					
pronominal	x					
non-pronominal	x					
dual	x					
non-dual	x					
itemized	x					
non-itemized	x					
singular	x			x		
non-singular	x			x		

Figure 1.63 Criteria motivating features in Halliday's DEIXIS network

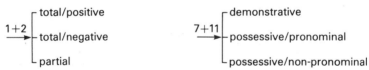

Figure 1.64 Systems 1 and 2 of Figure 1.62 collapsed

Figure 1.65 Systems 7 and 11 of Figure 1.62 collapsed

It seems prudent at present to treat stratification of this kind as a heuristic strategy. Should it turn out that most of the features and systems encoding semantic generalizations stand in a one-to-one relationship with formally motivated features and systems, then the two networks could be collapsed into a single network observing the notational proposals outlined above. If on the other hand it turned out that there was a good deal of alternation, neutralization and diversification between the networks, then one would conclude that in fact the simpler statement is achieved by not attempting to collapse the networks. In the 1970s the networks of certain systemicists (e.g. Hudson) became less and less semantic while those of others (e.g. Turner 1973) became increasingly abstract. It may be that the only way these developments can be incorporated into a descriptively adequate systemic model is through the stratification of non-phonological systems on the basis of criteria for motivating features.

1.5 SOCIO-SEMANTIC NETWORKS

In the past the focus of networks made up of non-formally motivated features has been on the process of socialization in parent/child interaction. The networks involved effect a very delicate analysis of illocutionary force, so delicate in fact as to be much more situationally specific than is common in linguistic descriptions. The systems in these networks are oriented to formalizing the options of control open to mothers in particular encounters with their children. An exemplary socio-semantic network appears in Figure 1.66 (Turner 1973: 155). The features in Figure 1.66 encode semantic distinctions which bear critically on the question of how language is structured to socialize a child. These features are realized through the preselection of lexicogrammatical and phonological options in a tri-stratal systemic model.

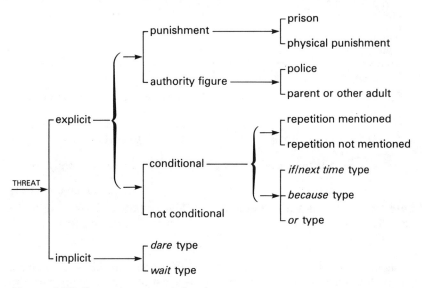

Figure 1.66 Turner's network for threat

Halliday has commented on the contextual specificity of socio-semantic networks as follows:

It must be made clear, however, that the example chosen was a favourable instance. We would not be able to construct a socio-semantic network for highly intellectual discourse, and in general the more self-sufficient the language (the more it creates its own setting as we explained earlier) the less we should be able to say about it in these broadly sociological, or social, terms. [Halliday 1973: 92]

These remarks underline the fact that networks of non-formally motivated features were initially designed with very particular descriptive and explanatory goals in mind. Certain types of social intercourse are more relevant to the process of socialization than others. Consequently, socio-semantic networks are easier to formulate for certain situations than for others. The most favourable instance of all is that approached by Halliday and Turner, i.e. situations in which the process of socialization is being carried on. Encounters in which social reality is sustained rather than transmitted are much less transparent to an already socialized investigator (cf. Berger and Luckman 1971).

Halliday's remarks need not, however, be taken to preclude the development of contextually neutral networks of non-formally motivated features. Less sociologically oriented descriptive and explanatory goals will lead to networks which lack the situational specificity of socio-semantic features. It is important to emphasize the point that stratification is motivated in light of certain descriptive goals, and that non-formally motivated features will reflect these goals. The more general the goals, the less non-formally motivated features will be bound by situation.

1.6 SPEECH FUNCTION AND MOOD

The clearest example of stratification in terms of formal and non-formal meaning which is not situationally specific is found in Halliday 1984. Here Halliday proposes an analysis of speech function and MOOD involving two strata of networks. His semantic network appears in Figure 1.67. Its features encode non-formal meaning relevant to the assignment of speech roles by a speaker in some context of situation.

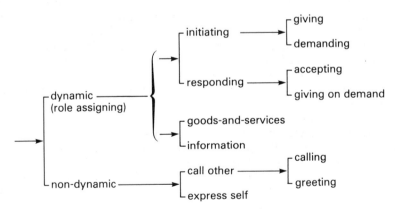

Figure 1.67 A semantic network for speech function

Options in Figure 1.67 are realized through the grammatical system of MOOD which appears in Figure 1.68. The features in Figure 1.68 are formally motivated; they in turn are realized in structures composed of the grammatical functions Finite, Subject, Predicate, Complement, and so on. The congruent interaction of the speech function and MOOD networks is outlined in Figure 1.69.

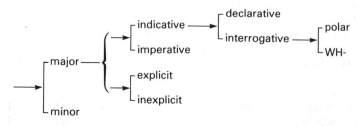

Figure 1.68 A MOOD network for English (partial)

speech function categories	⟍ *MOOD categories*
dynamic	major clause
non-dynamic (call/greet/	
exclaim)	minor clause
initiating (give/demand)	explicit
responding (accept/give)	inexplicit
offer	(various)
statement	declarative
command	imperative
question	interrogative

Figure 1.69 The exponence of speech function in MOOD

As Halliday points out, the two networks are oriented towards different types of description. The semantic network focuses on the speech situation and the grammar. The grammatical network looks towards the semantics and its own structural output. While the grammar of English has no exclusive structure encoding the giving of goods and services, this option is clearly present in the context of situation. On the other hand, the speech situation does not lead one to distinguish polar from WH-demands for information; but English structures these meanings very differently. Overall, the relation of formally to non-formally motivated features is not bi-unique. Giving goods and services is variously realized in the grammar. Accordingly, giving goods and services and giving information might be realized by the same structures. For example, the declarative structure 'There's some beer in the fridge' may be either an offer or a statement depending on the situation in which it is uttered. Interlocking diversification is present in Halliday's description and precludes the possibility of expressing the content of Figures 1.67 and 1.68 in a single network.

It is important to note the way in which Halliday's speech function network takes the non-formal meaning associated with his MOOD network, and reorganizes it in order to explain how English is structured to assign speech roles in any context of situation. Given the speech function network, features in the MOOD network need not be interpreted as encoding both formal and non-formal meaning. Any non-formal meaning they might once have been considered to encode is now exhausted by the speech function network. This analysis of speech function and MOOD presents a good example of stratification on the basis of the way in which features are motivated in systemic descriptions.

1.7 CONCLUSIONS

In this chapter two types of meaning associated with features in systemic linguistics have been distinguished: formal and non-formal. The formal meaning of features is in effect their place in a network of linguistic relationships relating meaning to sound. The non-formal meaning of features is the semantic/pragmatic information a systemicist uses them to encode.

A set of six criteria have been proposed for defining the formal meaning of features in extant systemic descriptions:

A. having a reflex in form;
B. being an entry condition for simultaneous systems;
C. being a disjunctive entry condition for a more delicate system;
D. being a conjunctive entry condition for a more delicate system;
E. being associated with a markedness convention;
F. being terminal, with all other terms in the system motivated by A through E.

On the basis of these critera three types of system network can be distinguished:

FIRST LEVEL NETWORKS: it is necessary and sufficient that all features are justified by A through F;
SECOND LEVEL NETWORKS: it is necessary and sufficient that all features encode non-formal meaning;
MEDIATED NETWORKS: it is necessary and sufficient that all features encode either formal or non-formal meaning.

First level networks are typically used for describing syntactic patterns (cf. Hudson 1971, 1976). Second level networks are typically used to answer contextually oriented questions such as how language is structured to socialize a child (cf. Turner 1973) or how language is structured to assign speech roles (cf. Halliday 1984). Mediated networks are so named because the scale of delicacy tends to mediate the position of features so that non-formally motivated features make generalizations about more delicate, formally motivated ones through which they are realized. Many of Halliday's descriptions, for example, the DEIXIS network considered in section 1.4, are of this type; that is, they include features encoding both formal and non-formal meaning.

First level networks may include features with non-formal meaning and second level networks may include features with formal meaning, but in neither case does this justify their presence there. The distinction between first and second level networks could be used to demarcate the boundary between non-phonological strata in a tri-stratal systemic model. Second level networks would be semantic, first level networks grammatical in such a theory.

In order to mark out explicitly the different types of meaning which features encode, the following notational conventions are proposed:

1. features motivated by A or E will be written in lower case letters (i.e. [feature]);
2. features motivated solely by B, C, D or F will be replaced with wiring;
3. features encoding non-formal meaning will be written in upper case letters (i.e. [FEATURE]);
4. features encoding formal and non-formal meaning will begin with a capital and continue in lower case (i.e. [Feature]).

These conventions are designed to make the linguistic content of systemic descriptions more readily interpretable. If systemic grammars are to function as explicit generative models, then consideration must be given to the way in which features are motivated in networks and realization rules expressing the exponence of these features must be provided. It is appropriate that systemic notation reflect these concerns.

BIBLIOGRAPHY

Anderson, J. (1969), 'A note on "rank" and "delicacy"', *Journal of Linguistics*, 5, No. 1.
Benson, J. D. and Greaves, W. S. (eds) (1985), *Systemic Perspectives on Discourse: Vol. 1 Selected Theoretical papers from the Ninth International Systemic Workshop*, Norwood, N.J., Ablex.
—— and—— (eds) (forthcoming), *Systemic Functional Approaches to Discourse: Selected Papers from the Twelfth International Systemic Workshop*, Norwood, N.J., Ablex.
Berger, P. L. and Luckman, T. (1971), *The Social Construction of Reality*, Harmondsworth, Penguin University Books.
Bernstein, B. (ed.) (1973), *Class, Codes and Control II: Applied Studies Towards a Sociology of Language*, London, Routledge and Kegan Paul (Primary Socialization, Language and Education).
Berry, M. (1977), *Introduction to Systemic Linguistics 2: Levels and Links*, London, Batsford.
Fawcett, R. P. (1973a), 'Generating a sentence in systemic functional grammar', in Halliday and Martin (1981: 146–83).
—— (1980), *Cognitive Linguistics and Social Interaction: Towards an Integrated Model of a Systemic Functional Grammar and the Other Components of an Interacting Mind*, Heidelberg: Julius Groos Verlag and Exeter University.
—— (forthcoming), 'What makes a "good" network good?—Four pairs of concepts for such evaluations', in Benson and Greaves (eds) (forthcoming).
Fawcett, R. P., Halliday, M. A. K., Lamb, S. M. and Makkai, A. (eds) (1984), *The Semiotics of Culture and Language: Vol. 1 Language as Social Semiotic*, London, Frances Pinter.
Halliday, M. A. K. (1967–8), 'Notes on transitivity and theme in English', Parts 1–3, *Journal of Linguistics*, 3, No. 1, 37–81; 3, No. 2, 199–244; 4, No. 2, 179–215.
—— (1969), 'Options and functions in the English clause', *Brno Studies in English*, 8,

81–8, reprinted in Householder (ed.) (1972) and in Halliday and Martin (eds) (1981: 138–45).

—— (1973), *Explorations in the Functions of Language*, London, Edward Arnold (Explorations in Language Study).

—— (1976), 'The English verbal group', in Kress (ed.) (1976: 136–58).

—— (1984), 'Language as code and language as behaviour: a systemic-functional interpretation of the nature and ontogenesis of dialogue', in Fawcett *et al.* (eds) (1984: 3–35).

—— *The Meaning of Modern English I: The Clause* (unpublished).

Harris, S. Z. (1948/66), 'Componential analysis of a Hebrew paradigm', *Language*, 24, 87–91, reprinted in Joos (ed.) (1966, 272–4).

Henrici, A. (1981), 'Some notes on the systemic generation of a paradigm of the English clause', in Halliday and Martin (1981: 74–98).

Hockett, C. F. (1954/66), 'Two models of grammatical description', *Word*, 10, 210–31, reprinted in Joos (ed.) (1966; 386–99).

Householder, F. W. (ed.) (1972), *Syntactic Theory 1: Structuralist*, Harmondsworth, Penguin.

Huddleston, R. D. (1981), 'Systemic features and their realization', in Halliday and Martin (eds) (1981: 58–73).

Huddleston, R. D. and Uren, O. (1969), 'Declarative, interrogative, and imperative in French', *Lingua*, 22, 1–26, reprinted in Halliday and Martin (eds) (1981: 237–56).

Hudson, R. A. (1968), 'Constituency in a systemic description of the English clause', *Lingua*, 18, 225–50, reprinted in Halliday and Martin (eds) (1981: 103–21).

—— (1970), 'On clauses containing conjoined and plural noun-phrases in English', *Lingua*, 24, 205–53.

—— (1971), *English Complex Sentences: An Introduction to Systemic Grammar*, Amsterdam, North Holland.

—— (1973), 'An item-and-paradigm approach to Beja syntax and morphology', *Foundations of Language*, 9, 504–48, reprinted in Halliday and Martin (eds) (1981: 271–309).

—— (1974), 'Systemic generative grammar', *Linguistics*, 139, 5–42, reprinted in Halliday and Martin (eds) (1981: 190–217).

—— (1976), *Arguments for a Non-Transformational Approach to Syntax*, Chicago, University of Chicago Press.

Joos, Martin (ed.) (1966), *Readings in Linguistics I*, Chicago, University of Chicago Press, 4th ed.

Kress, G. (ed.) (1976), *Halliday: System and Function in Language*, London, Oxford University Press.

Lamb, S. M. (1966), 'Epilegomena to a theory of Language', in *Romance Philology*, 19, 531–73.

—— (1971), 'The crooked path of progress in cognitive linguistics', in O'Brien (ed.) (1971: 99–124).

—— (1974), 'Mutations and Relations', in Makkai and Makkai (eds) (1974: 540–57).

Lockwood, David G. (1972), *Introduction to Stratificational Linguistics*, New York, Harcourt Brace Jovanovich.

Makkai, A. and Makkai, V. (eds) (1974), *The First LACUS Forum*, Colombia, S. Carolina, Horn beam Press.

Mann, W. C. (1985), 'An introduction to the Nigel text generation grammar', in Benson and Greaves (eds) (1985: 84–95).

Mann, W. C. and Matthiessen, C. M. I. M. (1985), 'A demonstration of the Nigel text generation computer program', in Benson and Greaves (eds) (1985: 50–83).

O'Brien, R. J. (ed.) (1971), *Report of the Twenty-Second Annual Round Table Meeting on Linguistics and Language Studies*, Washington, D. C., Georgetown University Press (Monograph Series on Languages and Linguistics: Developments of the Sixties— Viewpoints for the Seventies).

Turner, G. J. (1973), 'Class and children's language of control', in Bernstein (ed.) (1973: 135–201).

Winograd, T. (1972), *Understanding Natural Language*, Edinburgh, Edinburgh University Press.

Vachek, J. (1966), *The Linguistic School of Prague*, Bloomington, Indiana University Press.

Wojcik, R. (1976), 'Remarks on natural phonology', *CUWPL*, 3, 47–58.

Zwicky, A. M. (1975), 'Settling on an underlying form: the English inflectional endings', in Cohen and Wirth (eds) (1975: 129–85).

Part II
Discourse

2 Is teacher an unanalysed concept?

Margaret Berry
University of Nottingham

2.1 INTRODUCTION

The strength of systemic linguistics, as I have said elsewhere (Berry 1980, 1982, forthcoming a), lies in the devotion which it has always shown to the goal of relating language to its social context, in its attempt to bring together linguistic insights and sociological insights.[1] The weakness of systemic linguistics, as I have also said in the earlier publications, lies in its argumentation, particularly in its failure to confront its theories with relevant facts.

The strength of the work of the Birmingham discourse analysts (e.g. Sinclair and Coulthard 1975), or at any rate one of the strengths, would seem to lie in the bringing to light of a number of interesting, but hitherto unnoticed, facts about different types of discourse and their relation to their social contexts. The weakness of this work is that there is no overall theory of the relations between language and social context which could account for the facts that have been discovered. I would probably be only slightly overstating my case if I said that systemic theory (e.g. Halliday 1978: 108–26) was currently an explanation in search of some facts, while the facts of the Birmingham discourse analysts were currently facts in search of an explanation.

Since Halliday's theory is a theory about the relations between language and social context and since the facts of the Birmingham discourse analysts are facts about an aspect of language (discourse structure) and its relation to social context, it would seem that the latter ought to be relevant to the former. My eventual aim is to bring these two together in such a way as to produce a well-formed adjacency pair of FACTS and EXPLANATION.

I must emphasize, however, that this is a long-term aim. In a paper addressed to the Seventh International Systemic Workshop (Berry 1980: especially 36–56), I outlined a major research programme likely to take very many years to complete.

In the present chapter I shall be able to make only the smallest of small beginnings to such work. I shall review some of the facts brought to light by Sinclair and Coulthard and their associates. I shall put forward hypotheses which could account for such facts and I shall consider methods of testing the hypotheses. Discussion of the significance of the hypotheses for Halliday's general theory, should they stand up to testing, will, I am afraid, for reasons of space, have to await future publications (I hope to include some preliminary discussion of this kind in Berry forthcoming b).

2.2 SOME FACTS ABOUT CLASSROOM DISCOURSE

Among the facts that their analysis reveals, Sinclair and Coulthard themselves draw particular attention to the following:

(i) that a typical exchange in the classroom is not a simple adjacency pair, but consists of THREE moves: teacher INITIATION (I), pupil RESPONSE (R), teacher FEEDBACK (F), as in (1);

```
(1) Teacher:  Can you tell me why do          I
              you eat all that food?
              Yes.
    Pupil:    To keep strong.                 R
    Teacher:  To keep you strong.             F
              Yes. To keep you
              strong. [Sinclair and Coulthard 1975: 21]
```

(ii) that the feedback move includes among its constituents a type of speech act which Sinclair and Coulthard call EVALUATE. For instance, the feedback moves in examples (2) and (3) each consist of an evaluate (e), followed by another act which Sinclair and Coulthard call COMMENT (com);

```
(2) Teacher:  Can anyone have a              I
              guess, a shot at
              that one?
    Pupil:    Cleopatra                      R
    Teacher:  Cleopatra. Good girl.          F    e
              She was the most                    com
              famous queen, wasn't
              she, Cleopatra of the
              Nile. [Sinclair and Coulthard 1975: 80]
(3) Teacher:  Why did they build             I
              Pyramids?
              Paul.
    Pupil:    When they were dead            R
              they put all their
              riches and everything
              they owned in their
              Pyramid.
    Teacher:  Yes they did, yes.             F    e
              Right in the depth,                 com
              in the heart of the
              Pyramid there was
```

a special little room
where they had their
personal belongings.
Precious special things
that belonged to them.
[Sinclair and Coulthard 1975: 82]

In early work by the Birmingham discourse analysts, evaluate was characterized as follows:

Realized by statements and tag questions including words and phrases such as 'good', 'interesting', 'team point', commenting on the quality of the reply . . . also by 'yes', 'no', 'good', 'fine', with a high fall intonation, and repetition of the pupils' reply with either high fall (positive), or a rise of any kind (negative evaluation). [Sinclair and Coulthard 1975: 43]

Later, following work by Brazil (e.g. 1975, 1978) on KEY, positive evaluation became particularly associated with HIGH KEY (Coulthard and Brazil 1979: 30); that is, with high pitch at the beginning of the utterance.

(iii) that teachers also make a good deal of use of words such as 'now', 'right' and 'OK', which serve to indicate boundaries in the discourse. Sinclair and Coulthard call these boundary markers FRAMES. Examples of frames are:

(4) Teacher: Now,   Frame
             I want to tell you
             about a King who
             lived a long time
             ago in Ancient
             Egypt. [Sinclair and Coulthard 1975: 22]
(5) Teacher: Right,   Frame
             Here's the next
             quiz then if
             you're ready.
             [Sinclair and Coulthard 1975: 66]

2.3 THE NEED FOR AN EXPLANATION

The facts are interesting, not only in their own right as facts about the structure of a particular type of discourse, but also for their relevance to other types of enquiry. For instance, they are sociolinguistically and sociologically relevant via a study of social roles. As Stubbs says:

It is principally through conversational interaction, the give-and-take of everyday multi-party discourse, that social 'roles' are recognised and sustained. We can talk about intuitively recognisable social roles such as 'teacher' and 'doctor'. Clearly, in some sense, people ARE teachers or doctors—that is their job. But clearly, also, there is quite specific conversational behaviour attached to being a teacher—as teachers would soon discover if they talked to their families as they do to their pupils. Even in the classroom, a teacher cannot simply BE a teacher, without DOING quite specific and describable conversational activities . . . 'Roles' have to be acted out in social interaction. [Stubbs 1983: 7–8]

In drawing attention to the facts listed above, Sinclair and Coulthard are beginning to describe the 'describable conversational activities' that are entailed by being a teacher.

Also, perhaps more obviously, since they pertain to the role of teacher, the facts are educationally relevant. It can presumably be assumed that the better the social role of teacher is understood, the more that is known about the activities, conversational or otherwise, that are entailed by being a teacher, the more successful are likely to be any attempts to improve the effectiveness of teaching. (It should be noted here that French and Maclure (1981: 32) warn against TOO HASTY applications of discourse analysis of this kind.)

The facts, then, are already interesting. They would be even more interesting if we understood better the REASONS for the facts. Just why do teachers conversationally behave in these ways? What aspects of the teacher's role are being acted out in these particular forms of discourse structure? Are all three facts associated with the same aspect of being a teacher, or are they relatable to different aspects? Is 'being a teacher' really a rather complex matter, as the previous two questions would seem to imply?

Sinclair and Coulthard do discuss these issues informally, but they do not set up precise hypotheses and systematically investigate them. Yet if we really want to understand the relationship between certain forms of discourse structure and the role of being a teacher, and even more if we want eventually to be able to make recommendations leading to more effective teaching, then surely we must progress beyond informal speculation to more controlled attempts to provide an explanation for the facts.

2.4 THE TYPE OF EXPLANATION THAT COULD BE OFFERED

In asking questions such as 'What aspects of the teacher's role are being acted out in these particular forms of discourse structure?' and 'Are all three facts associated with the same aspect of being a teacher, or are they relatable to different aspects?', I am virtually complaining, as Goffman does of the speaker and hearer roles, that the role of teacher is at present an unanalysed concept, that it is a 'global folk category' which needs to be 'decomposed' into 'smaller, analytically coherent elements' (Goffman 1981: 129).

One way of decomposing the role of teacher would be to carry out a kind of 'distinctive feature' analysis of teacher and other social roles. It would seem unlikely that the role of teacher is totally different in all respects from other social roles. Much more probable is that it is like other social roles in some ways, different from them in others; like some other social roles in some ways, like others in others. A set of 'distinctive features' could then be proposed to capture the patterns of similarities and differences.

The aim of such a study would be to find features that could be used to predict the occurrence/non-occurrence of particular forms of discourse in different social contexts. If the predictions were successful, if in each case the evidence indicated that there WAS a link between the presence of a particular feature and the occurrence of a particular form of discourse, then we should have grounds for associating particular aspects of roles with particular types of conversational behaviour. We should be in a position to answer questions such as those with which I began this section. We should have the beginnings of an explanation for facts such as those cited in section 2.2.

I will illustrate the type of approach I have in mind by reference to the six roles for which the discourse structure has been most fully examined in Sinclair and Coulthard terms: teacher, pupil (Sinclair and Coulthard 1975); doctor, patient (Ashby 1973; Coulthard and Ashby 1975, 1976); chairman, committee member (Stubbs 1973, 1974).

Before I begin, however, I should make clear that I am not of course claiming to be the first systemicist to link social roles and language. There has been much discussion of this in the literature, and particularly notable in this connection is Davies 1979. I am also not claiming to be the first person to propose features for roles. Goffman (1981: 144–5) virtually proposes features and Di Pietro 1981 explicitly does so. I am not even claiming to be the first person to use features associated with roles in order to predict the occurrence/ non-occurrence of forms of discourse in different social contexts. Hasan 1978 effectively does this, though she does not call them features and she does not draw system networks to show how they are related. Of this earlier work, it is Hasan's to which my own approach owes most. As I explained in the 1980 paper, I see myself as working in the tradition which she has started, but as extending her approach beyond the limits which she herself envisaged.

There is one further acknowledgement that I should make before I begin. It will already be obvious from my use of the term ADJACENCY PAIR that I have been influenced by the work of the ethnomethodologists (e.g. Schegloff and Sacks 1973; Sacks, Schegloff and Jefferson 1974; for a recent survey see Levinson 1983, chapter 6).

I shall also follow them in looking for evidence that any principles of organization that I propose are oriented to by participants. Thus I shall be formulating my hypotheses in terms of occurrence/non-occurrence of forms of discourse, but I shall not be surprised to find counter-examples to these hypotheses. What will particularly interest me will be whether there is any evidence that the participants themselves regarded these counter-examples as breaks in a normal pattern. If so, since what I am looking for are normal patterns rather than unbreakable rules, I shall consider such counter-examples to be evidence FOR such normal patterns rather than evidence against. I shall have a little more to say on this point in section 2.8. However, for a full discussion see Berry forthcoming b.

2.5 SOME FACTS ABOUT DOCTOR–PATIENT INTERVIEWS AND COMMITTEE TALK

As I have indicated, my aim is to find features that will enable me to predict and account for the normal occurrence/non-occurrence of forms of discourse in different social contexts. My immediate concern in this chapter is to account for the occurrence/non-occurrence of the three forms of discourse discussed in section 2.2: three-move exchanges, evaluates and frames; to account for their occurrence/non-occurrence, that is, in the three types of social context indicated in section 2.4; classroom discourse, doctor–patient interviews and committee talk. At a later stage in the work I shall of course wish to be able to predict and account for the occurrence/non-occurrence of many other forms of discourse and in many other types of social context. For the moment, however, limiting myself to the three forms of discourse and the three types of social context, the first thing to do is to establish exactly what are the facts about occurrence/non-occurrence that need accounting for.

I have already indicated, in section 2.2, that all three forms of discourse occur in classroom discourse. A further point, which I have implied but which perhaps needs to be made explicit, is that they all occur in association with the role of teacher. It is the teacher, not the pupil, who initiates three-move exchanges; most pupil-initiated exchanges are two-move exchanges. And it is the teacher who provides evaluates and who uses frames.

Do these three forms of discourse occur in doctor–patient interviews and in committee talk? And, if so, in association with which roles?

Frames occur in doctor–patient interviews. They are used by doctors, but apparently not by patients:

(6) Doctor: Right.   Frame
                     I'd like you to
                     gargle frequently [Coulthard and Ashby
                     1976: 86]

(7) Doctor: Right.   Frame
                     Well, if you go
                     along with nurse
                     she'll give you
                     a cubicle and I'll
                     come and see you
                     in a little while
                     Mrs. A. [Coulthard and Ashby 1976: 87]

Frames also occur in committee talk. Stubbs (1974: 33) associates these with the role of chairman:

(8) Chairman: right (2)   Frame
                   so internal
                   self-consistency
                   is what you're after [Stubbs 1974: 33]

(9) Chairman: ((click))ᵛ   Frame
              well what's
              the general
              feeling then [Stubbs 1974: 33. Stubbs
              describes the click as a 'paralinguistically
              realised frame'.][2]

Three-move exchanges also occur in doctor–patient interviews. They are initiated by the doctor.

(10) Doctor: How long
                have you had those
                for?
    Patient: Well I had'm a
                week last Wednesday.
    Doctor: A week last Wednesday. [Coulthard and
                Ashby 1976: 80]
(11) Doctor: how long have you
                had these quick pains
                on the right side of your
                head?
    Patient: well again when this
                trouble started
    Doctor: again for about two
                years [Coulthard and Montgomery 1981: 21]

Three-move exchanges, however, do not normally occur in committee talk (Stubbs 1973: 5–7).

Evaluates do not typically occur in either doctor–patient interviews or committee talk.[3] In committee talk, as I have just indicated, there are not normally any third moves to contain evaluate acts. In doctor–patient interviews there are third moves, but these are usually different in character from the third moves of classroom exchanges.

To develop this last point. As I said in section 2.2, an evaluate which is typical of the third move of a classroom exchange, is an act of commenting on the quality of a reply (Sinclair and Coulthard 1975: 43). It is associated with high key (Coulthard and Brazil 1979: 30). A further point that can be made about it is that it appears to be heard by the pupils as terminating the exchange; they make no further contribution to the exchange after such an evaluate (Coulthard and Montgomery 1981: 19). The teacher goes on to initiate a new exchange.

If we look now at the third moves in the doctor–patient examples (10) and (11), it is true that they appear to be heard by the patients as terminating their exchanges. In each case the patient makes no further contribution to the exchange and the doctor goes on to initiate a new exchange with a new question (*do you bring up sputum* in the case of (10); *when did you first start noticing that you er were having attacks of coldness* in the case of (11) (Coulthard and Montgomery 1981: 20–1)). However, they are LOW key utterances, not high key utterances (Coulthard and Montgomery 1981: 20–1). And, intuitively, one feels that they are not so much acts of commenting on the quality of the patient's reply as acts of noting and/or reinterpreting the reply for the doctor's own benefit.

There are some occasions in doctor–patient interviews when doctors do produce a high key third move. On these occasions, however, the patient usually appears to hear the move as NON-terminal and produces a further move himself.

(12) Doctor: when did you first start
                 noticing that you er were
                 having attacks of coldness
     Patient: I've always been very cold
                 feet and hands
     Doctor   MOST OF YOUR LIFE (high key)
     Patient: yes I would say so doctor [Coulthard and
                 Montgomery 1981: 21]

In doctor–patient interviews, then, the third move is normally either a low key utterance which is heard as terminal, or a high key utterance which is heard as non-terminal. What is NOT typical of the third moves of doctor–patient exchanges is the high key utterance which is heard as terminal, i.e. the evaluate.

To sum up, the facts that appear to need accounting for are as follows:

  (i) frames are associated with the roles of teacher, doctor and chairman, but not pupil, patient or committee member;
 (ii) the initiation of three-move exchanges is associated with the roles of teacher and doctor, but not chairman, pupil, patient or committee member;
(iii) evaluates are associated with the role of teacher, but not doctor, chairman, pupil, patient or committee member.

2.6 SOME HYPOTHESES THAT COULD ACCOUNT FOR THE FACTS

There would seem to be a fairly obvious explanation for the first of these facts. The pairs of roles teacher–pupil, doctor–patient and chairman–committee member are each hierarchically ordered. In each case it is the higher member of the pair that is in control of the discourse and whose responsibility it is to mark off the stages in the discourse. It is not surprising, therefore, that the higher members of the pairs—teacher, doctor and chairman—make use of frames, while the lower members of the pairs—pupil, patient and commitee member—do not. I will accordingly propose a role feature [±HIGHER] and will hypothesize as follows:

Hypothesis I: In any language event involving a pair of roles which is hierarchically ordered, the person occupying the [+HIGHER] role will make use of frames, while the person/people occupying the [−HIGHER] role will not.

The feature [±HIGHER] can also be used in part to account for the occurrence/non-occurrence of three-move exchanges and evaluates, since these forms of discourse do not occur in association with any of the [−HIGHER] roles. The feature cannot fully account for the occurrence/non-occurrence of these forms, however, as it is not true that they do occur with all the [+HIGHER] roles. We appear to need additional features which will distinguish between the [+HIGHER] roles.

To account for the occurrence/non-occurrence of three-move exchanges, we need a feature which teacher shares with doctor, but not with chairman. Coulthard and Montgomery (1981: 18) suggest that similarities of structure between classroom discourse and doctor–patient discourse may be relateable to the fact that teachers and doctors are 'experts' compared with their pupils and patients, but that chairmen are the 'professional equals' of their committee members. Teachers and doctors are not only of higher status than their opposite numbers from the point of view of their responsibility for controlling the discourse; they are also of higher status from the point of view of their relative knowledge. It is true that a particular person occupying the role of chairman may know more than his committee members. But it is not true that he is NECESSARILY EXPECTED to know more BY VIRTUE OF HIS ROLE, as is the case with teachers and doctors. Indeed, a chairman of a committee may well know less about the field under discussion than those members of his committee who have been appointed specifically on account of their various types of relevant expertise. It must be remembered that it is ROLES to which I am attempting to assign features, not the occupants of the roles. The roles of doctor and teacher do seem to carry with them expectations of greater knowledge; the role of chairman carries no such expectations. I will propose a feature [±PRIMARY KNOWER] and I will assume that teacher and doctor are [+ PRIMARY KNOWER], while chairman is [−PRIMARY KNOWER].

Hypothesis II: The occupant of a role which is both [+HIGHER] and [+PRIMARY KNOWER] will initiate three-move exchanges; the occupant of a role which is not both [+HIGHER] and [+PRIMARY KNOWER] will not initiate three-move exchanges.

To account for the occurrence/non-occurrence of evaluates, we need a feature which will distinguish between teacher and doctor. Here I will make use of a distinction which I have introduced elsewhere (Berry 1981 a, b, c) in other connections. It is still a matter of relative knowledge, but this time instead of being a matter of relative knowledge with respect to a whole field, it is a matter of relative knowledge with respect to the propositional content of a particular exchange. It is perfectly possible to be primary knower with respect to the relevant field and yet not to be primary knower with respect to the actual items of information being exchanged in the discourse related to that field. This is true of the doctor in examples (10), (11) and (12). The doctor can be assumed to be primary knower in respect to the field of medicine in general. But what is being discussed in these examples are the patient's symptoms. And the form and duration of a patient's symptoms are something that the patient is in a better position to know about than the doctor. The doctor, then, is primary knower with respect to the general field, but is NOT primary knower with respect to the propositional content of these particular exchanges. From now on I will distinguish between these two senses of 'primary knower' by using capital letters for the larger-scale knowingness, which relates to a general field, and lower-case letters for the smaller-scale knowingness, which relates to the propositional content of individual exchanges: 'PRIMARY KNOWER', as opposed to 'primary knower'.

Let us make use of this distinction to contrast the roles of teacher and doctor. As I have already said, I am assuming that these two roles are alike in both being [+PRIMARY KNOWER]. They are not alike, however, from the point of view of the smaller-scale type of knowingness. Examples (10), (11) and (12) are in fact typical of doctor–patient interviews. Much of the discussion which takes place IS about the patient's symptoms. The doctor, though expected to be generally knowledgeable about medicine, is expected to need further information of a personal kind from the patient before being able to complete his diagnosis. The doctor, though PRIMARY KNOWER, is typically NOT primary knower.

The teacher, on the other hand, is expected to be not only more knowledgeable than the pupils about the general field under discussion, but also already in possession of all the main individual items of information that are to be exchanged during the lesson. The teacher in examples (2) and (3), for instance, is not only expected to be more knowledgeable than the pupils about Ancient Egypt in general, but is also expected to already know the answers to individual questions which she has asked. The teacher is typically not only PRIMARY KNOWER, but also primary knower.

I am, then, proposing a third feature: [±primary knower]. I am assuming that the role of doctor is [−primary knower], though [+PRIMARY KNOWER]; and that the role of teacher is both [+primary knower] and [+PRIMARY KNOWER].

Hypothesis III: The occupant of a role which is [+HIGHER] AND [+PRIMARY KNOWER] AND [+primary knower] will produce evaluates; the occupant of a role which does not possess all three of these features will not produce evaluates.

I will refer to the hypotheses of this section as Hypotheses Set A.

2.7 A FURTHER SET OF HYPOTHESES

One aspect of my work may surprise other systemicists. I intend to include among the features I propose ONLY THOSE which the evidence currently available suggests are NECESSARY for the purpose that I have in mind; that is, for predicting the occurrence/non-occurrence of forms of discourse in different social contexts. It seems to me that often, as systemicists, we clutter up our networks with features that we think just might perhaps conceivably be useful for some undisclosed purpose at some time in the distant future. It is not surprising that non-systemicists complain that they cannot see the motivation for systemic proposals. We fail to distinguish between those proposals for which we already have motivation and those which are part of some mystic vision for the future (see Berry 1980 for further discussion on this point).

As I have indicated, a study of the occurrence/non-ocurrence of frames, three-move exchanges and evaluates suggest that there is at least some prima-facie evidence that the features [±HIGHER], [±PRIMARY KNOWER] and [±primary knower] may be necessary to predict the distribution of such forms of discourse in different social contexts. I have therefore tentatively proposed such features. I am well aware that it is possible to think of many other kinds of similarity and difference between teachers, doctors, chairmen, pupils, patients and committee members. I shall resist including additional features to represent these other similarities and differences, however, unless or until I or someone else produces evidence that such features at least seem likely to be necessary for my purpose.

I shall, in fact, hypothesize at each stage of my work: (1) that the features I have so far proposed ARE necessary to predict the distribution of forms of discourse in different social contexts; and (2) that they are the ONLY features that are necessary for this purpose.

Thus my fourth and fifth hypotheses currently read as follows:

Hypothesis IV: The features [±HIGHER], [±PRIMARY KNOWER] and [±primary knower] are necessary to predict the distribution of different forms of discourse in different social contexts.

Hypothesis V: The features [±HIGHER], [±PRIMARY KNOWER] and [±primary knower] are the ONLY features that are necessary to predict the distribution of different forms of discourse in different social contexts. (I do not expect this last hypothesis to stand up for very long. However, see section 2.8 for discussion of the advantages of setting up precise hypotheses at every stage of one's work.)

Similarly, I shall include in my system network only those COMBINATIONS OF FEATURES that I have so far found to be necessary for my purpose.

My only use in this chapter so far of [+primary knower] was in circumstances in which it was associated with [+PRIMARY KNOWER] and [+HIGHER]. In my system network (Figure 2.1) I have accordingly made the opposition [±primary knower] dependent on the opposition [±PRIMARY KNOWER] and [±HIGHER].

I have twice made use of [+PRIMARY KNOWER]: to predict the occurrence of three-move exchanges, and to predict the occurrence of evaluates. On both occasions it was in association with [+HIGHER]. I have therefore shown [±PRIMARY KNOWER] as dependent on [±HIGHER]. It is NOT the case, however, that on both occasions [±PRIMARY KNOWER] was associated with [±primary knower]; on one occasion it was, but on the other it was not. Although [±primary knower] is dependent on [±PRIMARY KNOWER], the reverse is not true.

I have three times made use of [+HIGHER]: to predict the occurrence of frames, of three-move exchanges, and of evaluates. On one occasion it was associated with [+PRIMARY KNOWER] and on one occasion it was associated

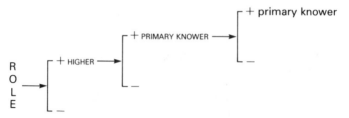

Figure 2.1 A system network for differentiating roles

with both [+PRIMARY KNOWER] and [+primary knower]. On the other occasion, however, it was associated with neither [+PRIMARY KNOWER] nor [+primary knower]. [±HIGHER] is not dependent on either of the other oppositions, although each of the other oppositions is dependent on [±HIGHER]. I have not so far discovered any opposition on which [±HIGHER] does depend.

The system network in Figure 2.1 thus reflects the following hypotheses:

Hypothesis VI: The combinations of features [+HIGHER], [+HIGHER and +PRIMARY KNOWER] and [+HIGHER, +PRIMARY KNOWER and +primary knower] are necessary to predict the distribution of forms of discourse in different social contexts.

Hypothesis VII: The combinations of features [+HIGHER], [+HIGHER and +PRIMARY KNOWER] and [+HIGHER, +PRIMARY KNOWER and +primary knower] are the ONLY combinations of these features that are necessary to predict the distribution of forms of discourse in different social contexts.

This arrangement of the system network also enables me to reflect two further hypotheses that I would wish to put forward.

I assume that it is the aim of a study of text–context relations not only to investigate the relations between particular forms of discourse and particular features, or combinations of features, of the social context, but also to arrive at some assessment of the relative strength of influence of the features under consideration in determining the general form of the discourse. I assume that the greater number of forms of discourse a feature is useful in predicting, the more influential that feature can be considered to be (see Berry 1980: especially 40, 46 and 58).

As I have said, I have so far made use of [+HIGHER] in predicting the occurrence of three forms of discourse, [+PRIMARY KNOWER] in predicting the occurrence of two forms of discourse, [+primary knower] in predicting only one form of discourse. My current hypotheses of this type are thus:

Hypothesis VIII: [±HIGHER] is more influential than [±PRIMARY KNOWER] in determining the forms of discourse used in particular social contexts.

Hypothesis IX: [±PRIMARY KNOWER] is more influential than [±primary knower] in determining the forms of discourse used in particular social contexts.

These hypotheses are reflected in the ordering in delicacy in the system network. The nearer to the lefthand side of the diagram a system is, the more influential I am claiming it to be. I shall refer to Hypotheses IV–IX as Hypotheses Set B.[4]

2.8 FUTURE WORK TO TEST THE HYPOTHESES

If this were an article on syntax, I should of course be expected immediately to go on and test my hypotheses by confronting them with further data. And in my view it is JUST AS IMPORTANT in studies of text–context relations as in studies of syntax that one's hypotheses SHOULD be tested. (A not altogether popular view in systemic linguistics. See Berry 1980, 1982 and forthcoming a for further discussion.) However, for two reasons, the testing of hypotheses about text–context relations is bound to be a much slower process than the testing of hypotheses about syntax.

In the first place we cannot rely on vast arrays of already widely known facts, discovered as a result of centuries of study. Many people have put forward ideas about text–context relations, but there are as yet regrettably few known facts. As far as I am aware, for instance, there is no store of already available facts about the occurrence/non-occurrence of frames, three-move exchanges and evaluates in social contexts other than those which I have already considered. There is thus no convenient supply of relevant facts that I can draw on to test my first set of hypotheses.

In the second place we cannot conjure up new facts just by sitting back in our armchairs with eyes closed and ears shut and peacefully introspecting. The original facts that I tried to account for—those of sections 2.2 and 2.5—were discovered as a result of much painstaking and time-consuming research on the part of the Birmingham discourse analysts. Any attempt to discover whether or not frames, three-move exchanges and evaluates are characteristic of the discourse associated with other types of social context will similarly necessitate much painstaking and time-consuming research.

I cannot, then, IMMEDIATELY go on to test my hypotheses, much as I would like to. In fact the systematic testing of such hypotheses is more than one person's work. This is the main reason why I have written first a conference paper and now chapters of a book at this early stage in my thinking—in the hope of interesting other people in my hypotheses, so that they will assist me in the testing!

This is of course the point of setting up explicit hypotheses at every stage of one's work. It makes clear to others exactly how far one has got in one's own thinking, so that they can see where they can be of assistance. Indeed, it seems to act as a challenge to other linguists! If one is vague, or if one hovers around on the tops of fences, other linguists are content to leave one in one's state of ignorance. If, on the other hand, one commits oneself to bold hypotheses, they rush to provide one with counter-examples. Such counter-examples are of great value in the process of weeding out unsatisfactory hypotheses and substituting better ones.[5]

I expect that almost every point I have made in this chapter will in due course be attacked. If so, in one way that will mean that I have failed and I shall have to revise my hypotheses hastily, maybe my whole approach. In another way, however, it will mean that I have succeeded. One of the main things I am trying to do in this chapter is to say something that is precise enough to be argued against. It seems to me that all too often in systemic linguistics we do not succeed in achieving that degree of precision. It seems to be assumed that because we are working in an apparently 'messy' field, we have to proceed in a 'messy' way. I cannot see any reason in principle why studies of text–context relations cannot be as precise and methodical as studies of syntax or studies of phonology.

(i) *Testing the first set of hypotheses*

The most obvious way to test the hypotheses of Set A would be to investigate other social contexts involving hierarchically ordered pairs of roles to see if the occurrence/non-occurrence of frames, three-move exchanges and evaluates follows the predicted patterns. The procedure would be: (1) to elicit informants' judgements about the expectations associated with the relevant roles—with regard to relative knowledge and relative responsibility for controlling the discourse—and to assign features to the roles on the basis of these expectations; (2) to carry out systematic analyses of the discourse to see if frames, three-move exchanges and evaluates regularly occur and, if so, in association with which role.

For instance, I have myself begun looking at the discourse of radio and television quiz programmes. Informants' judgements usually indicate: that they consider quizmaster and contestant to be a hierarchically ordered pair of roles; that they expect a quizmaster to be in control of the discourse; that they expect a quizmaster to be a generally knowledgeable person; that they expect a quizmaster to be already in possession of the individual items of information about which he is questioning the contestants—in all probability he has the answers to the questions written down on a piece of paper in front of him; that they expect a contestant not to be in control of the discourse; that a contestant may be a generally knowledgeable person but that it is equally possible that he may not be; that a contestant may know the answers to the individual questions but that it is equally possible that he may not. I have accordingly assigned to the role of quizmaster the features [+HIGHER, +PRIMARY KNOWER, +primary knower] and to the role of contestant the features [−HIGHER, −PRIMARY KNOWER, −primary knower]. My hypothesis would then predict: that a quizmaster will use frames but that a contestant will not; that a quizmaster will initiate three-move exchanges, but that a contestant will not; that a quizmaster will provide evaluates, but that a contestant will not.

It is now my task to carry out detailed analyses of the discourse of quiz programmes to see if these predictions are correct.

Early indications are that the hypotheses WILL BE SUPPORTED. However, I have already come across instances of what at first sight appear to be counter-examples, but which on closer inspection turn out not to be genuine counter-examples at all. It is probably worth discussing these in order to illustrate more general points about exactly what I would regard as evidence against hypotheses of the type in Set A and what I would not regard as evidence against such hypotheses. I will first discuss four instances of apparent counter-examples and then draw out the general points to which they relate.

(a) In a programme in BBC's *My Music* series, Denis Norden, one of the contestants, produced what sounded like the initiating move of a three-move exchange. The exchange did in fact turn out to be a three-move exchange, the quizmaster, Steve Race, providing the second move and Denis Norden himself providing the third move. Denis Norden's third move includes an evaluate. This looks like a counter-example both to the hypothesis that it will be the quizmaster, not the contestants, who initiates three-move exchanges and to the hypothesis that it will be the quizmaster, not the contestants, who produces evaluates.

However, this example is the ONLY example of its kind in the whole programme. All the other three-move exchanges were initiated by the quizmaster and all the other evaluates were provided by the quizmaster. One swallow does not make a summer and one counter-example does not refute a hypothesis, particularly when the hypothesis has been set up in the context of investigating which forms of discourse TYPICALLY occur in association with which role and which forms TYPICALLY do not. In spite of this one example, it is still true of the *My Music* programme AS A WHOLE that evaluates and the initiation of three-move exchanges are TYPICAL of the discourse of the quizmaster but NOT typical of the discourse of the contestants.

There is another way in which this one apparent counter-example can be shown to be untypical. It is not only NUMERICALLY untypical. It also appeared to be PERCEIVED as untypical by the studio audience. There was a good deal of laughter at this point. The audience apparently recognized and appreciated a humorous deviation from the normal pattern of events. What seemed to be happening was that Denis Norden was temporarily usurping the quizmaster's role for comic effect. It was in fact an example of ROLE-SWITCHING (cf. Stubbs 1974: 31–3).

(b) Another interesting point in connection with the *My Music* series is that Steve Race sometimes forgets to provide evaluates. The programme is really intended as an opportunity for the celebrity contestants to display their verbal wit and to indulge in reminiscences about musical events rather than to display actual knowledge. Steve Race seems to get so carried away by listening to the reminiscences and the wit that he forgets he is supposed to evaluate the answers to his questions.

However, numerical considerations can again be taken into account. The occasions on which Steve Race does provide evaluates are very much more frequent than the occasions on which he does not. (I have not yet carried out a strict count so I am not yet able to provide exact figures here.) It can therefore still be said that evaluates are TYPICAL of Steve Race's discourse, even though there are occasions on which they are missing.

And again there is evidence that other participants in the language event PERCEIVE as UNTYPICAL those occasions on which Steve Race does NOT produce an evaluate. The contestants do not let him get away with his lapses. If he attempts to move on to another question without evaluating the answer to the last, one or other of the contestants will usually interject *Well, was I/he right?* The absence of an evaluate in a quizmaster's discourse is evidently a NOTABLE ABSENCE, oriented to by participants (Schegloff and Sacks 1973).

(c) The first two apparent counter-examples were instances of untypical occurrences/non-occurrences of forms of discourse. The third is an instance of an untypical quizmaster from the point of view of the features assigned to the role.

I have said that informants' expectations of quizmasters led me to assign the features [+HIGHER, +PRIMARY KNOWER, +primary knower] to the role. And it certainly seems from my investigations so far that most quizmasters do match up to these expectations.

However, the quizmaster of one ITV quiz programme that I watched did not seem to match up to these expectations. He was a well-known television personality, but not one who was noted for his general knowledgeability. I found myself at the beginning of the programme comparing him unfavourably with such people as Bamber Gascoigne of ITV's *University Challenge* and wondering how he was going to cope. I was perfectly prepared to admit that he was likely to be well able to control the discourse, but I had doubts as to whether his general knowledge was such as to inspire confidence and I also wondered if he could really be said to KNOW the answers to the individual questions, even though he obviously had answers written down in front of him. In other words, I was accepting his ability to match up to the [+HIGHER] expectation, but I was placing mental queries against him from the point of view of [+PRIMARY KNOWER] and [+primary knower].

It is important to re-emphasize at this point that I am attempting to assign features to ROLES, not to occupants of roles. Although this particular occupant of the role of quizmaster may not have matched up to the expectations of the role, the expectations of the role remained the same. The feature analysis of the role thus remained the same. I assumed the features [+HIGHER, +PRIMARY KNOWER and +primary knower] for the ROLE of quizmaster—in the quiz programme I am at present discussing just as much as in any other quiz programme. And since the hypotheses of Set A are phrased in terms of features of ROLES, this means that the predictions about the occurrence/non-occurrence of forms of discourse remained the same. I predicted that this quizmaster would use frames, initiate three-move exchanges and provide evaluates just as much as other quizmasters. He was still a quizmaster, if not a quite typical one.

However, if my doubts about this particular quizmaster's ability to match up to the expectations were well founded, then I would expect that the mismatch too would be reflected in the discourse in some way. Since I did not have any doubts about his matching up to the [+HIGHER] expectation, I predicted that there would be no problems over his use of frames. However, since I did have doubts as to his matching up to the [+PRIMARY KNOWER] and [+primary knower] expectations, I predicted that, although he would initiate three-move exchanges and produce evaluates, there would be some problem over his use of these forms of discourse.

Both sets of predictions were borne out. This quizmaster, like other quizmasters, did use frames, did initiate three-move exchanges and did provide evaluates. There was no problem over the use of frames—there seemed to be no difference at all between the way in which this quizmaster used frames and other quizmasters use frames.

There was, however, a difference between this quizmaster's provision of evaluates and that of other quizmasters. This quizmaster frequently paused before producing the expected evaluate. He seemed to be hesitating over whether the answer which had been given was correct or not. My guess was that the contestant had used different words from the words in the answer that the quizmaster had got written down in front of him and the quizmaster was having difficulty in working out whether or not they meant the same thing.

Indeed, on a number of occasions he produced an incorrect evaluate (he said an answer was wrong when it was right, or vice versa); he was obviously corrected over his headphones by someone more knowledgeable in the background; and then had to apologize to the contestant and revise his ruling. On these occasions, the expected three-move exchanges became lengthened to more-than-three-move exchanges. This certainly did not contribute to the smooth flowing of the programme.

My own intuition is that this was not a very successful quiz programme. As support for my own intuition I will mention that I read a critical review of the programme. Like myself, the reviewer compared the programme unfavourably with *University Challenge*, though not of course in the same terms as I have been doing. And it is also true that this programme does not appear to have become a favourite with viewers. It does not recur every year, after the manner of *University Challenge* and BBC's *Mastermind*, so presumably ITV themselves do not regard it as one of their more successful efforts.

If it is agreed that this was an unsuccessful quiz programme, I would suggest that a role feature analysis such as I am proposing, together with a consideration of the extent to which occupants of roles match up to the expectations for the roles, can point to possible reasons for the lack of success: the occupant of the role of quizmaster did not match up to the expectation of [+PRIMARY KNOWER] and so was not able to inspire general confidence; he also did not match up to the expectation of [+primary knower] and so was not able to ensure the smooth flowing of the programme.

(d) I am not of course suggesting that any and every attempt to break with the stereotypic image of the quizmaster is inevitably doomed to failure. Indeed, I will now discuss an apparently successful attempt to depart from the usual pattern.

The programme in question is ITV's *Winner Takes All*. In this programme the role of quizmaster is apparently shared by two people: Jimmy Tarbuck and Geoffrey Wheeler. Jimmy Tarbuck, a well-known comedian, hosts the show. He makes a great parade of not being very knowledgeable and of not really knowing the answers to the questions—presumably with the intention of setting the contestants at their ease. He makes it clear that he regards Geoffrey Wheeler as the knowledgeable one, with the answers to all the questions. (It is probably interesting to note in this connection that Geoffrey Wheeler is well known for his appearance as quizmaster in more conventional quiz programes such as *Top of the Form*.) Geoffrey Wheeler stays in the background, contributing to the discourse only when Jimmy Tarbuck invites him to do so.

It would seem then that in this quiz programme there are two occupants of the role of quizmaster and that they share the responsibility for matching up to the expectations of the role. Jimmy Tarbuck fulfils the [+HIGHER] expectation; Geoffrey Wheeler fulfils the expectations of [+PRIMARY KNOWER] and [+primary knower]. If this is a correct analysis of the situation, then one would predict that it would be Jimmy Tarbuck who would use the frames and Geoffrey Wheeler who would initiate the three-move exchanges and provide the evaluates.[6]

It certainly does seem to be Jimmy Tarbuck who uses the frames and it certainly does seem to be Geoffrey Wheeler who provides the evaluates. I THINK it will also be possible to argue that it is Geoffrey Wheeler who initiates the three-move exchanges. However, the assignment of exchange boundaries is a very much more complex issue than the recognition of frames and evaluates and I shall have to wait until I have carried out a detailed analysis of the discourse before I am able to make any confident assertions on this point.

As I have indicated, my intuition is that *Winner Takes All* is a very much more successful attempt to break with the stereotypic image of quizmaster than was the programme I discussed under (c). Certainly *Winner Takes All* does recur every year, so it is presumably regarded as successful by the independent television authorities.

If one were attempting to account for the apparent difference in success, one might suggest that the moral of the story is that there must be SOME named person in the programme who matches up to the expectations of [+PRIMARY KNOWER] and [+primary knower], even if it is not the host and central figure of the show.

As I said above, I have only been discussing quiz programmes in order to illustrate more general points. I hope that in course of time it will be possible for myself or someone else to investigate in the same way the discourse of many other types of social context.

The general points that I would wish to draw out of this discussion are as follows:

1. The hypotheses of Set A are intended to be taken as hypotheses about which forms of discourse TYPICALLY occur in association with which role features and which TYPICALLY do not.

2. The word *typical* can mean two different things: it can mean *in accordance with the statistical norm*; and it can mean *perceived as typical* by the participants in the discourse (or by informants later asked to react to the

discourse). It may of course be the case that what is typical in one sense is also typical in the other sense. However, it cannot automatically be assumed that the two types of typicality will coincide. It would in fact be interesting to investigate to what extent they do coincide.

3. I regard BOTH types of typicality/untypicality as FACTS TO BE ACCOUNTED FOR by any theory of text–context relations. In other words I am assuming both textual data AND introspective data.

4. I would regard as a counter-example to one of my hypotheses any REGULAR occurrence/non-occurrence of a form of discourse which went against the predictions for the feature/combination of features under consideration, *provided that* there were no evidence that the text(s)/context(s) being investigated had been perceived as untypical by participants/informants.

5. I would NOT regard as a counter-example any merely OCCASIONAL occurrence/non-occurrence that went against the predictions, NOR any occurrence/non-occurrence in text(s)/context(s) that had been perceived as untypical.

(There is no room to discuss in this chapter where I should draw the line between regular occurrence/non-occurrence and occasional occurrence/ non-occurrence, though this is obviously a question I shall have to face in the near future.)

6. If it can be established that there ARE *typical* patterns of text–context relations, then this paves the way for interesting discussions of the *untypical*. Types of untypicality that can then be investigated include:
   (a) role-switches;
   (b) humorous deviations from the norm;
   (c) unsuccessful attempts to occupy roles;
   (d) deliberate attempts to break with the stereotypic images of roles.

While I am on the subject of deliberate attempts to break with the stereotypic images of roles, I will return briefly to the role of teacher. Some members of the audience to whom I gave the earlier versions of this chapter misunderstood the claims that I was making and therefore it is important to emphasize certain points.

Firstly, it was thought that I was claiming that ALL teachers were necessarily [+HIGHER, +PRIMARY KNOWER and +primary knower]. I hope it has become clear from my discussion of quiz programmes that this is not so. The features are intended to represent the expectations that members of a community have of a role. They are NOT a claim that all occupants of the role necessarily conform to the expectations.

Secondly, it was thought that I was suggesting that all teachers SHOULD be [+HIGHER, +PRIMARY KNOWER and +primary knower], that all occupants of a role OUGHT to conform to the expectations of the role. Again, this is not so. I hope it has become clear from my discussion of *Winner Takes All* that I am in sympathy with deliberate attempts to break with the stereotypic images of roles.

There are of course in educational circles at the present time increasing attempts to break with the traditions of the formal classroom and these seem to involve attempts to break with the stereotypic image of the teacher. It would be interesting to investigate such departures from earlier tradition in terms of such role features and forms of discourse as those I have been discussing in this chapter.

Interesting questions which immediately present themselves include:

Is a teacher who favours an informal approach attempting to shed one or more of the features associated with the role? If so, which? Is a teacher who arranges group work, where the pupils have the responsibility for controlling their own discourse, attempting to shed [+HIGHER]? Is a teacher who arranges a lesson on a sport or hobby, on which some of the pupils are experts but not the teacher himself, attempting to shed [+PRIMARY KNOWER]? Is a teacher who tries to draw out personal experiences of the pupils, before going on to relate the personal experiences to the main subject matter of the lesson, attempting to shed [+primary knower]?

CAN features easily be shed? I suggested in my discussion of the quiz programmes that there was some slight evidence that, if a quiz programme was to be successful, the responsibility for matching up to the features could not be entirely neglected, though it could be passed to someone else. Does this apply to classroom discourse?

In the light of the answers to the above questions, what predictions would one make about the occurrence/non-occurrence of frames, three-move exchanges and evaluates? Are these predictions borne out?

I must leave these questions to be answered by those people working on the discourse of informal classrooms.

I will conclude this subsection with a quotation from Halliday: 'There is always, in language, the freedom to act untypically—but that in itself serves to confirm the reality of the concept of what is typical' (Halliday 1978: 226).

(ii) Testing the second set of hypotheses

The real testing of Hypotheses Set B will begin when the investigation is extended to a consideration of the occurrence/non-occurrence of forms of discourse other than frames, three-move exchanges and evaluates.

For instance, if facts are discovered which cannot be accounted for in terms of the three features that I have proposed here, this will be evidence against Hypothesis V.[7] If facts are discovered which CAN be accounted for in terms of the three features proposed here, but NOT in terms of the COMBINATIONS OF FEATURES proposed here, this will be evidence against Hypothesis VII.

At this stage it is perfectly possible that I or someone else will discover features other than those proposed here, which can be used both to account for the facts discussed here and also to account for the new facts. This will make the features proposed here unnecessary. In other words, it will be evidence against Hypothesis IV. Similar evidence may be discovered against Hypothesis VI. If evidence is discovered against Hypothesis VI, this will also be evidence against Hypotheses VIII and IX.

In general it can be assumed that the best proposal for a set of features will be the one that most economically accounts for the facts. As I indicated in the

1980 paper (41 and 45–6), there are practical as well as theoretical reasons for allowing simplicity and economy to adjudicate between rival proposals in this way[8].

2.9 CONCLUSION

In this chapter I have continued the work of outlining an approach to the study of text–context relations. In the 1980 paper I discussed such an approach in general terms. In this chapter I have illustrated the approach by reference to a particular set of facts. My main concern is to develop an approach that will be both precise and methodical.

NOTES

1. This chapter is a revised version of a paper read to the Ninth Systemic Workshop, Toronto, August 1982. I am grateful to Christopher Butler, Ronald Carter and Michael Stubbs for discussing with me many of the points in it. I am also grateful for comments from members of the Toronto audience and from members of audiences at the universities of Essex and Birmingham, and for written comments from Malcolm Coulthard, Timothy Lane, Richard Mead and Lesley Milroy. My only regret is that space and time, particularly space, have prevented me from taking as much account of all the helpful suggestions as I would have liked to do.
2. In Stubbs's transcription conventions, (2) indicates a two-second pause, (( )) a description of a paralinguistic feature, and superior v a silent stress.
3. Coulthard and Ashby (1976: 79) cite one example of an evaluate in a doctor–patient interview, but indicate that such an occurrence is not typical of doctor–patient interviews in the way that it is of classroom discourse. Unfortunately, the Birmingham discourse analysts do not give precise figures for occurrences of the forms they discuss, but use expressions such as 'typical', 'more usually' and 'sometimes'. I would hope that in any future work of this kind exact counts would be made and precise figures given.
4. Hypotheses of the kind that I have discussed in this section, particularly IV and V, are of course taken for granted in most approaches to linguistics that work with features. They are NOT, however, taken for granted in systemic linguistics. I have therefore felt it necessary to spell them out.
5. At the time of going to press I am already beginning to receive information from other linguists as a result of an earlier version of this chapter which I circulated in mimeograph form. I look forward to inspecting this material to see to what extent it supports my hypotheses, to what extent it necessitates revisions.
6. Tim Lane points out to me that, strictly speaking, my existing hypotheses do not make these predictions. My claim is that Jimmy Tarbuck and Geoffrey Wheeler jointly occupy the role of quizmaster. What one would expect from my hypotheses, therefore, is that they will be jointly responsible for the initiation of three-move exchanges and for the production of frames and evaluates. There is some evidence that this is the case for three-move exchanges and evaluates. Although it is Geoffrey Wheeler who produces the acts which most obviously correspond to the teacher's elicitation and evaluate, he only does so in response to a direct invitation from Jimmy Tarbuck (e.g. *May we start tonight's show please Geoffrey* and *Geoffrey Wheeler's*

got the second question, both from *Winner Takes All* 26 August 1983). It is as if the two speakers combine to produce the necessary moves. I have not so far discovered any evidence, however, that they combine to produce frames. Frames appear to be the prerogative of Jimmy Tarbuck.

7. In Berry 1980, following Hasan 1978, I discussed facts relating to the occurrence/ non-occurrence of identifications and greetings. It is difficult to see how these facts could be accounted for in terms of the features which I have proposed in the present article. Thus Hypotheses IV and V already need revising to include the features proposed in the earlier articles by Hasan and myself: the features [±HIGHER], [±PRIMARY KNOWER], [±primary knower], [±visual contact], [±maximum social distance], [±future transaction] are necessary, etc.; these are the ONLY features that are necessary, etc.

8. I am again spelling out things that would be taken for granted in other approaches to linguistics, since they are NOT at present taken for granted in systemic linguistics.

BIBLIOGRAPHY

Ashby, M. (1973), 'Doctor–patient interviews', *Working Papers in Discourse Analysis*, No. 1, University of Birmingham, English Language Research (mimeo.).

Berry, M. (1980), 'They're all out of step except our Johnny: a discussion of motivation (or the lack of it) in systemic linguistics', University of Nottingham (mimeo).

—— (1981a), 'Systemic linguistics and discourse analysis: a multi-layered approach to exchange structure', in Coulthard and Montgomery (eds) (1981: 120–45).

—— (1981b), 'Polarity, ellipticity, elicitation and propositional development, their relevance to the well-formedness of an exchange', *Nottingham Linguistic Circular*, 10, No. 1, 36–63.

—— (1981c), 'Towards layers of exchange structure for directive exchanges', *Network*, 2, 23–32.

—— (1982), 'M. A. K. Halliday: *Language as Social Semiotic*', review article, *Nottingham Linguistic Circular*, 11, No. 1, 64–94.

—— (forthcoming a), 'Argumentation in systemic grammar'.

—— (forthcoming b), 'Towards an analysis of the social contexts of discourse'.

Brazil, D. C. (1975), *Discourse Intonation*, Discourse Analysis Monographs, No. 1, University of Birmingham, English Language Research.

—— (1978), *Discourse Intonation II*, Discourse Analysis Monographs No. 2, University of Birmingham, English Language Research.

Coulthard, M. and Ashby, M. (1975), 'Talking with the doctor', *Journal of Communication*, 25, No. 3, 140–7.

—— and—— (1976), 'A linguistic description of doctor–patient interiews', in Wadsworth and Robinson (eds) (1976).

Coulthard, M. and Brazil, D. (1979), *Exchange Structure*, Discourse Analysis Monographs No. 5, University of Birmingham, English Language Research.

Coulthard, M. and Montgomery, M. (eds) (1981), *Studies in Discourse Analysis*, London, Routledge and Kegan Paul.

Davies, E. C. (1979), *On the Semantics of Syntax*, London, Croom Helm.

Di Pietro, R. J. (1981), 'Discourse and real-life roles in the ESL Classroom', *TESOL Quarterly*, 15, No. 1, 27–33.

Dressler, W. U. (ed.) (1978), *Current Trends in Text Linguistics*, Berlin and New York, de Gruyter.

French, P. and MacLure, M. (1981), 'Teachers' questions, pupils' answers: an investigation of questions and answers in the infant classroom', *First Language*, **2**, No. 1, 31–45, reprinted in Stubbs and Hillier (eds) (1983).

Goffman, E. (1981), *Forms of Talk*, Oxford, Blackwell.

Halliday, M. A. K. (1978), *Language as Social Semiotic: The Social Interpretation of Language and Meaning*, London, Edward Arnold.

Hasan, R. (1978), 'Text in the systemic–functional model', in Dressler (ed.) (1978).

Levinson, S. C. (1983), *Pragmatics*, Cambridge, Cambridge University Press.

Sacks, H., Schegloff, E. A. and Jefferson, G. (1974), 'A simplest systematics for the organization of turn-taking in conversation', *Language*, **50**, No. 4, 696–735.

Schegloff, E. A. and Sacks, H. (1973), 'Opening up closings', *Semiotica*, **7**, No. 4, 289–327.

Sinclair, J. McH. and Coulthard, R. M. (1975), *Towards an Analysis of Discourse: The English Used by Teacher and Pupils*, London, Oxford University Press.

Stubbs, Michael (1973), 'Some structural complexities of talk in meetings', *Working Papers in Discourse Analysis*, No. 5, University of Birmingham, English Language Research (mimeo.).

—— (1974), 'The discourse structure of informal committee talk', University of Birmingham, English Language Research (mimeo.).

—— (1983), *Discourse Analysis: The Sociolinguistic Analysis of Natural Language*, Oxford, Blackwell.

Stubbs, M. and Hillier, H. (eds) (1983), *Readings on Language, Schools and Classrooms*, London, Methuen.

Wadsworth, M. and Robinson, D. (eds) (1976), *Studies in Everyday Medical Life*, London, Robertson.

3 Sociosemantic networks and discourse structure

Geoffrey J. Turner
Hatfield Polytechnic

3.1 INTRODUCTION

The past decade or so has seen something of a text/discourse explosion in
linguistics, to use Sandulescu's (1976: 349) evocative expression. As Dressler's
1978 volume indicates, a wide variety of approaches to text/discourse
analysis have been developed by groups of researchers working for the most
part independently of each other. Inevitably, there must come a time when
different approaches are compared, terminological barriers penetrated and,
where it seems profitable, attempts at synthesis made. Sandulescu 1976, in an
interesting comparison, pitches Bielefeld against Birmingham, establishing
points of similarity and dissimilarity in their approaches (chiefly as represented in Petöfi and Rieser 1973 and Sinclair and Coulthard 1975 respectively). The result is perhaps not too surprising: whilst it may not be a case of
'ne'er the twain shall meet', the gap between the two positions looks
discouragingly wide.

This chapter also deals with aspects of the Birmingham work on discourse
structure, but the work that I am interested in relating to it—the sociosemantic network approach (Halliday 1971/73, 1972/73; Turner 1973)—is by
no means so distant. This is because both approaches utilize the Hallidayan
linguistic model, though different versions of it, representing different stages
in development. The present comparison arose out of working with the
sociosemantic approach and considering Halliday's (1972/73: 94) question:
'Is it necessary to recognize "semantic structures"?'. This chapter will attempt
to tease out certain aspects of the answer to this question.

3.2 THE QUESTION OF 'SEMANTIC STRUCTURES'

The question of 'semantic structures' is an extremely complicated one, and it
is necessary to separate out a number of important issues.

(a) What is the relationship between the speech functions in the sociosemantic
work and the discourse functions in the Birmingham work?

Halliday's 1984 discussion of dialogue in terms of three levels—social–contextual, semantic ('speech function') and grammatical—has points of contact with this question, but does not address itself directly to the Birmingham work.

(b) What is the nature of the output of the sociosemantic networks?

Halliday (1972/73: 95) suggested that

> it may be unnecessary . . . to interpose another layer of structure between the semantic systems and the grammatical systems—given the limited purpose of the semantic systems, which is to account for the meaning potential associated with defined social contexts and settings.

He emphasized, however, that structure is to be defined as 'the "configuration of functions", since this is abstract enough to cover semantic structure if such a thing is to be formulated' (95).

(c) Do different kinds of meaning have different structural shapes?

Fawcett (1975: 34) has pointed out that a sociosemantic network seems to represent 'a rankless semantics' in that the network apparently relates to whole sentences. In his own work he has found it advantageous to recognize a hierarchy of two units, 'referent situation' and 'referent thing', which are prelinguistic units that serve as input to the linguistic system (Fawcett 1975, 1980). However, whilst a hierarchical analysis is appropriate for some kinds of meaning, it may not necessarily be appropriate for other kinds, as Halliday's 1979 discussion of modes of meaning emphasizes. Halliday's (1979: 11) observations on the interpersonal mode are of some relevance to the sociosemantic approach:

> Interpersonal meaning cannot easily be expressed as configurations of discrete elements . . . The essence of the meaning potential of this part of the semantic system is that most of the options are associated with the act of meaning as a whole.

Finally,

(d) Is it necessary to formulate semantic structure WITHIN semantic networks?

Fawcett (1980: 197) notes that Halliday's 1972/73 remarks relate to 'the structure of the OUTPUTS from the semantics, rather than to structure within it'. Fawcett stresses that in the kind of explicit generative grammar he proposes it is necessary to formulate structure within the semantic networks. This is because, in generating an expression, it may be necessary to pass through a network more than once. To achieve this, he introduces a flow chart procedure within the network. It should be noted, too, that Fawcett 1986 has also developed a 'systemic flow chart' for 'local discourse structure', with system networks being set within a flow chart. In the space of this chapter, it will be necessary to concentrate on the first question, which is concerned with the relationship between speech functions and discourse functions.

3.3 COMPLEMENTARY EMPHASES?

3.3.1 SocioLINGUISTIC and sociolinguistic

Both the Birmingham approach and the sociosemantic one are linguistic approaches to discourse: they are both concerned with language as situated social behaviour.[1] Burton (1981: 21) has characterized the Birmingham work as 'SOCIOLINGUISTIC', to emphasize its particular focus. There is a sense in which the sociosemantic approach could, by contrast, be characterized as 'sociolINGUISTIC', since it, unlike the Birmingham work, does emphasize the need for sociological criteria to identify social situations and behaviour patterns that are socially significant. The question is: to what extent can the two approaches be brought together?

3.3.2 Syntagmatic and paradigmatic relations

The framework for discourse analysis devised by Sinclair and Coulthard 1975 concentrates on syntagmatic relations. This reflects the fact that it is closely modelled on Halliday's 1961 early scale-and-category grammar rather than on later versions of systemic theory. In the Birmingham work the scales and categories of the early theory are applied to a new level of analysis, distinct from grammar, the discourse level, which is concerned with language function in social interaction. A rank scale of hierarchically ordered units is recognized: each unit, except that of lowest rank, has a structure representing combinations of the unit of the rank below; an element of structure is realized by a class of the unit of the rank below, but, at some of the elements, a system is identified which is realized by classes of the unit below. Sinclair and Coulthard's (1975: 26) summary table for the unit 'move (answering)' provides a neat illustration of the analysis (see Figure 3.1).

Elements of structure		Structures	Class of act	
pre-head	(pre-h)	(pre-h) h (post-h)	pre-h:	acknowledge
head	(h)		h:	system operating at h; choice of reply, react, acknowledge
post-head	(post-h)		post-h:	comment

Figure 3.1 RANK IV: Move (Answering)

It would be fair to say that the bulk of Sinclair and Coulthard's analysis is concerned with unit and structure: considerably less attention is paid to the establishment of systems and more delicate classes of unit, although some significant systems are identified. Importantly, Sinclair and Coulthard do not attempt to construct networks, that is, sets of interrelated systems. Butler (1985: 213) has observed that 'although discourse analysts have provided stimulating accounts of syntagmatic patterning in discourse, work on paradigmatic aspects is scanty'. He himself has sought to restore the balance by proposing a model for the description of discourse, based on daughter dependency grammar (Hudson 1976, 1978), in which system networks, with no formal distinction between 'categories' such as move, act, etc. and 'features' such as reply, react and acknowledge, are related to structures by explicit realization rules.

The sociosemantic approach concentrates on the construction of networks. The approach reflects the development of the concept of system in Halliday's later theoretical work. This development of system has been queried by some systemicists, who have wondered whether there is perhaps a danger of overemphasizing paradigmatic relations at the expense of syntagmatic relations. Berry (1980: 15) writes: 'Systems apparently no longer operate at places in structure but just float in space . . . This in my view undermines the whole basis of scale-and-category and early systemic grammar.' Gregory (1983: 1) argues that the emphasis on paradigmatic relations has led to 'an increasingly encoding perspective' and that there is a need to hold a balance between encoding and decoding perspectives:

. . . language in the communicative event does move from then to now; it has a horizontal dimension. System is, of course, a good way of characterizing the choices the encoder makes, but the decoder meets these choices realized in chains of units.

Halliday's (1972/73; 1974/77) view was that for certain limited purposes (such as the ones discussed in his papers) it may not be necessary to recognize semantic structures, but he pointed out that for more complex materials it is 'almost certainly' going to be necessary to recognize semantic structure (Halliday 1974/77: 41). It is of some interest here that he suggested that the study of institutional communicational networks (e.g. patterns of consultation and negotiation in an industrial firm) 'might be extended to a linguistic analysis if the semantic options were first represented in semantic structures' (Halliday 1972/73: 96).

3.4 DISCOURSE: LAYERS OF STRUCTURE

The Sinclair and Coulthard model of discourse seeks to capture the linear and hierarchical nature of discourse. The model is heavily dependent on the early scale-and-category theory of grammar and just a single layer of structure is recognized. Sinclair and Coulthard do not postulate a deep structure, and do not incorporate anything analogous to Halliday's three-function approach to the clause. On Halliday's 1970 functional approach, they comment:

He finds in the structure of the clause three functions: (a) the 'ideational'—expressing content; (b) the 'interpersonal'—maintaining social relations; and (c) the 'textual'— enabling links to be made with the situation and cohesive texts to be constructed. This approach to function did not provide us with a useful starting point. However, just as in Chapter 3 we return to *Categories of the Theory of Grammar* for a system of presenting our description so in some future time we may find this framework similarly useful. [Sinclair and Coulthard 1975: 12]

The case for recognizing more than one layer of structure has been strongly put by Berry 1981a, b, c. She argues that an account of discourse structure based on a single linear structure for each unit does not allow one to take account of enough similarities and differences between texts. It is also too limited to enable one to predict the distribution of surface forms, to generate 'grammatical' forms of discourse and to block 'ungrammatical' forms. For her work on exchange structure, Berry argues that it is NOT necessary to propose a new level of analysis, namely discourse. The observations that she wishes to make about sentences in exchanges can be made by identifying three layers of structure, textual, interpersonal and ideational, directly comparable to those recognized by Halliday for the clause. Each layer contributes a set of functions, for example, 'primary knower' and 'secondary knower' for the interpersonal layer, and the three sets of functions are mapped on to each other by means of realization rules.

Whilst Berry's work can be seen as advancing and refining the Birmingham approach, it is nonetheless a significant departure from it in that she herself does not propose a discourse level of analysis. Whereas Sinclair and Coulthard 1975 take the sentence to be the largest unit of grammar, Berry (1981a: 40) does not see any grounds for taking it as the cut-off point: 'In the absence of compelling arguments to the contrary . . . I am recommending that THE EXCHANGE RATHER THAN THE SENTENCE BE REGARDED AS THE HIGHEST UNIT OF SYNTAX, SEMANTICS AND PRAGMATICS' (her emphasis). There are, however, two points to consider alongside this recommendation:

(a) Berry allows that there may well be facts for which it is necessary to postulate a new level. She points out that it is not clear that relationships BETWEEN exchanges could be accounted for in her way.

(b) For the sake of simplifying the discussion, Berry's account is concerned with moves which consist of a single sentence (that is, a head only). The assumption is that moves consisting of combinations of sentences will also obey the rules outlined by Berry.

Berry's views on the likeness between an exchange and a clause may be compared with Halliday's (1981: 33) on text semantics and clause grammar:

Having insisted that a text is NOT like a clause, I now intend to suggest that it is. It is not that I have changed my mind on the issue. The point is rather that, once we have established that texts and clauses are of different natures, the one being lexico-grammatical (a construct of wording), the other semantic (a construct of meaning), we can go on to note that there are several important and interesting respects in which the two are alike. But the likeness is of an analogic kind; it is a metaphorical likeness, not the kind of likeness there is between, say, a clause and a word.

Halliday identifies two kinds of analogic likeness between texts and clauses: a metonymic likeness and a metaphorical one. In the case of the metonymic likeness, texts are seen as repeating on a larger canvas patterns identified in clauses, whereas in the case of metaphorical likeness a similarity is seen between the clause and the text that it serves to realize: features selected in the clause are seen as standing as a metaphor for the text.

The position I adopt owes much to Berry, but does not accept her recommendation to take the exchange as the highest unit of syntax. For reasons that will be made clear in sections 3.6 and 3.7, the view is taken that Sinclair and Coulthard are correct in establishing a discourse level of analysis. I find Berry's work on exchange structure invaluable, and adopt a similar multi-layered approach (textual, interpersonal and ideational), but I would stress that the three layers correspond BY ANALOGY with Halliday's three functions in the clause. It seems a useful analogy for discourse. I am aware, of course, that the number of functions recognized for the clause can be challenged; see Fawcett 1980 for alternative proposals.

Before discussing further how the Birmingham work and the sociosemantic work can be located in terms of a multi-layered analysis, it is necessary to examine how each approach deals with language function, more specifically, the function of particular utterances in particular types of social situation.

3.5 SPEECH FUNCTIONS AND DISCOURSE FUNCTIONS

3.5.1 Type of social function

It is important to note the social situations investigated and the criteria for selection. Sinclair and Coulthard (1975: 6), taking into account difficulties encountered in analysing desultory conversations, chose teacher–pupil discourse in teaching situations as their starting point:

... we decided it would be more productive to begin again with a more simple type of spoken discourse, one which has much more overt structure, where one participant has acknowledged responsibility for the direction of the discourse, for deciding who shall speak when, and for introducing and ending topics.

In subsequent research, the same descriptive principles have been applied to other, though usually comparable, types of social situation, including doctor–patient interviews, chaired committee meetings in industry, and chaired discussions on television (see Coulthard and Montgomery 1981). It is important to mention, however, Burton's (1980, 1981: 61) work on modern dramatic texts and casual conversation, which has sought to extend Sinclair and Coulthard coding scheme so that it can be applied to 'non-formal, non-authoritarian, non-collaborative contexts'. Burton has introduced the notion of challenging moves into the model in order to deal with conflict, but otherwise the Sinclair and Coulthard framework is little changed.

Concerning the sociosemantic approach, Halliday (1972/73: 80) has emphasized: '... in sociological linguistics the criteria for selecting the areas of study are sociological. We investigated those contexts and settings that are socially significant, for instance those concerned with the transmission of cultural values.' The sociological theory on which Halliday has based his discussions, and which I have been concerned with, is that of Basil Bernstein 1971. In particular, the sociosemantic approach has been illustrated and used in connection with Bernstein's work on mother–child control (Halliday 1971/73, 1972/73; Turner 1973).

3.5.2 Levels of analysis

A fundamental difference between the Birmingham approach and the sociosemantic approach emerges when one considers how each approach relates its categories to the speech functions of statement, question and command. Sinclair and Coulthard 1975 are at pains to stress that their discourse categories (e.g. 'informative', 'elicitation' and 'directive') are different from these 'situational' categories (to use their terminology), and represent a distinct level of analysis. The situational categories, it is said, do not capture information about the discourse value of an item. In the case of the situational categories, information about the NON-LINGUISTIC environment (which includes 'all relevant factors in the environment, social conventions, and the shared experience of the participants' (28)) is used to reclassify grammatical items as statement, question or command; thus an interrogative may be classified as question or command depending on the situation. But such a classification does not capture the value of an item in its LINGUISTIC environment: 'the DISCOURSE value of an item depends on what linguistic items have preceded it, what are expected to follow it and what do follow' (Sinclair and Coulthard 1975: 34). In the case of the discourse level, items classified as statement, question, etc. in terms of situation are reclassified according to the contribution they make to the developing discourse; thus a question may or may not be an elicitation.

The sociosemantic categories are, in these terms, situational categories, but are much more situation-specific than Sinclair and Coulthard's categories of statement, question and command. The sociosemantic approach was proposed by Halliday as a possible meeting point for the sociologist and the linguist concerned with language function in social situations. The aim was to try and get them to combine their insights concerning language function. It was suggested that for certain types of situation ('situation types') it may be possible to identify a 'meaning potential', that is, the range of socially significant options, 'behavioural semantic' options, that are available to the speaker in the context of the situation type. The options can be represented in the form of a network, which shows how various choices are systematically related to other choices. An important characteristic of the network is that it is open-ended; it allows the researcher to represent finer and finer distinctions in meaning, as many in fact as the research problem demands. For illustration I give (see Figure 3.2) part of a network devised for an empirical study of Bernstein's social control theory (Turner 1973: 153–6; cf. Halliday's 1971/73, 1972/73 related networks).

Halliday (1972/73: 80) states: 'The input to the semantic networks is sociological and specific; their output is linguistic and general.' Sociological theory, it is suggested, can help to identify social situations and behaviour patterns which are socially significant: a 'meaning potential' rests upon such information. Linguistic theory provides the network concept, and shows how selection in the 'meaning potential' is related to selection in the 'formal potential' of language, that is, within the linguistic code. Halliday (1971/73: 56) suggests that the relationship between a behavioural–semantic category, such as that of 'threat' and linguistic form, is comparable to that between 'statement', 'question', etc. and the grammatical categories of mood:

... the relationship between, say, 'question' in semantics and 'interrogative' in grammar is not really different from that between a behavioural–semantic category such as 'threat' and the categories by which it is realized grammatically. In neither instance is the relationship one-to-one, and while the latter may be rather more complex, a more intensive study of language as social behaviour also suggests a somewhat more complex treatment of traditional notions like those of statement and question.

For realization statements for the categories of threat depicted in Figure 3.2, see Turner (1973: 156–8); cf. Halliday (1972/73: 90–1). There is, however, a difference to be noted between categories like those of statement and question and a category like that of threat. The former are regarded as 'a special case in that they are a property of speech situations as such, and do not depend on any kind of social theory' (Halliday 1971/73: 56). By contrast, what constitutes threatening, for example, is far more dependent on the situation for its interpretation: ' "threat" in a mother/child context has a different significance from "threat" in another social context, such as the operation of a gang'; and this may affect its realization in language (Halliday 1972/73: 79).

3.5.3 Speech acts and discourse

The question of how the sociosemantic approach might be related to the Birmingham concept of discourse structure is part of a wider question: where should speech act information go, if at all, in a model for discourse analysis?

The Birmingham model does not make clear provision for the incorporation of such information. We have seen in section 3.5.2 how the situational categories of statement, question and command are reclassified according to the contribution they make to the developing discourse. These can be seen as speech acts which are reclassified according to their discourse function (see Butler 1985; Edmondson 1981), but it is a narrow range of speech acts and it is obvious that the interest is not in speech acts as such. Stubbs's (1979: 52) observation is of interest here:

The system is comprehensive in the sense that all utterances are coded from beginning to end: nothing is omitted and brushed under the carpet. But only one level of functions is coded. The system has nothing to say about the ways in which language is used to convey threats, irony, humour or whatever. Consequently, like all such systems, the description has an averaging effect: everything is coded according to one particular interest ...

The interest is in the discourse value of the utterance. At this point it is worth reminding ourselves of Bernstein's interest in control strategies such as 'threat of punishment' and 'cognitive appeal' (to use categories from Cook-Gumperz 1973). Arguably, Bernstein's concern is really rather similar, since he is interested in the amount of discretion that is accorded to the person controlled (the child). Control strategies are regarded as differing in the discretion they permit: thus, a cognitive appeal presents the child with a

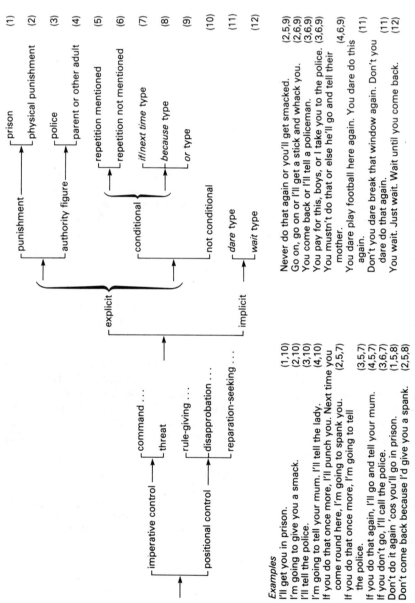

			┌ prison	(1)
			┌ punishment ┤	
			└ physical punishment	(2)
		┌ authority figure ┤	┌ police	(3)
			└ parent or other adult	(4)
			┌ repetition mentioned	(5)
			└ repetition not mentioned	(6)
			┌ if/next time type	(7)
		┌ conditional ┤ because type	(8)
			└ or type	(9)
	explicit ┤ └ not conditional		(10)
		┌ dare type	(11)
└ implicit ┤ └ wait type		(12)

┌ command ...	(1,10)
imperative control ┤	
└ threat	
┌ rule-giving ...	
positional control ┤ disapprobation ...	
└ reparation-seeking ...	

Examples

I'll get you in prison.   (1,10)
I'm going to give you a smack.   (2,10)
I'll tell the police.   (3,10)
I'm going to tell your mum. I'll tell the lady.   (4,10)
If you do that once more, I'll punch you. Next time you
  come round here, I'm going to spank you.   (2,5,7)
If you do that once more, I'm going to tell
  the police.   (3,5,7)
If you do that again, I'll go and tell your mum.   (4,5,7)
If you don't go, I'll call the police.   (3,6,7)
Don't do it again 'cos you'll go in prison.   (1,5,8)
Don't come back because I'd give you a spank.   (2,5,8)

Never do that again or you'll get smacked.   (2,5,9)
Go on, go on or I'll get a stick and whack you.   (2,6,9)
You come back or I'll tell a policeman.   (3,6,9)
You pay for this, boys, or I take you to the police.   (3,6,9)
You mustn't do that or else he'll go and tell their
  mother.   (4,6,9)
You dare play football here again. You dare do this
  again.   (11)
Don't you dare break that window again. Don't you
  dare do that again.   (11)
You wait. Just wait. Wait until you come back.   (12)

Figure 3.2 Part of the sociosemantic network given in Turner 1973

reason which he may challenge (e.g. 'Do you always have a headache when I want to play?' (Bernstein 1971: 159)); a threat does not. Strategies like cognitive appeals are regarded as keeping the discourse open; other strategies are seen as, in varying degrees, closing the discourse, that is, according the controlled a reduced amount of discretion.

Stubbs's comment that 'only one level of function is coded' could be interpreted as implying that illocutionary force information should be dealt with at a different level of analysis. Sinclair and Coulthard's situation level, as I have already implied, would seem to be the obvious candidate: this is the level at which the categories of statement, question and command are identified, and these stand in an interstratal relationship with the discourse categories. How speech act categories might be related to the existing situational categories is, in fact, suggested by Sinclair 1972, in the context of discussing grammar, not discourse. Discussing sentences and 'sentence-actions', he argues for recognizing four actions that sentences do (statement, question, command and response). These categories are 'comprehensive and clear-cut', but a category such as threat would lead to cross-classification:

A 'threat' is certainly an action that a sentence performs; but any threat can ALSO be:
(i)   a statement: I'll be angry if you do this.
or
(ii) a question: Do you think I'll let you do this without payment?
or
(iii) a command: Sit down or I'll get very annoyed.
'Threat' is a much more subtle action than 'question', and we cannot easily relate the idea of threatening to particular STRUCTURAL features. A great many threats have a clause in them beginning with *if* or *unless*, but such a criterion is not accurate enough—there will be many threats that do not, and many sentences with *if*-clauses that are not threats' (Sinclair 1972: 19).

There is a suggestion here of a distinction being drawn between semantics and pragmatics, and the 'comprehensive and clear-cut' categories are perhaps to be seen as semantic categories rather than as the pragmatic 'situational' categories of the later Birmingham work.

There are indications of a different line of approach in Sinclair and Coulthard's 1975 chapter 'Recent developments'. Here they introduce 'illocution' into the model, such that a move like 'directive' can be subdivided according to its illocutionary force. It should be observed, however, that they regard illocution as an internal matter, as a set of choices which do not affect discourse value. They give an illustration (example (1) below), which is of considerable interest:

(1) I was just wondering if you could have a look at this.

They point out that 'it is part of the job of discourse analysis to identify elements of structure such as GREETING, INITIAL MOVE, INTERRUPTION, and to categorize utterances on scales such as formality, politeness, embarrassment' (129) and suggest that an utterance like (1) could be given the features

[+interrupt]   [+transaction initial]   [+polite]

They state that the option is open to extend the feature list, and the utterance could be analysed as

DIRECTIVE: have a look at this: [+softener]   [+... etc.]

where 'softener' covers 'I was just wondering if you could'. Sinclair and Coulthard point out that their use of the conventions of feature analysis is purely a matter of convenience. What is noticeable about Sinclair and Coulthard's suggested analysis is that it groups together features which arguably belong to different 'dimensions' of meaning. The view I take is that the dimensions are best separated out and features located with respect to their appropriate layer of structure.

3.5.4 Elements of structure and classes of act

Sinclair and Coulthard's (1975: 134) position on illocution is reasonably clear, but there is a certain lack of clarity about whether they are talking about moves or acts:

An utterance that clearly requires some activity to satisfy its presuppositions is a DIRECTIVE, and the division of directive into all the many kinds involves a study of the illocutionary force of each. Only where there is a unique effect on the structure of exchanges are there grounds for recognizing a distinct category of move. We regard illocution as a set of choices derived from the internal structure of utterances.

In the system of analysis the directive is a class of act (not move), which can occur as head of an opening move. We have noted earlier the criticism of the development of the concept of system in Halliday's work: 'Systems apparently no longer operate at places in structure but just float in space' (Berry 1980: 15). Is the solution (or part of it) essentially that of tying the sociosemantic network to a particular class of act, namely, the directive operating as head of an opening move? Unfortunately, the solution is not quite so easy, and an examination of places in structure where, for example, a threat can occur, also raises some doubts about the stuctures recognized.

   The directive can only occur as head of an opening move, but there are some directive-like acts that serve subsidiary functions. Below is given Sinclair and Coulthard's (1975: 26) structure for the opening move, with the two classes of subsidiary act shown which could be associated with threats.

Opening move
signal	pre-head	head	post-head	select
	starter		clue	

In terms of Sinclair and Coulthard's (1975: 40–1) definitions, the starter is realized by 'statement, question or command' and 'its function is to provide information about or direct attention to or thought towards an area in order to make a correct response to the initiation likely'; and a clue is realized by 'statement, question, command, or moodless item' and 'it is subordinate to the head of the initiation and function by providing additional information which helps the pupil to answer or comply with the directive'. The starter is illustrated in the following extract (Text D, 76):

(2)

	Act	Move
These three then are for you to sort out for yourselves.	starter	Opening
Can you translate can you be an Egyptologist and translate these names from the chart.	directive	
I'll put them along here so that you can see them.	aside	No move assignment

The aside in the above example looks like a clue, but presumably there were paralinguistic clues that led to this assignment. The clue is now illustrated (Text D, 80):

(3)

	Act	Move
Try the last one	directive	Opening
NV	react	Answering
Come on, Isabel	prompt, nomination	Opening
You're nearly there	clue	Answering

There is no suggestion, of course, in Sinclair and Coulthard's definitions that the starter and clue could be associated with threats, but I would like to suggest that they could, and this need involve no significant distortion of the original categories. Below is given a pair of made-up examples to illustrate the point:

(4)

	Act	Move
I'm going to keep you in at break if you haven't finished your work.	starter	Opening
Answer all the questions in Section B.	directive	

(5)

	Act	Move
Answer all the questions in Section B.	directive	Opening
I'm going to keep you in at break if you haven't finished your work.	clue	

In each case the threat plays a subsidiary role in the discourse: it is subordinate to the head of the move. But does it play a different role according to whether it occurs before or after the head? Apparently not, and an examination of Sinclair and Coulthard's definitions of starter and clue reveals them to be remarkably similar. The question arises, then, whether there really are two functions here, as opposed to two positions in sequence.

Turning from the opening move to the answering one, there would appear to be no place here where a threat could occur, in terms of Sinclair and

Coulthard's categories. This seems counter-intuitive, and it is a matter to which I will return, having consider the follow-up move.

There is a place in the follow-up where a threat seems possible, namely, the post-head position associated with comment act. The structure for the follow-up move is now given (Sinclair and Coulthard 1975: 27):

Follow-up move
   pre-head   head   post-head
                         comment

To illustrate the comment in a follow-up move and to compare it with the directive in an opening move, two extracts are reproduced (Text H, 92, 94).

(6)

	Act	Move
What do we do with a saw?	elicitation	Opening
Cut wood	reply	Answering
Yes	evaluate	Follow-up
You're shouting out through	comment	

(7)

	Act	Move
Scissors	starter	Opening
What do I cut with scissors?	elicitation	
Paper paper	reply	Answering
Yes paper	evaluate	Follow-up
Somebody's shouting out at the back	directive	Opening
NV	react	Answering

For the given comment we could substitute a threat such as:

But I'll get annoyed   comment
if you keep shouting out

For the given directive in (7) it is possible to substitute a threat such as the following:

I'm going to get annoyed if you   directive
don't stop shouting out at the
back

Berry (1979: 57), in her discussion of Sinclair and Coulthard's classes of act, has suggested that comments like 'You're shouting out though' can be classed as 'controlling comments'; they are realized by 'second person statements referring to pupil ongoing activity' and their 'function is to direct the course of the discourse'. Edmondson (1981: 69), approaching the examples from a different angle, is reluctant to interpret 'You're shouting out though' as a statement (as Sinclair and Coulthard's definition requires). He emphasizes that both the comment and directive are commands in situation, and the difference between them is that the former has a subordinate role in its move, whilst the latter acts as head: this difference in status is built into the definition of the two categories. This point is of some significance for our discussion of threats and sociosemantic networks. Since the Sinclair and Coulthard analysis is imposing a further analysis on top of a situational analysis, it should not surprise that a situational (speech act) category such as threat can occur at several places in structure.

What is perhaps surprising, however, is that Sinclair and Coulthard's analysis appears to offer no scope for a threat to occur in an answering move. The head of an answering move may be a reply (realized by 'statement, question, moodless and non-verbal surrogates such as nods'), react (realized by 'a non-linguistic action') and acknowlege (realized by '"yes", "OK", "cor", "mm", "wow", and certain non-verbal gestures and expressions'). It is noticeable that the head is not associated with any class realized by commands. This is also the case for the pre-head and post-head, which are associated with acknowledge and comment respectively. Another point to notice is that, whilst the acts that can head an answering move can all be realized non-verbally, and one of them (react) only non-verbally, the acts that head an opening move are not realized non-verbally. This point is relevant, since threats often occur as responses to non-verbal actions ('If you do that again, I'll . . .'). Leaving aside the question of threats for a moment, consider the following interchange from Goffman (1976: 290):

(8) A: (Enters wearing new hat)
     B: 'No, I don't like it.'
     A: 'Now I know it's right.'

Goffman is bringing together spoken moves and non-linguistic ones to suggest that the notion of adjacency pair may be misleading:

What is basic to natural talk might not be a conversational unit at all, but an interactional one, something of the order of: mentionable event, mention, comment on mention—giving us a three-part unit, the first part of which is quite likely not to involve speech at all. [290]

One need not go quite so far as Goffman does to query the omission of non-verbal realizations for opening moves. I shall return to this point in section 3.6, when Berry's 1981 'primary actor' and 'secondary actor' roles are discussed.

The introduction of the notion of a challenging move into the model (Burton 1980, 1981) provides other places in structure where a threat could occur. Challenging moves function to hold up the development of the topic presented in the previous utterance; thus, for example, a speaker may not give a reply after an elicitation and may give a directive instead. A challenging move is similar to an opening move and, indeed, Butler (1985: 220) classifies both as initiating. As with the opening move, there seem to be three places at which a threat could occur:

Challenging move
     pre-head   head   post-head
     starter   directive   comment

Here is a possible example:

(9)		Act	Move
A:	Give me some of your sweets.	directive	Opening

B: If you don't leave me alone,   directive   Challenging
   I'll tell the teacher.

It should be noted that a challenging move in Burton's analysis does not necessarily imply hostility: it is simply that the interactional expectations set up by a previous move are not fulfilled by the move. The additional move is not designed to solve the problem of non-verbal openings, as no such openings are recognized.

To return to the question of floating systems and the possibility of tying systems to places in discourse, the inspection of Sinclair and Coulthard's classes of move and Burton's challenging move has revealed a somewhat complex picture. In the case of two of the moves, opening and challenging, a threat can occur as head or subordinately as pre-head or post-head; in the case of the answering move, a threat cannot occur, but questions have been raised about the appropriateness of the analysis; and, finally, in the case of the follow-up move, a threat can occur subordinately as post-head. Four classes of discourse acts are involved: directive, comment, starter and clue, but the functional distinction between the latter two has been queried. It should be made clear that much of the complexity is already present in the Birmingham analysis: three of the classes, directive, comment and starter, appear to be cross-classes; that is, they relate to more than one element of structure (see Berry 1979: 51 on Sinclair's introduction of the term). Introducing speech act categories such as threats with accompanying networks yields more delicate classes of these acts, an 'internal' classification from Sinclair and Coulthard's (1975: 134) point of view. The situation is far from neat—cross-classes never are. But we are certainly not saying that anything can occur anywhere, and we are moving from talking about sociosemantic options in a situation to sociosemantic options in the structure of situated discourse. The question arises, however, whether the concept of structure is adequate and whether there are advantages in adopting a multi-layered approach to structure. At this point it is important to consider Berry's (1981a, b, c) proposals for a multi-layered approach to exchange structure.

3.6 BERRY'S PROPOSALS

Berry (1981b) takes up Coulthard and Brazil's (1979: 43) suggestion that 'the exchange is the unit concerned with negotiating the transmission of information', and aims to show how the negotiation of information can be described with reference to three simultaneous layers of structure. It will be helpful to give the structures she recognizes and an example of the analysis—(10) below—before describing the categories:

	Structural formula[2]						
interpersonal layer:	dk1	k2	*k1*	(k2f)			
ideational layer:	pb	*pc*	ps				
textual layer:	*ai*	bi	aii	bii	...	an	bn

(10) Quizmaster: In England, which
                  cathedral has the
                  tallest spire   dk1   pb   *ai*
     Contestant: is it Salisbury   k2   *pc*   bi
     Quizmaster: yes   *k1*   ps   aii
     Contestant: oh   k2f   bii

[Berry 1981b: 127]

The interpersonal layer of structure is concerned with the interactants' knowledge in relation to the information negotiated. Berry takes the view that there must be someone who already knows the information (the primary knower role) and someone to whom the information is imparted (the secondary knower role), and she identifies four functional slots in this layer of structure, two of which can be occupied by the primary knower and two by the secondary knower: dk1 = delaying primary knower; k1 = primary knower; k2 = secondary knower; k2f = secondary knower follow-up. Berry claims that each of the four functions can occur only once in an exchange, and that they are sequentially ordered, as shown in the structural formula.

Berry (1981c) has also argued that essentially the same analysis can be applied to exchanges concerned with negotiating NOT INFORMATION, but action, the carrying out of action. For these she recognizes a primary actor, that is, the person who is going to carry out the action, and a secondary actor, that is, the person who is getting the other person to do it. Example (11), from Berry (1981c: 3), illustrates the categories:

(11) A: Would you like some coffee?   da1
     B: Yes, please   a2
     A: NV (Non-verbal action)   a1
     B: Thanks   a2f

Berry 1981c suggests that the four functional slots identified create increased opportunities, as compared with the 'adjacency pair' approach, for defining speech acts in terms of co-occurrence and sequencing restrictions. This she sees as creating possibilities for relating the work of Sinclair and Coulthard to that of other people working on speech acts. She gives the example of 'request': this is frequently regarded as a speech act, but it is difficult to handle in the Sinclair and Coulthard framework. Using the four functional slots, Berry (1981c: 13) offers the following definition of 'request' in terms of co-occurrence and sequencing restrictions:

request—CAN be preceded by da1 move, CAN be followed by a a2f move,
    followed by a a1 move which CAN contain assent.

Berry's proposals, though at an early stage of development, represent an important advance in defining speech acts and relating them to discourse structure.

The ideational layer of structure is concerned with the amount of information in an exchange. Berry asks: how much information is necessary in an exchange? She suggests that 'the minimum amount of information for an exchange is a completed proposition' (Berry 1981b: 139). She thus recognizes a functional slot pc, standing for propositional completion which is obligatory for all exchanges concerned with the transmission of information. If the first speaker in an exchange is not the one who completes the proposition, he may provide the basis for the completed proposition by producing an utterance which predicts the form of the completed proposition: this is function pb, standing for propositional base. Once the proposition has been completed, it may then be supported by the speaker who did not complete it: this is the final function ps, standing for propositional support. Berry claims that each of these functions can occur only once in an exchange and in the sequence shown in the structural formula.

Berry 1981c has offered a tentative proposal for an ideational layer of structure for directive exchanges. The differences are that a completed proposition is optional, but a completed action is obligatory, and propositional support is replaced by action support:

$$(pb) \quad (pc) \quad ac \quad (as)$$

The textual layer of structure is intended to 'reflect the view of discourse as speakers taking turns' (Berry 1981b: 131), and is the same for both information-oriented and action-oriented exchanges. There is one obligatory function, ai, which is the first contribution of the first speaker. This may be followed by bi, the first contribution of the second speaker, which in turn may be followed by aii, the second contribution of the first speaker, and so on.

Of particular significance for the sociosemantic approach is Berry's work on the interpersonal layer of structure. It is of interest that she has suggested that the structures for the informing/eliciting exchanges and the directive ones can be generalized:

$$((dx1)\ x2\ )\ x1\ (x2f)$$

x being interpreted as actor for directive exchanges, knower for informing/eliciting exchanges (Berry 1981c: 10). The set of options available to a person initiating an exchange are represented in a system at ai in the textual structure (see Figure 3.3). Berry provides realization statements for three of the systems.

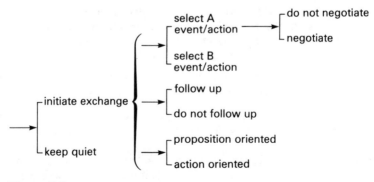

Figure 3.3

These specify which textual and interpersonal functions to include and how to conflate them. Below are given the realization statements for the following initiation:

(12) Father: Salisbury is the English cathedral which has the tallest spire.
     Realization statements
     initiate exchange: include x1 and *ai*
     do not negotiate: conflate x1 and *ai*

There are a number of observations to be made concerning Berry's work. I will first comment on a number of matters which seem to reflect the early stage of development of the work. I will then draw attention to the advantages it offers, if one wishes to try to relate sociosemantic networks to discourse structure.

The first observation concerns the textual layer and the relation between it and the other two layers. There is a sense in which Berry's (1981c: 15) attitude to this layer is rather negative: 'It is a layer of structure which is not so much interesting in itself as for the way in which other layers of structure are mapped on to it.' The textual layer, for Berry, is simply concerned with turns:

$$ai \quad bi \quad aii \quad bii \quad \ldots \quad an \quad bn$$

For the sake of simplicity, Berry assumes that each turn involves a single move which generally consists of a single sentence. Only in the case of the a1 move in a directive exchange does she recognize two classes of act in one move: the obligatory NV (non-verbal action) and the optional verbal contribution that may be given. Example (13) from Berry (1981c: 4) illustrates this combination:

(13) A: Take five paces to the left and there put in the first marker.
     B: Five paces to the left.
         NV

Such simplifying assumptions are necessary at the start of any new work, but in a more developed model of discourse, the textual layer of structure would have much more work to do. As the Birmingham work has shown, there are acts with subsidiary roles within the move (for example, starter, comment), and these also need to be taken into account.

It is worth noting that Berry's (1981c: 4) proposed description of the interpersonal layer does incorporate a kind of hierarchical structuring, as is indicated by the bracketing in the formula:

$$((dx1) x2) x1 (x2f)$$

Example (14) illustrates the use of the categories in an action-oriented exchange:

(14) A: Would you like some coffee?   da1
     B: Yes, please   a2
     A: NV   a1
     B: Thanks   a2f

It will be observed that the first two turns are interpreted by Berry as a check-request sub-sequence: the primary actor delays his action in order to check its acceptability to the secondary actor, and the secondary actor 'requests' the action. Although Berry does not comment on this, it is obvious that this sequence could in turn have been preceded by a further sequence also delaying the action, for example:

(15) A: Are you in a hurry?
     B: No.

Such sequences as the one in (15) have been termed 'pre-sequences' by conversation analysts and within them, pre-invitations, pre-requests, pre-arrangements and pre-announcements have been distinguished; see Levinson 1983 for a useful overview. In the case of pre-invitation, a question is used to check whether some precondition obtains for the action to be performed, and the answer indicates whether it does or does not obtain, encouraging or discouraging the foreseeable action. The question of hierarchical structure is crucial to the interpretation of such acts. On the face of it one could interpret (15) as 'proposition-oriented' and analyse it in terms of 'secondary knower' and 'primary knower' roles, with the structure k2 k1. It is only when one sees the sequence as a sub-goal leading to a main goal that the switch to an 'action-oriented' interpretation seems necessary. My view is that the textual layer of structure should capture not only turns but also the goal structure, both in the relationship with moves and the relationship between moves.

This leads me to a second observation about Berry's proposed analysis. The categories proposed do not take into account the possibility that an act may serve more than one goal. In an earlier paper (Turner 1985) I discussed a complex act, which I termed 'informative-elicitation', in which the speaker BOTH gives information (an expression of the primary knower stance) AND seeks information that he does not know (the secondary knower stance). I shall refer to aspects of this study later, but I want at this point to indicate how the question of multi-goals also arises in the case of action-oriented exchanges.

There seems to be one obvious slot in Berry's formula for the interpersonal layer where a threat could occur: this is the a2 slot, at which the secondary actor demands action of the primary actor. In a well-formed exchange this is followed by a1, the actual non-verbal action of the primary actor. If the primary actor does not provide the action demanded and, say, queries its necessity, this is regarded as the start of a further exchange (strictly, the initiating move in a bound exchange). This analysis is only partially satisfactory. It does not capture the fact that in the case of an explicit threat like 'If you don't go to bed at once, I'll smack you' there are two paths of action involved. The speaker's main goal is to get the child to go to bed, and this is supported by threatening the child with action on the mother's part if the child himself does not act. There are thus two action patterns to be described, one in which the child is the primary actor and one in which the mother is:

| a2 | a1 | | child primary actor |
| da1 | a2 | a1 | mother primary actor |

In this perspective the mother's use of a threat is seen as a way of delaying her action, of checking whether it is 'required' by the child. The child's refusal to carry out the action demanded is the signal that the condition for the mother's action obtains. It will be noticed that in carrying out this analysis I have used Berry's functions but I have departed from her requirement that each of the functions should occur only once in an exchange and in the order given in the structural formula. An explicit threat is seen as a2 in relation to the child's action and as da1 in relation to the mother's action.

There is a final observation to be made on Berry's proposals. This concerns the treatment of non-verbal action. Barry (1981c: 3) does allow an initiating move to consist of non-verbal action, provided that it is related to linguistic moves: 'An action is only linguistically interesting when it is syntagmatically related to other moves which are linguistically realized.' Example (16) below is taken from Berry (1981c: 3):

(16) A, on entering a room where B is working, sees papers flapping about on B's desk in a breeze from the window.
   A: NV
   B: Thanks.

In (16) NV is a1, the main contribution of the primary actor, and 'Thanks' is a2f, the move in which the secondary actor follows up and acknowledges the NV action. If B had queried A's action, this would have been the initiating move in a bound exchange. Whilst the analysis is satisfactory for Berry's purposes, certain doubts arise when one tries to apply it to control situations. If a child, for example, hits his brother, this action is likely to evoke a controlling response from his mother. To see the child as the primary actor and the mother as the acknowledger does not seem entirely appropriate. I would suggest that in some respects the situation is comparable to that in example (17):

(17) Son: Which English cathedral has the tallest spire?
   Father: Salisbury
   Son: Oh.

In (17) the son's question is k2, the father's reply is k1, and the son's 'Oh' is k2f. In the k2 slot the son indicates his state of knowledge in relation to the information and in the k1 slot the father indicates that he knows the information and confers upon it a kind of stamp of authority. It could be said, by analogy, that the child, in hitting his brother, indicates his state of knowledge in relation to action, and the mother, in responding to the child's action, indicates her knowledge in relation to the action, conferring upon it the primary knower's authority. This approach would capture the idea of a person being an 'authority' on action.

I have in the above observations questioned some aspects of Berry's work. I now wish to emphasize the advantages it offers, if one wishes to relate sociosemantic networks to discourse structure. Again it will be helpful to consider examples. Compare examples (18), (19) and (20):

(18) Father: Salisbury is the English cathedral which has the tallest spire.
     Son: Oh.
(19) Father: Salisbury is the English cathedral which has the tallest spire.
     Son: Yes.
(20) Father: Salisbury is the English cathedral which has the tallest spire.
     Son: No, it's not.

At first sight the son's replies in (18), (19) and (20) may seem easily relatable in terms of one system. But as Barry's (1981b) analysis makes clear, it is more revealing to characterize the differences in terms of different layers of structure. The choice between 'Oh' and 'Yes' is handled by Berry with a system at k2f in the interpersonal layer:

It is assumed that 'oh' means 'That's news to me' and that 'Yes' means 'That accords with what is already my understanding of the situation'. At the ideational layer of structure, 'Yes' is seen as positively supporting the proposition, and 'No, it's not' as negatively supporting. This choice is handled with a system at ps:

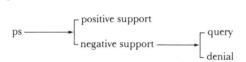

Finally, at the textual layer of structure the following system is recognized at bi:

As we have previously noted, the textual layer of structure is for Berry 'not so much interesting in itself as for the way in which other layers of structure are mapped on to it' (Berry 1981c: 15). The choices represented here clearly reflect choices in the ideational layer.

I believe that the model that Berry proposes, with its layers of simultaneous structure, is helpful, if one is interested in relating sociosemantic networks to discourse structure. The idea of having three layers of structure, where each comprises a 'configuration of functions', and each function can, in principle, be associated with a system, is helpful in avoiding the problem of floating systems. It offers the possibility of locating choices relating to the choice of speech act, its propositional content and its operational relevance in the appropriate layer of structure.

A number of questions remain, however, concerning the relationships between the layers of structure and the claims about the co-occurrence and sequencing restrictions. I shall consider certain aspects of the relationship between the ideational layer and the interpersonal, and between these two layers and the textual. I shall go on to suggest that the functions and roles proposed by Barry have a value, even when the co-occurrence and sequencing restrictions are apparently violated.

How distinct is the ideational layer from the interpersonal? In the case of Berry's proposition-oriented exchanges this may not seem much of an issue. These are concerned with statements and questions, and any propositional content can be stated or questioned. But in the case of the action-oriented exchanges this is much more of an issue. It is not the case that any propositional content can be used to make a threat or a promise, and so on. Discussing the structure of the ideational layer in proposition-oriented exchanges (namely, pb *pc* ps), Berry (1981b: 141) points out:

At the slot occupied by pb there is an almost unlimited range of propositions that can be introduced. The pb itself however narrows the range so that the range of propositions available for the pc slot is relatively limited. The actual completion of the proposition narrows the range even further—to one; at the ps slot only one proposition is negotiable.

Berry (1981c: 7) offers 'a first tentative proposal' for an ideational layer of structure in action-oriented exchanges: (pb) (pc) ac (as). The slot that would conflate with a2 in the interpersonal layer in the case of a threat is pc, propositional completion. It seems to me that it has to be admitted that a critical factor in narrowing down the range of propositions is the type of speech act involved.

The next question concerns the relationship between the textual layer and the other two layers. Is it possible for an exchange to violate co-occurrence and sequencing restrictions relating to the ideational or interpersonal layers and yet still be well formed? Consider the following example (21), which is discussed by Levinson (1981: 111):

A. What's the metric torque-wrench nipple-extractor look like?
B. It's on the bench in front of you.

There is a sense in which this exchange is ill formed with respect to the ideational layer of structure, in that B does not supply pc to A's pb: he does not actually give a description of the tool. However, B's 'answer' is cooperative (support rather than challenge), but

only on the assumption that the reason for A's question is that he wishes to identify and find the wrench and that B reckons that a statement of its location will serve A's purpose better than a description of the instrument itself. [Levinson 1981: 111]

In other words, B's 'answer' can be seen as a cooperative response to a higher-level goal. Examples such as (21) cast doubt on the value of defining the textual layer of structure in 'negative' terms, that is, as the layer on which the other two layers of structure are mapped. In my view, the textual layer of structure should be seen as the last court of appeal in judging whether a structure is well formed or not, that is, in judging whether a unit of discourse is 'operationally relevant' (to use a phrase that Halliday (1976: 27) has used in connection with the textual component in the linguistic system). The textual layer of structure is to be interpreted in terms of the pursuit of goals, and operational relevance is to be judged in terms of the goal structure.

On the question of co-occurrence and sequencing restrictions, I have in a previous paper (Turner 1985) argued that Berry's functions and roles are of value in analysing discourse, even when the restrictions she outlines are apparently violated.

My work on interview materials has suggested that, if one is considering the transmission of information in exchanges, it is not enough to see the initial speaker as adopting EITHER a primary knower stance OR a secondary knower stance, as Berry does. It is possible for the speaker to give information (an expression of the primary knower stance) in a complex speech act, which I have termed 'informative-elicitation', on analogy with Sinclair and Coulthard's 1975 acts. This complex act has important consequences for the structure of the respondent's answer, in that the respondent can give the information sought and comment on the information received. If one attempts to apply Berry's categories to the interview speech, in which interviewers asked mothers how they would solve certain problems of control, it becomes apparent that there is a sense in which the interviewer acts as primary knower and secondary knower and the mother acts as primary knower with the option of also acting as secondary knower. Below is given one of the interview questions with the associated functions alongside:

(22)	Interviewer	Mother
Supposing your husband forgot to bring — a present that he'd promised and he/she wouldn't talk to his/her father all day.	k1	(k2f)
What would you say or do?	k2	k1

The interviewer's utterance is interpreted as a complex act which seeks information but which also provides information as an essential part of it. Note that the informing part may either precede or follow the eliciting part; in example (23) it follows:

(23) What would you say or do	k2
if — wasn't watching what he/she was doing and spilt tea over the table-cloth?	k1

It is also the case that the two parts of the mother's answer (when there are two parts) can vary in sequence, independently of the sequence in the interviewer's speech. In (24) her comment on the reality of the problem (k2f) precedes the informing part (k1), and in (25) it follows:

(24) oh we have this yes   k2f
      I send him to bed . . .   k1
(25) . . . I would try to play middle fiddle   k1
      with my husband
      but it wouldn't happen I don't think   k2f
      quite honestly

If this interpretation of the inverview speech is accepted, Berry's claim about the four functions and their sequential order would seem to require adjustment. It could, of course, be objected that, in applying Berry's categories to conditional utterances, I have extended, and perhaps 'distorted', the original use of the categories. I would argue that the categories still illuminate the structure of the discourse, even though the original co-occurrence and sequencing restrictions are not met.

My work on the interview materials also suggests that Berry's claims concerning the ideational layer may need to be modified in parallel with her claims for the interpersonal layer. Berry 1981b claims that propositional completion may occur only once in an exchange. But she deals with exchanges with only one 'line' of propositional development (to use a term introduced in Turner 1985). Where there is an 'informative-elicitation' act, two lines of propositional development can be distinguished—the 'main line' and a 'related line'. In the interview materials, the main line of propositional development is concerned with 'solution of problem'. The 'elicitation' part of the interviewer's speech provides the propositional basis for the main line of propositional development. The main line is developed when the mother provides the completed proposition(s) which give her solution to the problem. This is the main line, since the mother must provide propositional completion if she is to be regarded as having answered the interviewer's question. The related line of propositional development is concerned with 'reality of problem'. The interviewer's 'informative' provides completed propositions, which the mother may or may not comment on. Important here is the fact that the problem situation is presented in hypothetical terms. This provides the mother with the opportunity to give information about the reality of the problem. If the mother takes up this opportunity, she is to be seen as developing the related line of propositional development by giving propositional support.

The analysis that I have been developing for the interpersonal and ideational layers of structure, with reference to the interview materials, is shown diagrammatically in Figure 3.4 (diagram reproduced from Turner 1985). The convention of placing the functions in linked circles (barbells) has been introduced to indicate that the sequential order of the functions may vary.[3] As we have seen, in the interviewer's 'informative-elicitation' act, in the interpersonal layer, k2 may precede or follow k1. Similarly, in the ideational layer, the functions which conflate with the interpersonal functions (mlb with k2, rlc with k1) are of variable sequence. When a function is optional (k2f and rls), it is placed in the upper circle, and $+/-$ is placed to the right of the link line. Concerning the ideational layer, mlb stands for propositional base for the

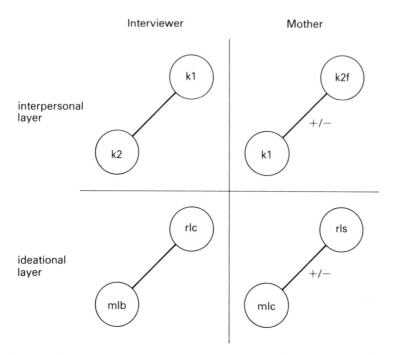

Figure 3.4 Analysis for the interpersonal and ideational layers of structure

main line of propositional development, mlc for propositional completion for the main line, rlc for propositional completion for the related line, and rls for propositional support for the related line.

In my earlier paper (Turner 1985) I made no new proposals concerning the textual layer of structure. However, it will be clear from the above discussion that the treatment of the interpersonal and ideational layers points towards a treatment of the textual layer in terms of goal structure. In a subsequent paper (Turner, forthcoming) I have offered an analysis of the textual layer in terms of goal structure.

3.7 LOCATING THE BIRMINGHAM WORK AND THE SOCIOSEMANTIC WORK

At this point I want to return to the claim that both the Birmingham approach and the sociosemantic approach can be located with respect to ·the three dimensions of meaning. The bulk of Sinclair and Coulthard's analysis I would interpret as relating to the textual layer of discourse, the rest as relating to the interpersonal layer. In making this interpretation I am drawing on Halliday's 1978 discussion of what is 'text' and what gives a text 'texture'. Halliday (1978: 133) argues that, in order to give a complete characterization of 'texture', it is necessary to make reference to 'generic' structure, that is, 'the form that a text has as a property of its genre', for example, narrative form. Halliday emphasizes that this kind of structure does not have its origins in the linguistic system (that is, language as code):

> The generic structure is outside the linguistic system; it is language as the projection of a higher-level semiotic structure. It is not simply a feature of literary genres; there is a generic structure in all discourse, including the most informal spontaneous conversation . . . [134]

The elements of the generic structure of discourse, being outside the linguistic system, cannot be defined in syntactical terms. As Hasan (1978: 29) points out: 'To be at all viable, the definition will have to be functional (Sinclair and Coulthard (1975)), the functions themselves being determined by the semiotics of the text genre . . .' Hasan mentions the well-known example of Aristotle's formula for texts belonging to the genre of Greek tragedy: there must be three elements, Beginning, Middle and End, and the elements must occur in that order.

In essence, the Birmingham approach to the description of discourse structure is very similar. To illustrate this, we may refer to Sinclair and Coulthard's 1975 description of RANK II: Transaction. Here they identify three elements, Preliminary, Medial and Terminal, and give the following formula:

$$P \ M(M^2 \ldots M^n) \ T$$

They comment:

> . . . this formula states:
>
> a) there must be a preliminary move in each transaction,
> b) there must be one medial move, but there may be any number of them,
> c) there can be a terminal move, but not necessarily. [25]

The same principles are applied to the definition of structures at the lower ranks, for example, the unit occurring at M ('exchange (teaching)') has the structure I (R) (F), but see the subsequent revisions in Coulthard and Brazil 1979 and Stubbs 1979.

If the Birmingham analysis is concerned with structures such as I (R) (F), where each successive part provides a frame of reference for what follows, it seems entirely appropriate to deal with the question of 'fit' within the textual layer (on 'fit', see Sinclair and Coulthard, 1975: 133). The basic question here, as I see it, is whether the person making a non-initial move (that is, one at bi, aii, etc. in Berry's terms) decides to play the game as the other person has set it up or decides to try and change it. In other words, does he allow the other person to have control of the interaction or does he try to gain control himself? I believe that it is useful to conceptualize this in terms of the offering and adoption of goals. The system that Berry 1981b, drawing on Burton (e.g. 1981), identifies as each place in the textual layer after *ai* is helpful, though I would see a goal analysis as going beyond Berry's 'negative' approach to the textual layer. It should be stressed that the actual communication roles that the speakers adopt in negotiating information and action, such as informing, acknowledging, questioning, answering, threatening, warning, are the concern of the interpersonal layer of structure. It is here that I would locate much of the sociosemantic work.

Both the Birmingham work and the sociosemantic are, of course, concerned with propositional content, though in differing ways. Halliday 1981, in fact, describes the Birmingham work as being concerned with ideational structure. I would want to qualify that description. I would want to say that Sinclair and Coulthard have identified a textual structure that reflects hierarchically ordered content, but they have not directly analysed the structure of that content: they have not been concerned with the proposition. The sociosemantic work in its sub-classification of speech acts, such as threats, has been concerned with content. It is to be noted that the sub-classification of threat in the network shown in Figure 3.2 is made in terms of ideational content. The recognition of an ideational layer of structure in discourse permits a more formal treatment.

3.8 CONCLUSION

In exploring the relationships between the Birmingham work and the sociosemantic work, the paper has suggested an approach to a discourse level of analysis which separates meaning into three 'dimensions', and recognizes for each a layer of structure. For each function in each layer of structure, in principle, a system, or network, can be identified, representing choices in meaning appropriate to the particular dimension of meaning. Berry's work on exchange structure has been vital, but it has been necessary to modify some of her claims. In the proposed approach the three layers of structure are concerned with the following matters:

Textual layer:	Turn taking
	Goal structure
Interpersonal layer:	Speech acts
Ideational layer:	Topic

NOTES

1. Fawcett 1975 presents five reasons for not regarding sociosemantic networks as a level of the linguistic code. Whilst certain points that Fawcett makes are, I believe, questionable (see Butler 1976; Turner 1976), I do not take issue here with Fawcett's main line of argument, since I do not claim that sociosemantic networks are part of the code, but rather are concerned with situated social behaviour.
2. In the representation of structure, brackets = 'optional under all circumstances', no italics = 'obligatory under certain circumstances', italics = 'obligatory'.
3. This convention owes something to Halliday's 1979 discussion of experiential structures: cf. 'The non-linear representation implies more of a molecular model of structure . . .' (9).

BIBLIOGRAPHY

Allerton, D. J., Carney, E. and Holdecroft, D. (eds) (1979), *Function and Context in Linguistic Analysis: Essays Offered to William Haas*, Cambridge, Cambridge University Press.

Beekman, J. and Callow, J. (1974), *Translating the Word of God*, Grand Rapids, Zondervan.

Benson, J. D. and Greaves, W. S. (eds) (1985), *Systemic Perspectives on Discourse: Vol. 1 Selected Theoretical Papers from the Ninth International Systemic Workshop*, Norwood, N.J., Ablex.

—— and —— (eds) (1985), *Systemic Perspectives on Discourse: Vol. 2 Selected Applied Papers from the Ninth International Systemic Workshop*, Norwood, N.J., Ablex.

Benson, J. D., Cummings, M. and Greaves, W. S. (eds) (forthcoming), *Linguistics in a Systemic Perspective*, Amsterdam, Benjamins.

Bernstein, B. (1971), *Class, Codes and Control: Vol. 1 Towards a Sociology of Language*, London, Routledge and Kegan Paul.

—— (ed.) (1973), *Class, Codes and Control: Vol. 2*, London, Routledge and Kegan Paul.

Berry, M. (1979), 'A note on Sinclair and Coulthard's classes of acts including a comment on comments', *Nottingham Linguistic Circular*, 8, No. 1.

—— (1980), 'They're all out of step except our Johnny: a discussion of motivation (or the lack of it) in systemic linguistics', University of Nottingham (mimeo).

—— (1981a), 'Polarity, ellipticity, elicitation and propositional development, their relevance to the well-formedness of an exchange', *Nottingham Linguistic Circular*, 10, No. 1.

—— (1981b), 'Systemic linguistics and discourse analysis: a multi-layered approach to exchange structure', in Coulthard and Montgomery (eds) (1981).

—— (1981c), 'Towards layers of exchange structure for directive exchanges', *Network*, 2.

Burton, D. (1980), *Dialogue and Discourse*, London, Routledge and Kegan Paul.

—— (1981). 'The socio*linguistic* analysis of spoken discourse', in French and Maclure (eds) (1981).

Butler, C. S. (1976), 'Some important aspects of the interpersonal function', University of Nottingham (mimeo).

—— (1985), 'Discourse systems and their place within an overall systemic model', in Benson and Greaves (eds) (1985), Vol. 1.

Christie, F. (ed.) (1986), *Language and the Social Construction of Experience*, Geelong, Deakin University.

Cook-Gumperz, J. (1973), *Social Control and Socialization*, London, Routledge and Kegan Paul.

Copeland, J. E.and Davis, P. W. (eds) (1981), *The Seventh LACUS Forum 1980*, Columbia, S. Carolina, Hornbeam Press.

Coulthard, M. and Brazil, D. (1979), *Exchange Structure*, Discourse Analysis Monographs No. 5, University of Birmingham, English Language Research.

Coulthard, M. and Montgomery, M. (eds) (1981), *Studies in Discourse Analysis*, London, Routledge and Kegan Paul.

Dijk, T. A. van and Petöfi, J. (eds) (1977), *Grammars and Descriptions*, Berlin, de Gruyter.

Dressler, W. U. (ed.) (1978), *Current Trends in Textlinguistics*, Berlin and New York, de Gruyter.

Edmondson, W. (1981), *Spoken Discourse: A Model for Analysis*, London, Longman.

Fawcett, R. P. (1975), 'Summary of "Some issues concerning levels in systemic models of language" (paper read to the Nottingham Linguistic Circle, December 1973)', in *Nottingham Linguistic Circular*, 4, No. 1.

Fawcett, R. P. (1980), *Cognitive Linguistics and Social Interaction: Towards an Integrated Model of a Systemic Functional Grammar and the other Components of a Communicating Mind*, Heidelberg, Julius Groos Verlag.

—— (1986), 'Children are choosers: a socio-cognitive framework, using systemic linguistics, for thinking about language in education', in Christie (ed.) (1986).

Fawcett, R. P., Halliday, M. A. K., Lamb, S. M. and Makkai, A. (eds) (1984), *The Semiotics of Culture and Language: Vol. 1 Language as Social Semiotic*, London, Frances Pinter.

French, P. and Maclure, M. (eds) (1981), *Adult–Child Conversation*, London, Croom Helm.

Goffman, E. (1976), 'Replies and responses', *Language in Society*, 5, 257–313.

Gregory, M. (1983), 'Sentence and clause as distinct units in the morphosyntactic analysis of English and their relation to semological proposition and predication', in Morreall (ed.) (1983).

Halliday, M. A. K. (1961), 'Categories of the theory of grammar', *Word*, 17, 241–92.

—— (1970), 'Language structure and language function', in Lyons (ed.) (1970).

—— (1971/73), 'Language in a social perspective', *Educational Review*, 23, No. 3, 165–88, reprinted in Halliday (1973).

—— (1972/73), 'Towards a sociological semantics', *Working Papers and Prepublications* (Series C, No. 14), Centro Internazionale di Semiotica e di Linguistica, Universita di Urbino, reprinted in Halliday (1973).

—— (1973), *Explorations in the Functions of Language*, London, Edward Arnold.

—— (1974/77). 'Text as semantic choice in social contexts', in van Dijk and Petöfi (eds) (1977), reprinted in Halliday (1978).

—— (1976), 'The teacher taught the student English': an essay in applied linguistics. In Reich (ed.) (1976).

—— (1978), *Language as Social Semiotic*, London, Edward Arnold.

—— (1979), 'Modes of meaning and modes of expression: types of grammatical structure, and their determination by different semantic functions', in Allerton, Carney and Holdcroft (eds) (1979).

—— (1981), 'Text semantics and clause grammar: some patterns of realization', in Copeland and Davis (eds) (1981).

—— (1984), 'Language as code and language as behaviour: a systemic-functional interpretation of the nature and ontogenesis of dialogue', in Fawcett, Halliday, Lamb and Makkai (eds) (1984).

Halliday, M. A. K. and Hasan, R. (1976), *Cohesion in English*, London, Longman.

Hasan, R. (1978), 'Text in the Systemic-Functional model', in Dressler (ed.) (1978).

Hudson, R. A. (1976), *Arguments for a Non-Transformational Grammar*, Chicago, Illinois and London, University of Chicago Press.

—— (1978), 'Daughter dependency grammar and systemic grammar', *UEA Papers in Linguistics*, 6, 1–14.

Leech, G. (1981), *Semantics*, 2nd edn., Harmondsworth, Penguin.

Levinson, S. C. (1981), 'Some pre-observations on the modelling of dialogue', in *Discourse Processes*, 4, No. 2, 93–110.

—— (1983), *Pragmatics*, Cambridge, Cambridge University Press.

Lyons, J. (ed.) (1970), *New Horizons in Linguistics*, Harmondsworth, Penguin.

Morreall, J. (ed.) (1983), *The Ninth LACUS Forum*, Columbia, S. Carolina, Hornbeam Press.

Nickel, G. (ed.) (1976), *Proceedings of Fourth AILA Congress: Vol. 1*, Stuttgart, Hochschulverlag.

Petöfi, J. and Reiser, H. (eds) (1973), *Studies in Text Grammar*, Dordrecht, Reidel.

Reich, P. A. (ed.) (1976), *The Second LACUS Forum*, Columbia, S. Carolina, Hornbeam Press.

Sandulescu, C. (1976), 'Theory and practice in analyzing discourse', in Nickel (ed.) (1976).

Sinclair, J. McH. (1972), *A Course in Spoken English: Grammar*, London, Oxford University Press.

Sinclair, J. McH. and Coulthard, R. M. (1975), *Towards an Analysis of Discourse*, Oxford, Oxford University Press.

Stubbs, M. (1979), *Observing Classroom Language*, O.U. PE232, Block 5, Open University Press.

Turner, G. J. (1973), 'Social class and children's language of control at age five and age seven', in Bernstein (ed.) (1973), Vol. 2.

—— (1976), 'M. A. K. Halliday: *Learning how to Mean*', review article, *Nottingham Linguistic Circular*, **5**, No. 2.

—— (1985), 'Discourse structure: social class differences in answers to questions', in Benson and Greaves (eds) (1985), Vol. 2.

—— (forthcoming), 'Social structure and social action', in Benson, Cummings and Greaves (eds) (forthcoming).

Winter, E. O. (1977), 'A clause-relational approach to English texts', *Instructional Science*, **6** (Special Issue).

—— (1979), 'Replacement as a fundamental function of the sentence in context', *Forum Linguisticum*, **IV**, No. 2, 95–133.

Part III
Meta-functions

4 Meta-functions: aspects of their development, status and use in systemic linguistics

Michael Gregory
York University, Toronto

The literature in linguistics concerned with a functional approach to language extends back at least as far as Malinowski, Bühler, Jakobson and the Prague school. It is being enlarged at present by systemic linguists, and not without controversy, For example, the Seventh International Systemic Workshop at Sheffield University, September 1980, made it clear that there were interestingly conflicting views among systemicists. Questions were raised about the number of meta-functions to be recognized, their relevance to system networks and possible generative forms of the semantics and/or lexico-grammar, and about the allocation of systems to functions. Their relationship to the concept of register and its field, mode and tenor was also discussed.

Here such matters will be addressed in three sections.[1] The first will sketch the development of the concept of meta-functions within linguistics in general and systemics in particular; the second will assess the importantly differing present positions of M. A. K. Halliday and R. P. Fawcett; and the third will discuss J. R. Martin's proposed revision of the register framework in relation to the meta-functions.

4.1 THE DEVELOPMENT OF THE CONCEPT OF META-FUNCTIONS

The use of the word FUNCTION in linguistics has been, and is, diverse. It is used in the description of internal language patterns: grammatical (e.g. Martinet 1977; Pike and Pike 1977) and phonological (e.g. Martinet 1960). Those influenced by Hjemslev have used FUNCTION for intersystemic relationships; Scale and Category linguists in the 1960s did not hesitate to say that a nominal group could function as the Subject element of structure in a clause. As well as its use in formal description, function meaning 'use' of language has been with us a long time. Important was Malinowski's 1923 idea of meaning as 'function in context'. This was developed by Firth in terms of a series of internal and external contexts. He wrote:

Meaning we use for the whole complex of function which a linguistic form may have. The principal components of this whole meaning are phonetic function which I call a 'minor function', the major functions—lexical, morphological and syntactical . . . and the function of a complete locution in the context of situation, the province of semantics. [Firth 1935/57: 33]

It is possible to discern here a view of function which is both intrinsic and extrinsic to language.

The two earliest and clearest modern statements on functions of language, in the sense of major abstract functions as opposed to functions in language, are both, however, extrinsic. Malinowski 1923, from an ethnographic point of view, first distinguished three: ACTIVE, NARRATIVE and MAGICAL, and later two: PRAGMATIC and MAGICAL (1935). Bühler 1934, from a psychological perspective, distinguished three: REPRESENTATIONAL, EXPRESSIVE and CONATIVE. Influenced by Bühler and particularly Mathesius 1928, INTRINSIC concepts emerged with the Prague school: Daneš 1964, Firbas 1964 and Vachek 1966 developed the concepts of FUNCTIONAL SENTENCE PERSPECTIVE, ORGANIZATION OF UTTERANCE and SEMANTIC STRUCTURE OF SENTENCE. Halliday 1969 recognized the development by Czechoslovak linguists of the 'functionalist' view of linguistic STRUCTURE. Introducing his work on the systems and structures of the clause in English, he wrote:

The systems having the clause as their point of origin group themselves into three sets which I have referred to elsewhere under the headings of transitivity, mood and theme [Halliday 1967]. These labels refer specifically to sets of clause systems, which are however relatable to these general components of the grammar. Those with transitivity belong to that area which Vachek derives from Bühler's 'Darstellungsfuncktion' and glosses as 'informing of the factual, objective and content of extralinguistic reality' [Vachek 1966]. Daneš calls it the 'semantic structure of the sentence' [Daneš 1964]. Those of mood express speech function, the relations among the participants in a speech situation and the speech roles assigned by the speaker to himself and his interlocuters; this includes most of Poldauf's 'third syntactical plan' [Poldauf 1964] and embraces both of Bühler's additional functions—the speaker's attitude and his attempt to influence the hearer—though excluding (as outside grammar) the paralinguistic indexical signals. Theme is the clausal part of Mathesius' 'functional sentence analysis' [Vachek 1966: 59ff.], Daneš' organization of utterance [Daneš 1964: 227ff.], which continues to be studied extensively by Firbas and others [Firbas 1966]; this concerns the structure of the act of communication within the total framework of a discourse, the delination of message units and the distribution of information within them. [Halliday 1969: 81/1972/1981]

Halliday (1970a: 147ff.) also recognized the implications of Sweet's 'logical' and 'grammatical subjects' (Sweet 1891:10ff., 89ff.) as indicating an awareness of the simultaneity of different structures in a clause.

In his 1969 article Halliday presented the functions as COMPONENTS OF THE GRAMMAR: 'Let us then suggest four generalized components in the organization of the grammar of a language, and refer to them as the components of extra-linguistic experience, of speech functions, of discourse organization and of logical structure' (Halliday 1969: 81–2); the logical component is concerned with the 'ands' and 'ors' and 'ifs' of language and should 'rather be considered separately' from extra-linguistic experience (ibid. 80). In Halliday

1970a, the components are now introduced as FUNCTIONS OF LANGUAGE, which 'are simply different kinds of meaning' and the labels IDEATIONAL, INTER-PERSONAL and TEXTUAL are used and 'for the sake of brevity . . . the logical component in linguistic structure, which is somewhat different in its realizations' (Halliday 1970a: 144) is left out. Both the 1969 and 1970a articles are concerned with the simultaneous configuration of structures in the independent clause: two different binary structures (mood, theme) and the multi-role transitivity structure.

Linguistic ontogeny is introduced with the discussion of function in Halliday 1970b: 'The link between function and structure is seen most clearly in the language of the child' (ibid.: 322). Halliday 1973 and 1975a extend the discussion in detail and trace a child's progress, starting with seven micro-functions or 'uses': INSTRUMENTAL ('I want'), REGULATORY ('do as I tell you'), INTERACTIONAL ('me and you'), PERSONAL ('here I come'), HEURISTIC ('tell me why'), IMAGINATIVE ('let's pretend') and REPRESENTATIONAL ('I've got some-thing to tell you'), which yield a 'content-realized-by-expression' proto-language. The child then generalizes these into MATHETIC (observation and learning) and PRAGMATIC (response-demanding and participatory) uses of language. This leads in turn to an acceptance of the adult system with its simultaneous and configured meta-functions (IDEATIONAL, INTERPERSONAL and TEXTUAL), which enables the user to mean more than one thing at once because of the intrusion between content and expression of FORM, the lexico-grammatical stratum which allows the different functions to be mapped on to one another, a process for which Halliday has used the analogy of polyphony in music (1978: 56).

From 1970 to 1977, there is growing emphasis in Halliday's work on the systems which underlie structure and the clustering of systems according to the functions; this is involved in an emerging concept of the description of behaviour as a description of POTENTIAL; what the individual can 'do' is the concern of semiotics, what he can 'mean' of semantics, what he can 'say' of lexico-grammar, and what he can 'sound' of phonology. Like the Prague linguists, Halliday is increasingly speaker-oriented; the speaker is seen as observer of life's experience, as intruder into other people's behaviour, and as maker of texts in situations—but these are linked respectively to the ideational, interpersonal and textual functions of LANGUAGE, rather than to Praguian ideas of function of UTTERANCE.

REGISTER, the configuration of field, mode and tenor of discourse, which was introduced as a language variety category (Halliday, McIntosh and Strevens 1964) is viewed more and more as a semantic concept of considerable abstraction: the semantic resources 'at risk' in a given type of situation (cf. Halliday 1975b). Field, mode and tenor are now regarded as more than just 'kinds of language use' or simple 'components of the speech setting'. They become 'a conceptual framework for representing the social context as the semiotic environment in which people exchange meaning' (Halliday 1975b: 26), and are related to the ideational (field), interpersonal (tenor) and textual (mode) functions. Halliday and Hasan 1976 emphasize TEXT seen as a semantic unit as a major concern in linguistics; textuality is described in terms of intra-sentential structure, inter-sentential cohesion, and consistency of register.

Meanwhile Hudson 1974 described Halliday's idea of the organizing link between functions and clusters of system as 'plausible' but in his own grammars makes no explicit use of functions. Fawcett (1973a, 1973b/81) made two important departures from Halliday's position. First, system networks are confined to the semantics, which is what the networks of transitivity, mood and theme comprise (Halliday having described these networks as belonging in both semantic and lexico-grammatical strata, and in 1973: 88–9 having used the term 'semantic' to describe the sociosemantic networks). Thus form (syntax and items for Fawcett) is seen in structural terms (cf. Butler 1979, 1985: 94–102 for a clear summary of Fawcett's syntax within systemics). Second, the number of functional components (of the SEMANTICS, therefore) is at this time expanded to six. Fawcett divides Halliday's ideational into two separate functions: EXPERIENTIAL and LOGICAL are not viewed as sub-components but as components in their own right; the interpersonal is bifurcated into the INTERACTIONAL (speech function) and the EXPRESSIVE (attitudinal), and the textual into THEMATIC and INFORMATIONAL.

4.2 TWO POSITIONS ON META-FUNCTIONS: M. A. K. HALLIDAY AND R.P. FAWCETT

Halliday's most recent published position can be found in Halliday 1977, 1978, 1979 and Halliday and Hasan 1980. Language is viewed as a semiotic system, as a code that has two or more realizational cycles in it. This means that it consists of at least three strata: SEMANTICS, which is realized by LEXICO-GRAMMAR, which is realized by PHONOLOGY. The term 'at least' allows for the addition of further strata above the semantic system,

since the semantic system itself can be regarded as the realization of some higher level semiotic. In principle this may be associated with any number of different orders of meaning, cognitive, social, aesthetic and other things besides. At any particular time, attention is likely to be focussed on one or other of these higher orders. [1979: 57–8]

The number of functions and 'where' they belong in the theory is dealt with this way: the functions are seen as 'modes of meaning' so they belong to the semantic stratum, and seen from this vantage point there are three functions: IDEATIONAL, INTERPERSONAL and TEXTUAL , with the ideational having the sub-components of EXPERIENTIAL and LOGICAL. It is argued that within the semantics the EXPERIENTIAL and LOGICAL are linked because 'there is greater systemic interdependence between these two than between other pairs' (1978: 131). Viewed from the vantage point of a higher-level semiotic than the linguistic one, the ideational and interpersonal are yoked together as 'extrinsic' (dealing in different ways with what goes on in behaviour), as opposed to the 'enabling' function, the textual. When the functions are viewed 'from below', i.e. from the lexico-grammatical stratum, the logical is distinct from all others 'since it alone is, and always is, realized through recursive structure' (1978: 170), and so is univariate as opposed to the multivariate, experiential, interpersonal and textual structures.

The 1979 article repeats the argument of Halliday 1969 and 1970a, that the functions are justified because they are limited to relatively independent sets of options, but now the options are seen as semantic rather than as components of the grammar (cf. Halliday 1979: 61). However, the most far-reaching hypotheses of this article are (1) that 'each of these semantic components typically generates a different kind of structural mechanism as its output, or realization'; and (2) that 'these different types of structure are non-arbitrarily related to the kinds of meaning they express' (ibid.: 61). The different 'modes of meaning' (which I interpret as semantic systems) are then claimed to be uniquely related to the nature of the 'modes of expression' (which I interpret as grammatical structures) they generate.

Halliday suggests that experiental systems give rise to CONSTITUENT, ROLE-type structures—in Pike's 1967 terms, 'particulate' structures—such as Actor, Process, Goal, which are in themselves unordered as regards sequence. It is argued that this is non-arbitrary, that it expresses how we order our experience when we want to deal with it linguistically; we split it up into discrete entities which interact with each other.

The interpersonal mode of meaning is seen to be reflected in structures that permeate the clause. In English, modalities, including swear words and obscenities, can be spread throughout the unit. Interpersonal meaning (e.g. the system of 'key') can also be expressed by intonational contours mapped on to the clause as a whole. The rationale behind this mode of expression is that interpersonal meanings represent 'the speaker's ongoing intrusion into the speech situation' (Halliday 1979: 67), so they are PROSODIC or CUMULATIVE—FIELD-like, in Pike's terms (although this is stretching Pike's meaning somewhat).

Textual structures, on the other hand, are seen as PERIODIC or CULMINATIVE. Typically in English, in the unmarked instance, THEME occurs at the beginning of the clause and the informational NEW towards the end. So

what the textual component does is to express the particular semantic status of elements in the discourse by assigning them to the boundaries . . . and so marks off units of the message as extending from one peak of prominence to the next. [Halliday 1979: 69]

They are seen to be WAVE-like, in Pike's terms.

As has been indicated, the logical mode is seen to be realized by structures different again from all of the other three because they are RECURSIVE and generate complexes rather than simplexes. Halliday recognizes that these associations of kinds of structures with semantic functions are typical tendencies rather than rules; whereas the functions themselves can be regarded as universal, the structural tendencies, although non-arbitrary, represent statements about English, and modes of expression may vary from language to language. Nevertheless, Halliday's argument is an attractive one: it goes a long way to giving credibility to his contention that 'functional variation [is] not just . . . variation in the use of language, but rather . . .

something which is built in, as the very foundation, to the organization of language itself, and particularly to the organization of the semantic system' (Halliday and Hasan 1980: 49).

Fawcett's *Cognitive Linguistics and Social Interaction: Towards an Integrated Model of a Systemic Functional Grammar and the Other Components of a Communicating Mind* (1980) presents rather different views and develops considerably some of his earlier ideas. Its very title contains language clearly within the systemic tradition and language redolent of the Chomskyan tradition, and there is a theoretical ambiguity about Fawcett's position. He sees linguistics as 'in principle a branch of cognitive psychology' (Fawcett 1980: 4), appeals to 'psychological reality' (ibid.: 7 ff.), and uses the term 'grammar' in the Chomskyan sense of a model of a particular language. As before, systems are located in the semantics and realized through syntax, items and intonation. He describes Halliday as having semanticized his lexico-grammatical stratum and argues 'that syntax is a level of language that can be described (though not explained) independently of the semantic system networks from what it is generated' (ibid.: 52). Although his networks and realization rules (to which he devotes considerable attention and which are richly rewarding) are still, as he recognizes, incomplete, it is apparent that Fawcett is much concerned with the generative form of the 'grammar' and, despite his disclaimer (ibid.: 8) about taking elegance criteria too seriously, many of his descriptive positions seem to be dictated by considerations of parsimony.

There is much to be said for semanticized grammars such as many of Halliday's own descriptive statements suggest. Pike and Pike's 1977 development of the four-cell tagmeme has made their kind of grammatical analysis more semantically revealing, and I am currently working on a grammar[2] developed from Gregory (1967/72) which attempts to combine systemic (semantic) and structural (syntactic) statements into a kind of tree diagram form containing most of the information given in both Halliday's 'structural analysis of a clause' (Kress 1976: 24, reprinted in Fawcett 1978: 53) and Fawcett's own 'displayed feature semantic representation of an English clause' (Fawcett 1980: 195). There are a host of purposes, such as stylistics, text description and language pedagogy, for which semantically revealing syntactic analysis has a place. Geoffrey Sampson, a non-systemicist, has pointed out that systemic grammars are amenable for use in literary study and language teaching because they are good at showing a mass of similarities and dissimilarities between sentences (Sampson 1980: 230–1). Even when chasing after generative goals, systemicists should not lose this quality of clarity and staged detail; which is why the scales of rank and delicacy remain important—as well as assignment to functions.

Fawcett is sensitive to Halliday's contribution towards formalizing the concept of function (Fawcett 1980: 25 ff.). However, he still disagrees as to the number of functions. His dominant criteria for recognizing a function seems to be what he considers a different type of meaning, rather than any paradigmatic or syntagmatic criteria or group of criteria. This leads him now to recognize eight functional components of the semantics, and three minor 'possible extras'. The eight are EXPERIENTIAL, LOGICAL RELATIONSHIPS, NEGATIVITY (these three corresponding to Halliday's ideational: negativity has been variously placed by Halliday in the logical, the interpersonal and the experiential); INTERACTIONAL (speech function, mood), AFFECTIVE (performer's emotional evaluation) and MODALITY (all of which Halliday includes in the interpersonal); THEMATIC and INFORMATIONAL (Halliday's textual). The three possible extras are the INFERENTIAL, the METALINGUAL (which seems to me from his example to be within Halliday's interpersonal), and the DISCOURSE ORGANIZATIONAL (which Halliday and Hasan 1976 and 1980 appear to deal with as matters of textual cohesion, text structure and register). This multiplying of the functions may help Fawcett's 'semantic-system-to-strucutral-realization' generative 'grammar', but there appears to be a loss of generality in that, unlike Halliday, he cannot claim that every sentence has to be dealt with in terms of ALL the metafunctions; he can only claim in terms of several. His functions are perhaps best seen as an increase in delicacy useful for certain purposes and preoccupations. Whether it is intended to do so or not, his own chart representing the comparison between his and Halliday's functions seems to suggest this (Fawcett 1980: 28, Figure 2).

4.3 J. R. MARTIN'S PROPOSED APPROACH TO REGISTER AND META-FUNCTIONS

Martin 1980/81 takes yet another stance, and that a provocative one. After examining fifteen different criteria that have been used by systemicists, he claims that there is 'no set of necessary and sufficient paradigmatic or syntagmatic reasons for locating systems in one meta-functional component or another' (Martin 1980/81: 1). He interprets the concept of meta-function 'as an empirical claim about the paradigmatic organization of clause systems in English' (1980/81: 1) and maintains that it is specifically synchronic, and tied to a particular rank, that of clause, in the closed system part of the lexico-grammar. (This may not be such a different position from Fawcett's or Halliday's as it at first appears: Fawcett's semantics is his first stratum of networks, his syntax being essentially structural, and Halliday seems recently to write as if lexico-grammar's concern is with structure rather than system.) For Martin, extensions of the concept of meta-function to kinds of meanings, to other grammatical ranks, and to lexis are by ANALOGY and once extended are not open to testing by writing optimal grammars and observing how systems cluster (as suggested by Hudson 1974).

To overcome some of these problems he proposes a reworking of the register categories 'so that they will correlate more closely with the clusters of systems to which meta-functional labels are applied' (Martin 1980/81: 1). His reworking involves maintaining my distinction between functional and personal tenor (Gregory 1967; Gregory and Carroll 1978); Halliday has variously included what is covered by functional tenor in field (e.g. Halliday 1965) or mode (e.g. Halliday, McIntosh and Strevens 1964). Martin differs from me, however, in placing functional tenor in a 'deeper' stratum underlying field, personal tenor and mode, and giving rise to the schematic structure of text, as his figure illustrates (Martin 1980:81: 25, Figure 28) reproduced as Figure 4.1. Unlike Fawcett, he sees each stratum as consisting of a full system-structure cycle at various ranks so that, for example, a SEMANTIC system of SPEECH FUNCTION would underlie LEXICO-GRAMMATICAL MOOD. He argues that whereas it is probable that Halliday's proposed link between field and the experiential system, mode and the textual, personal tenor and the interpersonal may be established by empirical research on texts, functional tenor is unlikely to have such a one-to-one relationship and so is 'deeper'. His hope is that if register 'could be shown to be linked to certain core well-motivated meta-functional components, it could be used to test the location of systems whose metafunctional address is unclear' (Martin 1980/ 81: 34).

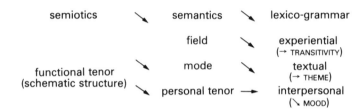

Figure 4.1 Martin's representation of register and meta-function relationships

I have modifications to suggest which emerge from some objections to Martin's interpretation of Gregory 1967 and Gregory and Carroll 1978. Martin writes, 'Gregory, following Halliday (1961), uses the term CONTEXT for the stratum called SEMANTICS and does not recognize a fourth stratum of linguistically significant patterning' (Martin 1980/81: 25). Certainly I would now use the term SEMANTICS for what was then called CONTEXT, but I maintain that a fourth stratum is to some extent recognized in both the 1967 and 1978 statements, and that is SITUATION, which I now regard as the concern of SEMIOTICS. SITUATION was described as 'the study of those extra-textual features ... which have high potential relevance to statements of meaning about the texts of language events' (Gregory 1967: 178). This refers, then, to 'patterns' of human social behaviour which have linguistic relevance, and seems quite compatible with the current use of 'semiotic' in linguistics. CONTEXT I described as 'the correlation of formally described linguistic features, groupings of such features within texts and abstracted from them, with those situational features themselves constantly recurrent and relevant to the understanding of language events' (Gregory 1967: 178). This seems quite compatible with the use of SEMANTICS (as was suggested in Gregory and Carroll 1978: 4, 9). The need for having both situational (semiotic) and contextual (semantic) categories is argued in Gregory (1967: 182–3) and, as

Martin seems to recognize (Martin 1980/81: 23), this is why functional tenor and personal tenor are both 'tenors': they are the SEMANTIC reflection of SEMIOTIC addressee relationships, personal and functional. Recently, Halliday appears to be placing field, mode and tenor in the semiotic stratum, and giving them what might be called portmanteau designations which combine what for Martin and me would be semantic categories: for example, 'field' combines with a semiotic category such as 'social process', so he writes about 'a field' of social processes (what is going on), a 'tenor' of social relationship (who are taking part), and a 'mode' of symbolic interaction (how the meanings are exchanged) (Halliday 1979: 189). What I suggest as an alternative to both Martin and Halliday is represented in Figure 4.2.

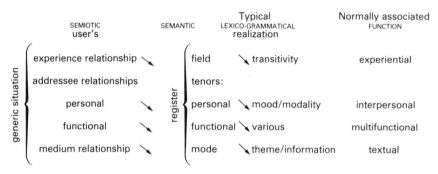

Figure 4.2 Proposed revisions of Figure 4.1

EXPERIENCE RELATIONSHIP is now preferred to PURPOSIVE ROLE (Gregory 1967; Gregory and Carroll 1978) or SOCIAL ACTIVITY or PROCESS (Halliday 1978, 1979) as the semiotic category related to field, to avoid possible confusion with personal or functional addressee relationships. Martin's suggestion that functional tenor underlies the other three and necessarily gives rise to schematic structure is rejected. In Gregory and Carroll 1978, it was recognized that, in some instances, functional tenor is the most determining category: 'The generic structure of text is often defined in terms of functional tenor . . . An advertisement is by definition an attempt to persuade through both linguistic and visual means' (1978: 53, cf. also 60). Also, Martin's own particular selection of examples support his case: they reflect generic situations in which functional addressee relationships have an important role. However, after a reasonably detailed description of a typical collect of the *Book of Common Prayer*, Carroll and I were able to point out that

such a configuration of field, mode and tenors indicates a register of the Christian Collect. This can be regarded as a FIELD-DETERMINED REGISTER, as the choices of mode and tenor can be seen as being consequentially related to the nature of the field of discourse. [emphasis added]

And we continued:

The activity of science is a recording activity, which means that it is committed to the written mode, and has its own conventions of impersonality of presentation, which means that there are few variations as regards tenors of discourse. Scientific texts tend to be expository in their functional addressee relationship and of mid-formality in their personal addressee relationship. [Gregory and Carroll 1978: 33]

These observations as regards the range of determining influence of the different dimensions I would still make. I do not want to separate schematic structure from considerations of genre and generic structure, and, as Martin recognizes and seems to think research will justify (Martin 1980/81: 24, 30), I prefer to characterize genre in terms of all dimensions of language variety (cf. Gregory and Carroll 1978: 45). Martin and I agree that Halliday is descriptively unwise to place genre considerations within mode (Halliday 1973). Genre I consider semantically as REGISTER and semiotically as GENERIC SITUATION. The need for both sets of categories, particularly in the study of literary genres, lay behind the following comment:

... great literature may often make its impact by constantly not meeting the linguistic expectations of the addressee. Writers will consciously alter normal patterns of form and substance, will 'play' with the semantic possibilities offered by language in order to create an innovative work that draws our attention afresh to human experience and its verbalization. [Gregory and Carroll 1978: 73]

But, of course, a playing-off of register choices against generic situation expectations is not confined to literature. The comedian, the advertiser trying to be creative, the teacher, the orator, and the cocktail party conversationalist also play this game.

In my scheme the relation of the register categories to the functions of language with which they are 'normally associated' and the lexico-grammatical features by which they are 'typically realized' is deliberately a guarded statement. As Martin points out, the detailed research has not yet been done to demonstrate empirically what we intuitively think is so (Martin 1980/81: 33); and elsewhere I have indicated that the links between the register dimension and the functions are likely to be a matter of tendency rather than exclusivity (Gregory 1980: 76); multi-valence can be expected everywhere. All this in no way invalidates Martin's central proposal; research and text description constitute the most important work to be done in systemics, in order to delineate the relationships between the meta-functions and the semantic and lexico-grammatical strata (cf. Berry 1980 and her discussion of the need for such a research programme). However, a non-exact match between the register categories and lexico-grammatical clusters of systems need not hamper the research; it will just make it a little more, perhaps necessarily, complex. I am confident that we need FUNCTIONAL TENOR as the semantic reflection of an important dimension of the social semiotic that surrounds language—the functional relationship of potential addresser to potential addressee—and I am confident that we need GENERIC SITUATION to represent semiotically what is semantically reflected by REGISTER. Nor will the meta-functions be empirically less well-established if one component of the semantics (functional tenor) is variably hospitable in its relation to lexico-grammatical systems; mismatches of various kinds are rather what we should expect. That is why I propose that as well as investigating clear-cut registers

and artificially constructed situation types as Martin suggests (1980/81: 33)—
and they are important for purposes of establishing major correlative
patterns—we also maintain the Firthian and neo-Firthian tradition of
investigating literature; then we will not make the mistake of over-neatness.

Perhaps, too, we ought to be cautious about attempting to PROVE the
existence of the meta-functions; this may be falling into the trap of
'scienticism'. Rather we should continue to USE them and see what they can
do for us. They have already shown themselves to be helpful organizing and
investigating concepts not only in grammatical analysis but recently also in
the linguistic study of literature (cf. Halliday 1971/73; Benson and Greaves
1981a, b; Gregory 1981) and in exchange structure analysis in discourse (cf.
Berry 1981). Fawcett's work seems to suggest that further distinctions within
the functions may also be useful for generative purposes. The meta-functions
are means of tackling the manifold complexity of meaning in both its formal
and non-formal aspects. Such means are always sorely needed in linguistics if
it is to be of any use to anybody.

NOTES

1. In the preparation of this article I had many useful discussions with my colleagues
   James Benson, Michael Cummings and William S. Greaves, and particularly with
   my research assistant, Karen Malcolm. They are, of course, not responsible for any
   of its shortcomings.
2. The name of this type of grammar is Communication Linguistics: a book describing
   its main features is at present in preparation.

BIBLIOGRAPHY

Allerton, D. J., Carney, E. and Holdecroft, D. (eds) (1979), *Function and Context in
    Linguistic Analysis: Essays Offered to William Haas*, Cambridge, Cambridge University
    Press.
Berry, Margaret (1980), 'They're all out of step except our Johnny: a discussion of
    motivation (or the lack of it) in systemic linguistics', Department of English Studies,
    University of Nottingham (mimeo.).
—— (1981), 'Systemic linguistics and discourse analysis: a multi-layered approach to
    exchange structure', in Coulthard and Montgomery (eds).
Benson, J. D. and Greaves, W. S. (1981a), 'Ideational, interpersonal and textual
    meaning in Melville's *Moby Dick*', Toronto, Applied Linguistics Research Working
    Group, Glendon College, York University, revised version of a paper read to the
    Seventh International Systemic Workshop, Sheffield, 1980.
—— and —— (1981b), 'Textual meaning in Trollope's *Barchester Towers*: the
    foregrounding of adversative conjunctions', Toronto, Applied Linguistics Research
    Working Group, Glendon College, York University.
Bühler, K. (1934), *Sprachtheorie: die Darstellungsfunktion der Sprache*, Jena, Fischer.
Butler, C. S. (1979), 'Recent developments in systemic linguistics', in *Language and
    Language Teaching Abstracts*, No. 12, 71–89, London, Cambridge University Press.
—— (1985), *Systemic Linguistics: Theory and Applications*, London, Batsford.

Chatman, Seymour (ed.) (1973), *Literary Style: A Symposium*, New York, Oxford University Press.

Coulthard, R. M. and Montgomery, M. (eds) (1981), *Studies in Discourse Analysis*, London, Routledge and Kegan Paul.

Daneš, F. (1964), 'A three level approach to syntax', *Travaux Linguistiques de Prague*, I.

Dijk, T. A. van and Petöfi, S. (eds) (1977), *Grammar and Descriptions*, Berlin, de Gruyter.

Fawcett, R. P. (1973a), 'Systemic functional grammar in a cognitive model of language', University College, London (mimeo. available through ETIC Archives).

—— (1973b), 'Generating a sentence in systemic functional grammar', mimeo., University College, London (mimeo., available through ETIC Archives), and in Halliday and Martin (eds) (1981: 146–83).

—— (1980), *Cognitive Linguistics and Social Interaction: Towards an Integrated Model of a Systemic Functional Grammar and the Other Components of a Communicating Mind*, Heidelberg, Julius Groos Verlag.

Firbas, J. (1964), 'On defining theme in functional sentence analysis', *Travaux Linguistiques de Prague*, I.

—— (1966), 'Non-Thematic Subjects in Contemporary English', *Travaux Linguistiques de Prague*, 2.

Firth, J. R. (1935/57), 'The Technique of Semantics', *Transactions of the Philological Society*, 1935, reprinted in Firth, J. R. (1957), *Papers in Linguistics, 1934/1951*, London, Oxford University Press.

Gregory, Michael (1967), 'Aspects of varieties differentiation', *Journal of Linguistics*, 3.

—— (1967/72), *English Patterns: Perspectives for the Description of English*, Toronto, Glendon College, York University, 1972 (individual chapters issued 1966–7).

—— (1980), 'Language as social semiotic: the recent work of M. A. K. Halliday', *Applied Linguistics*, 1, No. 1.

—— (1981), 'Linguistics and theatre: Hamlet's voice—aspects of text formation and cohesion in a soliloquy', *Linguistics and the Humanities Conference*, University of Texas at Arlington, to be published in the Proceedings.

Gregory, Michael and Carroll, Susanne (1978), *Language and Situation: Language Varieties in their Social Contexts*, London, Routledge and Kegan Paul.

Halliday, M. A. K. (1961), 'Categories of the theory of grammar', *Word*, 27, No. 3.

—— (1965), 'Speech and situation', *Bulletin of the National Association for the Teaching of English: Some Aspects of Oracy*, 2, No. 2.

—— (1967), 'Notes on transitivity and theme in English: Part 2', *Journal of Linguistics*, 3, No. 2.

—— (1969), 'Options and functions in the English clause', *Brno Studies in English*, 8, reprinted in Householder (ed.) (1972: 248–57), and in Halliday and Martin (eds) (1981: 138–45).

—— (1970a), 'Language Structure and Language Function', in Lyons (ed.) (1970).

—— (1970b), 'Functional diversity in language, as seen from a consideration of modality and mood in English', *Foundations of Language*, 6, No. 3.

—— (1971/73), 'Linguistic function and literary style: an enquiry into the language of William Golding's *The Inheritors*' in Chatman (ed.) (1973), reprinted in Halliday (1973).

—— (1973), *Explorations in the Functions of Language*, London, Edward Arnold.

—— (1975a), *Learning How to Mean: Explorations in the Development of Language*, London, Edward Arnold.

—— (1975b), 'Language as social semiotic: towards a general sociolinguistic theory', in Makkai and Makkai (eds) (1975).

—— (1977), 'Text as semantic choice in social contexts;, in van Dijk and Petöfi (eds) (1977).

—— (1978), *Language as Social Semiotic: The Social Interpretation of Language and Meaning*, London, Edward Arnold.

—— (1979), 'Modes of meaning and modes of expression: types of grammatical structure and their determination by different semantic functions' in Allerton, Carney and Holdecroft (eds) (1979).

Halliday, M. A. K., McIntosh, A. and Strevens P. (1964), *The Linguistic Sciences and Language Teaching*, London, Longman.

Halliday, M. A. K. and Hasan, R. (1976), *Cohesion in English*, London, Longman.

—— and —— (1980), *Text and context: Aspects of Language in a Social-Semiotic Perspective*, Tokyo, Sophia University.

Halliday, M. A. K. and Martin, J. R. (eds) (1981), *Readings in Systemic Linguistics*, London, Batsford.

Householder, F. W. (ed.) (1972), *Syntactic Theory 1: Structuralist*, Harmondsworth, Penguin.

Hudson, R. (1974), 'Systemic generative grammar', *Linguistics*, 139, 5–42.

Kress, G. (ed.) (1976), *Halliday: System and Function in Language*, London, Oxford University Press.

Lyons, J. (ed.) (1970), *New Horizons in Linguistics*, Harmondsworth, Penguin.

Makkai, A. and Makkai, V. B. (eds) (1975), *The First LACUS Forum*, Columbia, S. Carolina, Hornbeam Press.

Malinowski, B. (1923), 'The problem of meaning in primitive languages', in Ogden and Richard (eds) (1923).

—— (1935), *Coral Gardens and Their Magic*, Vol. 2, London, Allen and Unwin.

Mathesius, V. (1928), 'On linguistic characterology with illustrations from Modern English', in *Actes du premier congrès international de linguistes à La Hague*, reprinted in Vachek (ed.) (1964).

Martin, J. R. (1980/81), 'Register and Meta-function', Department of Linguistics, University of Sydney, revision of a paper read to the Seventh International Systemic Workshop, Sheffield, 1980.

Martinet, A. (1960), *Elements of General Linguistics*, Chicago, University of Chicago Press.

—— (1977), 'Les fonctions grammaticales', *La Linguistique*, 13, No. 2.

Ogden, C. K. and Richard, I. A. (eds) (1923), *The Meaning of Meaning*, London, Routledge and Kegan Paul.

Pike, K. L. (1967), *Language in Relation to a Unified Theory of the Structure of Human Behaviour*, The Hague, Mouton.

Pike, K. L. and Pike, E. G. (1977), *Grammatical Analysis*, Dallas, Texas, Summer Institute of Linguistics and the University of Texas at Arlington.

Poldauf, I. (1964), 'The third syntactical plan', *Travaux Linguistiques de Prague*, I.

Sampson, G. (1980), *Schools of Linguistics: Competition and Evolution,* London, Hutchinson.

Sweet, H. (1891), *New English Grammar: Part I*, Oxford, Clarendon Press.

Vachek, J. (ed.) (1964), *A Prague School Reader in Linguistics*, Bloomington, Indiana, Indiana University Press.

—— (1966), *The Linguistic School of Prague*, Bloomington, Indiana, Indiana University Press.

5 The logical and textual functions*

Jeffrey Ellis
Formerly of the University of Aston, Birmingham

5.0 INTRODUCTION

The purpose of this chapter is to examine (1) two of the four LANGUAGE FUNCTIONS as distinguished by Halliday, and (2) the RELATIONS between them (see Halliday 1969, etc.; cf. Ellis 1978 and forthcoming; but cf. Fawcett's six (1973a, 1974a), later eight (or more) (1980: 27 ff.; 1983: 112); see further in sections 5.1.2–4 and 5.3 below). Of the four—experiential and logical (both ideational), interpersonal and textual—the textual is essentially sharply set off from the others (see sections 5.2.1 and 5.3.1) and has already been much discussed in various aspects. The logical has not been so much discussed, and there is still considerable controversy about its status and scope. It will therefore be necessary to treat it at some length in section 5.1 before turning to its relation with the textual in section 5.3. At the same time, although the textual has been much discussed in various aspects, a comprehensive overview that draws together these aspects of it as one of the functions is needed to relate it to the logical (section 5.2).

Note that while a 'function' (also known as a 'meta-function') is a function of language, hence extra-linguistic, a '(functional) component' is within a language.

5.1 THE LOGICAL FUNCTION

5.1.1 The logical among functions and components in the model

When we consider the nature and place of the logical among the functions and components, two starting-points present themselves. One is the point made by Hudson, that the claim that the formal (lexico-grammatical)/semantic systems of a language can be grouped into components corresponding to functions 'is an empirical one, testable by writing optimal grammars for languages and seeing

---

* Based on papers given to the first two International Systemic Workshops. My thanks are due for discussion of various parts of my subject-matter to those who attended these workshops, and in particular to H. M. P. Davies, R. P. Fawcett, R. Haden, M. A. K. Halliday, Ruqaiya Hasan and Jean N. Ure.

whether their rules tend to fall into relatively independent sets' which 'reflect different functions of language' (cf. Halliday 1974a: 62–5; Fawcett 1973a: 16–17). The other is that whatever one's findings about components, the functions are as fundamental as the systems to the total model of language.[1] The functions are a necessary intermediary within the model between the grammar (or lexico-grammar or semantics) and extra-linguistic reality (Halliday *passim*; Fawcett 1973a: 17; 1974a: 41–5; 1980: 25f.).

One part of extra-linguistic reality is the aspects of thought, or aspects of the world of experience as thought about,[2] that constitute the subject-matter of logic.[3] Whether the relation between this part of 'reality' and grammar, etc. is to be made through a distinct 'function' will be treated below in section 5.1.3. First let us look in the opposite direction, as it were, from logic and its components or constituents to language.

5.1.2 The divisions of logic and their reflection in language

By LOGIC is meant here the subject as traditionally understood, including the mainstream of modern developments, and not for practical purposes any secondary or metaphorical understandings of the term.[4] Moreover, by LOGIC unqualified or tout court (as distinct from, e.g., THE LANGUAGE OF LOGIC) is meant the content of the subject and not its formulation, even in precise symbolization (though it is impossible to refer to it specifically without some such formulation), let alone by paraphrase of the symbolization in natural language, bringing with it language functions essentially absent from logic itself (cf. n. 6 and section 5.1.5).

By the components of logic we mean propositions and their constituents, and relations between propositions. This is the distinction made within modern logic between predicate and propositional calculus, etc. (Kleene 1967: 74; Kneale 1962: 175–6; von Wright 1957: 5–6).[5] What is absent from logic (in the non-natural-language sense indicated above) is anything interpersonal or textual (apart from 'logical structure of the text', see 5.2.3).[6]

The principal constituents of propositions may be distinguished as: relations[7] (or predicates), their terms (or arguments), quantifiers, and negation.[8] Of these the first two, relations and their terms, would seem to belong indisputably to the experiential in language (with the possible exception of a special case adduced below (sections 5.1.3, 5.1.4)), corresponding to Fawcett's referent-situation and referent-thing (1973b: 7, 1980: 47), just as inter-propositional relations seem to be the one thing indisputably assigned to the logical in the linguistic model (section 5.1.5).

It is with quantifiers and negation that controversy begins among systemic linguists. Fawcett (1974a: 40; 1973a: 19—'linguistic correlates of logical quantifiers') includes in the logical 'particularization' and 'quantification'. In Fawcett (1980: 95), however, particularization is in the 'informational' component. Particularization, as distinct from quantification, is absent from logical propositions in so far as it is textual; it includes the anaphoric and cataphoric uses of the definite article and other determiners (section 5.2.3), and in languages without the definite article other information-structuring devices such as sequence of elements in clause-structure. (Homophoric uses—which are simply absent in article-less languages—have no content separable from the treatment of proper names in logic, or generics, cf. Ellis 1971: 370–1, Biggs 1976: 10.[9] Ecphoric uses are interpersonal.) Quantification, like numeration, would seem to belong in the experiential.

The place of negation is even more disputed: polarity is claimed by Halliday for all of the three components, logical, experiential and interpersonal, though Fawcett 1973a would seem to be right in including it in the logical function (cf. section 5.1.4). In Fawcett 1980 (95), however, it is given a separate component of its own.

So far we have been speaking, if of language at all, of a FUNCTION: we come now to the distinct question of COMPONENTS.

5.1.3 Function and (sub-)component

To the question whether the logical is a function and whether it is a component there have been different answers. Halliday tends to the position that is not a function and that it is a sub-component (1977, 1969: 2.5–6). For Fawcett, it is both a function and one of six or eight components (1973a: 19, 1974a: 3, 1980: 27 ff.). There would seem to be both a logical function and a logical sub-component (see below on the scope of 'sub-'), but functions and components differ in that functions are inter-language, while components are language-specific and correspond to functions only as wholes, not in every constituent of the system network. In other words, when one carries out the test proposed by Hudson and others (see section 5.1.1 above) one will be likely to find that in some cases, and varying from language to language, 'the relatively independent sets of rules reflect different functions of the language' (Hudson) only as regards the majority—even if the overwhelming majority— of the meanings included.

As to the question of component or sub-component, assuming 'sub-component' means something less than a component and not a component corresponding to less than a function, and that 'less than a component' means 'less independent' in terms of 'the Hudson test' than the other components, then again a final decision would await the final carrying out of the test.

This leaves two questions outstanding about the logical function and sub-component:

(1) whether there can be a more precise extra-linguistic definition of the function (within the ideational function) than the kind of piecemeal attribution to certain constituents of logic that has been indicated above, demarcated only negatively, with reference to other functions, especially experiential; and

(2) the status of recursion (or univariateness of structure) in relation to the sub-component, and hence the function.

The first question will be considered further in section 5.1.5. But some indication of a possible line of attack might be gained from consideration of what Seuren (1974) says about his concept of 'universe of interpretation':

A universe of interpretation is a cognitive structure, which has a truth value with respect to the world: it is either true or false given actual states of affairs. We do not assign truth values to sentences, but to universes of interpretation. When we say, sloppily, that a particular sentence is true, we mean that when that sentence is interpreted in terms of some given universe of interpretation, it adds to it or modifies it in such a way that the resulting universe of interpretation is true with respect to the world. [Cf. Ellis 1966b, n. 27.]

Universes of interpretation allow for different levels of abstraction: elements are created which have no direct counterpart in the actual world, but are related to elements in the world by means of a complex apparatus of cognitive functions, including our natural logical powers. We can thus operate with an element such as 'the possibility that Jack is ill', although we know that there is no actual thing in the world which is the possibility that Jack is ill . . .

It is hardly necessary to point out that virtually nothing is known about the ways in which elements of semantic interpretations (analyses) map on to elements in inter-pretative universes, or about the ways in which such universes are related to the world. This is practically uncharted territory. But mention has to be made of these matters in the present context if we are to provide any reasonable basis for the intuitive notion 'referential expression' employed in the formulation of constraint [on the incorporation of semantic material into lexical islands].

Referential expressions are of a nominal, not a verbal character. That is, they map on to ELEMENTS in the interpretative universe, not on to RELATIONS. [Cf. von Wright 1957: 1–18]

So far, Seuren. Similarly, it might be argued, we could say, for example, that there is an actual thing in the world which is Jack's being ill, but there is not an actual thing in the world which is Jack's not being ill. Hence polarity (by virtue of its marked member—Fawcett) is logical (in function) and not experiential, whereas singularity or plurality, duality, etc. of objects is as actual as the objects; hence numeration is experiential (cf. von Wright 1957: 6 ff.; Kneale 1962: 479).

As for the second question, recursion will be discussed under specific headings in section 5.1.4. It certainly characterizes the one undisputed part of logical meaning, inter-propositional relations. But Halliday has more and more taken the position (culminating in Halliday 1979) that 'recursive' and 'logical' are identical, i.e. necessarily coextensive (e.g. 1977 in comparison with 1969: 2.5–6)—meaning by 'logical' presumably the sub-component if indeed the function is to be distinguished in this respect as proposed above. Fawcett finds this unacceptable: some of his logical meanings are non-recursive, and some of his recursive rules may be non-logical (Fawcett 1974b: A, section 6; see also Fawcett 1980: 182; in 1974b, A, section 2, 6 Fawcett rejects altogether hypotactic clause-complexes).

Again, the only possible solution at present seems to be to entertain the possibility that the Hudson test will result in components in which the 'logical' (sub-component) alone and entirely (although this is less likely, if the component is to include all meanings formally drawn into the 'set') is recursive, while classifying extra-linguistically in the function meanings which may or may not have recursive counterparts in the grammar (but see section 5.1.5).

5.1.4 Possible systems in the sub-component

Systems that have been claimed for the sub-component (in English at least) include: polarity, secondary tense and unit complexes generally (clause, group, word).

POLARITY: In section 5.1.3 it was said that it might be argued that polarity belonged to the logical FUNCTION because there is not an actual thing in the world which is Jack's not being ill. This view is supported (indirectly) by Taylor (1974), who treats negatives with 'uncertainties' like Seuren's 'possibility that Jack is ill'.

But does polarity belong to the logical COMPONENT—in English, for example? Fawcett (1980: 30) points out that Halliday first put it in the logical component (1973: 141); then in the early 1970s in the interpersonal (1973: 40); and in 1978 (132) in the experiential. To this should be added that in 1977 (84) it appears with person in the interpersonal at group rank, verbal group, as well as with transitivity and modulation in experiential at clause rank.

SECONDARY TENSE: This was mentioned in section 5.1.2 as a possible special case in the relation between language functions and logical propositions (cf. Halliday 1969: 2.6, referred to in section 5.1.5 on different formulations in language of the same logical relation).

What corresponds in logic to tense in natural language, primary or secondary? It is propositions in which the relation is one of relative position in time, and the terms 'time spoken of' and 'time of speaking', primary, or 'secondary time spoken of' and 'primary time spoken of', secondary. To the extent that tense is not experiential, this would be the exception mentioned in section 5.1.2, but it is a special case because such a proposition is stated only as a qualification of another proposition stated as a full clause or process-referent. (On the relativity of proposition-constitution, cf. Fawcett, 1974b: A, section 5, on propositions and presuppositions; on tense and time in logic, see further Harman 1976, and the reference to Reichenbach in Ellis 1966a.)

There are two arguments for including secondary tense in the logical function (as Halliday does in 1969: 29, 11 and 1970: 327, but not in 1977: 84): (1) that it is recursive in English; and (2) that it is further from experiential reality than primary tense. There are also two arguments for including primary tense in the logical component in English: (1) that it is tense generally that is recursive; and (2) that secondary tense is already qualified to be in the logical component by being in the logical function, and primary tense should be with it.

The experiential reality from which secondary tense would be at one remove is the experience of present, past and future. But, of these, future is already at one remove from the reality of present and past, which is part of the extra-linguistic argument against the ternary analysis of primary tense in English (cf. Fawcett 1973a: 16 and Lyons as discussed in Ellis 1966b). In fact secondary tense seems to be removed from reality in a sense less radical than this: the ordering of reference points that it embodies arguably belongs to the same universe of interpretation as that of primary tense itself, present and past as well as future.

As to whether secondary tense, or tense altogether, is recursive, the latter depends on the status we accord the identification of 'present', etc. and 'present in', etc., and both on whether what can be analysed as recursion only with severe constraints can be counted as recursion. The identification of 'past' and 'past in', 'future' and 'future in', is clearly logically justified (the relation in the logical proposition—with different terms—is the same), but the identification of 'present' and 'present in' is justified descriptively as a convenience of economy of systematization with past and future (see Ellis 1966a: 88 and n. 51; Turner and Mohan 1970: 106–7). Fawcett, however, has a network for English tense without recursion (though it is arguable that there are forms it will not yield that are acceptable in some registers and that are yielded by Halliday's recursion).

UNIT COMPLEXES, or UNIVARIATE STRUCTURES, or RECURSIVE SYSTEMS: Recursion here, in complexes, in general is without the severe restrictions ('stop rules', as Halliday 1965 calls them) that have to accompany a recursive treatment of secondary tense. Stop rules restrict not the number of elements as such, but combinations of particular choices at the elements. Halliday (1977: 66–9) has examples of the various kinds of complexes he includes in the general notion. But according to Fawcett (1974b: A, section 6), complexes are only coordinate, not in apposition or indirect speech or hypotactic for all of which he uses embedding. Of all these he admits to the logical component only (1) coordination and (2) subordination when conditional, causal or concessive.

RECURSION IN CLAUSE AND SENTENCE: Fawcett and others welcome the implication at one point in Halliday 1977 that there is no sentence on the rank scale, clause and clause-complex being enough. But on p. 66 Halliday does say 'clause-complex (= sentence)', which is surely to be interpreted as those clause-complexes which function as sentences. For even with Fawcett's restricting complexes to paratactic ones there are complexes within complexes (as treated in Halliday 1965), so that not all complexes are co-terminous with the sentences in the kind of analysis it is proposed to supersede. And certainly in the study of textual and logical structure of written texts it is necessary to distinguish parataxis of sentences from parataxis of clauses. One may still argue whether this is 'grammar' in the rank-scale sense or something else (say 'rhetoric') which one may or may not include in grammar generally.

Halliday (1977: 66–8) has examples of the relations of expansion, identity and projection in both paratactic ($\alpha\alpha$) and hypotactic ($\alpha\beta$) relations. As mentioned in section 5.1.4, Fawcett (1974b: A, section 6) opposes the $\alpha\beta$ treatment. Independently of this, we have his network for inter-propositional relations, with his discussion in C.

RECURSION IN GROUPS: Originally Halliday included in the logical component some aspects of the structure of the individual group, e.g. in 1970 (327), 'nominal group: classification, sub-modification'. Note that the separation of 'sub-' from 'primary' modification (in experiential) parallels primary and secondary tense (sections 1.42). Now he includes only the relation between groups in a group complex. As regards the structure of the group, Fawcett (1974b: A, section 2; cf. 1975: 25) includes in informational 'ad hoc classification', and this is a point where his informational corresponds either to the logical or to the experiential in Halliday's functions.

Halliday (1977: 68) gives examples of group complexes (not actually in the Thurber text that is the subject there): (1) *as soon, or sooner*; (2) *her inamoratus, the male hippopotamus*; (3) *one African afternoon, at half past four*. Only the first of these apparently would be a complex for Fawcett.

RECURSION IN WORDS: Word-complexes, or rather groups, for Halliday (1977: 68–9), may be simultaneously structured as both constructions (multi-variate) and complexes (uni-variate), except prepositional groups, which are like clauses. Examples are given by Halliday (1977: 69) of expansion and identity, paratactic and hypotactic (not projection as clause).

RECURSION IN MORPHEMES: Finally, let me mention morpheme complexes, included by Halliday in the old table as logical 'word: compounding, reduplication'. Word morphology is relatively neglected in systemic theory, but see Ward 1966 and Tittensor n.d. On recursive and non-recursive reduplication in languages like Akan, and their respective functions, see Ellis forthcoming.

5.1.5 Conclusions: logic and the 'language-logical'

We speak of logic being reflected (however imperfectly) in language as if logic came first and natural languages later. Historically, however, logic as a human activity, like its congener, mathematics (cf. note 2), is a refinement of symbolism standing on the shoulders of language. Indeed, the way in which it brings out what is already latent in language is illustrated by von Wright's (1957: 5) comment on the question of 'semantic relations':

... there are logical constants for which ordinary language has no name [but which appear in language with varying explicitness; see section 5.2.3] and for which the logician must invent a technical term. This fact probably offers a partial explanation why some branches of logic were much retarded in their development before the rise of so-called symbolic logic.

As indicated in section 5.1.2, logical propositions are pre-textual: sequence of the elements within them is not significant, except in arranging the terminals of an asymmetrical relation. (On alternative conventions for arbitrary sequence and their relation to natural languages, cf. Ellis 1966a: 93, notes 34 and 36.)

But can there be said to be a textual relation BETWEEN propositions in a logical discourse as such, as distinct from its formulation in natural language or the kind of symbolization intermediate between natural language and logical symbolsim that may be used in spoken realization (where of course phonological information structure is unavoidable)?

It seems possible to argue that the relation between propositions in logic can be syntagmatic only in an attenuated sense, the only relation between any two propositions being a logical one already given, as it were, paradigmatically. If this should be so, an analogy might be drawn between the relation in this respect between language and logic and that between the surface structure of language and its deep grammar in systemic theory (as opposed to the deep STRUCTURE of transformational grammar). (On the general subject of the relation between paradigmatic and syntagmatic, cf. Fawcett 1983: especially 78–82, 92, 104.)

Since language itself is not logic, and 'reflects logic imperfectly', the expression of logical relations in language is complex and not clear-cut, and not a matter of the logical 'function' or sub-component alone (cf. Ellis 1978). As Halliday (1969: 2.6) puts it: the logical options [in the linguistic sense of the logical function or sub-component] are those whereby the speaker expresses in "pure" (abstract) form relations which appear experientially as processes (linking "things") and textually as conjunctives (linking propositions).' He gives the example *Tomorrow is New Year's Day* (identity) (experiential relation); *Tomorrow, New Year's Day* . . . (apposition) (logical relation); *Tomorrow is their great day. That is to say, New Year's Day is the day when* . . .' (commentary) (textual relation).

The part of logic as a whole to which the logical function of language would appear to correspond is propositional calculus rather than predicate (e.g. *Tomorrow is New Year's Day*) calculus. We may define the distinction of this function or (sub-)component from the others—especially the other ideational sub-component, the experiential—by criteria (for the FUNCTION) within the CONTENT of logical or linguistic discourse in some such way as that referring to Seuren in section 5.1.3, or (for the SUB-COMPONENT) within linguistic FORM as in Halliday's criterion of recursiveness of structure (sections 5.1.3, 5.1.4).

An example of the problems in applying these generalities to actual languages, and of functions being inter-language and components language-specific (section 5.1.3), with possibly fuzzy boundaries to their co-terminousness, is provided by polarity. (On the content criterion and polarity, see sections 5.1.3 and 5.1.4.) Negation is logically recursive (though as with minus in mathematics, the actual mechanism will be a flip-flop between negated/minus and unnegated/plus); natural language with its multi-dimensional complexity (including interpersonal aspects to negation) finds it necessary to negate negatives explicitly, but it may do this in a separate clause like 'it is not the case that . . .' and it depends on the particular language whether a 'double negative' within the clause realizes a logical negated negative or a particular case of single negation.

5.2 THE TEXTUAL FUNCTION

5.2.1 The textual function and text linguistics

The textual function is alone among the functions of systemic grammar in having devoted to it, outside the systemic model, a whole new discipline, a branch of linguistics generally which goes under the names of 'text grammar', 'discourse analysis', etc.; on the other hand, systemic grammar is alone, at least among what we might term the 'deep-grammar' schools of linguistics, in its treatment of the other functions, and in its perspective of integrating the textual with them. What explains these singularities is the fact that, as Halliday puts it, the textual function is an enabling function in relation to the other functions, which are directly extra-linguistic, 'extrinsic', functions.

To put it another way, text in the sense of A text is itself (now) a unit of linguistic analysis, so that one now sometimes speaks of SENTENCE-GRAMMAR as distinguished from TEXT-GRAMMAR, the latter meaning relations between sentences (or between larger parts of texts) or grammatical features of sentences themselves that have a textual function (cf. Ellis 1976). This unit, according to Halliday and Hasan (1976), is a semantic and not a grammatical unit, but the considerations involved in the distinction will be touched on later (sections 5.2.3, 5.2.4).

5.2.2 Text demarcation

Demarcation of or into texts is not, as a matter of theory, altogether the straightforward thing it might appear, as is evidenced by the amount of space in the literature taken up by definitions of a text—though this does not necessarily mean that all the essential points are adequately covered. For example, Dressler writes (1970: 68): 'M.E. stellt sogar ein ganzer Dialog einen einheitlichen Text dar', which implies that what might have been thought to be an obvious solution is not familiar to text-linguists in general, namely that text-demarcation might be multi-layered (Ellis 1976: 91–2). To the question 'which is a text, the individual utterance (or the individual's utterances) or the whole dialogue?', the answer is 'both'. This of course leaves open the more detailed questions involved in relations between texts one within another, and questions of their sub-classification and terminology, questions perhaps best taken up again in connection with text-structure (section 5.2.3, also 5.3.2).

That situation is essential in an adequate conception of what constitutes a text, complementary to (e.g. van Dijk 1972: 8) its linguistic constitution, and including, for example, speech-act classification (cf. van Dijk 1972: 318), is brought out by Dressler (1972a: 92–101), van Dijk (1972: 316–18), Hartmann (1975: 98, 102–4), and by Widdowson's distinction between 'text' in his sense and 'discourse' (1973, 1975; Ellis 1976: n. 1 and 93, 97).

Here again, not all is straightforward: a one-to-one relation between texts and situations and equal discontinuity between them is disturbed by such factors as changing situation within linguistically cohesive discourse, or discontinuous discourse in largely the same situation. Cf. Halliday and Hasan's point that textuality (in their sense of being A text, being demarcated as a text) is not all or nothing, and their criterion of text-boundaries found in texture (see section 5.2.4).

5.2.3 Ingredients of textualness

The ingredients of textualness I should like to divide for present purposes (and much less delicately than Halliday and Hasan) into:

> PHORA: GRAMMATICAL and LEXICAL
> INFORMATIONAL STRUCTURING
> STRUCTURE OF TEXT (textual structure, distinguished in
> section 5.3.2 from other kinds of structure of text),

where the first and second, together with the conjunction of sentences in the third, contribute to, go to make up formal expression of, or correlate with (are ingredients in) the various kinds of overall structure of the text.

PHORA: Of the relevant classes of phora (see Ellis 1971 and references therein; Ellis forthcoming; Martin and Rochester 1975), HOMOPHORA (i.e. 'pointing at itself') has to do with the text, in that a part of the situational demarcation of the text is the universe of discourse within which a reference is unique—e.g. in the following text A: *the Caprice*, and possibly *the airport*. (For a more delicate treatment of homophora see Ellis 1971.)

Text A
> Frank Mannon had called him from the airport that morning, a few minutes before he left for his date at the Caprice with Judy. He found him up in the first floor general office, dictating notes to Maureen Brooks, when he got back from lunch. There was a brandy glass in Mannon's free hand and his grey worsted suit looked as if it had been slept in. [F. Mullally]

Text B
> wanpela man i tromwe gutpela pikinini bilong wit long gaden bilong en.
> Tasol taim ol manmeri i slip, birua bilong dispela man em i kam, na em i tromwe pikinini bilong gras nogut namel long wit, na em i go. [New Guinea Pidgin translation of Matthew 13: 24–5]

Phora that is actually textual is either anaphoric (pointing back) or cataphoric (pointing forward) in the text.

CATAPHORA in English is either textual in the narrow sense, beyond the sentence, or at least beyond the clause, or within the nominal group, e.g. text A above: *the (first floor) general office*, or as regards the phoric feature of the deictic *his*: *his free hand* (*his other hand* would have been classed in Halliday and Hasan's category of 'comparative' with *same, next, last*, etc.), but not *his grey worsted suit*, his only suit in the immediate situation. In languages where the article follows the element epithet (also, as in some West African languages, classifier, when it occurs, or qualifier, as in *at the Caprice with Judy*), the relation within the nominal group is not strictly CATAphoric, and we use the term ESPHORIC (or eisphoric, Ellis 1976: 93, 103, n. 5), INTO the group (Ellis ;1971; Martin forthcoming).

Cataphora is usually grammatical, in the sense of their being no lexical item in the cataphoric expression. Expressions like *the following*, as an alternative to *these* cataphoric, contain a group-cataphoric (esphoric) article and meta-linguistic, textual use of the lexical item *follow*.

But the principle distinction between grammatical and lexical in phora is in ANAPHORA. We may classify anaphora (again less delicately than Halliday and Hasan) in a sequence with lexis playing an increasing part:

(1) pronominal and other purely grammatical anaphora;
(2) as a less lexical case of the following, what Halliday and Hasan term 'general nouns' on the grammar–lexis borderline, like *thing, stuff, person*;
(3) article or deictics generally with lexical items in direct (repetition or synonym) and indirect (defined below) anaphora;
(4) in languages without definite article (e.g. text B above, *wit*, also possible *dispela wit*), or in conditions of use without article, including proper names (Halliday and Hasan: restricted), lexical items alone in direct or indirect anaphora.

As to pronominal and other purely grammatical anaphora (of which generally Halliday and Hasan have a highly elaborated analysis), the complex co-textual conditions of acceptable freedom of use of pronominal anaphora are examined by van Dijk (1972: 75–9). Examples in text A are: *him* twice, once for Bill Griffith, not named in this extract, once for Frank Mannon; *he* three times, all Bill Griffith; *his* once for Bill Griffith and once after *Mannon's*. Examples in text B are: verse 24 (*bilong*) *en*, referring to *wanpela man*; verse 25 *em* referring to *birua bilong dispela man* (*i* is not a pronoun but at most a person-marker like Latin —(*n*)*t*).

By direct and indirect anaphora are meant respectively: (1) reference to the same referent, by repetition of item or use of synonyms, including hyperonyms as instantial synonyms (Halliday and Hasan's 'superordinate'), e.g. *his enemy . . . this man*; and (2) anaphora 'to an implicit bringing of it [the referent of the anaphoric item] into the universe of dicourse by some expression or expressions [the item that anaphora is to] referring to some associated referent' (Ellis 1971), the items belonging to some common lexical set(s). Hawkins (1978) terms indirect anaphora 'associative anaphoric usage'. An example is *free* in *his free hand*, indirect anaphora to *dictating notes*, linkage being between lexical sets: *free* and *occupied* etc.; *occupied* hyperonymous to *dictating notes*, etc., etc. (cf. Dressler 1972a: 4 (7.4)).

Dressler (1972a: 21–2) cuts across the distinction by classing direct anaphora by synonym ('Paraphrase') with indirect anaphora, as against (20–1) direct anaphora by repetition (or 'Rekurrenz' of 'Bedeutungsinhalte' in the form of identical words, 'Satzteile' or 'Sätze'). However, he does (39) list some necessary raw material for distinctions needed in semantic relations, for example synonyme/homoseme (*Brille, Augenglas*), paraseme (*stallion, mare*), hyperseme (*horse, stallion*), antiseme/antonyme (*victory, defeat*), Teil-Ganzes-, Teil- Teil-, Actio- Agens- Relationen, etc., and he discusses Harweg's taxonomy of contiguities.

Besides the primary distinction of direct and indirect anaphora, that is to say, we need, as Haden puts it, 'a semantics which handles synonymy, hyponyms and hyperonyms, the part–whole relationship etc'.[10] On 'semantic relations' and logic see section 5.1.2 above. Here I offer some further tentative observations on semantic relations in anaphoric reference. We already have (1) synonyms, (2) antonyms and (3) what Lyons calls converses (reversible, e.g. *victory* and *defeat*, and irreversible, e.g. *give* and *take*; cf. Hurford and Heasley 1983: 114–19) as well as (4) hyponyms and hyperonyms.

Part and whole are to be distinguished from hyponym and hyperonym, and might be termed MERONYM and HOLONYM. Items hyponymous to the same hyperonym or meronymous to the same holonym might be termed, so long as it does not suggest 'pun' as Dressler's PARASEME above does not, PARONYMS (or PARAHYPONYMS, PARAMERONYMS). We also need to distinguish from whole and part, e.g. *house* and *door*, a more general relation of belonging, e.g. *house* and *garden*, including Lyons's converses like *father*, *child* (relative) as opposed to *question*, *answer* (complementary). For the moment I will use QUASI-HOLONYM and QUASI-MERONYM and QUASI-PARAMERONYM.

An example of the kind of data the terminology is needed to cope with is to be found in Dressler (1972b: section 4.6), unusual semantic relation in anaphora: 'eine ungewöhnliche Koreferenz zwischen *Samen* und *Weizen*' translating Greek σπέρμα and σῖτος in the parable of the sower, Matthew 13 (*seed* and *wheat* in the Authorized Version). It is usual, as he says (and as indicated above by including hyperonym and not hyponym in anaphoric instantial synonym), for co-referent antecedent to have a greater meaning content and a lesser meaning range than co-referent consequent. But *wheat* (*seed*), hyponymous to *seed*, has the greater meaning content and lesser meaning range.

So far Dressler. But let us look at the New Guinea Pidgin version in text B above. New Guinea Pidgin tends to have a more explicit expression of structural semantics in Lyons's sense (or semantic components as in Leech's treatment, cf. Dressler 1972a: 39) than most languages. (On general lexical TYPOLOGY, including explicitness in hyponymy, and equivalence between lexical series (e.g. *bandstand*, *hatstand*) and sets, cf. Halliday 1966: 157.)

In this case, the relevant most general term, which does not itself appear in the text, is *gras*, hyperonymous both to *wit* (hyponymy not explicit), which is in the text, and to *gras nogut* ('weeds') (hyponymy explicit), which is not itself in the text. Quasi-meronymous to these we have, not in the text, *pikinini bilong gras* 'seed' (in general), *pikinini bilong wit* '(wheat) seed' in the text, and *pikinini bilong gras nogut* 'tares' in the text. In the New Guinea Pidgin text, instead of Dressler's (Greek-German-English, etc.) hyperonym followed by hyponym, direct anaphora of anomalous kind, we have a normal sequence of explicit quasi-meronym *pikinini bilong wit* followed by repetition of the quasi-holonym *wit*, direct anaphora to that part of the antecedent expression. Should then perhaps the original (or translations into most languages) be looked upon rather as IMPLICIT quasi-meronym followed by quasi-holonym that was implicit in it, indirect anaphora that is not anomalous if *seed* is understood instantially (from the context of sowing one's own land) as *wheat seed*?

INFORMATIONAL STRUCTURING comprises both information structure in Halliday's (e.g. 19678) strict sense, expounded phonologically by intonation, with elements of structure 'Given' and 'New', and thematic structure of the clause, expounded by sequence, with elements of structure 'Theme' and 'Rheme', with various possibilities of marked theme, and what Halliday terms 'theme' generally (as in the title of 1967/8), including various constructions picking out elements of grammatical structure (cf. Ellis 1978). This structuring of sentences is determined by their place in a text, and may be said to determine their potential placing in texts (cf. Ellis 1976: 97, with n. 16). See further section 5.2.4 below.

TEXTUAL STRUCTURE: In so far as textual structure includes reference to conjunction of sentences (grammatical as well as logical—see Jones 1974: section III, and Halliday and Hasan's fuller networks) as one constituent of the grammatical surface of whole-text structure, it raises the question of the status of sentence as a grammatical unit and of clause-complexes. I shall use the term 'sentence' for a clause-complex not entering into a higher clause-complex.

In section 5.3.2 we shall distinguish between the textual and logical structure of a text. It seems necessary, in considering the textual function, to discriminate further than this and ask what kinds of textual structure there are and (here and in section 5.3.2) what their relation is to other kinds of structure of a text including the logical.

Jones distinguishes:

(1) conceptual structures, underlying and realized by (2);
(2) rhetorical strategies, patterns of function, rhetorical coherence;
(3) grammatical realizations, patterns of form, grammatical cohesion; (2) and (3) constitute discourse analysis.

Hartmann (1975: 101) distinguishes (in different order, which I adapt to Jones's):

(1) notional-semantic content 'information' [exemplified as paraphrase];
(2) rhetorical-pragmatic intent 'functions' (e.g. setting the scene; summarizing information);
(3) formal-syntactic units 'propositions' exemplified as instantial text exponents.

Sinclair and Coulthard (1975: 24) distinguish:

(1) non-linguistic organization;
(2) discourse;
(3) grammar.

I would include under (1), Jones's conceptual, depending on the genre of the text: (a) logical structure (not to be confused with possible 'logical linguistic' structure, i.e. linguistic structure belonging to the logical subcomponent (see below, section 5.3.2)); (b) literary structure in general and poetic, narrative and other kinds of literary and non-literary structure (as van Dijk (1972: 284) points out, narrative and literary are not co-terminous in either direction) like van Dijk's narrative macrostructures (1972, 1975). Category (3), i.e. grammar, refers to sentence-grammar, our 'ingredients' and the conjunction of sentences, the immediate sentence-relations distinguished in the first part of van Dijk 1972 from global text structure, macrostructures. (Cf. Dressler 1972a: 10–12, 15, 83, including the question, now it is to be hoped historical, of regarding a text as a long sentence; cf. van Dijk 1972: 9, 14.) Somewhere between (1) and (3) we have to locate whatever linguistic structures—formal and/or semantic—can be set up for whole texts. Both Jones's 'rhetorical strategy' and Sinclair and Coulthard's 'discourse structure' have the kind of general properties that sentence-grammar structures on the rank scale have (as distinct, for example, from the clause 'structures' of theme–rheme or participant roles). But other linguistic structures of text (in a wider sense of 'structure', but in a strict sense of formal linguistics) are possible (see Ellis forthcoming): chains of anaphora (cf. Halliday and Hasan's 'cohesive chains'), which yield division into topics and topic units—which involve 'structure' in which divisions overlap syntagmatically—and which are relatable to both participant roles and thematic and information structure and to sentence conjunction. Is Jones–Sinclair discourse structure formal in this sense, establishable by criteria of what formal items or other exponents of linguistic categories are observable in the text? Some of Sinclair and Coulthard's criteria involve specific lexical and grammatical items, e.g. in the impressive 'functional definition and characteristic formal features' (40–4), but to some extent one might think that it was arrived at semantically (cf. the discussion, 23, 27–39, 118–25); and Jones's rhetoric seems avowedly semantic in basis. (The use of 'semantic' here is possibly to be distinguished from Halliday and Hasan's use, when they say a text is a semantic, not a grammatical unit.)

If, then, what we might call the formal/semantic structure of Sinclair, Jones and others is of a kind (a strict category of structure) like a sentence-grammar structure that has units and classes, what are the textual UNITS, and what CLASSES do they have?

Sinclair and Coulthard (1975: 24) have for spoken classroom discourse:

UNITS: act; move; exchange; transaction or (135) sequence; lesson or (135) interaction. (Act is lined up approximately with clause in the Grammar column, move with sentence; transaction with topic in the Non-Linguistic Organization, lesson with period; nothing with course (and nothing with group and below in Grammar))

CLASSES: act: e.g. marker, starter, elicitation, directive, informative . . .
move: framing, focussing; opening, answering, follow-up
exchange: boundary, teaching
transaction: lessons are unordered in discourse structure

Jones, explicitly adapting Sinclair et al. (1972), has for written exposition:

UNITS: act (in his example corresponding to one (graphic) sentence)
move (a number of sentences) (structure I(S)R(S))
stage (a number of paragraphs),
plan

CLASSES: act: ascription—I(nitiating), differentiation—R(esponding), exemplification/justification—S(upporting)

move: contrastive analysis, problem deduction, amplification of problem

stage: problem identification, solution presentation

If we accept both of these as valid for their kind of text, it is possible that we may generalize (as do Sinclair and Coulthard, and to some extent Jones) from the difference between them (explicit in Jones) and say that the scale of units for texts in general begins (going upwards) with act and move, but then depends on the GENRE of the text (cf. Jones: Sinclair *et al.*'s 'units above the level of move are concerned with patterns of interaction between inter-locutors.'). This holds not only for the number of units (Sinclair and Coulthard 1975: 134: 'Higher up there is a possibility that more units for the rank scale will be postulated, or that some discourse types will not require all those that are available in the language as a whole . . .'), which will include larger ones in larger-scale kinds of texts, but also for the nature of a given unit like transaction/sequence, and in the classes of all units (cf. Hartmann 1975: 100; also Halliday and Hasan 1976: macrostructure establishes a text as belonging to a particular kind of text, though their macrostructure seems possibly more towards Jones's (1) than I am wanting to place LINGUISTIC structure). (On genre structure, Halliday's generic structure, cf. Ellis 1976: 93.) Presumably correlation with such graphic units as paragraph, chapter, part, 'book', volume, is greater with higher units.

At this point we may return to the question of multi-layer text-demarcation (section 5.2.2). The structure of complex texts like a sequence of poems or a church service (the latter additionally complex in the genres of texts included) consists in the first instance (going downwards) of included texts, themselves with a structure beginning (going downwards) with the appropriate high unit. Texts embedded in the sentence-grammar of other texts are another matter; cf. Dressler (1972a: 88–91).

The interesting question, which I owe partly to R. Hasan, is how far linguistic cohesion continues to parallel content-coherence across these higher boundaries (cf. van Dijk 1972: 138 quoting Bever and Ross's insistence that coherence of discourse is not accounted for by linguistic devices alone), including, for example, comparison of situationally 'free' units, i.e. that could be independent texts, and 'bound' units that could not. Nothing has been said about quantification up to this point, but some quantitative measure of cohesion (if not of coherence!) would be useful here, as elsewhere.

5.2.4 Text and register

The relation between the functions of language and the classification of texts into registers is a subject of recent and current development in systemic theory. Besides defining the TEXTURE of a text as combining TEXTUAL COHESION and REGISTER, Halliday postulates the following correlations between FUNCTIONS and his three[11] dimensions of register classification, which are also presented as dimensions of the semiotic structure of a situation-type (1974a: 25): field of discourse, tenor of discourse and mode of discourse:

ideational with field;
interpersonal with tenor;
textual with mode.

This is not to say that the textual function is not, or may not be, an aspect of the linguistic variation correlating with EACH of the dimensions. We have just seen that textual structure, units, etc. appear to depend upon genre (5.2.3); that and other textual features are part of the linguistic features of register.

But the most fundamental difference in the textual function is one of mode, between spoken and written language. In so far as spoken language is unprepared or unpremeditated, and written language worked over before completion (more complex cases being language written to be read out and spoken language reported in writing), there are of course differences in kinds of textual structuring, etc., involving other register-dimensions than mode. But what distinguishes all spoken from written registers textually, in English at least, is that spoken English has information structure phonologically expounded by intonation, and written English has to rely on other ways of structuring its informational aspect, the punctuation of writing absent in speech being only a partial reflection of the distinctions present in speech (cf. Dressler 1972a: 80–4). These ways include, notably, the systems of theme which are bound up with information structure in spoken English (cf. section 5.2.3). There is also in spoken language what Halliday and Hasan term the COHESIVE function of intonation.

The relation between spoken and written informational structuring, involving their differences and what corresponds between them, is being investigated by H. M. P. Davies (e.g. 1975) in his research on how school-children and others interpret in reading aloud the informational aspect of written texts and in general the role of textuality in learning to read and write (cf. Ellis 1976: 97).

5.3 RELATIONS BETWEEN THE TWO FUNCTIONS

5.3.1 General relations between functions

Fawcett (see references in the Introduction above) divides the two non-ideational components of Halliday's each into two, making six components in all, but this (and his eight in Fawcett 1980) would appear to affect only in detail the relations between the logical, experiential, interpersonal and textual functions themselves.

Relations between functions/components are dealt with in general by Halliday (1977: section 1.3). Semiotic-functionally ('from above'), ideational and interpersonal are extrinsic; textual is enabling. Semantically, logical is with experiential in being ideational. Lexico-grammatically ('from below'), logical is uni-variate, the others multi-variate. See further Halliday 1979, distinguishing between the structural characteristics of the non-logical components themselves. And as to the ideational and textual, Halliday (1969: section 2.6) says that the logical is intermediate between the experiential and the textual (see also Ellis forthcoming (Appendix), and on language-specific relations between the experiential and textual involving logical relations ('being'), see Ellis 1978, and Ellis and Boadi 1969).

A particular case is touched on by Halliday (1969: section 2.6): 'The logical options are those whereby the speaker expresses in "pure" (abstract) form relations which appear experientially as processes (linking "things") and textually as conjunctives (linking propositions).' In its relation to the structure of text, this is taken up in section 5.3.2 (see also section 5.1.5).

The textual function is closest to the logical in the sense that the textual component is least easy to disentangle from the logical sub-component. But at various levels of analysis and ranks (of sentence-grammar and text-grammar) the textual function is entwined also with the interpersonal and the experiential, and a full account of the textualness of a text will tend to be an account of all its functions with the emphasis on the textual (Halliday 1977: section 2.1).

In other words, the linguistic options involved in textual meaning (instantial in a given text and potential in the resources available in the language, register or genre) are not limited to those of the textual component (which organize the textual meaning, together with items derived from elsewhere, like *following* derived from otherwise experientially functioning lexis). For example, tense and especially aspect (in the Slavonic sense in languages that have it), which contribute to the textual integration of clauses and sentences (cf. van Dijk 1972: 81–8), themselves belong to the ideational, and at least partly to the experiential component.

5.3.2 Kinds of structure of text(s)

On structure in components in general, see Halliday 1979. Structure above the sentence (i.e. of texts or parts of texts) is a subject currently in development and full of controversy, with some confusion of terminology. For example, different writers mean different things by 'rhetoric' (some within linguistics, others outside), by 'semantics' (some within (lexico-)grammar, others outside), and, of course, by 'structure'. But it seems possible to distinguish the following relevant kinds of structure:

(1) linguistic structure:
    (i) logical, indifferently above or below sentence;
    (ii) textual, not 'structure' in the strict sense of the grammatical (or phonological) category;
(2) the 'discourse structure' of Sinclair/Jones/Hartmann (see section 5.2.3; on its linguisticness see below);
(3) Halliday's 'generic structure' (see below);
(4) non-linguistic structure:
    (i) logical;
    (ii) narrative, poetic, etc., depending on genre ('rhetorical' in one sense).

('Graphic' and 'phonological' structure (invoked in sections 5.2.3, 5.2.4 and cf. Ellis 1976: 94), are not included here, as not being structures of the text as belonging to the level of form—or 'semantic' in Halliday's sense; cf. section 5.2.3; Ellis 1976: 95—but of the organization of its substance.)

By non-linguistic structure is meant structure of the 'content' of a text, to be distinguished (though they may interact) from 'structure of situation' (of the speech event of which the text itself is another constituent), which Ure 1973, 1974 invokes in determining the demarcation of certain kinds of language-occurrence (cf. section 5.2.2 on multi-layering, and Ellis (1976: 91–2). Sinclair/Jones/Hartmann's third column (numbered (1) in section 5.2.3) corresponds to this, Sinclair's (school organization) also partly to 'structure of situation'.

All texts will have all of these kinds of structure ((4) (i) and (ii)) in varying degrees: a 'logical' text within natural language (cf. section 5.1.5) will have maximum logical structure, but also share 'exposition structure' with expository texts on other subjects; texts of less logical genres will still have some looser logical structure beside the structure of content of their genre. (We assume a wide interpretation of 'genre' in ascribing (3) to all texts.)

(1) (i)—logical linguistic structure—comprises relations between propositions represented by clauses and sentences in parataxis and hypotaxis, with their conjunctions and relevant adjuncts. It has some counterpart in a 'text' of logical propositions, in so far as in logic inter-propositional relations are to be conceived syntagmatically at all (see section 5.1.5), whereas (as said in section 5.1.2) (1) (ii)—textual linguistic structure—has none (with the possible kinds of exception noted in section 5.1.5). It would seem to be nearer to being co-extensive with a non-linguistic structure (4) (i) than any other linguistic structure with any non-linguistic one; we limit the co-extensiveness by defining (1) (i) as being within the 'logical sub-component' of the lexico-grammar, which corresponds to part only of 'logic' (see section 5.1.5). Some linguistic features may prove difficult to disentangle between (1) (i) and (ii) (see Halliday 1969: 2.7). In particular (for discussion see Halliday and Hasan 1976), and, and the 'and' feature in the meaning of other conjunctions, is arguably recursive in some uses and not others.

(1) (ii)—textual linguistic structure—is the overall textual structure (in the sense of the textual function/component) of a text, or structure of presentation of information (in the linguistic sense of information in INFORMATION STRUCTURE, as opposed to the CONTENT of (4)). It would involve (1) division into chains of anaphora, topic units (constituting 'structure' not in the strict sense of the grammatical category, because of overlapping divisions; see Ellis 1966a: 84–5); (2) topics (defined by the overlap of topic units: see Ellis 1966a: 84), etc., relatable to (1) participant relations (transitivity in the experiential sub-component); (3) sentence-conjunction; and (4) thematic and information structure (see section 5.2.3 and Ellis forthcoming).

(2)—'discourse structure'—is discussed at length above in section 5.2.3, where it is argued that it is structure in the strict sense of the grammatical category, but that it is doubtful whether it is purely linguistic-formal in the criteria of its demarcation, classes, etc.

(3)—Halliday's 'generic structure' 1977; (Ellis 1976: 93, 96: 'genre structure')—comprises linguistic features of textual structure possessed by a text in virtue of belonging to a genre ('the form that a text has as a property of its genre'), and hence straddles (1) and (2)—while both particularizing and generalizing by explicit reference to genre—rather than constituting an additional separate structure. For an exemplification of this, as of (4) (ii) (content structure of haikus), see Ellis (1976: 93, 96, 94–5).

(4) (i)—logical non-linguistic structure—is distinguished from (4) (ii), other non-linguistic structure(s), by being concerned with truth-value relations (cf. section 5.1, especially n. 4). For further categorizations of (4) (ii), cf. Section 5.2.3 above and Ellis (1976: 93) and references given.

As indicated in section 5.1.5, logical relations may appear in language in various guises: see Halliday (1969: section 2.6) quoted there. As also indicated in section 5.1.5 (and 5.1.2), it is the inter-propositional (corresponding more to the above-sentence, textual aspects of language) part of logic that is most unquestionably reflected in the logical sub-component; hence the points of contact between the logical and textual functions above.[12]

NOTES

1. To say that a total model of language implies a model of 'language in use' is surely unnecessary in the context of this book, but it is perhaps worth making explicit that the descriptive linguistic model in question is a model of LANGUAGE (in abstraction from 'use') understood in such a way that the descriptive linguistic model can be the basis of a sociolinguistic model (or psycholinguistic model, etc.) of language IN USE, or of language AND USE OF language. (For discussion of the relation of descriptive linguistics and sociolinguistics (etc.), which lies outside the subject of this chapter, see Halliday *passim*, e.g. 1973a, b, 1974a, b, 1977; Hasan and others in Bernstein 1973; Ure and Ellis 1974; Ellis 1965; Fawcett 1973a, 1974a; Davies 1975; Turner and Mohan 1970.) But it should be emphasized that the functions belong to the descriptive linguistic model (cf. Fawcett 1973a: 17, 1974a: 41–5, 33, with the difference of emphasis that 'the concept of SYSTEM is more basic'), where they play an essential role in its underlying the sociolinguistic (etc.) model, as well as in the rationale of its own components.
2. For such a distinction, and its application to the differentiation of mathematics (on which, numeration, as experiential, cf. sections 5.1.2, 5.1.3) from logic itself (both standing on the shoulders of language, cf. section 5.1.5), see Quine (1974: 5), and cf. Kneale (1962: 739).
3. On definition of the subject of logic cf. Quine (1974: 5), Copi (1961: 4–6), Kleene (1967: 3), Kneale (1962: XII.5) and Mates (1972: 205).
4. Secondary in general, such as R. M. W. Dixon's notion of developing language-specific logics (Ellis 1966a: n. 15); metaphorical, such as G. Turner's notion of interpersonal logic(s). Both senses (strict and secondary/metaphorical) appear in S. Hall's 'Ideologies do not operate by logic; they have logics of their own' (BBC2, 18 July 1978). Cf. Kneale (1962: 741); also Harman 1976. The crucial distinction seems to be that logic in the narrow sense is concerned essentially with truth conditions (cf. references in n. 3) in ratiocinative concatenation: these are independent of which natural language the logic is formulationally associated with, as some of the other considerations, e.g. in Harman, are not.
5. von Wright (1957: 5–6) distinguishes the logic of relations as a 'province of logic (and of logical truth)' from that of properties as well as of propositions.

6. In saying this, as regards textual, I am rejecting Fel'dman's conception (1954: 121, 122, 126), according to which LOGICAL content of sentences includes what we should call informational, if not thematic, structures. It is in fact symptomatic of the late development of understanding of the textual function (but cf. section 5.2.1) that Fel'dman's threefold division is into MATERIAL content (in which he is right not to include informational structuring), EXPRESSIVE content and, as already said, LOGICAL content (in which he includes what we should call mood as well as the textual).

7. Cf. Quine (1974: 245–7), Kneale (1962: 41, 185, 259), von Wright (1957: 4f, 15–18, 20, 28, 46–57).

8. von Wright (1957: 3–4) extends the logical form of propositions (defined as that on which truth-relations depend irrespective of variables ('independently of its content', 5), 1–2) from quantifiers, connectors, copulas, negation, etc. (his examples: *if–then*, *all*, *are* and *some*) to include what we term (section 5.2.3) semantic relations, specifically 'two (primitive) logical constants of relational logic' (1, n. 2), converse (does not belong to logic of properties, 5–6) and 'relative product' or 'chain', e.g. relation called *uncle*, *grandfather*: chain-relation of relative *brother*, *father*, and *father* with itself. The linguistic expresssion of these does not belong to the logical component as defined by Halliday, which does not appear to include this lexical part of the lexico-grammar (cf. Hasan in the present volume; Ellis 1966b).

9. Biggs's distinction between universal and G = a generically significant number (which he concedes may be pragmatic and not in the semantics itself) is arguably a matter of register application of the strict logical quantifier.

10. Parts of the discussion of semantic relations themselves, as distinct from their application in anaphoric reference, have also benefitted from discussion with A. Duthie. Cf. also Enkvist 1976.

11. J. R. Martin has suggested a way of relating FOUR register dimensions to the functions; cf. Gregory's chapter in this volume.

12. It should be pointed out that this chapter was completed before the publication of Halliday's *Introduction to Functional Grammar* (1985). However, this in no way weakens its relevance, as most of the ideas relating to the logical function presented there had already appeared elsewhere, and are frequently referred to here. [Editorial note]

BIBLIOGRAPHY

Allerton, D. J., Carney, E. and Holdecroft, D. (eds) (1979), *Function and Context in Linguistic Analysis: Essays Offered to William Haas*, Cambridge, Cambridge University Press.
Bazell, C. E., Catford, J. C. and Halliday, M. A. K. (eds) (1966), *In Memory of J. R. Firth*, London, Longman.
Bernstein, B. (ed.) (1973), *Class Codes and Control: Vol. 2 Applied Studies: Towards a Sociology of Language*, London, Routledge and Kegan Paul.
Biggs, C. (1976), 'A generic/generics/the generic', paper to Linguistics Association, Edinburgh meeting.
Candlin, C. (ed.) (1974), *The Communicative Teaching of English*, Lancaster, Lancaster University.
Copi, I. M. (1961), *Introduction to Logic*, New York, Macmillan.
Davies, H. M. P. (1975), 'A way in to language study', DES Summer School for English Teachers, Oxford.

Dijk, T. A. van (1972), *Some Aspects of Text Grammars*, The Hague, Mouton.
—— (1975), 'Narrative macro-structures: logical and cognitive foundations', Thaxted Symposium of Neo-Formalists, Dept. of Language and Linguistics, University of Essex.
Dijk, T. A. van and Petöfi, J. (eds) (1977), *Grammars and Descriptions*, Berlin, de Gruyter.
Dressler, W. (1970), 'Textsyntax und Übersetzen', *Commentationes Societatis Linguisticae Europaeae*, 3: 64–77.
—— (1972a), *Einführung in die Textlinguistik*, Tübingen.
—— (1972b), 'Textgrammatische Invarianz in Übersetzungen?', Rhoda Colloquium, mimeo.
Ellis, J. (1961), 'Some recent work on German grammar', *Archivum Linguisticum*, 13.
—— (1965), 'Linguistic sociology and institutional linguistics', *Linguistics*, 19.
—— (1966a), 'On contextual meaning', *In Memory of J. R. Firth*, London, Longman.
—— (1966b), 'Lyons, *Structural Semantics*', review article, *Linguistics*, 24.
—— (1971), 'The definite article in translation between English and Twi', M. Houis (ed.), Eighth West African Linguistic Congress, Abidjan.
—— (1976), 'The role of the concept of text in the elaboration of linguistic data', York Papers in Linguistics.
—— (1978), 'Identification and Grammatical Structure in Akan and Welsh', in Wurm and McCormack (eds) (1978).
—— (forthcoming), 'Textual meaning in an Akan folktale and its English translation'.
Ellis, J. and L. Boadi (1969), ' "To be" in Twi', in Verhaar (ed) (1969).
Enkvist, N. E. (1976), 'Linearity and text strategy', lecture University of Aston, May 1976.
Fawcett, R. (1973a), *Systemic functional grammar in a cognitive model of language*, University College London (mimeo.).
—— (1973b), 'Generating a sentence in systemic functional grammar', University College London (mimeo.), reprinted in Halliday and Martin (eds) (1981).
—— (1974a), 'Two concepts of function in a cognitive model of communication', in Candlin (ed.) (1974).
—— (1974b), 'Notes on the logical component of a systemic grammar of English', paper to First Systemic Workshop, Walsall, West Midlands College (mimeo.).
—— (1974–6), 'Some proposals for systemic syntax', *Midlands Association for Linguistic Study Journal*, 1, No. 2, 2, No. 1, 2, No. 2.
—— (1980), *Cognitive Linguistics and Social Interaction*, Heidelberg, Julius Groos Verlag and Exeter University.
—— (1983), 'Language as a semiological system', in Morreall (ed.) (1983: 59–125).
Fel'dman, N. I. (1954), 'A. V. Fedorov, *Vvedenie v teoriyu perevoda*', review article, *Voprosy Yazykoznaniya*, 117–27.
Firbas, J. (1972), 'On the interplay of prosodic and non-prosodic means of functional sentence perspective', in Fried (ed.) (1972).
Fried, V. (ed.) (1972), *The Prague School of Linguistics and Language Teaching*, Oxford, Oxford University Press.
Gazdar, G. and Pullum, G. (1976), 'Truth-functional connectives in natural language', paper to Linguistics Association, Edinburgh meeting.
Halliday, M. A. K. (1965), 'Types of structure', Nuffield Programme, University College London.
—— (1966), 'Lexis as a Linguistic Level', in Bazell, Catford and Halliday (eds) (1966).
—— (1967/8), 'Notes on transitivity and theme in English, *Journal of Linguistics*, 3, 4.
—— (1969), 'An outlook on English grammar', Dept. of General Linguistics, University College, London.
—— (1970), 'Functional diversity in language', *Foundations of Language*, 6.

—— (1972), 'Options and functions in the English clause;, in Householder (ed.) (1972).

—— (1973), *Explorations in the Functions of Language*, London, Edward Arnold.

—— (1974a), 'Language as Social Semiotic', *LACUS* 1.

—— (1974b), *Language and Social Man*, London, Longman.

—— (1975), *Learning How to Mean*, London, Edward Arnold.

—— (1977), 'Text as Semantic Choice in Social Contexts', in van Dijk and Petöfi (eds) (1977).

—— (1978), *Language as Social Semiotic: The Social Interpretation of Language and Meaning*, London, Edward Arnold.

—— (1979), 'Modes of meaning and modes of expression', in Allerton, Carney and Holdecroft (eds) (1979: 57–79).

Halliday, M. A. K. and Hasan, R. (1976), *Cohesion in English*, London, Longman.

Halliday, M. A. K. and Martin, J. R. (eds) (1981), *Readings in Systemic Linguistics*, London, Batsford.

Harman, G. (1976), 'Logic and language', *Current Trends in Philosophy*, 3, *The Listener*, May.

Hartmann, R. (1975), 'Understanding Texts', *System*, 3, No. 2, 98–105.

Hawkins, J. A. (1978), *Definiteness and Indefiniteness: A Study of Reference and Grammaticality Prediction*, London, Croom Helm.

Householder, F. W. (ed.) (1972), *Syntactic Theory 1: Structuralist*, Harmondsworth, Penguin.

Hudson, R. (1972), *Systemic Generative Grammar*, University College London (mimeo.).

Hurford, J. R. and Heasley, B. (1983), *Semantics: A Coursebook*, Cambridge, Cambridge University Press.

Jones, K. (1974), *The Role of Discourse Analysis in Devising Undergraduate Reading Programmes in English for Science and Technology*, London, The British Council (mimeo.).

Kleene, S. C. (1967), *Mathematical Logic*, New York, Wiley.

Kneale, W. and Kneale, M. (1962), *The Development of Logic*, Oxford, Oxford University Press.

Makkai, A. and Makkai, V. B. (eds) (1975), *The First LACUS Forum*, Columbia, S. Carolina, Hornbeam Press.

Martin, J. (forthcoming), 'Phoricity: a systemic analysis of reference'.

Martin, J. and Rochester, S. (1975), 'Cohesion and reference in schizophrenic speech', in Makkai and Makkai (eds) (1975: 302–11).

Mates, B. (1972), *Elementary Logic*, 2nd edn., Oxford, Oxford University Press.

Morreall, J. (ed.) (1983), *The Ninth LACUS Forum*, Columbia, S. Carolina, Hornbeam Press.

Quine, W. V. (1974), *Methods of Logic*, 3rd edn., London, Routledge and Kegan Paul.

Seuren, P. A. M. (1974), 'Referential constraints on lexical islands', *Nottingham Linguistic Circular*, 3, No. 2, 8–20.

Sinclair, J. et al. (1972), *The English used by Teachers and Pupils*, SSRC Project Report, University of Birmingham.

Sinclair, J. and Coulthard, R. M. (1975), *Towards an Analysis of Discourse: The English Used by Teachers and Pupils*, London, Oxford University Press.

Taylor, N. M. (1974), 'Speculations on bilingualism and the cognitive network', Working Papers on Bilingualism, 2, 69–124, March, Ontario.

Tittensor, D. (n.d.), *Systemic Morphology of Old English*, Edinburgh (mimeo.).

Turner, G. and Mohan, B. (1970), *A Linguistic Description and Computer Program of Children's Speech*, London, Routledge and Kegan Paul.

Ure, J. N. (1973), 'Register and Unit of Discourse', draft working paper, Language Use in Ghana (SSRC project), Legon (mimeo.).

—— (1974), 'Self-reporting and the question of reliability', International Congress of Sociology, Toronto.

Ure, J. N. and Ellis, J. (1974), Register in descriptive linguistics and linguistic sociology', in Uribe-Villegas (ed.) (1974).

Uribe-Villegas, O. (ed.) (1974), *La Sociolingüística Actual*, Mexico City, University of Mexico.

Verhaar, J. W. M. (ed.) (1969), *The Verb 'Be' and its Synonyms 3*, Dordrecht, Reidel.

Ward, D. (1966), *Pronominal Systems*, Problems of the Grammatical Analysis of Contemporary Russian 3, Essex, Contemporary Russian Language Analysis Project.

Widdowson, H. (1973), *An Applied Linguistic Approach to Discourse Analysis*, unpublished Ph.D. thesis, Edinburgh.

—— (1975), *Stylistics and the Teaching of Literature*, London, Longman.

Wright, G. H. von (1957), *Logical Studies*, London, Routledge and Kegan Paul.

Wurm, S. and McCormack, W. (eds) (1978), *Approaches to Language*, The Hague, Mouton.

Part IV
System networks in the lexico-grammar

6 The semantics of clause and verb for relational processes in English

Robin P. Fawcett

University of Wales Institute of Science and Technology

6.1 BASIC PROBLEMS

6.1.1 The theoretical and descriptive setting: some problems to be addressed

A central problem—perhaps THE central problem—facing linguists today is that of how to characterize meaning.[1] What types of 'meaning', in the broadest sense of the term, should be included in a model of the semiotic system that we call 'language'? How should this 'meaning potential' be modelled? How far should an attempt to understand language push the explanation towards the realm of the various kinds of 'knowledge' (including knowledge of the 'co-text', the immediate situation and the culture) that guide the choices within the language itself? And if there is a distinguishable semantic level of langauge—as we shall assume there is—how closely, and by what means, are meanings to be related to forms?

The problem of meaning is a problem of both theory and description. We approach it here through attempting a description of a part of the English language which is, I would claim, absolutely central—in terms of both its functions in the grammar and the frequency of its use. This is the grammar of RELATIONAL processes. Indeed, such processes, as defined here, are in many natural texts more frequent than the combined totals of the other two main TRANSITIVITY types, MATERIAL and MENTAL processes.[2]

The system network and realization rules for relational processes are chiefly concerned to model the possible configurations of PARTICIPANT ROLES, to use Halliday's (1985: 102) term (roughly, in the terms of Fillmore 1968, etc. 'cases'), together with the MAIN VERBS that occur with them. Halliday's *Introduction to Functional Grammar* includes a valuable contribution to our understanding of relational processes and how they are used (1985: 112–28), and we shall refer to this work at many points. But I shall suggest that a far larger share of the grammar of transitivity should in fact be included in the relational processes than Halliday does; I shall, for example, propose that clauses with *give* and *sell* do NOT realize a type of 'material' process that has the addition of a 'Beneficiary' (as does Halliday 1985: 132), but that they are relational processes, just as much as clauses with *be* and *have* are. I shall show that a systemic grammar provides a natural means of bringing out the remarkable similarities in the semantic features of clauses with (a) *have*, *get* and *give*, etc. (b) *be*, *become* and *make*, etc., and (c) *be*, *go* and *send*, etc. Many of these process-types involve the role of Agent, so that an important corollary of the model offered here is that the presence of an Agent is in no way a marker of a material process. It is in fact a role that is relevant across all three major process-types, including mental processes. (Thus *look at* is to *see* as *go* is to *be*; mental processes will be the topic of another paper.)

This chapter, then, offers 'another interpretation' of relational processes to set alongside the approach taken in Halliday 1985, and it is offered in the same spirit in which Halliday himself offers 'another interpretation' of transitivity in general and material processes in particular, in Halliday (1985: 144f.).

The expression 'relational processes' will perhaps seem strange to a reader unfamiliar with the systemic tradition. The term 'relational' was introduced by Halliday in 1968 (202) to label what was then seen as a relatively minor area of the grammar, chiefly concerned with 'ascriptive' and 'equative' clauses with *be*. The term 'process' dates from 1967a (38), and from the beginning Halliday interpreted it in a broad sense that included 'states and relations' as well as 'actions and events' (1970: 146). Hence the apparent anomaly of referring to a clause such as *Ivy is the boss* as a 'process'. In the present approach, then, the term 'process' is not to be contrasted with terms such as 'state' or 'event', as it has been in some other studies.

The proposals made here have been developed out of Halliday's earlier work in this area. At various points I offer analyses of examples that are different from Halliday's analyses, but there are indications in Halliday 1977 and 'unpublished' that in the 1970s his thinking was in some respects—but certainly not all—moving in a direction parallel to that which I was independently taking, as presented in Fawcett 1975a, Fawcett (1980: 138–9), and here. Halliday (1985: 112ff.), however, while giving an impressively thorough coverage to relational process (sixteen pages, with only four on material and six on mental processes), does not in fact develop these ideas.[3]

Nonetheless, Halliday 1985 offers the major alternative description of relational processes to the present one. It is full of penetrating insights, including some not found in his earlier writings on this topic. However, it includes a number of complex distinctions which, it seems to me, are not needed for a full specification of the language system itself. Where some of them come into their own is, in my view, at the next stage 'up', as it were: in specifying the states of 'KNOWLEDGE' under which a speaker would appropriately choose a particular bundle of features in the system networks at the SEMANTIC level of language. Thus Halliday's insights should contribute to specifying the PROCEDURAL FELICITY CONDITIONS (to use the term first employed in Fawcett 1983: 97 and exemplified in Fawcett 1984: 166f.) or INQUIRIES (in the terms of Mann and Matthiessen 1983: 17/1985: 52) that guide the choices of a user of a language (and their interpretation). If this is right, we might say that some of Halliday's complex distinctions will find their appropriate place in this latter component of a computer model of language; in shorthand form the insights could be said to be PRAG-MATICALLY relevant, but not necessary for the SEMANTIC level of a purely linguistic description. (We shall meet a number of examples of this in what follows.)

I would therefore claim (1) that the descriptive framework to be presented here is considerably simpler than that in Halliday 1985 (which, if I can persuade you of its adequacy, may be something of a relief!); and (2) that it provides an insightful account of a wide range of semantic variables realized in the clause—including many that are found in Halliday 1985 outside the account of relational processes, and some that are not met there at all.

It would double the length of what is already a long chapter to present arguments for every proposal in relation to those of Halliday 1985—let alone those of other scholars. Nonetheless, I shall try to indicate briefly the main points of difference. In particular I shall adopt the strategy of using examples taken from various sections of Halliday 1985 and from his earlier works to indicate where, in the present framework, these examples are covered.

Beyond Halliday the debt is to J. R. Firth, for the concepts of system and structure, and beyond him again to Saussure. It is unusual for a systemic linguist to claim Saussure explicitly as an antecedent, but I have argued (Fawcett 1983) that systemic and stratificational grammar in fact provide the fullest and most explicit developments in linguistics today of Saussure's basic concepts. The particular type of systemic model with which I work is perhaps more Saussurean than that of some other systemicists, in that it has consistently and explicitly built into it the concept that a language, like other semiotic systems, consists essentially of two levels, corresponding to the two-halves of the Saussurean 'sign'. The first level consists of a set of 'signifieds', i.e. a mutually defining set of semantic 'values' (features) in complex systemic relationships to each other of choice, dependency and simultaneity, and the second is the set of 'signifiers' that realize them, i.e. lexical and structural items, syntactic arrangements of those items, and intonational phenomena. It is the lack of a one-to-one relationship between the two sets of phenomena that is one of the chief fascinations of language, and that provides the challenge to which this paper offers one response.

We may say, then, that a clause is generated from a set of SEMANTIC FEATURES such as [relational, locational etc.]. While the more delicate of these specify the MAIN VERB, the primary ones specify the configuration of ROLES, such as CARRIER + LOCATION, with which the clause is associated. The term 'semantics', then, as defined here, is restricted to that relatively abstract level of the grammar—which is, however, still relatable by explicit REALIZATION RULES to the level of form—where we find the options in transitivity, mood, theme, etc.; it is being used, therefore, in precisely the sense commended in Butler (1979: 80).

Halliday's own position in his writings of the 1970s and 1980s is not fully clear. As Butler comments (1985: 94): '. . . it is frankly difficult to know what counts as semantic and what as syntactic in this latter work.' The problem is still unresolved in Halliday 1985. On the one hand, the whole book exemplifies persuasively the fact that, as Halliday says (1985: xx): 'this book is a "functional" grammar based on meaning'—and, indeed, the chapter on transitivity is introduced as an exploration of 'the different types of process that are built into the semantics of English' (1985: 102). On the other hand, Halliday suggests in his introduction that, while we may have a reasonable understanding of the lexico-grammar, 'we cannot yet describe the semantic system of a language' (1985: xx). And this seems to imply that there is a level of semantic explanation beyond that which he is offering. Halliday's own resolution of the dilemma is that 'there is no clear line between semantics and grammar, and a functional grammar is one that is pushed in the direction of semantics' (1985: xix). And, as he then says, 'this one has been pushed fairly far.'

Here we shall make the assumption—as did Hasan in her valuable paper on 'the semantics of the Urdu verb *honaa* (to be)' (1971: 1), and as Halliday himself seems to do when involved in the nitty-gritty of description itself—that the account of the clause that we shall consider here is the result of a 'push' that has reached the semantics. Perhaps, on the issue of levels, we should let the grammar decide. That is, if we construct a level of explanation that is not in a one-to-one relationship with the level of items and structures, we need a name for it. Even though it is a label that has been unforgivably overstretched by some scholars, there seems to be no real alternative term for this level to 'semantics'.

We should note, however, that this is in marked contrast to other uses of the term in the systemic literature, where it may refer, for example, to socio-semantic networks (of the sort presented in Turner's chapter) or to register options (as in Gregory's). My *Cognitive Linguistics and Social Interaction* (Fawcett 1980) offers a fuller picture of the overall framework assumed here, including proposals as to how other aspects of 'meaning', including register, referents, knowledge, intended deductions, etc., can be modelled in an integrated model of a systemic functional grammar and the other components of a communicating mind. Thus, if you find the model for relational processes outlined here persuasive, this description provides support for a particular sub-class of systemic grammar. We might call this sub-class SYSTEMIC SEMANTIC grammar; such a grammar may of course also be a SYSTEMIC FUNCTIONAL grammar.

Three issues in systemic theory on which the present chapter bears are therefore:

(a) How many levels of system networks are needed in a systemic model of language?
(b) What conditions are necessary and sufficient for including a feature in a (semantic) system network?
(c) should an explicitly semantic network seek to capture ALL conceptual equivalences and, if not, how should we decide which to capture and which to leave aside?

And a fourth issue which this paper addresses is:

(d) How high a priority should be attached to the idea of 'elegance' when constructing system networks (and their realization rules)?

We shall return to these questions in section 6.5.2.

6.1.2 Seven basic descriptive concepts

First, following Halliday (1967a: 38–9) and all his later writings on the topic, we shall take the notion of 'transitivity' to be relevant to realizations in the CLAUSE as well as in the MAIN VERB—rather than merely in the latter, as in most other grammars, including Quirk *et al.* (1972: 38). But, unlike Halliday, we shall treat all of those elements that most systemic linguists regard as elements of the 'verbal group' as direct elements of the clause (cf. Hudson 1971: 26; Fawcett: 1980: 47–9). (Note, however, that Halliday (1977: 212 and 1985: 71 f.) suggests that the element 'Finite' is an element of clause structure as well as of 'verbal group' structure.) The advantage for our present purposes in abolishing the verbal group is that we can generate the items that expound the element Main verb directly and simply from the same network as the participant roles.

Second, we shall assume that there is a prime distinction between PARTICIPANT and CIRCUMSTANTIAL roles, such that the participant roles are specified by the transitivity network.[4] The circumstantial roles are specified in a set of networks that are separate, though in some cases dependent: cf. Figure 6.3 in section 6.3.2 and Hasan's chapter in this volume. Note that the term 'participant role' must be taken as including what Halliday earlier (1970: 149) termed 'inner circumstantial' roles. In Fawcett (180: 135 f.) I referred to them as 'inherent roles'; they are those that are inherently associated with the process expressed by the Main verb.

Third, we shall follow a MINIMAL LABELLING principle. Thus the goal is to introduce the minimum number of labels for roles (or any category) in order to get the grammar to work insightfully. Ideally, then, there will be one label for each role type. Thus, if two types of process are adequately distinguished from each other through having different configurations of roles, we shall not need to recognize sub-categories of, say, Agent. In cases where it IS necessary to recognize two types, we shall in fact find that we can treat these as primary categories without loss of significant generalization (e.g. the four terms suggested in section 6.3.2 to replace 'Beneficiary'). Note that while we shall recognize here certain two-function roles, the two labels involved are NOT ordered in delicacy; the role is simply a compound one, with two equal parts.

Fourth, we should note that participant roles may be present in a clause without being realized overtly, as in (1) where all three participant roles are COVERT, i.e. unrealized; see further Fawcett (1980: 98 f, 145–6, 147).

(1) Give generously!

(Examples illustrating key concepts in the framework being proposed are set out on a separate line and numbered, but in addition many other illustrative examples will be included in the running text.)

Fifth, the term COMPLEMENT is taken to be an element of syntactic structure, and so to belong at the level of FORM. But its definition is ultimately dependent on semantic criteria (cf. Fawcett 1975b/81: 4–5, reproduced and discussed in Butler 1985: 94 f.); Complements simply realize participant roles that have not been given the additional 'mood-marking' role of Subject. Thus *by Sir Christopher Wren* in (2) (taken from Halliday 1973: 43) and *in the garden* in (3) (taken from Halliday 1967a: 71) are in the present grammar both Complements—and not Adjuncts, as Halliday suggested in those earlier works.

(2) this gazebo was built by Sir Christopher Wren
(3) John is in the garden

Halliday's (1985: 79) position is that a Complement is an element 'that has the potential for being Subject but is not'. But he goes on: 'there is one exception to this general principle: that is the attributive Complement, as in *King Alfred was a noble king* or *its fleece was white as snow*.' From this it might appear that (*by*) *Sir Christopher Wren* in (2) should now be classed as a Complement. However, the only analysed examples, which come in the section entitled 'Transitivity and voice: another interpretation', still make the Agent an Adjunct, e.g. *the cat* in *the glass was broken by the cat* (p. 151). So the position is not clear.[5] A similar position to mine on these two clause types is taken by Young (1980: 129 and 121 respectively).

Sixth, we are now in a position where we can see why the notion of participant roles is so crucial to the grammar. When it is established through the selection of the relevant features in the network that a given participant role is to be realized OVERTLY, as either a Subject or a Complement, this leads to a RE-ENTRY to the semantic system, and so, on a second cycle, to the generation of a syntactic unit that will fill that element of syntactic structure, and so realize that role. Typically, this unit is a nominal or other type of GROUP, but it may on occasion be another CLAUSE. (Choices on this subsequent cycle will be limited, where this is appropriate, by re-entering at a given point or points—e.g. to generate either a nominal group or a non-finite clause with the item *to*, after *want*.) Thus, abstract though the participant roles may seem, the features in the network that specify them do ultimately have a reflex at the level of form, just as surely as do the more delicate features that determine the phonological (or graphological) shape of the Main verb.

The seventh and final concept is that each role in a process must be different from the others. It may well be that this plays a role in keeping apart in our minds the various units that are being generated on those subsequent passes through the semantics.

6.1.3 Descriptive strategies

Every grammarian works on the basis of certain assumptions about how to go about the business of describing language. It may be helpful to state explicitly those that have governed the description offered here.

(a) The description is text-based. While only some of the examples are natural texts reproduced in unmodified form, my general approach is to scour texts for examples. However, in order to save space, they often need to have their nominal groups reduced to a proper name, and their Adjuncts removed.

(b) Of all the various types of linguists, the systemic linguist is probably the most committed to the importance of the paradigmatic dimensions of language. But one could spend a lifetime scouring the texts for minimally contrasting examples that are suggested by the network but are not there in one's collection of examples, so that in fact I fairly often invent examples to fill out the paradigm—as, I am sure, ALL linguists do in reality.

(c) Where I am not absolutely sure that such creations would be unquestionably accepted by all native speakers, I conduct informal experiments on friends, family and students. (Sometimes—and less satisfactorily—I simply ask if there is anything odd about the example under scrutiny.)

(d) In constructing system networks, and so in deciding which systems to make PRIMARY, I give more weight to the patterning suggested by HIGH-FREQUENCY process types and lexemes, and less to low-frequency ones.

(e) A second such consideration is that I give more weight to process types that are LEXICALLY PRODUCTIVE (i.e. that have associated with them more different forms expounding the Main verb) and less to those that are lexically restricted to one or two lexemes.

(f) I construct the grammar so that it will have the MINIMUM NUMBER OF CATEGORIES, both in the system networks, in the roles, and in the sytax that realizes them.

(g) If there is a clash between capturing generalizations with respect to roles and verbs, I give PRIORITY TO ROLES (e.g. *he burnt the cakes dry* is here related to *he made the water dirty*, not *he burnt the cakes*; see section 6.3.3).

6.2 SOME PRIMARY CHOICES IN THE RELATIONAL PROCESS NETWORK

6.2.1 An overview

The starting point in systemic linguistics for what were later termed 'relational processes' was Halliday's distinction (1967a: 66–7, 77) between three classes of the verb *be*. Two of these (his Classes 2 and 3) correspond to his later transitivity distinction between clauses that are 'attributive' and 'equative' (later still, 'identifying'), as in *Marguerite is a poet* and *Templecombe is the treasurer* (Halliday 1970: 154–5). We shall reappraise this distinction shortly. Halliday's third (his Class 1) is the so-called 'existential' *be*. Here we shall treat this as a sub-category of 'locational' process, i.e. one with a covert, recoverable location, rather as Lyons suggests (1968: 388 f.); see section 6.3.4.

Interestingly, Lyons includes in the same discussion 'possessive' clauses with *have*, such as *John has a book*. One of his reasons for doing so is that there is, among the languages of the world, a considerable overlap between what one might term 'having' and 'being with' (393 f.). However, as I hope to show, there is also compelling internal evidence from the semantics and syntax of English for treating 'possessive' clauses as relational. On this basis, then, there might appear to be four main types of relational process: 'attributive' 'identifying', 'locational' and 'possessive'. These are exemplified in (4–7). The first term after each is a possible semantic feature specifying the process type; this is followed by a structural description (where + means 'is in the unmarked sequence followed by'), specifying the roles that might appear to be inherently associated with each—but see below for some changes.

(4ai) Ivy is successful   'attributive'   Attribuant + Process + Attribute
(4aii) Ivy is a doctor   'attributive'   Attribuant + Process + Attribute
(5a)   Ivy is the boss   'identifying'   Identified + Process + Identified
(6a)   Ivy is in Peru   'locational'   Located + Process + Location
(7a)   Ivy has the key   'possessive'   Possessor + Process + Possessed

Let us now examine some basic issues concerning each.

The process-type in (4ai) and (4aii) is concerned with a class-inclusive relationship: the Subject 'Ivy' is being classified as a member of the class identified in the Complement, i.e. 'successful (ones)' or 'doctors'. In terms of the mental referents involved, the two are normally different, in that one referent is the whole class of 'successful ones' or 'doctors' (cf. below). It is irrelevant to the definition of the participant role 'Attribute' that the Complement in (4ai) is filled by a unit with an adjective at its apex (an 'adjectival' or 'quantity–quality' group: see Fawcett 1980: 92 and Butler 1985: 101), whereas the Complement in (4aii) is filled by a unit with a noun as head (a nominal group). However, we shall return to this distinction in section 6.4.4. Until the publication of Halliday 1985 I used the trio of terms 'classificatory', 'Classified' and 'Classifier' instead of 'attributive', 'Attribuant' and 'Attribute', because they seemed more transparent. Here, however, we shall use Halliday's terms, though in a sense that corresponds in his (1985: 112) terms to the type of 'attributive' process that is also 'intensive'. In section 6.5.2 I shall summarize the main differences between the two models; here all I need say is that these differences mean that in effect I am using the term in a fairly similar sense.

The process-type in (5a) is 'equative', to use Halliday's 1967a term, or both 'intensive' and 'identifying', in terms of Halliday (1985: 112 f.).[6] Here we shall take the view that from a LINGUISTIC viewpoint (as distinct from that of the philosopher or psychologist who is modelling 'knowledge of the world'), what matters is not the 'real world' relationship of the referent(s) of the two referring experiences, but that each needs to have assigned to it a DIFFERENT role in the semantics of the linguistic system. Indeed, the roles MUST be different (*pace* Huddleston 1970; cf. Fawcett 1980: 138 n.), because it is part of the purpose of uttering the clause to relate, in a particular semantic relationship, two referents that were previously NOT necessarily so related.

What, then, is the difference between (4a) and (5a)? Halliday (1985: 114) expresses a widely held view when he says 'the fundamental difference between the two is in the fact that identifying clauses are reversible, whereas attributives are not'. Thus we do not use constructions corresponding to (4ai) and (4aii) such as *successful is Ivy and *a doctor is Ivy (except in an archaic literary register), whereas we can and do say the boss is Ivy as well as (5a) Ivy is the boss.

Throughout the period of almost twenty years since first making this distinction, it has remained for Halliday a primary one. It is a distinction which is also made by Lyons (1968: 388 f.), and, as he shows, it reflects the modern logical tradition. In fact, though, as we shall see in section 6.3.2, the LINGUISTIC differences between the two are rather few, in comparison with the differences between these two and each of the other two major types of relational processes. The model to be developed here will explore the advantages of NOT treating the identifying/attributive distinction as primary.

Long after I had decided to amalgamate the two categories, I found myself reading—or, almost certainly, re-reading—the following words, which express neatly the basic reason for not making the distinction: 'identity may be merely the limiting case of inclusion'. Surprisingly, perhaps, in view of his long adherence to the 'identifying-attributive' distinction, these words come from Halliday himself (1967a: 190). And the same idea resurfaces in Halliday (1985: 124), when, having spent twelve pages on a persuasive case for making the distinction, he explores another interpretation of identification and attribution in which he suggests that 'first having separated them we can bring them together again'. In precisely the approach adopted in my own work, he writes:

the distinction between attribution and identification is not quite as clearcut as we have made it seem . . . The . . . means of identifying something by assigning it to a class is to make it a one-member class . . . The consequence of this is . . . that the relationship can be turned around.

The essence of what is proposed here, then, is that what makes certain attributive clauses identifying (or 'equative') is NOT the process realized in the clause, but the equativeness of the two nominal groups. To see this we need to distinguish between IMMEDIATE meaning and INFERRED meaning. The immediate meaning of (5a) is simply 'the class of "the boss" includes Ivy'. But since Ivy and the boss are identical for number and 'definiteness', so that the one may NOT in fact be 'included in' the other, we can further draw the inference that 'the boss' is to be equated with 'Ivy'. It is in this indirect way, I suggest, that English expresses the 'logical' notion of 'identification' or 'equation' (Lyons 1968: 389).

It is often assumed that it is the reversibility of 'equative' clauses with be that establishes identifying processes as a separate class. But the more fundamental distinction, as Halliday rightly suggests (1985: 116), is that many types of identifying clauses can be re-expressed as passive constructions (though not in fact all types, as we shall shortly see). Thus, as Halliday points out,

(8a) *Mr. Garrick played Hamlet* is to (8b) *Hamlet was played by Mr. Garrick* as
(9a) *Mr. Garrick was Hamlet* is to (9b) *Hamlet was Mr. Garrick*.

However, as we shall shortly see, the distinction that Halliday makes so central begins to break down when the clauses have anything other than a simple Carrier.

One problem for the passivisability and reversibility critera is that they do not always work. Halliday's list (1985: 116) of 'intensive identifying' verbs rightly includes *make*, and *add up to*. Yet, while we can say *two and two makes/adds up to four*, we do not say *four makes/adds up to two and two*, or *four is made/added up to by two and two*. Here, then, is a case of the lack of a 'clearcut' distinction of which Halliday has reminded us (1985: 1214).[7]

Moreover, while the criterion of entry to the VOICE system is without doubt an important one that needs to be provided for in any self-respecting grammar, the reversibility criterion is, I suggest, no more than an accidental by-product of the equativeness of the nominal groups that fill the two roles, when suitable options are chosen on RE-ENTRY for each, coupled with the Main verb expressing an equative meaning such as *be*, *become*, *equal* and perhaps *resemble*. The fact is that we find odd cases of reversibility, where the semantics of both the Main verb and the two nominal expressions are appropriate, at various otherwise unrelated points in the grammar. Examples include *the bank faces the hardware shop* (a 'locational' process) and *Phoebe will marry Fred* (a 'material' process). And it is perhaps suggestive that the reversibility test produces odd effects when applied to clauses IN A TEXT. This is because the producer of a text is likely to have rather clear ideas as to which of the two referents of an 'equative' clause (and note that there ARE TWO MENTAL referents before the utterance of the clause identifies one with another) is to have the role of Subject-theme, and which, if any, is to be marked as New information. This variation in the THEME and INFORMATION FOCUS systems is a source of rich variation in the particular sub-category of attributive clauses that happens to be reversible, as the tables on pp. 126–7 of Halliday 1985 elegantly demonstrate (see further note 7).

In what follows, then, we shall treat 'identifying' processes simply as involving Attributes consisting of a one-member class. However, in order to demonstrate the natural way in which 'identifying' clauses can be handled as attributives, we shall continue to include examples of them at every point, in order to make the case explicitly.

The process type in (6a) is LOCATIONAL, and the two suggested roles are LOCATED and LOCATION. Here there is another significant difference from the approach in Halliday 1985 (119f.); instead of my term 'location' he uses 'circumstance'. But these 'circumstances' are not in fact circumstantial roles but participant roles, because they are roles systematically associated with particular types of process (cf. Halliday 1985: 102). Nonetheless, the list of sub-categories of circumstances is for Halliday the same: they are, in his terms (103, 137–44), Time, Place, Manner (with the sub-sub-categories Means, Quality and Comparison), Cause (with sub-sub-categories Reason, Purpose and Behalf), Accompaniment, Matter and Role. Note, however, that while *be* clauses can be constructed with a participant role as Complement that corresponds in its INTERNAL semantics to these, there is a significant difference between (6a) *Ivy is in Peru* and *the best place is in Peru*. The latter is in fact 'identifying', in that the purpose of the clause is to assert that 'the best place' (the Attribuant) is a member of the one-member class 'Peru' (the Attribute), and we shall assume here that its semantic structure is the same as that of (5a) *Ivy is the boss*. That is, in the semantics of the CLAUSE—its participant roles and its process types—the two are identical; where the difference lies is in the semantics of the lower units, such as nominal groups that fill the elements of structure of the clause.

Other cases that Halliday 1985 treats as circumstances can be regarded in the same light: *tomorrow is the tenth*, *the best way to get there is by train*, and *the real reason is you're scared* (all from Halliday 1985: 120) are, as he says, 'identifying'—but in the present framework there is no need to say that they are also 'circumstantial'. Notice that they have no correlate of (6a) *Ivy is in Peru*; there is no **Ivy is by train* or **Ivy is you're scared*.

Here, then, we shall treat what is by far the most frequent of the 'circumstances'—location—as a primary category, and we shall explore the considerable advantages of constructing our grammar around it, together with the other two major types of relational process. Location, of course, includes location in time as well as in space, as in clauses such as *the fair is on a Tuesday* (Halliday 1985: 113). Place, however, is overwhelmingly more frequent as a participant role (though time is as a circumstance), so that our examples from now on will therefore normally be locations of place.

In (7a) the process type is POSSESSIVE. Till the publication of Halliday 1985 I used the term 'associative', with 'Associated' for 'Possessed'. My reason was that the concept of 'possession' is too narrow, perhaps suggesting little more than ownership. Yet the verb *have*, as is well known, is used for a wide range of relationship-types—as discussed, for example, in Fillmore (1968: 61f.). They may even involve the reverse of ownership, as in *that slave has had two owners* (Possessor + Process + Possessed). Some of these distinctions have syntactic repercussions, and one of these will need to be introduced in Section 6.4.2.

So far we have introduced six roles for just three types of relational process. Are we missing a generalization? I think we are; and it is, moreover, the one that shows (a) what the relational processes have in common, and (b) what differentiates them from material and mental processes. It is that the FIRST role in each of (4a)–(7a) can be regarded as the same in each case. It is around this role that relational processes are constructed, it being the SECOND role which distinguishes them. We may call this first role the CARRIER. The equivalent term introduced in Halliday (1967a: 39) was 'Attribuant' (later 'Attribuend'); 'Carrier' first appeared in the useful glossary in Halliday and Martin (181: 337).

There is thus another difference here from Halliday. For him 'the Medium is obligatory in all processes' (1985: 146); for me there is no single obligatory participant role. In my view what unites all these processes is precisely that they are PROCESSES; it is the differences in participant roles—or, more precisely, in the configurations of participant roles—that are the prime distinction between them. Our analysis will therefore now be as in (4b)–(7b).

(4b) Ivy is successful Carrier + Process + Attribute
(5b) Ivy is the boss   Carrier + Process + Attribute
(6b) Ivy is in Peru   Carrier + Process + Location
(7b) Ivy has the key   Carrier + Process + Possessed

As for the system network from which these are generated, it is as shown in Figure 6.1. (Notice that a row of dots after a feature in a network indicate that it is NON-TERMINAL; that is, there are dependent systems to come to the right of it.)

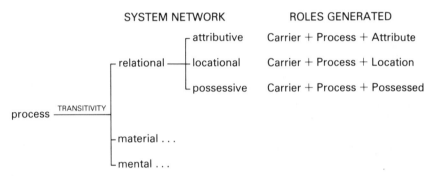

Figure 6.1 A first relational process network for English

6.2.2 Re-expression tests for participant roles

As we progress further into the complexities of relational processes it will become increasingly important to establish some rule-of-thumb method of checking that the roles that we recognize do not vary from clause to clause. We shall use tests for ROLES rather than for types of PROCESS, because the latter are (in part) defined in terms of configurations of the former, rather than vice versa. It is, moreover, easier to test for roles, because there are, in the transitivity network as a whole, far fewer roles than process types. Here, for example, we shall use only six roles (plus four compound roles constructed from them) to specify fifteen process-types.

Let us begin with the two roles of Agent and Affected, since there are already well-established tests for these (e.g. Fawcett 1980: 142). Although these roles are normally thought of in connection with the MATERIAL network, we shall shortly meet them in the expansion of the present network. (It should not be assumed that such notions are CONCEPTUALLY simple: see Cruse 1973: 11 f.)

In such tests it is helpful first to make any changes in the clause under consideration that are necessary to make it a simple active affirmative information-giver with a simple finite tense such as 'past'. (Non-finite clauses should be made 'finite' and 'past'). In addition, metaphorical interpretations need to be discounted. The fact that we have to deal with problem cases such as *ice-creams turn Ike on*, which we may well see as having recently crossed the boundary between being metaphor and a new lexical item, merely points up the validity of the distinction. In doubtful cases the more literal interpretation should be used.

Assuming the candidate element is X, the tests are to discover whether the clause can be re-expressed in the wording of the test, without changing its EXPERIENTIAL meaning, perhaps introduced by 'in other words': e.g. *Ike kissed Ivy; in other words, What Ike did was to kiss Ivy*.

T1 for Agent: 'What X did was to . . .'
T2 for Affected: 'What happened to X was that . . .' (plus failure in Agent test; note too that Agents may sometimes be 'affected' by their own actions, but they remain simple Agents).

Only when the re-expressed clause is acceptable is the test said to be passed and the candidate role confirmed.

(Note that T2 only works if the Affected is an entity which is in existence prior to the time when the process occurred, i.e. if it is 'dispositive' rather than 'creative' in the terms of Halliday (1985: 104). So we need to introduce the role 'Created' for entities such as *this gazebo* in *Sir Christopher Wren built this gazebo* (taken from Halliday 1970: 46). But we shall not need this role here.)

T3–T6 do not have the attractive simplicity of T1 and T2, which is due to the existence of the verbs *do* and *happen*. However, they seem to work equally well, and there is no reason why a participant role should necessarily be identified by a verb rather than by some other verbal expression.

T3 for Carrier: 'The thing about X was that . . .' plus failure to pass the Agent and Affected tests. (By this test Agents and Affecteds might also seem to be Carriers. But this is not necessarily so; Carriers are always entities associated with an Attribute, a Location or a Possessed, as in T4–T6 below.) Very occassionally more precise tests are need, derived from T4–T6, e.g. (for the Carrier in a possessive process with *belong*) 'X had . . . (Possessed).'
T4 for Attribute: '. . . (= Carrier) belonged to the class of Xs/X ones/was equivalent to X.'
T5 for Location: 'X is the place/time where/when . . . (= Carrier) was/went to/from/past.'
T6 for Possessed: 'X is what . . . (= Carrier) had/lacked.'

Note: the tests for compound roles are essentially as for their component roles; see the next section.

6.3 FURTHER PRIMARY CHOICES

6.3.1 Possessive processes

We shall now consider the three relational process-types in turn, beginning with the possessive. In each case I introduce (a) a set of semantic features they exemplify (some in the form of notes), and (b) certain problematical examples for which the present proposals seem to provide a helpful framework.

Consider (10a)–(13b). We begin, however, not with (10a) but with (13a). Note that it is to be taken in a sense where it is experientially equivalent to (13b), i.e. *to Ivy* rather than *for Ivy*, as one is almost certain to do with these examples. (We shall discuss the *for Ivy* type of 'Beneficiary'—a circumstantial role—in the next section.)

(10a) Ivy has/owns the key	Carrier + Process + Possessed
(11a) Ivy got/received the key	Affected-Carrier + Process + Possessed
(12a) Ivy got/took/obtained the key	Agent-Carrier + Process + Possessed
(13a) Ike gave/sent/took/ brought Ivy the key	Agent + Process + Affected-Carrier + Possessed
(13b) Ike gave/sent/took/ brought the key to Ivy	Agent + Process + Possessed + Affected-Carrier

Halliday (1985: 132) discusses clauses such as (13a), e.g. *I gave my love a ring that has no end* and *she sent her best wishes to John*, but only in the framework of material processes. I hope to show that such clauses are the realization of part of a general pattern in all three major types of relational process, and that they belong unequivocally in the present part of the grammar.

To do this we need to introduce the concept of causation, which is manifested in role terms as an Agent. Sometimes the Agent will be a separate role, as in (13a) and (13b), which we might gloss as 'Ike caused Ivy to have the key'. But sometimes it will be part of a COMPOUND role, as in (12a), which could be glossed as 'Ivy caused herself to have the key'. There are never more than two roles in a compound role. The re-expression test for a compound role is essentially as for each of its two components—except that one of the tests is applied to one of the re-expressions. Consider *Ike took the key*. We can use T6 to show that *the key* is a Possessed because we can say 'the key is what Ike had' (i.e. as a result of the process). And, now that we have introduced *have*, we can show by T3 that *Ike* is a Carrier—as well as being, by T1 on the original clause, also an Agent.

We can now add the system shown in Figure 6.2 to Figure 6.1, depending on the feature [possessive]. As you see, the features simply name directly the inherent roles generated when they are selected. Notice that we could, if we wished, use different labels in the network, such as 'simple', 'acceptive', 'causative' and 'third party causative', and this is often done in transitivity

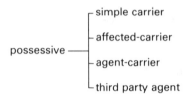

Figure 6.2 A first possessive process network for English

networks. The effect would be to avoid any possible danger of confusing FEATURES (in networks) with ROLES (in structures). But this seems to be to introduce an unnecessary extra set of terms, and so to increase unnecessarily the load on the memory of the user of the grammar. Here we simply mark the distinction by using a capital initial letter for a role, just as we do for Subject, Complement, etc.

Notice that in this approach the concept of causation is built neatly and naturally into the SYSTEM NETWORK itself. There is therefore no need to generate an extra level of STRUCTURE, separate from that at the formal level, as is done in some approaches to causation derived from logic (e.g. Bendix 1966 and much subsequent work in transformational grammar).

Notes

(a) We need to distinguish (11a) and (12a)—not only because *get* has two senses, similar to each of the most typical senses of *receive* and *obtain*, but because *Ivy* satisfies the Affected test more naturally in (11a) and the Agent test more naturally in (12a).

(b) The reason for the label 'third party agent' for (13a and b) is probably plain: it is that, whereas in (12a) Ivy herself acts to obtain the key, in (13a and b) a third party (Ike) takes on the role of Agent to enable Ivy to possess the key. Ivy, then, has a compound role: she is Affected in relation to Ike as Agent, and Carrier in relation to the key, which she comes to possess through the agency of Ike. (You may check this claim by applying the tests in section 6.2.2 in the way described above.)

(c) In a clause such as *Ivy has got the key* (cf. (12a)), where the Main verb is also *get*) the tense makes it PRAGMATICALLY similar to *Ivy has the key* (10a). That is, since Ivy has caused herself to have the key, and since the tense signals 'current relevance', the likelihood is that she still has it at the time of speaking. The result of this similarity in the conditions for choosing *has got* (with *has* as an auxiliary and *got* as the Main verb) and *has* (with *has* as the Main verb) is that *have/has got* and *had got* have become highly FACILITATED (cf. Fawcett 1980: 65–6), with the result that they have come to be thought of as variants of *have/has/had*. The two sets of forms, however, are associated with different tense variables, so that they can be shown to be SYSTEMICALLY different. Thus *Ivy has got the key* has the same tense as *Ivy has acquired the key* (cf. issue (c) in section 6.1.1).

(d) Examples (13a and b) list four of the most common verbs that occur in this type of process. (There is a discussion of problems relating to the potential ambiguity of *send*, *take* and *bring* in section 6.3.4.) Other verbs that occur here include *sell*, *lend*, *hire*, *let*, *leave* (as in the delightful *the Duke left my aunt this duckpress*) from Halliday 'unpublished'): these are lexically fuller verbs of the same type.

(e) The sequence of elements (except in (10a) with *have*) is not fixed, so that any role can be made Subject-theme or placed at the end of the clause to receive the unmarked tonic, signifying that this is 'new' information. See (10b), (11b), (12b) and (13c, d, e and f), the last four being directly relatable to Halliday's discussion of the variables in *the duke gave my aunt this teapot* (1985: 32f.). (Note that from now on we shall use abbreviated forms for the roles, as in (10a)–(13d).)

(10b)	the key was owned by Ivy	Pos + Pro + Ca
(11b)	the key was received by Ivy	Pos + Pro + Af-Ca
(12b)	the key was obtained by Ivy	Pos + Pro + Ag-Ca
(13c)	Ike gave the key to Ivy	Ag + Pro + Pos + Af-Ca
(13d)	The key was given (to) Ivy by Ike	Pos + Pro + Af-Ca + Ag
(13e)	The key was given by Ike to Ivy	Pos + Pro + Ag + Af-Ca
(13f)	Ivy was given the key by Ike	Af-Ca + Pro + Pos + Ag

(f) There is in fact one small but significant problem in the regularity of assigning these roles, to which we shall return in section 6.4.2.

The major area of difficulty associated with possessive clauses involve the problematical concept of 'Beneficiary', and we shall give the next section to this. However, there are two problem clauses in Halliday (1985: 135) for which we can now suggest a solution. Consider (13g) and (13h):

(13a)	Ike	gave	Ivy the key	Ag + Pro + Af-At + Pos
(13g)	The hotel	charged	me two dollars	Ag + Pro + Af-At + Pos
(13h)	The call	cost	me two dollars	Ag + Pro + Af-At + Pos

As section 6.4.2 will bring out more fully, possessive clauses are about 'lacking' as well as 'having'. So, just as we might gloss the analysis of (13a) as 'Ike caused Ivy to have the key', so we can gloss (13g) as 'The hotel caused me to lack two dollars' and (13h) as 'The call caused me to lack two dollars'. A call is a less typical Agent than a hotel, and a hotel is less typical than a person (such as *Ike*), but in fact we frequently endow events with Agent-like qualities, as with *the call* in *the call gave me some good news*. Halliday too makes no requirement that Agents be animate, of course, as is shown by his analysis (1985: 146) of *the news weakened my resolve* as Agent + Process + Medium (= Affected). However, Halliday (1985: 134) in fact has not (13g) but (13i). In the present framework, *for the call* would be a circumstantial role of Reason (cf. Halliday 1985: 140); it answers the question *Why?* (circumstantial roles are shown here by square brackets).

(13i) The hotel charged me two dollars for the call	Ag + Pro + Af-At + Pos + [Reason]

Halliday's analysis is essentially similar, except that he makes *two dollars* an Attribute and, surprisingly, *for the call* a Carrier. Since Carriers are always participant roles, all four would have this status in the present framework— and yet no other process type appears to need more than three. Moreover, Halliday's analysis of (13g) seems not to explain the generalization that is brought out in the analysis offered here. (13h), where Halliday has *the call* as Carrier, seems open to the same comment; the meaning of 'something costing someone something' is not necessarily closely related to the meaning of 'something cost something': cf. section 6.3.3.

Finally, note that 'wearing' is a type of 'having' (10c and d) and 'putting on' and 'taking off', when used of clothes, are ways of causing oneself to have or lack something (12c and d)—but again see section 6.4.2.

(10c) Ivy wore her jeans   Ca + Pro + Pos
(10d) Ike had his kilt on   Ca + Pro + Pos
(12c) Ivy put on her jeans Ag-Ca + Pro + Pos
(12d) Ike took his kilt off   Ag-Ca + Pro + Pos

6.3.2 Supplement: the 'Beneficiary' problem

We are now in a position to offer a reinterpretation of the vexed notion of 'BENEFICIARY'.

Halliday (1970: 147) presents the problem of characterizing adequately the difference between (14a) and (15a), and this will make a useful starting point. In (14b) and (15b) I give the nearest equivalent examples from Halliday (1985: 132).

(14a) I've given Oliver a tie
(14b) (Fred) gave John the parcel
(15a) I've made Frederick a jacket
(15b) Fred bought his wife a present

Clearly, (14a and b) will in the present framework be analysed like (13a), i.e. as Agent + Process + Affected-Carrier + Possessed—as also will *they paid John the money* (Halliday 1967a: 54). But why do I not use the widely employed term 'Beneficiary', in place of the clumsier 'Affected-Carrier'? The former certainly seems more semantically transparent—even though, as Halliday points out (1985: 133), there may be no 'benefit' for the 'Beneficiary', as in *Jocasta gave Claudius a dose of poison*. There are four reasons.

(a) It would obscure an important generalization concerning participant roles in all three relational process types (which will be demonstrated in the next two sections for attributive and locational process)—unless we were to extend the sense of the term so that it could be used there also. But this might well meet with resistance, because it would be stretching the term far beyond the usual usage.

(b) It suggests a similarity in the roles of *Oliver* in (14a) and *Frederick* in (15a) that is linguistically unwarranted (see immediately below).

(c) It would increase the number of participant roles needed to explain the phenomena concerned by one more than is otherwise necessary (Affected-Carrier being needed anyway for cases such as (11a)).

(d) Its use would obscure the fact that the re-expression test for it involves the use of TWO of the tests given in section 6.2.2, as described in the previous section. (No test using expressions such as *benefit from* or *gain from* could be used, because the 'Beneficiary' does not necessarily benefit, as we have seen, and blander expressions such as *be affected by* bring us too close to simple Affecteds.)

In what follows we shall refer for the moment only to (14a) and (15a), in order to simplify the discussion; the same principles, however, hold for (14b) and (15b).

I suggest that (14a) and (15a) are NOT closely related in transitivity terms, i.e. that *Oliver* and *Frederick* do NOT simply expound two sub-categories of Beneficiary, marked by *to* and *for* in the related prepositions (cf. Halliday 1970: 147, 1985: 132), but that, while *Oliver* in (14a) is a PARTICIPANT role, *Frederick* in (15a) is CIRCUMSTANTIAL—even though it is not preceded by a preposition and can be made the Subject.[8] Let me expand on this. In the grammar of English that I work with (much of which is still unpublished), I distinguish a number of types of role—all circumstantial—which have in other treatments been subsumed under the term 'Beneficiary'. The one that is relevant here is what I formerly termed 'Intended Recipient' (Fawcett 1974: 3; see also Huddleston 1971: 90, and especially Allerton 1978: 21–33). This role appears to correspond closely to Halliday's (1985: 132) CLIENT, so we shall here adopt his term. The re-expression test is as follows:

T7 for Client: Delete 'X' or 'for X' and add 'for X to have' to the end.

Thus (15a) can be re-expressed as *I've made a jacket for Frederick to have*, and (15b) as *Fred bought a present for his wife to have*. (15a), then, is simply a material process, where the two inherent roles are Agent and Created (cf. section 6.2.2 on Affected). The analysis is Ag + Pro + [Cl] + Cr, just as the analysis of (15c) would be as shown. (You will recall that square brackets indicate a circumstantial role.)

(15c) I've made a jacket for Frederick (Ag + Pro + Cr + [Cl])

The process in (15b), on the other hand, is a possessive clause: 'buying something' is a more heavily lexicalized way of 'causing oneself to have something'. The analysis is therefore Ag-Ca + Pro + [Cl] + Pos.

There is in fact a fairly wide range of process types to which the role of Client may be added, and Young (1980: 129–30) and Halliday (1985: 132–3) go some way to identifying the more frequent types. These include (a) 'creative' material processes (15a); and (b) the 'agent-carrier' type of 'possessive' process (15b). And there are certainly also (c) 'third party agent' possessive processes, such as *I've given Oliver a tie for Frederick* (in the sense of 'for Frederick to have', as in T7), and perhaps others. Yet no one, I take it, would wish to propose that whenever such clauses LACK a Client we must assume that a participant role of this sort is nonetheless inherently involved, covertly. Despite this there seems to be a temptation in cases such as (15a and b), where there is no preposition, to think that the role of Client has become a participant role. And that temptation is even stonger when the Client is made the Subject, as in (15d).

(15d) Frederick was made a jacket by his aunt

The temptations are of course based on what is normally the case; thus (a) participant roles are normally realized by nominal groups that are not preceded by a preposition; and (b) Subjects are normally associated with participant roles. But these associations are not absolute. Examples such as (10b)–(13f) illustrate the limitations of generalization (a). As for (b), the Subject may in fact be disassociated from ANY role: for example, as with *it* in *it's nice to see you* where *to see you* is Carrier and *nice* is Attribute: compare the British TV personality Bruce Forsyth's *nice to see you; to see you—nice*). Indeed, it seems to me that we simply cannot allow the ability of a role to be realized as Subject, as in (15d), to make it automatically a participant role (Halliday 1967a: 53; cf. Halliday 1985: 132), because if we did so we would be opening the door to the development of a transitivity system that was over-influenced by systems offering options in various types of 'Beneficiary' (two of which can occur without a preposition, as we shall see).

Why does this pattern occur? I suggest that the similarity in the FORM of (15a) and (15d) to *give*-clauses is used to invoke the SEMANTICS of such processes. Building someone a house, then, almost becomes giving someone a house—it ALMOST does, but in fact it does not.

There are two other types of circumstantial 'Beneficiary' besides Client. These are (1) Pleasee (i.e. 'one who is to be pleased'), for which Halliday's nearest equivalent term is 'Behalf' (which is somewhat misleading, as we shall shortly see); and (2) Replacement (for which he has no equivalent).

Let us take PLEASEE first. Halliday (1985: 132) describes the role of *Mary* in (16) as 'not a Client but a type of Cause (Behalf)'.

(16) I'm doing this for Mary

This makes it a Circumstance for him, so that there is agreement on this. The re-expression test that I suggest is given in T8.

T8 for Pleasee: Delete 'X' or 'for X' and add 'to please X' to the end (or, less naturally but perhaps preferably when X is unaware of the process, 'for X's good').

Note that Halliday's term 'Behalf' would invite the test 'on X's behalf', which is, as we shall see, more appropriate for our term Replacement.

Our use of Client as one who is intended to 'have' something (cf. T7) has in fact been narrower than Halliday's at first appears. For him a Client is marked by *for* and receives a service (as opposed, you will recall, to a 'Recipient', who is marked by *to* and receives a thing—and is handled here as the participant role Affected-Carrier, as we have seen). But he also in fact includes within the notion of 'service' a type of service that results in X having something rather 'goods'-like, so that the grounds for his basic Recipient vs. Client distinction become unclear. Examples are his labelling *John* and *Mary* as Clients in *he painted John a picture* and *he built Mary this house*—and rightly so, in my view. Here too, then, there is common ground. What, however, about cases such as (17a and b)? According to our tests, Mary is a Pleasee (not a Client, as in Halliday 1985: 132).

(17a) Play a tune for Mary
(17b) Play Mary a tune

We need in fact to recognize two classes of process which accept Pleasee as a circumstance (the first of which brings together process-types from many different parts of the transitivity network): (a) ALL processes with an Agent, to which the Agent's purpose 'to please X' can always be optionally added; and (b) a small sub-class of these, prototypically what I have termed the 'agent only' category of material processes, when they have a Process-Range element (Halliday 1985: 134 f.), as in (17a and b). It is only in the sub-class that the structure illustrated in (17b) may be chosen; again, I suggest that the reason for its use is to evoke the semantics of the vastly more frequent *give*-type structure, where *Mary* is a participant role, as in *give Mary a tune*.

Finally, there is the problem of Mae West's famous line *peel me a grape* (Halliday 1985: 133). Peeling is a material process that does NOT have a Range, as in *play Mary a tune*, but an Affected. We might ask: Is *me* a Client ('for me to have') or a Pleasee ('to please me')? Notice that, if it had been *peel a grape for me*, the same question could be asked and the answer would simply have been that it could be either; both roles occur naturally with *for*. The problem with examples such as *peel me a grape* is that they force us EITHER to extend the list of process-types given above for Clients, so that it includes all processes of the type that have the two roles Agent and Affected inherently associated with them (*hit*, *kill*, *kiss*, *touch*, *wash*, etc.), OR to interpret grape-peeling as Process plus Process-Range, like playing a tune and singing a song—or, of course, to declare the clause ungrammatical. The first solution seems fairly plausible in the present case, and similar examples such as *could you iron me a couple of shirts* would have a similar analysis (and perhaps express the same presumption that others are at one's service). But if we take the view that the grammar should also in principle be open to generating *kill me that guy*, *kiss me two boys*, etc., where only a Pleasee interpretation of *me* is plausible (since 'that guy' and 'the boys' are not to be given to 'me'), Mae West's utterance may be perceived as an innovatory extension of the grammar that is part of a wider pattern of making possible the INTEGRATION as pseudo-(or semi-?) participant roles of both Clients and Pleasees. Furthermore, if *he opened her door* (in the sense of 'to please her' is also possible, then the structure would be extended to a further large set of process-types ('affected-centred' in Fawcett 1980: 140–1). No doubt it is our sense of 'systemic ungrammaticality' or, preferably, 'systemic innovation' that makes Mae West's utterance particularly memorable.

The third type of 'Beneficiary' is the REPLACEMENT, as in the case of *for her* in (18). The test is as in T9. To demonstrate that this is not simply a type of Pleasee, consider the following situation.

(18) Ivy's arms were full, so Phoebe opened the door for her

T9 for Replacement: Replace for X by 'in place of X'.

Ike, being a true gentleman, would normally open the door for Ivy, who is heavily laden, but he isn't able to do so because of the narrowness of the hallway and so he calls to Phoebe, who is in front, as in (19).

(19) Could you open the   Agent + Process + Affected +
     door for Ivy for me?   [Pleasee] + [Replacement]

It is even just about possible to include all three types in one clause, as in (20).

(20) I've made Frederick a jacket   Agent + Process + [Client] +
     for the overworked tailor   Created + [Replacement] + [Pleasee]
     for you

The complete grammar will specify (a) which process types may select for each of the three systems [plus client] vs. [- - -], [plus pleasee] vs. [- - -], and [plus replacement] vs [- - -], (where [- - -] is the option NOT to have the role); (b) for some process types, in relation to Client and Pleasee, whether to permit the new role the further integration into the clause of occurring without *for*, rather as if it were a *give*-type process; and (c), in a very limited number of types, whether to further permit the role to become so integrated as to take on the role of Subject. Figure 6.3 suggests how some of the relevant systems may be related. But it makes no attempt to specify what process types provide the entry conditions to each, since it is not our task here to formalize this part of the grammar; our purpose has simply been to clear the ground, as it were, in order to show what phenomena we are and are not covering within the relational processes. (See Hasan's chapter in this volume for an alternative approach to some of these phenomena.)

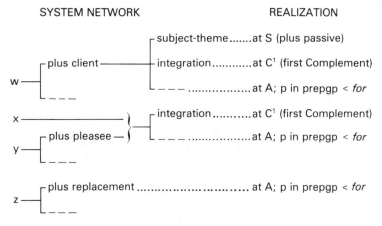

Figure 6.3 A first sketch towards a network for the circumstantial roles of Client, Pleasee and Replacement

6.3.3 Attributive processes

I suggested in section 6.2 that Halliday's 'identifying' processes can be treated as the limiting case of attributive processes. In order to demonstrate the extent to which this generalization holds, we shall continue throughout this section to consider examples of both types.

We look now at a type of process in which, like the possessive processes, the compound role of Affected-Carrier also occurs. Here, however, it would be rather odd to term it a 'Beneficiary'. Indeed, the striking semantic parallels between the clauses in (10a)–(13a) and those in (21a)-(24b) exemplify the prime reason for treating possessive processes as relational. That is, the system shown in Figure 6.2 that we added to the network for possessive processes is equally relevant to attributive processes.

(21a) Ivy is/looks/sounds successful	Ca + Pro + At
(22a) Ivy became/got/grew successful	Af-Ca + Pro + At
(23a) Ivy became/got/grew successful	Ag-Ca + Pro + At
(24a) Ike made/called Ivy successful	Ag + Pro + Af-Ca + At
(21b) Ivy is/represents the boss	Ca + Pro + At
(22b) Ivy became the boss	Af-Ca + Pro + At
(23b) Ivy became the boss	Ag-Ca + Pro + At
(24b) Ike made/called/elected Ivy the boss	Ag + Pro + Af-Ca + At

Notes

(a) *Ivy* in both (24a) and (24b) fills the same role of Affected-Carrier as in the *give* clause in (13a): *Ivy* is the Affected in relation to *Ike* as Agent, and is Carrier in relation to the Attributes *successful* and *the boss*, as the tests in section 6.2.2 show.

(b) In the attributive sub-network there is a tendency to collocational restrictions between the verb and some semantic feature of the Complement, including restrictions that prevent one from saying *he turned/went successful/ happy*. The main distinction is not the one between 'equative' and 'class-inclusive' types, but between two types of Attribuant, for which I use the labels 'thing' and 'quality of thing'. These are realized in nominal and quantity–quality groups ('adjectival' in Butler 1985: 101) respectively (see Fawcett 1980: 93). It is particularly significant that, in the case of the two high-frequency verbs *become* and *get*, the patterning follows this second distinction. Thus (22c) shows that *become* accepts both 'equative' and 'class-inclusive' Complements, while (22d) and (22e) show that in attributive processes *got* and *grow* cannot be used with a Complement that expresses a thing (cf. *got* in a possessive process, as in *Ivy got the ice-cream*).

(22c) Ivy became the doctor/a doctor/successful

(22d) Ivy got/grew more successful

(22e) *Ivy got/grew the doctor/a doctor (not starred, of course, in other senses!)

This difference corresponds to what Lyons (1968: 389) describes as one between 'characterizing' (*apples are sweet*) and 'sortal' (*apples are fruit*). Similarly we shall attest (in a chess setting) (22f) but not (22g).

(22f) This lump of plasticine represents/resembles a bishop/the bishop
(22g) *This lump of plasticine represents/resembles useful.

In other cases, some of which will be exemplified shortly, the Complement is much more narrowly restricted—sometimes to one or two lexical items. Here, then, we see at work the principles (d) and (e) from section 6.2.3, so that the grammar is constructed around process-types that are both frequent and lexically productive. Thus, examples of lexically restricted process types, as found among (26c)–(25j) below, will be explained within this framework.

(c) In contrast with the possessive processes, there seem to be no verbs that distinguish [agent-carrier] from [affected-carrier] attributive processes—i.e. (22a) and (22b) from (23a) and (23b). Yet the Agent and Affected tests still show that the distinction exists.

(d) Note that, in the present framework, clauses like (21c) are, like all other 'equative' clauses such as *Ivy is the boss* (21b), attributive and not possessive—the meaning is 'the piano is Peter's piano', and the 'possessive' quality of the example resides in the nominal group *Peter's* (*piano*), not in the transitivity (cf. Halliday 1985: 122–3).

(21c) The piano is Peter's   Ca + Pro + At

Peter's in (21c) is in fact ambiguous: it can mean 'the piano is one of Peter's pianos' or 'the piano is Peter's one piano': this suggests that the sense of term 'Attribute' used here, which covers both, is more appropriate than a terminology which forces a decision between an 'equative' and a 'class-inclusive' interpretation.

(e) Similarly, the various types of 'circumstance' that Halliday introduces in 'identifying' clauses are simply 'equative' types of attributive processes, as in (21d) and (21f). But, as a comparison with (21e) and (21g) shows, the difference between the two can be handled in the internal semantics of the Complement.

(21d) on the mat is the best place
(21e) on the mat is good
(21f) by train is the best way
(21g) by train is good

(Compare the reasons given in section 6.2.1 for abolishing the 'identifying' vs. 'attributive' distinction.)

(f) What is the relationship between (22) and (21h)—and for that matter (21i)? (21h) was originally an advertising slogan for beer, and it comes from Halliday (1967b: 224). The present grammar treats each of the last two in the same way, i.e. as attributive clauses of the 'equative' type, which happen to have embedded clauses as Subject or Complement—or both, as in (21j) (see also Fawcett 1980: 160).

(22)   we want Watney's
(21h) what we want is Watney's   Ca + Pro + At
(21i) Watney's is what we want   Ca + Pro + At
(21j) what we want is what you want   Ca + Pro + At

I do not deny, of course, that there is a PRAGMATIC similarity between (22) and (21h). As Halliday perspicaciously points out (1967b: 224), it is the fact that (21h) has *what we want* as Subject-theme that makes it a more effective advertisement for beer than (22) (which has *we* as Subject-theme), because its complex theme of *what we want* is more interesting than *we*. Moreover, the referential meaning is in fact different, in that in (21h) the ONLY thing that we want is Watneys. He makes a similar point in relation to (21k) in Halliday (1985: 43).

(21k) what the duke gave my aunt was that teapot

$$\underbrace{\overset{\text{Pos}\quad\text{Ag}\quad\text{Pro}\quad\text{Af-Ca}}{}}_{\text{Ca}}\qquad\text{Pro}\qquad\text{At}$$

Here, then, we have opted to build one set of generalizations into the grammar rather than another: those to do with embedded clauses, that relate (21h) to (21i and j) rather than those that relate (21h) to (22) by what is called, in the transformationalist literature, the 'pseudo-cleft' transformation. The fact that the meaning of (22) and (21i) are in fact REFERENTIALLY different, as indicated above, is support for the approach taken here.

(g) For simplicity's sake, we have assumed in (21a)–(24a) that the Attribute is a simple quality. The quality may be 'tempered' by an expression that tells us the quantity of that quality, as in *Ivy is extremely successful* or *Ivy is as successful as Phoebe is*. Alternatively, it may be expressed in a prepositional group, as in (21l–n). We have already seen that the Attribute may also take the form of a nominal group (21b)–(24b) or a clause (21i and j).

(21l)   Ivy is like Phoebe   (= 'Phoebe-like')
(21m) The story is about a fish   (= roughly 'fish-centred')
(21n)   Ivy is in a rage   (= 'angry')

The attributive network provides a simple way of explaining, within a central portion of the grammar, a number of problematical clauses (25a–c) which have been analysed by Halliday (1967a: 63) as 'action' (later 'material') clauses with the feature 'resultative'—which would clearly involve introducing a further participant role. The present framework avoids this. Thus (25a) might be glossed as 'He caused the door to become green—and the method was by painting it'.

(25a) he painted the door green   Ag + Pro + Af-Ca + At
(25b) he boiled the kettle dry   Ag + Pro + Af-Ca + At
(25c) he grew his hair long   Ag + Pro + Af-Ca + At

(25d) he rubbed (himself) dry   Ag + Pro + (Af-Ca) + At
(25e) the heat turned the milk sour Ag + Pro + Af-Ca + At
(25f) the sun made the bananas ripe Ag + Pro + Af-Ca + At
(25g) they voted Tom captain   Ag + Pro + Af-Ca + At
(25h) she called the baby Ann   Ag + Pro + Af-Ca + At

Halliday (1985: 152–3), however, takes a broadly similar approach to this with (25e and f), reinterpreting his earlier (p. 149) description of the role of *the heat* and *the sun* as not 'Attributor' (which would appear to introduce a further type of role) but Agent, with *the milk* and *the bananas* as 'Medium' (= our Affected). With (25g and h), however, he suggests (p. 153) that we 'have to recognise a distinct function, say that of ASSIGNER' for *they* and *she*. It is a little surprising to find *Tom* and *the baby* subsequently described as 'Agents'; the explanation can only be that these are regarded as sub-categories of Agent. The roles expounded by *captain* and *Ann* are described simply as 'Mediums' (= Affecteds).   Yet these two are clearly also processes in which a third party Agent causes a Carrier to 'be' (if only by name) some Attribute. (26a and b) are taken from Halliday 'unpublished':

(26a) the cakes burnt dry   Af-Ca + Pro + At
(26b) the kettle boiled dry Af-Ca + Pro + At

The relationship between (26b) and (25b) is clearly that (25b) has the additional role of Agent, both being attributive processes (not material, as in Halliday 'unpublished').

Other examples that find a natural analysis in the present framework include (26c)–(25j) below: note that the verbs, here quite restricted collocationally, are very frequent and collocationally unrestricted in other types of relational process, where they often occur with similar patterns of roles (see section 6.3.5).

(26c) She went mad   Af-Ca + Pro + At
(25i) He sent/drove her mad   Ag + Pro + Af-Ca + At
(26d) She kept quiet   Af-Ca + Pro + At
(25j) He kept her quiet   Ag + Pro + Af-Ca + At

Here too we can explain the temptation to handle *she's called Ivy* (25k) as if it were simply *she's Ivy* (21o); compare the participant roles.

(21o) she's Ivy   Ca + Pro + At
(25k) she's called Ivy   Af-Ca + Pro + At (+ Ag)
(25l) They call her Ivy Ag + Pro + Af-Ca + At

Occasionally there are lexical items that occur in both material and relational processes, as in (26c)–(28), and that could be used in pragmatically similar situations.

(26c) Ike's face became/turned/went white   Af-Ca + Pro + At
(25m) The lightning made/turned Ike's face white Ag + Pro +
                                                   Af-Ca + At

(27)   Ike's face whitened   Af + Pro
(28)   The lightning whitened Ike's face   Ag + Pro + Af

What distinguishes (26c) from (27) and (25m) from (28) is that in the first of each pair the concept 'white' has been expressed as an Attribute, while in the second it is a Process, marked by the suffix -*en*. What they have in common, apart from the item *white*, is the participant role structure; the analysis brings out nicely this similarity between the two pairs. This is there, even though the two are generated from two different parts of the transitivity network, (27) and (28) being affected-centred processes from the material process network.

It is here too that we can explain the difference between (29) and (30).

(29) She made him a good husband   Ag + Pro + Af-Ca + At
(30) She made (him) a good wife   Af-Ca + Pro (+ [Cl]) + At

As the analyses demonstrate, it is NOT, as proposed in some earlier grammars, that *a good husband* in (29) is an 'Object-Complement' whereas *a good wife* in (30) is a 'Subject-Complement'—as the optionality in (30) of the circumstantial role *him* clearly shows. *Him* in (30) is in fact a Client, in that one can say *she made a good wife for him to have*.

In conclusion we should note that, while the literature contains many problematical examples which can be explained naturally in the attributive framework, none of those examined here seems in fact to require the 'equative-attributive' distinction.

6.3.4 Locational processes

We turn now to the third of the three process types: LOCATIONAL processes. Here too the system shown in Figure 6.2 is directly applicable, as (31a)–(34a) clearly illustrate.

(31a) Ivy is/lives in Peru/with Ike   Ca + Pro + Loc
(32)   Ivy went/came/got to Peru   Af-Ca + Pro + Loc
(33a) Ivy went/came/got to Peru   Ag-Ca + Pro + Loc
(34a) Ike sent/took/brought Ivy to Peru   Ag + Pro + Af-Ca + Loc

Notes

(a) Once again, the notion of 'Beneficiary' is irrelevant to *Ivy* in (34a), *Ivy* being Affected in relation to *Ike* and Carrier in relation to the Location to which *Ike* is causing *Ivy* to go. (If *Ivy* seems too Agent-like, imagine her as a small child, or replace *Ivy* by *the package*.) Here, then, we have a completely natural place for Halliday's (1985: 132) sentence, she *sent her luggage to Los Angeles*.

(b) The Location may be specified as 'with' a person or institution, as (31a) shows. This is not to be confused with the circumstantial role Accompanier, which can be added to many process types, e.g. *Ivy went to Peru with Ike*, or even *She's staying with her mother with her husband*.

(c) The location is quite frequently COVERT, as in (33b) and (34b):

(33b) Ivy arrived   Ag-Ca + Pro (+ Loc)
(34b) Ivy has brought the sandwiches   Ag + Pro + Af-Ca (+ Loc)

(Here, as always in the analyses, rounded brackets indicate a covert, and so unrealized, inherent role). This occurs particularly frequently where, as in these examples, the semantic specification of the verb includes a feature with locational information.

(d) Note that in (33c) and (34c) *to Peru* is the Location, whether or not it is overtly present, and *out* is a PART of the process. 'Particles', such as *out* in these two cases and *away* in *they ran away*, etc. are analysed syntactically as 'Main verb-completing Complements', but are semantically part of the Process.

(33c) Ivy went out (to Peru)   Ag-Ca + Pro (+ Loc)
(34c) Ike brought Ivy out (to Peru)   Ag + Af-Ca (+ Loc)

Note, however, that they are Complement-like in being thematizable, as in (*and so*) *out Ivy went to Peru*, and *out he brought her* and *away they ran*.

(e) Occasionally, Range-like constructions occur (cf. Halliday 1985: 134), such as *go for a walk* in (33d). Without the element represented *to the church* in our example, they are in my framework 'Agent + Process + Range'.

(33d) Ivy went for a walk (to the church)   Ag + Pro + Ra

They are not relational, but material, and they have the features [agent-centred, material, plus range] (cf. Fawcett 1980: 137). But when *to the church* is present a problem arises: does the presence of *to the church* make them a relational process with the participant role of Location? Or does it simply tell us more about the reification of the process that is expressed in *walk*, so that the Range is *a walk to the church*? Informal informant testing suggests that the second of these is the more appropriate analysis, and this is the approach adopted here.

(f) Just as the location may be covert in the process types illustrated in (32)–(34a), as (33b) and (34b) have shown, so too it may be covert in the 'simple Carrier' type in (31a). These are the so-called 'existential' clauses that are often distinguished as a separate type (e.g. in the excellent summary in Halliday 1985: 130–1). But Lyons (1968: 388–90) suggests a different line and, while there is something to be said for both views, Lyons's approach, which is adopted here, has the advantage of avoiding the problem of having to decide, in certain problematical cases, whether there is a covert Location or simply no Location at all. We can approach the question by asking: is *in the garden* in (31b and c) a participant role, inherent in this type of 'being', or a circumstance, like *this morning*? (The *there* makes no difference to the transitivity; it is a weak *there*, pronounced exactly as if it were *the*, as the contrast in (31d) shows. It is in fact a thematic device that announces that the substantive theme in the process of 'being' is coming shortly; it is a type of what we might term 'thematic build-up.)

(31b) a sheep was in the garden (this morning)   Ca + Pro + Loc (+ Time)

(31c) there was a sheep in the garden (this morning)   Ca + Pro + Loc (+ Time)

(31d) there's a sheep over there   Ca + Pro + Loc

If we analyse (31b and c) as shown, we must surely analyse (31e–h) in the same way, even though they may typically occur without the portion in brackets.

(31e) unicorns don't exist (anywhere in the world).   Ca + Pro (+ Loc)
(31f) there aren't any unicorns (anywhere in the world). Ca + Pro (+ Loc)
(31g) has there been a phone call (since we last spoke)? Ca + Pro (+ Loc)
(31h) there followed an angry debate (after that).   Ca + Pro (+ Loc)

(g) Once again only the tests for inherent roles reveal a transitivity distinction between (32) and (33a); as with attributive processes there are not the distinctions of verb that there were with the possessive processes.

(h) While the locational space in (34a) is relatively large, (35a) (taken from Halliday 1970: 150) illustrates the locational verb that is most frequently used for small-scale locational actions.

(35a) he put all his jewels in the wash   Ag + Pro + Af-Ca + Loc

Underlying this, however, is the fact that with *put* the Agent is marked as being in control of the movement until the Medium-Carrier reaches the Location, whereas with *send*, he is not so marked.

(i) Finally, notice that while almost all the examples so far have related to location in SPACE, a subset of these process types are in frequent use to locate events in TIME, as in (31i and j). All the 'space' choices are in principle available for 'time'; the apparent limits are imposed by our conceptions of what is possible. These may be expanded by imagination and science, as in (33e) and (34d).

(31i) Phoebe's party will be on Tuesday   Ca + Pro + Loc
(31j) It will last for two days   Ca + Pro + Loc
(33e) We'll go back to the first century A.D.   Ag-Ca + Pro + Loc
(34d) The time machine took him to 2050
       A.D.   Ag + Pro + Af-Ca + Loc

We turn now to the problems that can be resolved in this framework. Let us look first at the problems associated with verbs such as *bring*, *take* and *send*, as in (36).

(36)   Ike sent the package to the college   { (a) Ag + Pro + Af-Ca + Loc
                                                 { (b) Ag + Pro + Pos + Af-Ca

First, however, we should remind ourselves that problems of ambiguity in ANAYLSIS do not necessarily mean that there are corresponding problems in constructing a grammar that GENERATES such clauses. With this in mind we can ask: is (36) like (13b) (*Ike gave the key to Ivy*) or like (34a) (*Ike sent Ivy to Peru*)? The answer, as (36a and b) show, is that it may be like either. The answers to such problems will normally be related to the fact that expressions such as *the college* which denote institutions have both a 'social group' interpretation, so that it is as appropriate for them to be given things as it is for individuals, and a simple 'Location' interpretation. If in addition the second participant role in the clause is non-human (e.g. as *the package*), then a possessive interpretation is completely plausible. But note that if it had been *the messenger* that was sent the probability of a locational interpretation would rise, because in our culture one does not normally give people away. Adherents of the 'localist hypothesis' (see, for example, Anderson 1971 and the discussion in Ikegami 1984) might argue that ultimately the analysis in (36b) is a more superficial form of (36a) and that we do not need both. But the systemic difference is clearly there, in English at least, because it is only the possessive processes that are open to the full range of thematic and informational options illustrated in (13a–d).

Halliday (1970: 147), in discussing the problems of *I've brought Percival a pullover* (37), rightly points out that 'the more categories one sets up, the more indeterminate instances will arise'.

(37)   I've brought Percival a pullover   { (a) Ag + Pro + Af-Ca + Pos
                                              (b) Ag + Pro + [Cl] + Af-Ca (+ Loc)

Here our goal is to set up no more semantic features than are required. But in fact we already have enough participant roles to provide an answer to the question that Halliday puts, i.e.:'Is (37) like *I've given Oliver a tie* (14a) or *I've made Frederick a jacket* (15a)?' The answer, as the two analyses in (37) show, is that while it may be like (14a) it cannot be like (15a). The second interpretation is in fact that it is locational process with (a) a covert Location, like (34b); and (b) an optional Client role (cf. the re-expression test: *I've brought a pullover for Percival to have*).

Another problematical example that can be explained in this framework is the apparently simple *John threw the ball* (Halliday 1968: 184). It may be locational with an overt Location (cf. *John threw the ball at the tree*), where 'throwing something somewhere' is seen as 'causing something to be somewhere', or it may be possessive with a covert Affected-Carrier; cf. *John threw the ball to Mary* and Berry's (1975: 158) example of *cover point threw (the ball) wildly to the wicket-keeper*. What these clauses with *threw* are NOT, as Berry's introduction of the Location *to the wicket-keeper* perhaps suggests, is a type of process with Agent and Affected only. Consider also (35b), taken from Halliday (1970: 149), where *at the bridge* is called an 'inner circumstance'. (But see further section 6.4.5 for an addition to this analysis.)

(35b) he was throwing stones at the bridge   Ag + Pro + Af-Ca + Loc

Finally, we can now suggest a new solution to the problem of *the prisoners marched* and *he marched the prisoners* (Halliday 1967a: 47 f.). The verb *march*, like the other 'verbs of motion' such as *walk*, *drive* and *fly*, is simply a lexically fuller version of both *go* and *send*, and it normally occurs in a clause with a Location as a participant role. This may be covert, as in Halliday's examples, or overt (compare (38) and (39)). What confuses matters is that many of the SAME verbs can also occur in material processes, as in (40), when the 'walking', 'driving', 'flying', etc. is regarded as pure action (cf. Fawcett 1980: 137, 139).

(38)   the prisoners marched (to the barracks)   Ag-Ca + Pro (+ Loc)
(39)   he marched the prisoners (to the barracks)   Ag + Pro + Af-Ca (+ Loc)
(40)   he walks/runs/jogs/marches (to keep fit)   Ag + Pro (+ [Purpose])

6.3.5 The systemic unity of the relational processes

We have seen in sections 6.3.1, 6.3.3 and 6.3.4 the impressive extent to which the three primary process types of attributive, locational and possessive have in common a set of features that determine whether there shall be an Agent, an Agent-Carrier, a Medium-Carrier, or a simple Carrier. If we put together all the features introduced so far we shall have the network shown in Figure 6.4. It is a DISPLAYED system network, and it can be contrasted with the more traditional but notationally equivalent CONSOLIDATED form shown in Figure 6.5 (see Fawcett in press (a) for a discussion of these terms). However, there are at least two more pieces of evidence that the three process-types of

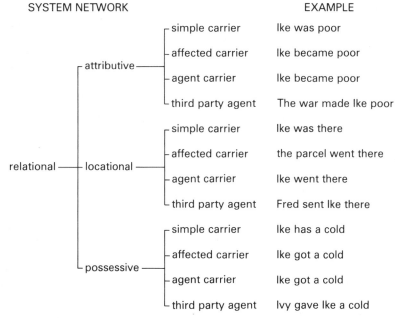

Figure 6.4 A displayed system network for relational processes in English

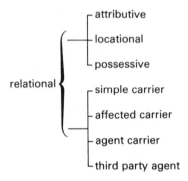

Figure 6.5 A consolidated system network for relational processes in English

attributive, locational and possessive belong together: we shall examine these in the next two sections.

6.3.6 Changing and maintaining in relational processes

There is yet another system that applies to all three process types—and in fact at TWO places in each. We shall call its features 'change' and 'maintain'. A clause such as *Ivy got the key* (12a) has the feature [change], in that it could be glossed as 'Ivy caused the situation to change to one where she had the key', whereas *Ivy kept the key* (41a) might be glossed as 'Ivy caused the situation of her having the key not to change', and is therefore [maintain]. Consider (41a)–(44b); in each the feature [maintain] has been selected. The four (a) examples illustrate [maintain] as it applies to 'compound' Carriers (i.e. Agent-Carrier or Affected-Carrier), while the four (b) examples show that exactly the same system is open to 'third party agent' processes.

(41a) Ivy kept the key   Ag-Ca + Pro + Pos
(41b) Ike left Ivy with the key   Ag + Pro + Af-Ca + Pos
(42a) Ivy stayed (remained) very quiet   Ag-Ca/Af-Ca + Pro + At
(42b) Ike kept Ivy very quiet   Ag + Pro + Af-Ca + At
(43a) Ivy stayed/remained (as) the boss   Ag-Ca/Af-Ca + Pro + At
(43b) Ike kept Ivy (as) the boss   Ag + Pro + Af-Ca + At
(44a) Ivy stayed/remained in Peru   Ag-Ca/Af-Ca + Pro + Loc
(44b) Ike left/kept Ivy in Peru   Ag + Pro + Af-Ca + Loc

You will notice that so far we have generally been assuming that [change] has been chosen in such cases; you should therefore find it easy to supply [change] equivalents for each of (41a)–(44b).

There is one point to draw attention to. The existence of (41b) is predicted by the system network, and it might be glossed as 'Ike caused the situation of Ivy's having the key not to change'. It is a clause-type that I have not found discussed in the literature, but it is not unusual; cf. (41c) and the more frequent type shown in (41d).

(41c) He left her with a bit of a problem
(41d) She was left with a bit of a problem

Note too that it is NOT closely related to (45), as one might think, which is in fact locational (cf. Note (b) in section 6.3.4).

(45)   Ike left the key with Ivy   Ag + Proc + Af-Ca + Loc

The consolidated network that incorporates this new system is as shown in Figure 6.6. This layout is preferred to alternatives, in that the feature [compound carrier] can additionally be used to capture the generalization (noted in sections 6.3.1, 6.3.3 and 6.3.4) that it is almost always the same lexical verbs that are open to Agent-Carriers that are open to Affected-Carriers, in each of the three process types.

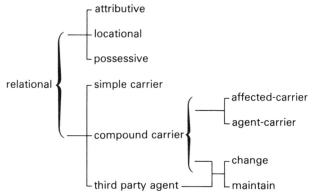

Figure 6.6 A maximally economical system network for relational processes in English

This, then, is as far as an elegantly economical system network can take us. In section 6.4. I shall introduce certain important features to the networks for each of the attributive, locational and possessive networks that are peculiar to that process type. Note, however, that this is in no way negates the essential findings established so far.

6.3.7 Lexical unity in the relational processes

There is yet more evidence of the unity of these three types of process. It is less systematic, but it is in its way equally impressive, and it is exemplified particularly clearly in (41a)–(44b). It is the repeated occurrence of a small set of high-frequency verbs, all with a minimal semantic specification, i.e. one that can be stated fully by the addition of only one or two extra features to the present networks (cf. Hasan's chapter). Each of the following occurs in either two or all three of the major relational process types: *be*, *bring*, *get*, *go*, *keep*, *leave*, *remain*, *send*, stay and *take*, and others such as *grow* and *make* occur in two or more sub-types within one major group. Note too the clear semantic and formal parallels between *come* and *become*.

6.3.8 Summary so far

Taken together, all this evidence supports strongly the main contention of this chapter: namely, that all the twenty-one types of process summarized in Figure 6.6 are relational processes. I hope that I have also demonstrated the elegance with which a system network can model their semantic unity, as well as the model's ability to explain, without setting up special categories, a fairly large number of otherwise problematical examples.

It would be tempting to conclude the chapter at this point, but to do so would be to avoid what I see as one of the linguist's major responsibilities. This is that one should not just point out elegant generalizations, but one should also produce a usable grammar for the area of language under discussion. This, then, is the goal of section 6.4. It is, however, an essential part of the argument being developed in this chapter, and it carries with it, as we shall see, certain theoretical implications.

6.4 FROM ELEGANCE TO USABILITY: SOME MORE DELICATE CHOICES

6.4.1 The turning point: a theoretical and notational issue

The attempt to expand the networks further brings us to an important turning point: from now on we shall no longer be able to generalize across the three transitivity types of attributive, locational and possessive. In other words, we shall need to REPEAT the lower network in Figure 6.6 for each of the three, because different dependent systems are involved for each. At times this will involve the same systems appearing in more than one place in the network, i.e. obligatorily introducing some of the characteristics of a DISPLAYED system network into what otherwise might be an elegantly CONSOLIDATED network (cf. Fawcett in press (a)). Indeed, once we make these additions it is no longer possible to draw a consolidated network that avoids repeating systems—except by introducing additional wiring and bracketing of such complexity as to obscure the communicative purpose of drawing system networks! To use a network that repeats systems may seem sacriligious to some systemic linguistics, but I would strongly maintain that to do this is NOT to fail to capture a generalization, but simply to capture it in a notationally less economical way. (In fact the features in the similar systems have to be labelled SLIGHTLY differently to enable the realization rules to work; cf. section 6.4.3.) Our networks from now on will therefore be less ELEGANT and more MESSY than those seen so far, but also much more USABLE—in terms of the clines suggested in Fawcett in press (a).

Two major limitations will remain, however. The first is that I shall not have space to introduce all of the many systems that offer choices between making participant roles OVERT or COVERT (i.e. unrealized); my approach to this question (in relation to material or 'action' processes) is, however, set out clearly in Fawcett (1980: 145–6).

The second is that I can only indicate for a small proportion of the relevant lexical verbs the sort of way in which they may be generated from the more delicate features in these networks. However, I shall provide sufficient realization rules to show how the grammar can be made to operate generatively, and this, I think, will indicate the way in which the present description bears on the theoretical issues referred to in section 6.1.1.

6.4.2 Possessive processes

First let me illustrate some of the main features that need to be added to the POSSESSIVE network. Please look at Figure 6.7.

Notes

(a) Till now our possessive network has been concerned with 'having' and with 'changing in order to have'. But for Y to lack Z, or for X to cause Y to lack Z, is as much of a relationship of 'possession', in the sense used here, as it is for Y to have Z. We therefore add this new system at the appropriate places. (Note the shorthand suffixes, as on some other repeated systems, which differentiate the features from each other to enable the realization rules to work.) One interesting result of this addition is the fact that clauses with *lack*, etc. are PRAGMATICALLY similar to ones with *have*, etc. plus the feature [negative]. But this does not mean that 'lacking' and 'not having' should be brought to a close SYSTEMIC SEMANTIC relationship, as a comparison of *we don't lack cabbages* and *we don't not have cabbages*, etc. clearly shows. To do so would be to lose a generalization about negation that is of far wider relevance.

(b) We have assumed, so far, that a Possessed is always simply a Possessed. But alert readers who have been applying the tests proposed in section 6.2.2 will have noticed that in examples such as (12a) and (13a) the Possessed entity (*the key*) is affected by the agency of *Ike*—just as is the Carrier *Ivy* in (13a).

(12a) Ivy got/took/obtained the key   Ag-Ca + Pro + Af-Pos
(13a) Ike gave Ivy the key   Ag + Pro + Af-Ca + Af-Pos

Thus one may reasonably say *What happened to the key was that Ike took it*, or *What happened to it was that Ike gave it to Ivy*. On the other hand, some types of Possessed entities that are not material objects such as *colds* or *ideas* (13g) are not 'affected' by the process of giving, and in such cases the original analysis stands.

(13g) Ike gave Ivy a cold/an idea   Ag + Pro + Af-Ca + Pos

In a fuller treatment we might additionally wish to examine questions such as the distinctions between (a) alienable and inalienable possession, and (b) literal and metaphorical having and giving, such as are referred to by Fillmore (1968: 61f.), and Halliday (1985: 327f.), cf. Halliday's 'cognate range' interpretation of *he gave the paint a stir* (1967a: 60) and other such examples. But whatever the effect of these other distinctions, we need to add the system shown in Figure 6.8 to the network in Figure 6.7.

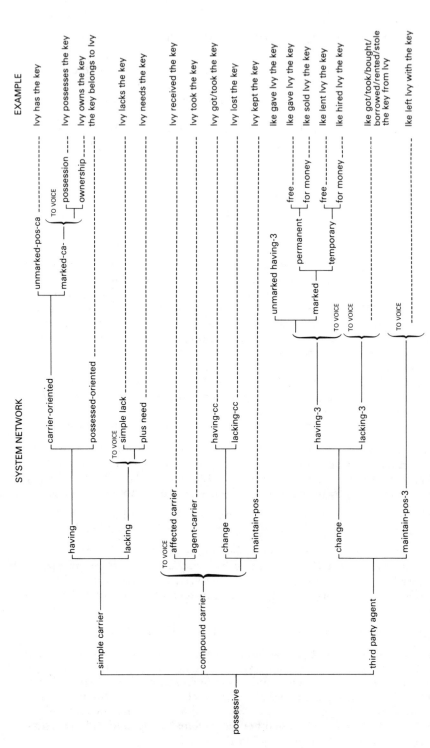

Figure 6.7 A partial possessive network for English (but see Figure 6.8)

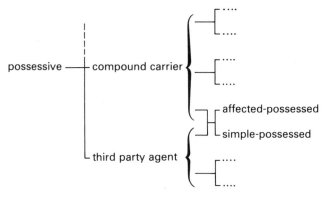

Figure 6.8 A modification to the possessive network for English (see Figure 6.7)

(c) The network shows that the process of X getting/taking/borrowing/ stealing/grabbing Y from Z is regarded here as 'X causing Y to lack Z'. But because one may normally infer that if X causes Y to lack Z, then X ends up with Z, this selection expression is PRAGMATICALLY similar to X causing X to have Z. See (12a) and (46): the analyses show the role parallels nicely, the Medium-Carrier (e.g. *from Ike*) being covert.

(12a) Ivy got/took/obtained the key   Ag-Ca + Pro + Af-Pos
(46)   Fred got/took/obtained/stole the key   Ag + Pro + Af-Pos (+ Af-Ca)

(d) the top system network shows an efficient if obvious way of modelling the distinctions between six closely related lexical verbs; notice that we need to separate out *have* and *belong to* from the others, because they do not occur in 'passive' constructions. (See the realization rules.) These examples illustrate how more features specifying lexical verbs could be added to the lower systems. It is here that the verbs listed in Halliday (1985: 122) under 'possession as process' enter the picture. These include, in addition to those illustrated: (i) for [simple carrier] *carry* ('have with one'?), *contain*, *include* ('have within') and *exclude* ('lack within'?), *involve* ('have to do with'), *comprise* ('have as parts'), *wear* ('have on'); (ii) for compound carrier, *acquire*, *get*, *grab*, *pinch*, *put on* (clothing) *steal*; (iii) for [third party agent, having-3]: *owe* ('ought to give'); *hire*, *let*, *rent*, *lease* and *charter*, i.e. culturally recognized ways of temporarily causing someone to have something in exchange for money: with (iv) their equivalents for [lacking-3] *hire*, *rent*, *lease* and *charter* (but not *let*), in many people's usage, as well as *charge* and *cost*.

(e) The most important omission is the specification of whether roles are to be realized overtly, or to be merely covert. These systems are particularly complex in the system entered from [third party agent, change, having -3], i.e. for *give*-type processes. Here many combinations have to be provided for, as we saw in (13c–f). The importance of the 'overt' vs. 'covert' choices lies in the fact that it is only when these decisions have been made that we know the answer to these questions:

(a) Are we to RE-ENTER part of the system network to generate a unit (such as a nominal group) that will fill the clause elements Subject and Complement?

(b) Will there be two or even three overtly realized roles, and so will we enter the relevant THEME, INFORMATION FOCUS and 'passive' systems?

The places where these choices are required are shown in the network by TO VOICE, in a sense of 'VOICE' that includes the question of the overtness and covertness of roles. In the present framework, where the configurations of roles involved are different for most (but not all) of the process types, it seems inappropriate to make the ability to enter the VOICE system the criterion for setting up a primary distinction between categories of process that it is (along with reversibility) in Halliday (1985: 114).

6.4.3 How the realization rules work

In order to provide complete realization rules, we would need to include here the full system networks that specified which participant roles may be covert, and then, of the overt roles, which will be Subject-theme and, with *give*-type processes, which will receive the unmarked tonic to mark it as 'New' information. This is a complex portion of the grammar, and one that is important in its own right. To introduce it here would, however, demand a chapter of its own; we shall therefore assume in what follows (a) that all the roles are overt and (b) that the only further system is a simple VOICE system, which allows one to choose which role will be Subject-theme. For example, the choice in the higher three VOICE systems shown in Figure 6.7 is [carrier-S-theme] vs. [possessed-S-theme], while the choice in the *give*-type system entered from [having-3] adds [agent-S-theme].

Because it is not the topic of this chapter, we shall also omit here the rules by which the appropriate forms of *be* and the appropriate past participles are chosen for the Main verb.[9] Instead we shall concentrate on the rules (a) that specify the Main verb, and (b) that associate the relevant participant with the Subject (S) or the Complement (C) or, in the case of the *give*-type processes, with the First and Second Complement (C^1 and C^2).

The rules given in Figures 6.9a and 6.9b presuppose certain 'starting structures' (Fawcett 1980: 47–8), which show the sequence in which the elements in any given unit appear unless there is good reason for them to occur in a different sequence. All that we need here is the limited structure for the clause shown in (47), and that for the prepositional group in (48).

(47) Subject + Operator + Main verb + First Complement + Second Complement

(48) preposition + completive

The effect of applying the rules is threefold: (a) they begin to build the elements of structure of a clause, by associating given SEMANTIC elements with

FEATURE	CONDITIONS	REALIZATION
unmarked-pos-ca		M < *have* /Ca BY S FOR S: RE [thing] /Pos BY C FOR C^1: RE [thing]
marked-ca	carrier-S-theme	/Ca BY S FOR S: RE [thing] /Pos BY C^1 FOR C^1: RE [thing]
	possessed-S-theme	/Pos BY S FOR S: RE [thing] /Ca BY C^1 FOR C^1 $\underline{\text{prepgp}}$ p < *by* FOR cv: RE [thing] O < *be* M < + *ed*
possession		M < *possess*
ownership		M < *own*
possessed-oriented		/Pos BY S FOR S: RE [thing] /Ca BY C^1 M < *belong* FOR C^1 $\underline{\text{prepgp}}$ p < *to* FOR cv: RE [thing]

Key
S   = Subject
O   = Operator
M   = Main verb
C^1 = First Complement
C^2 = Second Complement
p   = preposition
cv = completive
<   = is expounded by
RE = Re-enter the network
        at the feature . . .

$\underline{\text{prepgp}}$ = 'is filled by a prepositional group'

Figure 6.9a Some partial realization rules for possessive relational
            processes

the SYNTACTIC elements just listed (and, if certain choices are made, to build
the structure of a prepositional group that fills one of the clause's Complements); (b) they specify the Main verb; and (c) they specify the point of RE-
ENTRY to the overall system network (specifically, here, in the CONGRUENCE
network: see Fawcett 1980: 92–4, etc.). Notice that although the choice that

FEATURE	CONDITIONS		REALIZATION
having-3	permanent	free	M < *give*
		for money	M < *sell*
	temporary	free	M < *lend*
		for money	M < *hire*
	agent-S-theme		/Ag BY S FOR S: RE [thing]
		possessed new	/Af-Ca BY C^1 FOR C^1 RE [thing] /Af-Ca BY C^2 FOR C^2 RE [thing]
		affected-carrier new	/Pos BY C^1 FOR C^1 RE [thing] /Af-Ca BY C^2 @ C^2: $\overline{\text{prepgp}}$ p < *to* for cv: RE [thing]

Figure 6.9b Some partial realization rules for *give*-type clauses

the Subject will be a Carrier, for example, is known by the time of the re-entry, the temptation to limit Carriers to persons or animate entities is firmly resisted: the probability that the relationship expressed by *have* or *belong to*, for example, will involve a human Carrier is a type of knowledge that is handled in the present model in terms of KNOWLEDGE OF THE UNIVERSE (see Fawcett 1980: 63–4 and especially 1984).

Let us work an example. If we assume that the topmost pathway through the network in Figure 6.7 has been chosen, we generate a SELECTION EXPRESSION that comprises [possessive, simple carrier, having, carrier-oriented, unmarked-pos-ca]. If we now apply the realization rules for these features that have one (which in this case is only the last one), we shall have generated the structure marked A in Figure 6.10. (The clause symbol (C1) has already been generated by the choice of a feature to the left of [possessive] in the overall network.) Notice that the realization rules associate the relevant participant role with the Subject or a Complement, using a slash notation. Next, the network will be re-entered, to choose features in the [thing] part, to generate a nominal group (typically) to fill the Carrier and the Possessed.

Suppose that next we follow the pathway ending with [ownership]. This time we will have selected the feature [marked-ca], which, as the rules in Figure 6.9a show, has CONDITIONAL realizations. One of these is [possessed-S-theme], which is the choice in the THEME system that makes the Possessed entity the Subject-theme. One result of this is that a prepositional group fills the Complement, as in B in Figure 6.10. The structure labelled C shows the

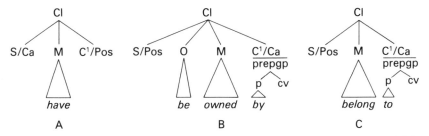

Figure 6.10 Three sample structures generated from Figures 6.7 and 6.9a

result of choosing [possessed-oriented] in Figure 6.7; it generates clauses with *belong*.

Notice that these last two examples show how we can handle participant roles where the unit that realizes the 'thing' is not one but TWO layers down the tree diagram. (The rules as they stand are probably clear, but a little clumsy; in the fully integrated grammar it is possible to express them rather more economically.)

Figure 6.9b shows, in a similar way, how a simplified version of part of the sub-network that generates *give*-type clauses works; it provides for the new distinction between *Ike gave Ivy the book*, where the Possessed is 'New', and *Ike gave the book to Ivy*, where *Ivy* is 'New'.

Finally, note that EVERY feature in the network is relevant to the generation of the formal output, even if only as a contrast to one that has a realization, or as an entry condition to such a system (cf. issue (b) in section 6.1.1 and Martin's chapter in this volume). We only know that the meanings of a language are actually there if they have some reflex in form or intonation. Or, in Saussurean terms: there must be some signifier for each signified.

6.4.4 Attributive processes

Some major systems of the attributive network are shown in Figure 6.11, as well as some systems illustrating how the sub-networks specifying the Main verb can be expressed. As with the possessive processes, it will be seen that the distinction between those sub-systems which select for VOICE and those that do not are handled naturally as non-primary choices. This network in fact suggests that, of the [simple carrier] process types, it is only in those where a 'thing' REPRESENTS another 'thing' that passives occur. The network provides for a number of clause types that in Halliday(1985: 119f.) are handled as 'circumstantial'. These include (i) what Halliday analyses as 'manner', e.g. *Ivy is like a/the doctor*; (ii) the various types of [measure] processes, e.g. *it weighs five kilos* (cf. *it's five kilos*); and (iii) Halliday's 'matter', e.g. *my story concerns a poor shepherd boy* (cf. *my story is about a poor shepherd boy*).

Notes

(a) The particular preoccupation of this network is with the nature of the Attribute. In some types it may be a 'thing' or a 'quality of a thing'. Note that

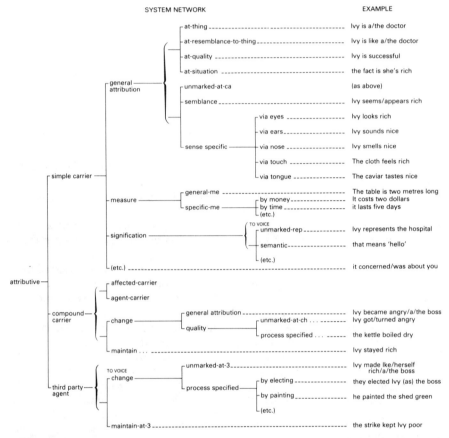

Figure 6.11 A partial attributive network for English

like a/the doctor is in fact systemically a quality, as much as is *successful*; consider *Ivy is very/more/too like a/the doctor/successful*. In others, such as [measure] and [representation], the Attribute is a 'thing' realized typically in a nominal group. In yet others, such as *Ivy got/turned angry*, it MUST be a quality. You will recall that, in the possessive realization rules, re-entry was, somewhat repetitively, always to [thing]. Here, however, re-entry is more varied. The effect of the features in the topmost system is in fact to 'pre-select' what options are to be available in the generation of the unit filling the Complement. This is done, as before, by having a re-entry rule for [at-quality] for example, that specifies re-entry at [quality of thing]. Re-entry will then be at the appropriate feature in the CONGRUENCE network, thus generating a unit with an adjective at its apex—and similarly for the other options. The distinction drawn by Halliday between 'attributive' and 'identifying' processes that is realized in, for example, *a doctor* and *the doctor* therefore comes in the 'thing' network, in which these nominal groups are generated.

(b) No realization rules are supplied, to save space. They are in fact much simpler than those for possessive processes, and correspond precisely to the first two in Figure 6.9a, which provides for processes that do not select for VOICE and that do respectively. There is no need for the complexity found in Figure 6.9b.

(c) Notice that while cases such as (21p) can be analysed simply as Ca + Pro + At, cases such as (49) involve an embedded clause *to be rich*, because there are two Main verbs: *seems* and *be*.

(21p) Ivy seems/appears rich
(49)   Ivy seems/appears (to me) to be rich.

The matrix process involves a MENTAL process; with *Ivy* ...... *to be rich* realizing a discontinuous Phenomenon and *to me* a Cognizant (cf. *it seems to me that Ivy is rich*).

(d) Notice too the somewhat similar cases of embedding in (50a and b), which are to be contrasted with (24a and b) *Ike made Ivy successful/the boss* (Ag + Pro + Af-Ca + At). Here too there are two main verbs in each; 'Ivy's becoming the boss' is what is brought about (or allowed to come about in the case of *let*) by the agency of Ike; it is a situation that he creates (or permits).

(50a) Ike made/got/had/let Ivy become successful/the boss
(50b) Ike caused Ivy to become successful/the boss

The embedded process thus has the role 'Created' in the higher process, that process being a material one.

(e) We can now explain the transitivity of problematical examples such as *She had her hair cut* (NOT *She had a haircut*, which is simple) and *She had her hair cut short*—and *She had the shed painted (green)*, etc.: see (51a–c). (Note that the analysis is only for the italicized embedded process.)

(51a) She made *her dad cut her hair (short)*   Ag + Pro + Af-Ca (+ At)
(51b) She had *her dad cut her hair (short)*   Ag + Pro + Af-Ca (+ At)
(51c) She had *her hair cut (short) (by her dad)* Af-Ca + Pro (+ At) (+ Ag)

(f) Some other verbs that would be specified by more delicate features in this network include: (i) for [simple carrier, measure] *cover (two acres)*, *measure (a mile)*, *weigh (a ton)*, (ii) for [signification] *betoken*, *express*, *play (Hamlet)*, *signify*, *symbolize*; (iii) for [affected-carrier] *burn (dry)*, *end up (poor)*, *go (red) grow (sleepy)*, *keep (still)*, *remain (blind)*, *turn (into) (a frog)*, *turn out (to be) (quite handsome)*; for [third party agent] *boil*, *burn*, *call*, *drive (me wild)*, *grow (one's hair long)*, *leave (her unattended)*, *send (me crazy)*.

(g) Note that each of the forms realizing the lower three 'sensory' options (*smell*, *feel* and *taste*) are highly ambiguous, each also realizing TWO types of mental process. Thus *smell*, for example, may correspond to *look*, *see* or *look at*, as follows (cf. section 9 of Fawcett in press (b)):

    the roses smelled nice   is to   *the roses look nice*

	as	*Ike smelled the roses*	is to	*Ike saw the roses*
and as		*Ike smelled the roses*	is to	*Ike looked at the roses*

6.4.5 Locational processes

Figure 6.12 illustrates some of the principal systems in the locational network. Yet again, the distinction between systems in which VOICE options may be simultaneously selected and those where the system is irrelevant are handled easily as non-primary systems.

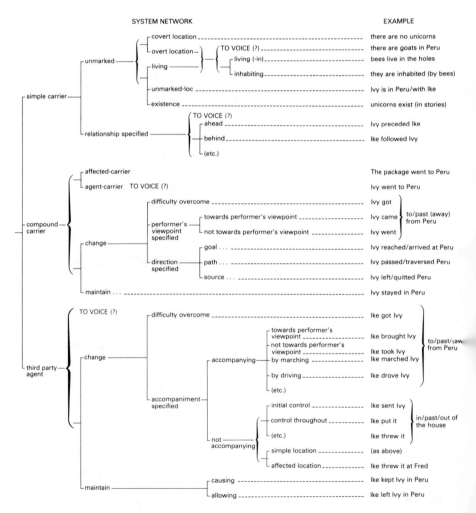

Figure 6.12 A partial locational network for English

Notes

(a) In this network most of the main sub-systems are concerned with specifying the meanings of certain high-frequency verbs with minimal lexical content. The predominant meanings include (i) the direction of movement in relation to the viewpoint of the performer (the speaker or writer); (ii) whether or not the performer accompanies the movement; and (iii) the direction of movement in terms of its source, path and goal (terms adopted from Bennett 1975).

(b) As with attributive processes, the types of realization rules needed correspond precisely to the first two in Figure 6.9a.

(c) Notice that, while the source, path or goal of a locational movement can be specified as part of the PROCESS, as in (52) with clauses with *reach*, *pass*, *leave*, etc., they are more frequently specified through a preposition within the expression realizing the Location, as in (53)—e.g. *to*, *into*; *past*, *through*, *via*, and *from*, *out of*.

(52) Ivy reached/passed/left the house	Ag-Ca + Pro + Loc
(53) Ivy went/came to/past/(away) from the house	Ag-Ca + Pro + Loc

In the latter preference has been given to expressing the performer's viewpoint in the Main verb, i.e. in *go* or *come*. Thus the directional meanings in (53) are not handled in the clause, but as a combination of (i) *come/go* (generated in this network) and (ii) a similar [source] vs. [path] vs. [goal] system in the separate network that generates prepositions. The similarities and distinctions are thus both clearly shown in the overall grammar.

(d) Figure 6.12 adds a distinction between two types of Location: that when the Location is affected by the process, and the more frequent type where it is not. The former is introduced to characterize the fact that the entity at which stones, arrows, spears etc. are thrown is typically affected by the process. The places where things are put can also sometimes be 'affected'.

(e) In cases such as (54) there are three Main verbs and so, clearly, three processes. Problems arise in cases such as (55) and (56a and b).

(54) Ivy left the school, passed the shops and arrived at her home at 5.30.	
(55) Ivy walked out of the school, past the shops, and into her home at 5.30.	
(56a) Ivy walked down the road to the shops.	Ag-Ca + Pro + Loc
(56b) Ivy walked down the road and to the shops.	Ag-Ca + Pro + Loc

I suggest that (56a) is a case of a compound Location, so that there will be a single Complement/Location that is filled, at the lower rank, by two coordinated locational expressions. This is supported by the possibility of inserting *and*, as in (56b). (55), however, could be like (54), with *She walked* ellipted from each of the second two clauses, or like (56). On the principle of ascribing minimum complexity, it would be analyzed like (56a and b). But note that if any item requiring a clause framework to explain its presence occurred (e.g. a manner Adjunct such as *quickly* before *past*), a three-process analysis would be required.

(f) If the network were to be extended to the right, more delicate features would specify, among others, the following more heavily lexicalized Main verbs (cf. Halliday's 1985: 120 category of 'circumstance as process'): (i) for [simple carrier] *accompany* (= 'be with'), *follow* and *succeed* (= 'be/go/come after'), *precede* (= 'is/go/come before') and possibly *cover* (= 'be over') *run* (= 'go to', of a road) and *span* (= 'be/go across'); (ii) for [compound carrier] *remain* and *sit* (*up*) (of a baby); (iii) for [third party agent], in addition to those shown, *cast*, *fling*, *fly*, *jog*, *march*, *project*, *run*, *sit* (of a baby), *throw*, *walk*.

(g) The case of clauses such as *the bridge spans the gorge*, *the tarpaulin covers the whole court* and *the road runs to the horizon* may not be quite as simple as we have assumed in note (f). An alternative analysis might regard them as meta-phorical versions of simple material processes, with the structure Agent + Process + Affected. Compare *these columns support the weight of the pediment*, which is taken from Cruse's useful discussion (1973: 11 f.) of the factors that may contribute to 'doing' (here taken as a criterion for agentivity). It seems reasonable to analyse *these columns* as an Agent, and *the weight of the pediment* as Affected. Moreover, it is possible to argue that

Ike opened the door with a key	is to	*the key opened the door*
as *Brunel spanned the gorge with*	is to	*the bridge spanned*
the bridge		*the gorge*.

Thus one might reasonably take *the key* and *the bridge* in the pair on the right not to be 'Instruments' as suggested by Fillmore 1968, but a type of surrogate Agent, and so to have some of the qualities of a more typical animate Agent (cf. Fawcett 1980: 155–6). In other words, it is possible to see processes such as *the bridge spans the gorge* either as metaphorical material processes, or as simple relational processes. Here the second solution is preferred, on the grounds that these constructions have crossed the divide between metaphor and new lexical items—but perhaps only just, in some cases.

6.5 SUMMARY AND CONCLUSIONS

6.5.1 Summary of the description

Despite the limitations of the three networks that have just been introduced, what has been said should enable them to be used (a) in a limited generative grammar (if more realization rules are added on the model of those provided), and (b) as a tool for the analysis of texts, in the sense that the options shown specify the participant roles associated with the Subjects and Complements of clauses.

The fifteen configurations of inherent roles generated are (assuming that all are realized overtly and in their unmarked sequence) as in Figure 6.13. The two pairs of variants under 'possessive' are for non-material and material Possessed entitities respectively, and the variant under 'locational' is to provide for *throw*-type processes, as described in note (d) in section 6.4.5. In

semantic features	possessive	attributive	locational
simple carrier	Ca + Pro + Pos	Ca + Pro + At	Ca + Pro + Loc
affected-carrier	Af-Ca + Pro + Pos	Af-Ca + Pro + At	Af-Ca + Pro + Loc
agent-carrier	Ag-Ca + Pro + Pos/Af-Pos	Ag-Ca + Pro + At	Ag-Ca + Pro + Loc
third party agent	Ag + Pro + Af-Ca + Pos/ Af-Pos	Af + Pro + Af-Ca + At	Ag + Pro + Af-Ca + Loc/Af-Loc

Figure 6.13 Participant roles in English relational processes

many examples, however, and especially in those in natural texts, one or more roles may be unrealized, and this may sometimes make it hard for the analyst to identify the process type. We have discussed a number of such cases in the course of this chapter.

But the true summary, in a systemic grammar, is captured in a system network. The essential characteristics of the meaning potential for English relational processes realized in the clause are as we showed them in Figure 6.6. (In fact Figure 6.6 over-generalizes slightly, as note (b) on Figure 6.7 points out.) But for the fuller picture, incorporating the additional, non-primary systems that are distinctive of each of the three types, we need the networks in Figures 6.7, 6.8, 6.11 and 6.12. Each has its own preoccupations: the possessive with 'having' and 'lacking'; the attributive with the type of Attribute and how solid the evidence is (*is* vs. *seems* vs. *looks*, etc.); the locational with the relationship of movement to the performer's viewpoint, and with accompaniment and direction.

6.5.2 The main differences from Halliday 1985

As we saw in section 6.1.1, these proposals arise in part out of Halliday's early work on this part of the grammar. They extend the area of relational processes greatly, in ways in which there are occasional interesting parallels in 'asides' in Halliday's subsequent writings, but they differ quite considerably from the main thrust of the presentation in Halliday 1985. It may be helpful to summarize the main differences. Some of the reasons for not incorporating the additional complexity of Halliday's approach, e.g. in 'identifying' clauses, have been given earlier; here we shall focus mainly on describing the differences themselves.

First, in Halliday 1985 the primary choices and examples of prototypical realizations are as shown in Figure 6.14. Halliday's category of 'identifying' clauses, you will recall, is marked by the reversibility of the participant roles in *be*-clauses and the passivizability of the others. In the present approach the reversibility is handled in terms of thematic choice (so that it does not appear in the relational process network) and VOICE systems are entered, as appropriate, as non-primary choices (as in other transitivity networks; cf. Fawcett 1980: 137, Berry 1975: 189). We could diagram this as in Figure 6.15.

In essence, the claim is that the distinction between [attributive] and [identifying] processes does not apply to 'circumstantial' (here [locational])

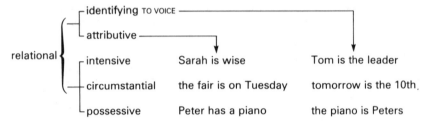

Figure 6.14 The primary relational systems in Halliday 1985

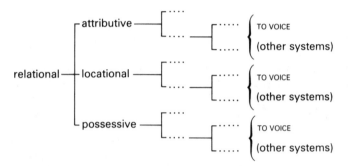

Figure 6.15 The non-primary statues of VOICE in the present approach

Figure 6.16 Where Halliday's prototypical examples of 'identifying'
processes are handled in the present approach

and [possessive] processes; the place in which the prototypical examples from
Figure 6.14 are handled here is shown in Figure 6.16.

Second, we do not make here the fine distinctions that Halliday makes, in
those clauses that are in his terms both 'identifying' and 'attributive', between
the different configurations of 'Identified' and 'Identifier', on the one hand,
and 'Token' and 'Value' on the other. It might simply be that for some
purposes (e.g. some types of textual analysis) such fine distinctions are not
needed. But, as I have suggested earlier, it may also be that they are not
needed in a fully generative grammar, because they appear to relate

systematically to choices in other components of the grammar: 'Identified' and 'Identifier' to THEME and 'Token' and 'Value' to INFORMATION FOCUS. Finally, it may be that the concepts behind the terms 'Identifier', 'Identified', 'Token' and 'Value' may relate to some aspects of higher order planning.

The third main difference is that many of Halliday's 'circumstantial' process types are handled in the attributive network, as we have seen, leaving only locational processes of space and time in the equivalent part of the network here. Even these are not differentiated in the present relational process network, because the two have the same transitivity potential. The claim implied in the present approach is that it is NOT the case that all the types of meaning found in circumstantial roles (realized as Adjuncts in clauses) can also occur with all the types of relational process that, on other grounds, we wish to introduce (i.e. the system that introduces 'third party' Agents, etc.). Thus, roles that, on INTERNAL grounds, can be distinguished as 'manner', 'cause', 'matter' and 'role' are all handled here as 'attributive', while 'accompaniment' is seen as a type of location. The difference can be summarized as in Figure 6.17.

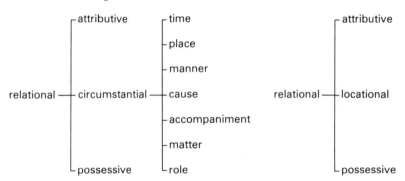

Figure 6.17 Halliday's and the present approaches to 'circumstance/location'

The fourth significant difference is the addition, as a primary system in the network, of the options that introduce Affected-Carriers, Agent-Carriers and third party Agents, as in Figure 6.18. As I have emphasized earlier, there are occasional hints in Halliday's writings of the possibility of incorporating this sort of approach in the relational process network. Indeed, in Halliday 1977

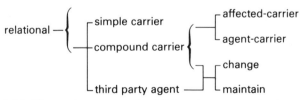

Figure 6.18 The main source of additional coverage in the present approach

we even find a system [neutral] vs. [imperfective] vs. [perfective], such that [neutral] appears to correspond to our [simple carrier], and the last two to our [maintain] and [change]. But this is not carried through in Halliday 1985.

In sum, we may say that the range of process types covered here is very much broader than in Halliday's 1985 approach to relational processes, including many types that would for him probably be 'material', while he makes many fine distinctions that are not here seen as necessary—particularly in the area of the intersection, in his terms, of 'identifying' and 'attributive' processes. Both approaches have been widely used for purposes of textual analysis; in terms of generation, we still await the publication of Halliday's system networks and realization statements.

6.5.2 Theoretical conclusions

Let us ask, finally: what are the theoretical implications of this exercise in description? Four issues were raised at the end of section 6.1.1.

Regarding issue (a); the model of relational processes presented here appears to support the case for a model of language in which structures at the level of FORM are generated directly from SEMANTIC system networks, as advocated in Fawcett 1980 and 1983, and without the intermediary of a 'purely formal' system network.

Let us now briefly relate this issue to Martin's very useful chapter in this volume, since there is one point (in his 'Conclusions') on which the present chapter bears. There Martin proposes that, if the features in a system meet his criteria A–F, which include 'having a reflex in form' (as I believe the features given here do), then the network in which they appear is 'grammatical'. This is as opposed to being 'semantic', this term being reserved for 'contextually-oriented' networks such as Turner's 1973 socio-semantic networks, which are at the 'second level'. Yet there is in fact no a priori reason why a feature that is a semantic option should NOT have a reflex in form; indeed, I would assume, with Saussure, that this is the usual position. One purpose of Fawcett 1980 and of this chapter is precisely to argue that systemic linguists have everything to gain and very little (if anything) to lose by recognizing that the central networks for TRANSITIVITY, MOOD, THEME, etc. that we operate with are in fact SEMANTIC networks. It does not matter much if we include both these networks of meanings and their realizations in the 'lexico-grammar', as Halliday does—unless, that is, we imply by so doing that we have still not reached the semantic level of language: in fact we HAVE reached it—and what lies beyond, including the various discourse grammars (cf. Fawcett in press (b)) need to be interpreted as semiotic systems in their own right.

Issue (b) concerned the necessary and sufficient conditions for including a feature in a semantic system network. My proposals, which are very similar to those of Martin in this volume, are that every feature should either have some 'reflex at the level of form' (cf. Fawcett 1974/81: 157) or should be in contrast with one that has, or should be an entry condition to a system. (Martin does not in fact include the second in his list, but it is surely necessary and is perhaps implied.) The networks offered here have been constructed in such a way that the above criteria collectively specify the necessary and sufficient conditions for including features.

As for issue (c), there have been a number of instances in this study where it became clear that there are indeed some types of pragmatic equivalence (e.g. 'not having' and 'lacking') which should be kept apart in a systemic model of language, on the crucial grounds that they are not open to the same co-selections in the rest of the grammar; we might say that they have different complementary meaning potentials.

Issue (d) concerns ELEGANCE. The present study illustrates particularly clearly an important fact (as I take it to be) about using system networks to model language. This is that it typically happens that, when we develop our system networks beyond a certain point in delicacy—and in particular when we reach the point of generating specific lexical items—elegance, including the traditional systemic devotion to what I term CONSOLIDATED networks, may have to be abandoned (cf. Fawcett in press (a)). Instead we find networks that are more complete but less ELEGANT—and that even include repetitions of systems. But these networks are more USABLE for both generation and analysis and also, in my view, more exciting to work with. This is because they are now explicit enough for one to try to incorporate them in a computer program: they are, in a word, falsifiable (cf. Fawcett 1980: 12 f., and, for a similar but fuller line of argument, Johnson Laird 1983: 4–22).

In fact, I would argue that these networks are NOT in any serious sense less elegant. It is not that generalizations such as those shown in Figures 6.6 are not captured in Figures 6.7, 6.8, 6.11 and 6.12, because the systems that are in common are there for anyone who reads the networks with due attention to see. The elegance is there, then, as well as the apparent 'messiness' that results from making the network usable.

Elegance in a grammar is an attempt to capture tendencies; sometimes, but only sometimes, these tendencies are so strong that they constitute absolute generalizations. The grammarian is always tempted to economize by applying the same sets of options to different areas of meaning—but this temptation must not be given free rein. If we want our grammars to be USABLE, in any of the various senses defined in Fawcett forthcoming, we must capture not only the generalization but also the exceptions and the variations.

The final theoretical implication of this study is that if you find the present description (or one not too unlike it) of this central area of the grammar of English persuasive, it should be taken as another piece of evidence for the SYSTEMIC SEMANTIC type of SYSTEMIC FUNCTIONAL grammar proposed in Fawcett 1980 and outlined in section 6.1.1.

NOTES

1. It was back in 1972–3 that I first established the main framework of the proposals to be presented here; though detailed modification has continued since then. My aim was to develop a generative model for relational processes in English that would be usable in a principled manner for the analysis of natural texts—most immediately

by my students and myself. But it may be of interest that the approach to participant roles given here (and complemented by a description of material (or 'action') roles substantially as in Fawcett 1980 and one of mental processes that is not yet in published form) is currently being used as the basis for this type of analysis by the EUROTRA-D team of the large European Community project in machine translation.

The proposals derive in part, of course, from the writing of other scholars, chiefly in the earlier work of Halliday, especially 1967a, 1967b, 1968, 1970 and 1973. Thus, when the basic distinctions in the present network were being hammered out, I had no idea of the way that Halliday's own ideas for this area were developing, as set out, for example, in Halliday 1977, 'unpublished' and 1985. (It may be of interest to point out that I was in a similar situation for the 'action' processes—which Halliday renamed 'material' in 1973—but that the result was different. Thus, while there is a fundamental similarity between my 'action' process network (Fawcett 1980: 134–51) and Halliday's material process network (e.g. that in Halliday 'unpublished' and that underlying Halliday 1985: 144f.; cf. also Berry 1975: 189 and the comparison in Fawcett 1980: 140–7), Halliday's and my networks for relational processes seem to have some fairly fundamental differences—as well, of course, as many points in common.) I have also drawn on and adapted certain ideas of Bendix 1966 and Lyons 1968. Other sources in the earlier stages of developing the network were: Jesperson 1933, Fillmore 1968, Turner and Mohan 1970, Hudson 1971 (for the importance of realization rules), Huddleston 1971, Sinclair 1972 and Quirk et al. 1972. Works consulted subsequently include, among others, Ellis and Boadi 1969, Burt 1971, Hasan 1972, Bennett 1975, Lyons 1977, Leech 1974/81, Allerton 1978, and, for some proposals with interesting similarities to my own but reached independently, Young 1980 (especially 118–23 for 'intensive clauses' and 130–1 for 'transitive-intensive' clauses).

I am grateful to Ray Cattell, Mick Perkins, Erich Steiner and members of the Cardiff Linguistics Linguistic Circle for their helpful comments on an earlier draft of this chapter.

2. Terminology is a major problem in this area. My criterion is to use Halliday's 1985 terms, wherever the sense seems to me to be wholly or, from my viewpoint, essentially the same. Wherever this is not possible I try to coin new terms (rather than using Halliday's or someone else's term in a potentially confusing new sense). Part of the problem is that Halliday's own terminology has changed over the years, and till now I have in general adhered to his terminology of the early 1970s (e.g. in Fawcett 1980). However, with the publication of his long-awaited *Introduction to Functional Grammar* (1985), it seems the appropriate time to switch to the terms used there, within the conditions stated above. In 'material' (formerly 'action') processes, however, I continue to take the line proposed in Fawcett 1980: 141, i.e. that it is unnecessary to think in terms FIRST of an 'Actor + Process + Goal' view of the transitivity of 'material' processes, which can if one likes LATER be reanalyzed in 'Agent + Process + Affected' terms (Halliday 1985: 144f.). Indeed, Halliday himself describes this 'ergative' approach to the grammar of processes as 'how it appears in the contemporary language' (1985: 146). Thus it seems to me that it is fully adequate to use ONLY the terms 'Agent' and 'Affected'. In Halliday 1985 the term 'Medium' replaces the term 'Affected', as used in Halliday 1970, 1973, 1977, etc. and in Fawcett 1980. This may be because Halliday regards this role as occurring in ALL process types, and it is odd to regard cases such as *Ivy* in *Ivy is rich* as an 'affected entity'. Note the oddness of *what happened to Ivy was that she was rich* (see the re-expression tests in section 6.2.2). Here we shall adopt a different view from Halliday's, suggesting that what all process types have in common is simply the

element Process, while it is the participant roles that distinguish them (cf. section 6.2.1). Here, then, we shall continue to use the term Affected (and also, following Halliday 1985, 'Created' for cases such as *this gazebo* in *Sir Christpher Wren built this gazebo*).

3. Two exceptions are on pp. 149 and 153 of Halliday 1985, where he considers the *heat turned the milk sour* and *they made/voted Tom captain* respectively. The 'distinct function' of 'Attributor' is introduced on p. 149 for *the heat* and the 'distinct transitivity function' of 'Assigner' on p. 153 for the second. But since *the sun* in *the sun made the bananas ripe* is described on p. 153 as an Agent, we may perhaps infer that we have here two sub-categories of Agent. In section 6.3.3 we shall find that the process types are adequately differentiated with the sole use of the term Agent for these cases.

4. The fact that is occasionally hard to decide, when analysing a text, whether a given element is a participant or a circumstantial role does not necessarily mean that the distinction is not there in the grammar itself.

5. A further difference is that in Halliday 1985 the familiar Scale and Category terms (Halliday 1961) of Predicator, Complement and Adjunct are introduced as a part of the 'interpersonal' structure of the clause, along with the Subject (as indeed they were in 1973: 43). They are therefore being treated as functional elements at the same level of analysis as the participant roles, rather than as syntactic elements that realize them, as here. I find it hard to see why these terms are needed at all at a level of analysis that is PARALLEL to transitivity; all three will be completely specified in other networks—Complements, for example, from the transitivity networks in the experiential meta-function.

6. See section 6.5.2 for a brief summary of the relevant part of Halliday 1985.

7. Incidentally, these examples show one of the reasons why we shall not need to recognize Halliday's 'Token + Value' versus 'Value + Token' distinction; just as 'Mr. Garrick' is Theme in (8a) while Hamlet is Theme in (8b), so with (9a) and (9b). The choices in the THEME system therefore already specify the difference between (9a) and (9b). In a rather similar way, variation in the placement of INFORMATION FOCUS in the tables on pp. 126–7 of Halliday 1985 co-varies quite regularly with what Halliday presents as an 'Identifier + Identified' versus 'Identified + Identifier', and can therefore be regarded as capturing the LINGUISTIC, and so SEMANTIC, difference between the pairs.

8. Thus we are here seeking to tighten up Halliday's (1985: 132) description, where he describes the Beneficiary as 'not so much an inherent element in the process, and as usually (but not always) an optional extra'. Thus he does not make the distinction being emphasized here between ones that are participant roles and ones that are circumstantial roles.

9. This part of the grammar, including also the relevant features in other networks specifying tense, aspect, etc. were presented, and in fact implemented in a computer demonstration, in a talk to the Spring 1984 Meeting of the Linguistics Association of Great Britain. At the time of writing that paper has unfortunately still not been written up for publication.

BIBLIOGRAPHY

Allerton, D. J. (1978), 'Generating indirect objects in English', *Journal of Linguistics*, 14, No. 1, 21–33.
Anderson, J. M. (1971), *The Grammar of Case: Towards a Localistic Theory*, London, Cambridge University Press.

Bach, E. and Harms, R. T. (eds) (1968), *Universals in Linguistic Theory*, New York, Holt, Rinehart and Winston.

Bendix, E. H. (1966), 'Componential analysis of general vocabulary: the semantic structure of a set of verbs in English, Hindi and Japanese (Part 2 of *IJAL*, 32), Bloomington, Indiana University and The Hague, Mouton.

Bennett, D. C. (1975), *Spatial and Temporal Uses of English Prepositions: An Essay in Stratificational Linguistics*, London, Longman.

Benson, J. D. and Greaves, W. S. (eds) (1985), *Systemic Perspectives on Discourse: Vol. 1 Selected Theoretical Papers from the Ninth International Systemic Workshop*, Norwood, N.J., Ablex.

—— and —— (eds) (in press), *Systemic Functional Approaches to Discourse: Selected Papers from the Twelfth International Systemic Workshop*, Norwood, N.J., Ablex.

Bernstein, B. (ed.) (1973), *Class, Codes and Controls: Vol. 2 Applied Studies Towards a Sociology of Language*, London, Routledge and Kegan Paul.

Berry, M. (1975), *An Introduction to Systemic Linguistics: 1 Structures and Systems*, London, Batsford.

Burt, M. K. (1971), *From Deep to Surface Structure*, New York, Harper and Row.

Butler, C. S. (1979), 'Recent developments in systemic linguistics', *Language Teaching and Linguistics: Abstracts*, No. 12, 71–89, and in Kinsella (ed.) (1979).

—— (1985), *Systemic Linguistics: Theory and Application*, London, Batsford.

Cruse, D. A. (1973), 'Some thoughts on agentivity', *Journal of Linguistics*, 9, No. 1, 11–23.

D'Addio, W. D., Ciliberti, A. and McRae, J. (eds) (in press), *Levels of Grammar*, Florence: La Nuovo Italia.

Dijk, T. A. van and Petöfi, J. S. (eds) (1977), *Grammars and Descriptions*, Berlin, de Gruyter.

Ellis, J. O. and Boadi, L. (1969), '"To be" in Twi', in Verhaar (ed.) (1969).

Fawcett, R. P. (1974/81), 'Some proposals for systemic syntax, Part 1', *Midlands Association for Linguistic Study Journal*, 1, No. 2, 1–15, reissued with light amendments (with Parts 2 and 3) in monograph form as Fawcett 1981.

—— (1975a), 'Relational networks: aspects of the experiential function', paper presented to the Second Systemic Theory Workshop, University of Essex, July 1975.

—— (1975b), 'Some proposals for systemic syntax, Part 2', *Midlands Association for Linguistic Study Journal*, 2, No. 1, 43–68.

—— (1980), *Cognitive Linguistics and Social Interaction: Towards an Integrated Model of a Systemic Functional Grammar and the Other Components of a Communicating Mind*, Heidelberg, Julius Groos Verlag and Exeter University.

—— (1981), *Some Proposals for Systemic Syntax* (revised version), Cardiff, The Polytechnic of Wales.

—— (1983), 'Language as a semiological system: a reinterpretation of Saussure', invited lecture to the Linguistic Association of Canada and the United States 1982, in Morreall (ed.) (1983: 48–125).

—— (1984), 'System networks, codes and knowledge of the universe', in Fawcett, Halliday, Lamb and Makkai (eds) (1984: 135–79).

—— (in press (a)), 'What makes a "good" system network good?'—four pairs of concepts for such evaluations', in Benson and Greaves (eds) (in press).

—— (in press (b)), 'An overview of cognitive systemic functional linguistics', in D'Addio *et al.* (eds).

Fawcett, R. P., Halliday, M. A. K., Lamb, S. M. and Makkai, A. (eds) (1984), *The Semiotics of Culture and Language*, Vols 1 and 2, London, Frances Pinter.

Fillmore, C. J. (1968), 'The case for case', in Bach and Harms (eds) (1968).

Halliday, M. A. K. (1961), 'Categories of the theory of grammar', *Word*, 17, 241–92, and the Bobbs-Merrill Reprints Series.

—— (1967a), 'Notes on transitivity and theme in English, Part I', *Journal of Linguistics*, 3, No. 1, 37–81.

—— (1967b), 'Notes on transitivity and theme in English, Part II', *Journal of Linguistics*, 3, No. 2, 199–244.

—— (1968), 'Notes on transitivity and theme in English, Part III', *Journal of Linguistics*, 4, No. 2, 179–215.

—— (1970), 'Language structure and language function', in Lyons (ed.) (1970).

—— (1973), *Explorations in the Functions of Language*, London, Edward Arnold.

—— (1977), 'Text as semantic choice in social contexts', in van Dijk and Petöfi (eds) (1977).

—— (1985), *Introduction to Functional Grammar*, London, Edward Arnold.

—— (unpublished), 'An outlook on modern English: the meaning of modern English', unpublished typescript prepared in the 1970s, partly but not wholly superseded by Halliday 1985.

Halliday, M. A. K. and Martin, J. R. (eds) (1981), *Readings in Systemic Linguistics*, London, Batsford.

Hasan, R. (1971), 'The verb "be" in Urdu', in Verhaar (ed.) (1972: 1–63).

Huddleston, R. D. (1970), 'Some remarks on case grammar', *Linguistic Inquiry*, 1, No. 4.

—— (1971), *The Sentence in Written English*, London, Cambridge University Press.

Hudson, R. A. (1971), *English Complex Sentences: An Introduction to Systemic Grammar*, Amsterdam, North Holland.

Ikegami, Y. (1984), 'How universal is a localist hypothesis?', in Fawcett *et al.* (eds) (1984: 49–79).

Jesperson, O. (1933), *The essentials of English Grammar*, London, Allen and Unwin.

Johnson-Laird, P. N. (1983), *Mental Models*, Cambridge, Cambridge University Press.

Kinsella, V. (ed.) (1979), *Language Teaching and Linguistics Surveys*, Cambridge, Cambridge University Press.

Leech, G. N. (1974/81), *Semantics*, Harmondsworth, Penguin.

Lyons, J. (1968), *Introduction to Theoretical Linguistics*, Cambridge, Cambridge University Press.

—— (ed.) (1970), *New Horizons in Linguistics*, Harmondsworth, Penguin.

—— (1977), *Semantics*, Vol. 1, Cambridge, Cambridge University Press.

Mann, W. C. and Matthiessen, C. M. I. M. (1983/85), 'A demonstration of the Nigel text generation computer program', Marina del Rey, University of Southern California Information Service Institute, and in Benson and Greaves (eds) (1985: 50–83).

Morreall, J. (ed.) (1983), *The Ninth LACUS Forum 1982*, Columbia, South Carolina, Hornbeam Press.

Quirk, R., Greenbaum, S. Leech, G. and Svartvik, J. (eds) (1972), *A Grammar of Contemporary English*, London, Longman.

Sinclair, J. McH. (1972), *A Course in Spoken English: Grammar*, London, Oxford University Press.

Turner, G. (1973), 'Social class and children's language of control at age 5 and age 7', in Bernstein (ed.) (1973).

Turner, G. and Mohan, B. (1970), *A Linguistic Description and Computer Program of Children's Speech*, London, Routledge and Kegan Paul.

Verhaar, J. W. M. (ed.) (1969), *The Verb 'Be' and its Synonym*, Dordrecht, Reidel.

Young, D. J. (1980), *The Structure of English Clauses*, London, Hutchinson.

7 The grammarian's dream: lexis as most delicate grammar

Ruqaiya Hasan

Macquarie University, Sydney

7.1 THE LEXICO-GRAMMATICAL STRATUM

It was over two decades ago that Halliday remarked: 'The grammarian's dream is . . . to turn the whole of linguistic form into grammar, hoping to show that lexis can be defined as "most delicate grammar"' (Halliday 1961: 267). This chapter briefly explores the reality of that dream by examining two questions: (1) is the project feasible? and (2) what would be the implications of 'turning the whole of linguistic form into grammar'? This formulation, by implication, rejects the views that (a) lexis is not form, and (b) that its relation to semantics is unique.

Drawing upon Halliday 1977, I shall make the following assumptions:

(1) Language consists of three strata: semantics, lexico-grammar and phonology.
(2) These strata are related by 'realization': meanings are coded as wordings, wordings are coded as sound patterns.
(3) Each stratum is describable as a network of options; the description is, therefore, paradigmatic, with environments for options also being defined paradigmatically.
(4) The semantic stratum is organized into four meta-functional components: experiential, logical, interpersonal and textual.
(5) Each meta-function specifies a particular (set of) option network(s) as its output at the lexico-grammatical stratum.
(6) Each act of choice—the selection of each option—contributes to the formation of a structure.
(7) A unified structure in its totality is the output of selections from four distinct (sets of) lexico-grammatical networks, specified by the four meta-functions.
(8) 'It is the function of the lexico-grammatical stratum to map these structures one on to another so as to form a single integrated structure that represents [the output of (R.H.)] all [meta-functional (R.H.)] components simultaneously' (Halliday 1977).

Assumption (6) is immediately relevant. Grammars have traditionally been concerned with describing the formation of syntagms, using the syntagm itself as the starting point for explaining the syntagm-formation phenomena. The Systemic Functional model has abandoned this approach in favour of one foreshadowed by Saussure 1916, Hjelmslev 1961 and Firth 1951, where the grammar of a language is viewed as a network of paradigmatic relations. If 'systemic options contribute to the formation of structure', and if the description of structure-formation is what characterizes grammar, then such system networks ARE the grammar. The question of feasibility can, then, be paraphrased as: 'Is it possible to extend a lexico-grammatical network in delicacy so as to turn it into a device for the description and generation of units of form called "lexical item"?' If so, then we shall have shown that lexis is delicate grammar.

This argument shifts attention to mechanisms whereby the paradigm and the syntagm—the option network and the structure—are brought into relation. (Henceforth the 'options' and 'networks' referred to are lexico-grammatical ones, unless otherwise stated.) An option can be viewed as instruction(s) to operate in a certain way; a specific structure is the outcome of following these operations. The technical term for such instructions is 'realization statement'. So realization statement is a mechanism mediating between networks and structures.

Six categories of realization statement will be used here:

(1) *insert* structural function x;
(2) *conflate* two/more functions into one element;
(3) *order* elements a and b (and . . . n) *vis-à-vis* each other;
(4) *sub-categorize* some function or feature;
(5) *pre-select* some feature as a concomitant of some insertion/sub-categorization;
(6) *outclassify* some function/feature as incompatible with some insertion/sub-categorization.

This view implies that options have consequences: they are justified by what they 'do'. And, since the doing takes cognizance of relations within the language, an option's justification is intra-linguistic. Simplifying greatly, the options for the description and generation of *enquire* and *ask* might differ in some respects; if so, the justification would not arise from the two activities differing physically, psychologically or socially, but from the differential lexico-grammatical patternings of the two lexical verbs. So ultimately, a delicate network is an enquiry into what Whorf 1956 called 'reactance'.

The network examined here is a minute part of the experiential meta-function's output, known as TRANSITIVITY, whose entry condition is [major] clause. (The technical terms in what follows are used as in Halliday 1985; features are shown in square brackets except in the networks themselves.) Figure 7.1 places TRANSITIVITY in relation to other systems applicable to [major] clause. Systems concurrent with TRANSITIVITY, e.g. MOOD, THEME, etc., will be ignored. Within TRANSITIVITY itself, VOICE options will be constantly assumed as [effective:active]. The portion of the network discussed

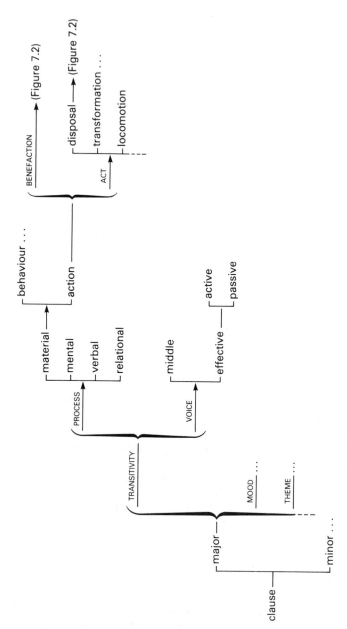

Figure 7.1 The entry condition for transitivity

belongs to PROCESS, and it has [disposal] as its entry condition. It is part of the lexico-grammar which constructs the semantic area that can be informally described as 'activities whose completion results in gain/loss of access to things'.

7.2 THE LEXICO-GRAMMAR OF ACQUISITION: GATHER, COLLECT, ACCUMULATE

[disposal] entails the options [material:action], which are built into its history, with the implication that the contribution they have made to the formation of the structure, remains a constant wherever [disposal] itself is selected. No part of this contribution can be negated by any instruction attached to [disposal] or options dependent upon it. This principle operates across the system, irrespective of the degree of delicacy. Part of the contribution made by [effective:active] VOICE in conjunction with [material:action] PROCESS is:

A: 1. the functions Process, Medium and Agent are inserted
    2. Process pre-selects Event
    3. Medium and Agent each pre-select Thing
    4. Event is sub-categorized as /material action/

By virtue of having to follow a particular systemic path, the selection of [disposal] inherits the bundle specified in A1–4. This I shall call PI, for 'systematic path inheritance', to keep it distinct from SI (semantic inheritance) (Brachman 1979; Collins and Quillian 1972) and 'conceptual dependency' (Schank 1972, 1975; Schank and Abelson 1977) in the AI literature. PI differs from both, in that it is not item-centred and is more rigorously defined. To see how PI works, imagine a network with options 1 through 7 as in Figure 7.1a. If (a, b) are the contribution of [1], (c, d) of [2], and (e, f) of [3], then the PI for [2] and [3] is (a, b); for [4] and [5], (a, b, c, d), and for [6] and [7] it is (a, b, e, f). Each progressive step in the network specifies both identity and uniqueness between classes of structures. When the network reaches a point where further uniqueness cannot be postulated, this is the logical endpoint; and the total selection expression—i.e. path specification—will, among other things, specify some formal structure(s) known as 'lexical item(s)'. The uniqueness of each lexical item is widely recognized (Berry 1977; Fawcett 1980; Fillmore 1977; Leech 1974; Lyons 1977). In this chapter I begin by concentrating on the identities of, for example, *give*, *share*, *collect*, *lose* etc., and work toward their uniqueness.

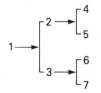

Figure 7.1a A simple system network

The realization statements attached to [disposal] are:

B: 1. sub-categorize Event as /(material action) of disposal involving change in location of Medium/
   2. sub-categorize Medium Thing as /alienable object/
   3. sub-categorize Agent Thing as /human, person(s) or institutions/

For lack of precise formal information, sub-categorization is expressed informally. It should not be confused with Chomsky's selection restriction rules (1965): the latter operate on items; possess directionality, e.g. assign 'features of the Subject and Object to the Verb'; (1965: 92); and their non-observance leads to linguistic malaise. None of these is necessarily true of sub-categorization. However, if B1–3 are not followed, the semantics of the resultant clause would be distinct from that of a clause whose underlying selection expression contains [disposal]. Consider:

(1a) Susan collected a lot of leaves.
(1b) The roof collected a lot of leaves.
(1c) She collected her thoughts.

(1a) is in keeping with B1–3; most speakers will 'read' it as Susan gaining access to a lot of leaves when the collecting is done; Susan is the 'doer', and the leaves are 'done-to'. In (1b), instruction B3 is not followed; the Agent is not human. Note that the roof is no longer 'doer', but 'location'. (1b) contains a grammatical metaphor (Halliday 1985), whose congruent pair would be *A lot of leaves collected on the roof*. The non-following of B3 will not always produce the semantic value of 'location' for the Agent (compare *These pipes distribute steam into the system* or *Her room carries the most amazing trash*); it will, however, produce a metaphorical effect. In (1c), B2 is not followed: the Medium is not an object, but rather a concept/abstraction. The clause is a good example of Whorf's 'objectification' (1956), where something itself not an object is treated as such. In English, a standard objectifying device is to use an abstract noun as the Medium of a Process, which normally requires a concrete noun as Medium. But this Medium-like thing, e.g. *her thoughts* in (1c), is not the Medium, as it would fail most of the heuristic tests applicable to that function. (Consider *What is she doing to her thoughts?—Collecting them* and *It is your thoughts you need to collect*.) (1c) is an instance of a complex metaphor, where the entire expression *collect+ . . . thoughts* must be seen as a unit, since in another such occurrence *collect* may bear little or no resemblance to *collect* in (1c). (Consider *She collected a good deal of kudos from that*.) This discussion, incidentally, justifies the validity of B1–3.

The system of BENEFACTION applies concurrently with that of ACT and is developed in Figure 7.2 below, where the systems dependent on [disposal] are also presented. This device will ensure that all systemic options relevant to [disposal] can be seen at one glance. The selection of [disposal] will demand the selection of one path from each of the three systems developed in Figure 7.2; while the systems of ACCESS and CHARACTER are directly dependent on [disposal], that of BENEFACTION is entailed by virtue of the dependence of [disposal] on [action].

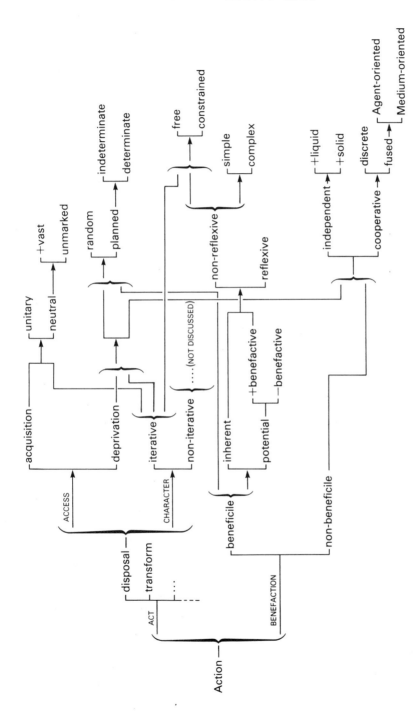

Figure 7.2 The process type [disposal:iterative]

ACCESS options are concerned with the result of the activity. The selection of [acquisition] implies the Agent's gain of access to the Medium, unless otherwise indicated. [deprivation] implies the reverse—the Agent loses access to the Medium. Indicating PI within brackets as before, the instructions for these options are:

C: 1.   [acquisition]
    a. sub-categorize Event as /(material action of disposal involving change in location of Medium) leading to Agent's gain of access to Medium/
   2.   [deprivation]
    a. sub-categorize Event as /(material action of disposal involving change in location of Medium) leading to Agent's loss of access to Medium/

CHARACTER options are concerned with the nature of the activity. The selection of [iterative] implies an inherently repetitive activity, in which the Agent–Medium configuration inherently remains identical; [non-iterative] implies an activity that is not inherently repetitive. The instructions are:

D: 1.   [iterative]
    a. sub-categorize Event as /(material action of disposal involving change in location of Medium) inherently repetitive/
    b. sub-categorize Medium Thing as /(alienable object) divisible
   2.   [non-iterative]
    a. sub-categorize Event as /(material action of disposal involving change in location) NOT inherently repetitive/

BENEFACTION options are concerned with specifying the benefit of the activity. [beneficile] implies that the activity is capable of permitting the indication of some benefiting party; [non-beneficile] implies that the activity is not capable of permitting such indication. On [beneficile] depend the options [inherent] or [potential]. [inherent] implies that the benefiting party MUST be specified; [potential] that the benefiting party MAY be specified: the resource is there; it may or may not be taken up. [+benefactive] implies that the resource is to be positively deployed, and a benefiting party is to be specified. [−benefactive] implies that the resource has been passed up, and so no benefiting party is to be specified. When the benefiting party is specified—as entailed by the selection of either [inherent] or [+benefactive]—the option between [reflexive] and [non-reflexive] operates. It is concerned with the specification of the benefiting party's identity. [reflexive] implies that the Agent and the benefiting party are one and the same; [non-reflexive], that they are not the same. The selection of the latter permits the selection between [simple] and [complex]—both being concerned with providing further details about the benefiting party. [simple] implies that only one benefiting party is to be specified; [complex], that two discrete benefiting parties are to be specified. The remaining two options—[free] and [constrained]—will be discussed later. Here I provide the instructions attached to the BENEFACTION options presented so far:

E: 1. [non-beneficial]
    a. sub-categorize Event as /(material action) INCAPABLE of requiring function Benefiter/
    b. outclassify function Benefiter
2. [beneficile]
    a. sub-categorize Event as /(material action) CAPABLE of requiring function Benefiter(s)/
3. [inherent]
    a. insert function Benefiter-1
    b. sub-categorize Benefiter-1 as Recipient
    c. Benefiter pre-selects nominal group with Thing animate
    d. sub-categorize Event as /(material action) NECESSARILY requiring Benefiter/
4. [potential]
    a. sub-categorize Event as /(material action) NOT NECESSARILY requiring Benefiter/
5. [+benefactive]
    a. sub-categorize Event as /(material action) requiring Benefiter/
    b. insert function Benefiter-1
    c. sub-categorize Benefiter-1 as Client
    d. Benefiter pre-selects nominal group with Thing animate
6. [−benefactive]
    a. sub-categorize Events as /(material action) not needing Benefiter/
7. [reflexive]
    a. Benefiter pre-selects (nominal group with Thing animate) and co-referential with Agent
8. [non-reflexive]
    a. Benefiter pre-selects (nominal group with Thing animate) NOT co-referential with Agent
9. [simple]
    a. outclassify Benefiter-2
10. [complex]
    a. insert Benefiter-2
    b. Benefiter-2 pre-selects (nominal group with Thing animate not co-referential with Agent)
    c. sub-categorize Benefiter-2 as Ultimate Client
    d. Ultimate Client pre-selects prepositional group with preposition *for*
    e. conflate functions Ultimate Client and Prepositional Complement
    f. order Prepositional Complement to follow *for*

The notion 'benefiting party' or Benefiter is not self-evident. As Halliday (1985: 135) points out, the Benefiter does not necessarily benefit in the every-day sense of the word as shown by *Jocasta gave Claudius a dose of poison*. Again, in *John drove to the office*, from a common-sense point of view, John could be said to benefit from his driving. So it is important to point out that not only is the function Benefiter at the 'receiving end', but also it is recognized only if there is a dissociation between it and the Agent. The limiting case of the Benefiter is with the option [reflexive], where the benefiting party is co-referential with the Agent (see E7a above). But even here the meaning of Agent^Process^Medium is not the same as Agent^Process^Benefiter^Medium. Consider:

(2a) Susan bought a dress   (Agent^Process^Medium)
(2b) Susan bought herself a dress (Agent^Process^Benefiter^Medium)

Although in the absence of Good Reason, (2a) would be interpreted as Susan buying the dress for herself, the possibility is always open that this may not be the case; with (2b) this indeterminacy does not exist. Compare:

(3) Susan couldn't find a better present for Pam,
    (a) So she bought a dress.
    (b) so she bought herself a dress.

Because Susan's buying a dress does not have to be interpreted as Susan buying it for herself, so (3a) in this context can be 'read' as 'she bought a dress as a present for Pam'. (3b) does not permit this reading and will remain odd unless further appropriate speech work is done. The impossibility of conflating the Agent and Benefiter roles is important, as we shall see later.

The differences between [beneficile:inherent] and [beneficile:potential: +benefactive] are also important. Consider:

(4) I gave John a book.   [beneficile:inherent]
(5) I bought John a book. [beneficile:potential:+benefactive]

In (4), the function Benefiter is entailed (E3a and d); in (5) it is simply permitted. *I gave a book* implies an implicit Benefiter (Hasan 1984, for implied vs. implicit); *I bought a book* does not. This aspect of the meaning of *buy* is captured by assuming that the BENEFACTION options underlying this item are [beneficile:potential]. Note the difference in the Benefiter roles inserted in response to [inherent] (E3b) and [+benefactive] (E5c) respectively. When combined with the option [simple], the Benefiter role for the former is more specifically Recipient, for the latter, Client. If the selection expression contains both the option [non-iterative] and [simple], then under certain specifiable conditions, the Recipient and Client-roles can be mapped on to Circumstance. If so, Circumstance will pre-select a prepositional group, which in the former case will pre-select the preposition *to* and, in the latter, *for*, with the Benefiter nominal group as its Complement. The result in the case of (4) and (5) would be:

(4a) I gave a book to John.   [non-iterative; . . . :inherent:
                                                  simple . . .]
(5a) I bought a book for John.   [non-iterative; . . . :+benefactive:
                                                  simple . . .]

The difference between [inherent] and [+benefactive] is displayed even more sharply if, instead of [simple], the option [complex] is selected. This option inserts the function Ultimate Client (E10c), which can only pre-select a prepositional group, initiated by *for*, with the Benefiter nominal group as Complement. (4) and (5) would then be:

(4b) I gave John a book for Iona.   [non-iterative; . . . inherent:
                                                                    complex]
(5b) I bought John a book for Iona.   [non-iterative; . . . +benefactive:
                                                                    complex]

Again, under certain specifiable conditions (4b)- but not (5b)- can take the following forms:

(4c) I gave a book to John for Iona.
(4d) I gave a book for Iona to John.

Parallel to the above we do not have:

(5c) I bought a book to/for John for Iona.
(5d) I bought a book for Iona to/for John.

A related observation is that while underlying (4e) would be [complex] (with Recipient implied and implicit), (5e) can only be read as [simple]:

(4e) I gave a book for Iona.
(5e) I bought a book for Iona.

The distinction between Recipient and Client as well as that between Client and Ultimate Client appears motivated. Note that when Ultimate Client is inserted, this creates a point of identity in the semantic value of Recipient and Client: both are a means whereby the Medium is passed to the Client. Many interesting questions arising from these details must be shelved, as this much will suffice for the discussion of the [iterative] processes, which is the main focus here. But two generalizations appear appropriate: first, a function inserted by two distinct options—e.g. Benefiter-1 inserted by [inherent] or by [+benefactive]—is not identical in ALL respects; and second, the semantic value of an option—the meanings that it constructs—depends on the environment of that option.

Returning to systems of ACCESS and CHARACTER, the combination of [iterative] and [acquisition] is the entry condition for choice between [unitary] and [neutral]. The combined PI of [iterative;acquisition] is the conjunction of C1 and D1a–b. The instructions for the [unitary] and [neutral] are:

F: 1.   [unitary]
    a. Medium pre-selects nominal group with Thing /(alienable, divisible) and plural/
    2.   [neutral]
    a. Medium pre-selects nominal group with Thing /(alienable, divisible) and plural OR non-count/

Ignoring BENEFACTION, the selection expressions of PROCESS up to this point are:

(i) [material:action:disposal:acquisition;iterative:unitary]
(ii) [material:action:disposal:acquisition;iterative:neutral]

Note that [unitary] is the endpoint of one path in Figure 7.2. Does it specify any unit of form that may be a recognizable lexical item? I claim that the linguistic unit capable of realizing the Event in selection expression (i) must refer to an activity which is concrete, involves change in the location of the Medium, is inherently repetitive, leads to the Agent's gain of access to the Medium, and is such that the Medium is constrained to be 'plural'. In English the only linguistic form that can meet all these requirements is *gather*. The formulation of the realization statement (C1;D1a–b;F1a), while permitting (6c), throws light on the source of the oddity of (6a–b):

(6a) Leonie gathered the water/meat in the bowl.
(6b) Leonie gathered one book from her shelf.
(6c) Leonie gathered some roses from the garden.

Selection expression (ii) does not represent the endpoint of a path; dependent upon [neutral] are the options [+vast] and [unmarked]. Nonetheless, taking the selection expression as it stands, it can be said confidently that a form capable of functioning as Event here must differ from *gather* at least in one respect: it should be capable of 'taking' a Medium in which the Thing may be either [plural] or [non-count]. Ignoring the archaic *amass* altogether, in English there appear to be only two lexical items suiting these requirements: *collect* and *accumulate*.

I believe we need to recognize that the orthographic word *collect* is the expression for two distinct—even if related—lexical items: *collect-1*, which is an antonym of *deposit*, and *collect-2*, which is an antonym of *scatter/strew*. Only the latter *collect* is [iterative] and thus subject to the requirement D1b. You can deposit one book or collect it from the library, but you cannot scatter/strew one book or collect it in the sense of *collect-2*. Again, *collect-1* appears to be [non-beneficile]; this is not true of *collect-2* (compare *I collected Iona her son from the school*, which is odd, with *I collected Iona some flowers*, which is quite unremarkable). Given F2, the following are perfectly ordinary English clauses:

(7a) Susan collected the water in the bowl.
(7b) Susan collected some leaves from the garden.

But what about *accumulate*? It is at this point that the final option between [+vast] and [unmarked] is needed. Compare:

(8a) Susan collected some solution.
(8b) Susan accumulated some solution.
(8c) Susan accumulated gallons of solution.
(9a) Leonie collected two dollars.
(9b) Leonie accumulated two dollars.
(9c) Leonie accumulated thousands of dollars.

Of these triplets, only the member (b) appears odd, and traditionally it would be described as 'stylistically infelicitous'. But style is not independent of grammar; a delicate grammar can point to the source of stylistic infelicity, as in this case. The instructions for [+vast] and [unmarked] are:

G: 1.   [+vast]
   a. Medium pre-selects nominal group with Thing /(alienable, divisible, plural or non-count) NECESSARILY indicating high degree of extent/
   2.   [unmarked]
   a. Medium pre-selects nominal group with Thing /(alienable, divisible, plural or non-count) indicating any degree of vastness/

These instructions provide a basis for explaining why, side by side with (8a), (8c) and (9a), (9c), we may also have:

(8d) Susan collected gallons of the solution.
(9d) Leonie collected thousands of dollars.

and why of (8a–d) and (9a–d) only the (b) member appears stylistically infelicitous. Note also that of the three lexical items yielded by the network so far, *collect* is the most 'versatile', by virtue of the options [neutral:unmarked] (see F2a/G2a). I would suggest that of the three [acquisition;iterative] processes, *collect* would be the most frequently used and *accumulate* the least. If this hypothesis is empirically substantiated, this would imply that a delicate grammar can point to a non-random relationship between the frequency of a particular linguistic unit and its selection expression.

[disposal] options are concurrent with the BENEFACTION ones. Thus although the unique identity of three lexical items has been already established, more can and must be said about them. In the environment of [disposal] BENEFACTION options carry implications for ACCESS. The combination of [acquisition] and [beneficile] implies that the Agent's gain of access to the Medium can be passed over to some Benefiter(s). Interestingly, [acquisition] combines most frequently with [beneficile:potential], though some exceptions can be found, e.g. *snatch*, *grab* or *inherit*. The combination of [deprivation] and [beneficile] implies that the Agent's loss of access to the Medium is some Benefiter's gain of access to that Medium. [deprivation] combines readily either with [beneficile:inherent] or with [non-beneficile]; it is rare for it to combine with [beneficile:potential], though, again, exceptions can be found, e.g. *scatter* or *throw*.

Assuming that the systemic paths originating at the conjunction of [acquisition;iterative] lead to the selection of Event which can only be expressed as *gather*, *collect* or *accumulate* as shown above, we may claim that the conjunction of options [acquisition;iterative] carries an instruction:

C1a–D1a: [acquisition;iterative]
   a. Process pre-selects options [beneficile:potential]

This is tantamount to claiming that there is no process in English whose selection expression contains [acquisition;iterative], but not [beneficile:potential]. If this is true, then *gather*, *collect* and *accumulate* should each be capable of 'taking' the function Benefiter; and this is indeed the case. In the examples of these lexical items above, the BENEFACTION selection has been [beneficile:potential:−benefactive]; but the selection [beneficile:potential:+benefactive] is also possible. But at this point some delicate distinctions between *accumulate* and the other two lexical items come to light. Consider:

(10a) I gathered Jenny some flowers.
(10b) I gathered some flowers for Jenny.
(11a) I collected the kids some water in the bowl.
(11b) I collected some water in the bowl for the kids.
(12a) ? Leonie accumulated John great wealth.
(12b) Leonie accumulated great wealth for John.

To use traditional terminology, of the three items, *accumulate* alone cannot 'take a direct beneficiary'. There are at least three possible ways of interpreting this difference: First, underlying *accumulate* is the option [nonbeneficile] instead of [beneficile:potential]. If so, we imply that *for John* (12b) has a radically different function from *for Jenny* (10b) and *for the kids* (11b), but this is dubious. Second, *for John* is the Ultimate Client because this Benefiter function is always realized only prepositionally (see E10c–d) where the prepositional group takes the form *for + Benefiter*. Against this solution, I would draw attention to (4e)–(5e), and the fact that according to E10c, Ultimate Client is a more specific label for Benefiter-2. Unlike *gather* and *collect*, *accumulate* cannot take a Benefiter-2:

(10c) I gathered Jenny some flowers for her mother.
(11c) I collected the kids some water in a bowl for their dog.
(12c) ? Leonie accumulated John great wealth for his children.

To treat *for John* as an Ultimate Client in (12b) would contradict the generalization that this function is inserted only if the function Recipient/Client is systemically 'present' as in (4b) and (5b). Third, in the final interpretation, *for John* (12b) is a Client, implying that its function is similar to *for Jenny* (10b) or *for the kids* (11b). Each has the role Benefiter-1 (=Client); however, to (10) and (11) apply certain systemic options from INFORMATION, to which (12) is not susceptible. If the option [beneficile:potential:+benefactive] combines with [(acquisition;iterative):neutral:+vast], then the item capable of acting as Event—i.e. *accumulate*—cannot take a direct Benefiter; it is constrained to take a Benefactive Circumstance, as in (12b) but not in (10) or (11). In this respect, then, *for John* (12b) differs from *for Jenny* (10b) and *for the kids* (11b). I take the last solution as the most acceptable, largely because cases comparable to (12b) will be found at least in the environment of the option [iterative].

   This insight is built into the network by indicating that, concurrent with the option [simple] vs. [complex], another systematic choice operates open to any clause whose selection expression contains both [iterative] and [... nonreflexive]. The terms are [free] and [constrained]. The instructions for [constrained] are:

H. 1.   [constrained]
     a. Client pre-selects prepositional group with preposition *for*
     b. Recipient pre-selects prepositional group with preposition *to/ between/amongst*

    c. conflate Benefiter-1 with Prepositional Complement
    d. order Prepositional complement to follow preposition

Option [constrained], then, acts upon function Benefiter-1 alone, irrespective of whether it combines with [simple] or [complex]. The two important aspects of the option are (a) that Client/Recipient are constrained as specified above (H1a–d), and (b) that certain specific INFORMATION options do not apply to it. In passing, note that characteristic (b), but not (a), is common also to clauses whose selection expression contains [potential:+benefactive:non-reflexive:complex]; but if characteristic (a) is lacking, they would not be said to contain option [constrained]. The point of similarity between the [constrained] and [potential:+benefactive:non-reflexive:complex:free], as exemplified by (5b), (10c) and (11c), can be indicated by a realization statement which would demand pre-selection of some specific INFORMATION option(s).

To summarize the discussion so far, the following array of selection expressions will require that the Event be expressed either by *gather* or *collect* or *accumulate*. Common to each member of the array are the following options:

[material:action:disposal:acquisition;iterative;beneficile:potential]

These options are not repeated but assumed present in each member of the array below:

    I: [:unitary;−benefactive]
                  Event = *gather* e.g. (6c)
    II: [:unitary;+benefactive:non-reflexive:simple;free]
                  Event = *gather* e.g. (10a–b)
    III: [:unitary;+benefactive:non-reflexive:complex;free]
                  Event = *gather* e.g. (10c)
    IV: [:neutral:+vast;−benefactive]
                  Event = *accumulate* e.g. [8c, 9c)
    V: [:neutral:+vast;+benefactive:non-reflexive:simple;constrained]
                  Event = *accumulate* e.g. (12b)
    VI: [:neutral:unmarked;−benefactive]
                  Event = *collect* e.g. (7a, 7b)
    VII: [:neutral:unmarked;+benefactive:non-reflexive:simple;free]
                  Event = *collect* e.g. (11a, 11b)
    VIII: [:neutral:unmarked;+benefactive:non-reflexive:complex;free]
                  Event = *collect* e.g. (11c)

7.3 THE LEXICO-GRAMMAR OF DEPRIVATION I: SCATTER,
    DIVIDE, DISTRIBUTE

Turning now to the options permitted by the combination of [deprivation] and [iterative], the BENEFACTION options have to be taken into account from the very start. This implies that the basis of distinction between the various [deprivation] processes lies not only in whether they are [iterative] or not but also whether they are [beneficile] or not. When [deprivation;itera-tive;beneficile] combine, this presents a complex entry condition for a choice between [random] vs. [planned]. The former implies that there is no particular design to the disposition of the Medium, while the latter implies an activity in which the disposition of the Medium follows a more or less equitable design. Note the PI for these options is a combination of C2,D1a–b,E2a; and the instructions attached to them are:

J: 1.   [random]
   a. (co-select option [potential]
   b. sub-categorize Medium Thing as /(alienable, divisible) plural or
      non-count, solid/
   2.   [planned]
   a. co-select option [inherent]
   b. sub-categorize Benefiter-1 as /(animate) non-singular/

As [random] represents the endpoint of one systemic path, the selection expression containing the option can be stated as follows:

(iii) [material:action:disposal:deprivation;iterative;beneficile:potential]

In English, the only lexical item capable of functioning as the Event in a clause with the above selection expression is *scatter*. Although the item *strew* resembles it in certain respects, it will not suit the requirements of [beneficile:potential], for this implies that a clause of this kind can 'take' the function *Benefiter*. With *strew* this possibility is not open (consider *she strewed the pigeons some breadcrumbs*).
    Given J1a–b, (13a–b) are normal clauses of English; (13c) is not:

(13a) she scattered her clothes all over the place.
(13b) she scattered the toys on the floor.
(13c) she scattered juice on the table.

Given the presence of [potential] in (iii), the option between [−benefactive] and [+benefactive] applies. (13a–b) present examples of the former option, while underlying (14) is the option [+benefactive]:

(14) she scattered the pigeons some breadcrumbs.

The selection of [+benefactive] has a somewhat interesting by-product: it creates an impression of intentionality, which is absent from (13a–b). This may not be just an accidental feature of this particular lexical item; so compare *she broke a stick* vs. *she broke them a stick* and *she found a sixpence* vs. *she found them a sixpence*.
    When the options [random] and [+benefactive] combine, this seems to bear a consequence for the nominal group pre-selected by the Benefiter: not only does the Thing have to be animate, but there is a very strong probability of it being non-human. Compare (14) with (15):

(15) she scattered the children some bread.

(15) conjures up a picture of a nasty female—perhaps the traditional stepmother in a fairytale. Again, [+benefactive:non-reflexive] allows either the selection of [simple] or of [complex], though with [random] the probability of the selection of [simple] is much higher than that of [complex]. We would rarely find clauses such as (16):

(16) She scattered the pigeons breadcrumbs for their chicks.

Although (15) and (16) may be less frequent than (13a) or (14), neither is odd, unlike (13c). So while (13c) would be attributed to a mistake, (15) will be seen as playing upon that part of the meaning of *scatter*, constructed by [random], while the rarity of (16) might arise from a combination of [random] and [+benefactive:non-reflexive:complex]. The former implies that the Medium is being disposed of without any particular design, whereas the selection of the option [+benefactive] raises the possibility of the Agent having a particular design for the disposal of the Medium. Specifically, the selection of the Ultimate Client (which is inserted in response to [complex]; see E10a–f) goes against the lack of a particular design for the disposal of the Medium. So it would appear that all these important facts about *scatter* can be stated without adding any more options to the network in Figure 7.2. The array of selection expressions which would require that the Event be expressed as *scatter* are now described.

Common to each member of the array are the following options, which will be assumed present in IX–XI:

[material:action:disposal:deprivation;iterative;beneficile:potential]

IX: [:random;−benefactive]
$$\text{Event} = scatter \text{ e.g. (13a, 13b)}$$
X: [:random;+benefactive:non-reflexive:complex:free]
$$\text{Event} = scatter \text{ e.g. (16)}$$
XI: [:random;+benefactive:non-reflexive:simple:free
$$\text{Event} = scatter \text{ e.g. (14)}$$

There may be one problem with the description of *scatter* presented here. I have implied that if option [free] is present, then with the selection of certain options from the INFORMATION system, the function Client would be realized as a Benefactive Circumstance. More specifically, the prepositional group would take the form *for*+Benefiter-1 nominal group. The proportion between (14) and (14a) is the same as that between (10a) and (10b):

(14a) she scattered some breadcrumbs for the pigeons.

But is (14b) also an equally normal clause?

(14b) she scattered some breadcrumbs to the pigeons.

If so, then *scatter* would appear to allow a Benefactive Circumstance, which is allowed to occur only if the Benefiter-1 role is sub-categorized as Recipient; and I have argued that this role only occurs if the option [inherent] is selected (see e.g. 4b–4e). If *scatter* is neutral as between taking Recipient or Client, then the instruction J1a is incorrect; and the network is misleading. However, while I am certain that (14a) is a perfectly normal clause, I am not certain about the status of (14b). So I shall leave the discussion of *scatter* with this query.

[planned] permits a choice between [indeterminate] and [determinate]. The instructions are as follows:

K: 1. [indeterminate]
    a. sub-categorize Medium Thing as /(alienable, divisible) singular, plural or non-count/
    b. co-select options [inherent] and [constrained]
   2. [determinate]
    a. sub-categorize Medium Thing as /(alienable, divisible) plural or non-count (i.e. outclassify singular)
    b. co-select options [inherent] and [free]

The implication is that if the option [indeterminate] is selected, then any item capable of acting as the Event can take a singular/plural/non-count noun as Thing in the Medium; the activity must imply a Recipient (as for *give*, cf. e.g. (4a–4e)); and the Recipient can only take the form of a Benefactive Circumstance, where the prepositional group begins with *to/between/among*. The only lexical item in English capable of meeting these requirements is *divide*. Like *collect*, *divide* expresses two distinct lexical items: *divide-1* which is roughly synonymous with *cut*, and is an antonym of *join*; the closest in meaning to *divide-2* is the item *distribute*, or the archaic *apportion*; its closest antonym is the iterative *collect*, and possibly *hoard*. I am concerned only with *divide-2* here. Together with the PI of [indeterminate], K1a–b explicitly allow for the following

(17a) she divided the apple between John and Jenny.
(17b) she divided the sweets amongst the children.
(17c) the Head of School divided the money between the two research directors for their assistants.

Note how (17a) differs from (18a–b):

(18a) she divided John and Jenny an apple.
(18b) she divided an apple for John and Jenny.

The *divide* in (18a–b) is *divide-1*, not a material action of disposal but of transformation. This *divide* does not have [inherent] BENEFACTION; so it is also possible to say (18c) without implying a Benefiter role:

(18c) she divided an apple (in half).

How right Whorf was in maintaining that 'we are all mistaken in our belief that any word has an "exact meaning" . . . the reference of the words is at the mercy of the sentences and the grammatical patterns in which they occur.' (Whorf 1956: 258–9). It is only by constructing delicate grammars that we can show which grammatical patterns determine what reference for some linguistic form. The description of *divide* as of *collect* perhaps shows clearly that it is more important to devise ways of making explicit 'reactances' between units of linguistic form than to concentrate on ways of segmenting given strings, and reordering and labelling the products of the segmentation.

The combination of [deprivation;iterative;beneficile:inherent] has another consequence, captured in J2b: the nominal group pre-selected by the Benefiter must have the feature plural. Note the difference between (17a) and (18d–e):

(18d) she divided John an apple.
(18e) she divided an apple for John.

The [iterative] *divide* is said to have the option [constrained] precisely because Benefiter-1 can never occur as a direct beneficiary. The option [inherent] is said to be pre-selected because Benefiter-1 will always be interpreted as a Recipient (as with *give*, *sell*, *lend*). These features, together with the option [planned], might explain why the Benefactive circumstance can be realized only by a prepositional group with *between* or *amongst*. But I believe that another aspect of [planned] processes is important here. Just as the selection of [+benefactive] with [random] (*scatter*) creates the impression of intentionality, so also the combination of [inherent] and [planned] is capable of creating an impression of 'exhaustivity'. (17b), for example, creates the impression that after the dividing is done 'the sweets' are exhausted, though this impression can be overridden by indicating otherwise (e.g. *she divided some of the sweets amongst the children*). Note, however, the difference between:

(19a) she distributed some medicine to the refugees.
(19b) she distributed some medicine amongst the refugees.

I feel that only (19b) creates the impression that 'some medicine' was exhausted after the distributing was done. If this is so, this may provide a better explanation for the selection of *between/amongst* with *divide*, which may be said to carry the connotation of exhaustivity, unless otherwise indicated. Note that further detail will be needed to differentiate between the selection of *between* and *amongst*, but perhaps the lines along which this may be done are clear enough not to need discussion.

The array of selection expressions requiring that the Event be expressed as *divide* are entered below (XII–XIII). Common to each are the following selections, which are not repeated in the individual arrays:

[material:action:disposal:deprivation;iterative;beneficile:inherent:non-reflexive]

XII: [:indeterminate;simple;constrained]
                                Event = *divide* e.g. (17a, 17b)
XIII: [:indeterminate;complex;free]
                                Event = *divide* e.g. (17c)

If the option [determinate] applies, the implication is that any item capable of acting as the Event cannot take a singular noun as Thing in the Medium; the activity must imply a Recipient (this is, of course, in addition to all the characteristics inherited through the PI up to this point). The lexical item that will meet all of the requirements is *distribute*. Compare (17a) and (20a):

(20a) she distributed an apple to the children.

Again, if we have *they distributed some medicine*, a Recipient is implied in the same way as it is in *I'm giving a book (as a present)*. I am treating *distribute* as having the option [free] (see K2b). This implies that it can take a direct Benefiter-1, as in:

(20b) the government distributed the peasants a new high-yielding variety of wheat seeds.

The option between [simple] and [complex] also applies:

(20c) to celebrate the event, they distributed everyone bags of sweets.
(20d) on Mother's Day, we distributed the children presents for their mums.

Note that the non-singularity of the Benefiter can be indicated in different ways, and it is likely that the sub-categorization statements in K1a–2a will need to be formulated more carefully. Consider:

(21a) she distributed pamphlets to the students.
(21b) she distributed a pamphlet to each student.
(21c) ? she distributed pamphlets/a pamphlet to a student.

The array of selection expressions requiring that the event be expressed as *distribute* are entered below (XIV–XV). Common to each are the same selections, shown above for XII–XIII, and these are not repeated:

XIV: [:determinate;simple;free]
                    Event = *distribute* e.g. (20a, 20b, 20c)
  XV: [:determinate;complex;free]
                    Event = *distribute* e.g. (20d)

7.4 THE LEXICO-GRAMMAR OF DEPRIVATION 2: STREW, SPILL, SHARE

The above section concludes the description of processes which combine [deprivation;iterative;beneficile]. When [deprivation;iterative] combine with [non-beneficile], this acts as a multiple entry condition for the options [independent] vs. [cooperative]. The option [cooperative] implies that the activity cannot be carried out without a 'co-doer'. So that just as a Recipient is always 'present' in a clause with the option [inherent], so a function I shall call Cooperant is always 'present' in a clause with [cooperative] as in (*Eric is so sweet) he always shares his toys*. When the option is [independent], the function Cooperant is not permitted; in this sense, then, I am making a distinction between 'joint' doing as in *Eric and Jim played with the toys*, and cooperancy as in *Eric shared his toys with Jim*. The instructions for the two are:

L: 1.　　[independent]
　　　a. sub-categorize Event as /(material action inherently repetitive, leading to Agent's loss of access to Medium, incapable of requiring Benefiter) and NOT INHERENTLY REQUIRING a co-doer/
　　2.　　[cooperative]
　　　a. sub-categorize Event as /(material action inherently repetitive, leading to Agent's loss of access to Medium, incapable of requiring Benefiter) and INHERENTLY REQUIRING function Cooperant/

[independent] is the entry condition to two options, which are so obvious they do not need much discussion. They lead to the sub-categorization of the Medium as follows:

M. 1.　　[+solid]
　　　a. sub-categorize Medium Thing as (alienable, divisible) plural or count, solid/
　　2.　　[+liquid]
　　　a. sub-categorize Medium Thing as (alienable divisible) liquid

The options [independent:+solid] require that the Event be realized by *strew*, while the options [independent:+liquid] require that it be realized by *spill*. It may be argued that *scatter* is a possibility for the former; but note that *scatter* has also the options [beneficile:potential]. When this combines with [. . . :−benefactive], there would appear to be some inter-changeability between *strew* and *scatter*. So we can have:

(22a) she had scattered everything on the floor.
(22b) she had strewn everything on the floor.

But, as lexical items, *scatter* and *strew* cannot be said to be exactly alike. There are no such clauses as:

(23a) she strewed the pigeons some breadcrumbs.
(23b) she strewed some breadcrumbs for the pigeons.

Another question may be raised: why should option [independent] be recognized in the case of *strew* but not in that of *scatter*? This is because it is only in the environment of [deprivation;iterative;non-beneficile] that the contrast carries any significance, since all other [disposal] processes are uniformly like *strew* in not being able to require the function Cooperant. As a lexical item, *strew* appears far less frequently than *scatter*; and this may be because *scatter* can do everything that *strew* can and also some more things which *strew* cannot do, e.g. take a Benefiter.

Spill differs from *strew* only in that its Medium must 'be' liquid. Note the metaphoric nature of *spill the beans* and *spill his guts*. Here is an example of *spill* comparable to (22b):

(22c) the waiter spilt soup on her dress.

Turning to the option [cooperative], it is best first to develop the notion of the function Cooperant. A Cooperant differs both from a Benefiter and from the informal notion 'joint doer'. A Benefiter, I have argued above, is not only always at the receiving end but must also be dissociated from an Agent. This is not true of Cooperant. Consider:

(24) they shared the sweets.

This clause would be interpreted as *they shared the sweets between/amongst themselves*. But if so, this is because the functions Agent and Cooperant are both systemically present and realized by *they*. Compare (24) with:

(24a) he shared the sweets.

Here the Cooperant is both implied and implicit; notwithstanding the absence of explicit mention of a Cooperant, the assumption is that the function is essential, since in the absence of the Cooperant the activity of sharing cannot be undertaken. So, unlike a Benefiter, a Cooperant is neither at the receiving end nor does it necessarily have to be disassociated from the Agent, though it can be as in:

(24b) John shared the sweets with Jenny.

In (24b) the function Cooperant is realized by *with Jenny*, that of the Agent by *John*.
    Cooperant is also different from 'joint doer'. In

(25a) they walked together to the station.
(25b) Eric walked to the station with Jim.

there is no cooperant function. In the first place, the activity of walking can be carried out without two or more persons' involvement; secondly, no matter how many persons function as the Agent, each is responsible for his/her own action. Not so with *share*. Sharing cannot be done without involvement of at least two persons; and the action of one is a condition for that of the other. There are certain non-disposal-type processes that resemble *share* in this respect, e.g. *marry*, *fight*, *meet*, *agree*. But of the disposal process as *share* alone has this characteristic. And although *sell*, *lend* might appear to be like *share*, there is an important difference. In

(26) John sold/lent Melanie a car

although John and Melanie are involved in the same exchange, their roles *vis-à-vis* the Event are not the same. If John shared sweets with Jenny, then it follows that Jenny shared sweets with John; but if John sold Melanie a car, it does not follow that Melanie sold John a car.
    But if the relationship of the Cooperant and the Agent to the activity is the same, then why should two separate functions of Agent and Cooperant be recognized? The simple answer is because the functions can be separated from each other. We would not need to dissociate the functions Subject and Actor and Theme, if, under certain specifiable conditions, each could not be realized by a different constituent of the clause. Moreover, there is a meaningful distinction between (24b) and (24c):

(24c) John and Jenny shared the sweets.

In (24b), John is likely to be seen as the one who had prior access to the sweets; (24c) is neutral about the prior ownership of the sweets. Moreover, (24b) leaves no room for indeterminacy; (24c) does, as comparison with (24d) shows:

(24d) John and Jenny shared the sweets with Benny.

It is important, then, to recognize a distinction between [discrete] and [fused]—the two options shown to depend on [cooperation]. The option [discrete] would carry the following instructions:

N: 1.   [discrete]
    a. insert function Cooperant
    b. Cooperant pre-selects prepositional group with preposition *with*
    c. conflate Cooperant with Prepositional Complement
    d. Prepositional Complement pre-selects nominal group animate not co-referential with Agent
    e. order Prepositional Complement to follow preposition *with*

Underlying (24b) then would be the options [:cooperative:discrete], while underlying (24c) would be [:cooperative:fused]. The only instructions for [fused] are:

N. 2.   [fused]
    a. insert function Cooperant
    b. Cooperant pre-selects nominal group animate

This option is the entry condition for a further systemic choice between [Agent-oriented] and [Medium-oriented]. (24c) exemplifies the former; an example of the latter would be:

(24e) John shared Jenny's sweets.

I suggest that in the absence of a Good Reason, (24e) would be interpreted as 'John and Jenny shared the sweets and the sweets were Jenny's'. This is one reason why it is possible to clinch the matter by saying:

(24f) John shared Jenny's sweets with her.

The instructions for the last pair of options are as follows:

P: 1.   [Agent-oriented]
    a. pre-select nominal group complex
    b. pre-select additive complexing conjunction *and*
    c. order Agent to precede *and*
    d. order Cooperant to follow *and*
  2.   [Medium-oriented]
    a. Cooperant pre-selects possessive - *'s*
    b. conflate Cooperant with Possessive Modifier in Medium

The difference between (24d) and (24f) is important. In the former, *with Benny* is Cooperant, while John and Jenny are (joint) Agent. In (24f), the function of *with her* is different; it is a kind of 'marking' and I am assuming that the option(s) that govern its appearance do not belong to TRANSITIVITY, but to options from some other system network which is the output of textual meta-function. Such marking can also occur with [Agent-oriented] as in:

(24g) John and Jenny shared the sweets with each other.

Note that the prepositional groups here are constrained to be co-referential with the Cooperant; thus if (24f) had been *John shared Ben's sweets*, then the prepositional group would have been *with him*. I shall not pursue this any further here, but conclude with the comment that the only lexical item capable of acting as the Event in a clause with options [deprivation;iterative;non-beneficile;cooperative] is *share*.

The array of selection expressions requiring that the Event be expressed as *strew* or *spill* or *share* is presented below (XVI–XX). The selections common to each and so not repeated are:

[material:action:disposal;iterative;non-beneficile]

XVI: [:independent:+solid]

Event = *strew* e.g. (22b)

XVII: [:independent:+liquid]

Event = *spill*   e.g. (22c)

XVIII: [:cooperative:discrete]

Event = *share* e.g (24b, 24d)

XIX: [:cooperative:fused:Agent-oriented]

Event = *share* e.g. (24c, 24g)

XX: [:cooperative:fused:Medium-oriented]

Event = *share* e.g. (24e, 24f)

7.5 THE CONTINUITY OF GRAMMAR AND LEXIS

The above discussion has, hopefully, established nine distinct lexical items:

gather	scatter	strew
collect	divide	spill
accumulate	distribute	share

Common to these lexical verbs is the characteristic that they can function as the Event in clauses whose selection expression contains the options [disposal] and [iterative]. There appear to be some seventy-odd [non-iterative] [disposal] processes. It has not been possible to discuss any of these for reasons of space; this is a natural concomitant of attempting to write a delicate grammar. However, I hope that the description will permit the claim that the project of turning the whole of linguistic form into grammar is feasible. In fact I believe that I have demonstrated not only that 'lexis' equals 'delicate grammar' but also that there is [grammar beyond lexis]. So far as *gather*, *collect* and *accumulate* are concerned, their unique identity *vis-à-vis* each other can be established by virtue of the options [unitary], [neutral], [+vast] and [unmarked]. To show the combination of these with BENEFACTION options is to do grammar after lexis, which has hopefully led to a better understanding of the identities and differences between members of the paradigm.

It needs to be made quite clear that the description presented here of the nine items is not complete. This follows from assumption (7) in section 7.1. The account is simply the output of one meta-function—the experiential. In the description of larger linguistic units, e.g. the clause, the validity of assumption (7) has been demonstrated by Martin 1984, Fawcett 1980, Halliday 1969; 1970; 1977; 1985, Mann and Matthiessen 1983, Young 1980, and others. It remains to be seen whether the postulate of concurrent multiple structures extends right down the rank scale to the smaller units, e.g. the lexical item. A priori there seems no reason to rule out this possibility; rather there is some favourable suggestive evidence. For example, synonymy is a well-recognized concept, though a troublesome one (Leech 1974; Lyons 1977). If pairs such as *ask*, *enquire/ buy*, *purchase/ smile*, *grin/ cry*, *bawl* are examined closely, we are likely to find that while their experientially motivated grammatical structure is the same, their interpersonally motivated structure differs. A similar phenomenon is evident in *day*, *today* and *two*, *both*: both members of each pair are likely to have the same experientially motivated structure, though they most probably differ in their textually motivated structure. Unlike larger structures, the lexical item is unsegment-able; but if we accept that, in principle, different functions can be conflated on to the same segment, there would appear to be no reason for denying that a lexical item could be the expression of two or more conflated grammatical functions. These remarks are speculative, and are intended as an invitation to closer examination.

One may ask: What exactly is the basis of these options? Where do they come from? And isn't there some circularity? Is one simply pretending to start from the network as if it were *sui generis*, while in fact the options appear to be postulated precisely because certain lexical items are known to exist? I would answer this by saying that no matter what aspect of the lexico-grammar we describe, we are in the last analysis describing the possibilities of only that which is known to us, and this knowledge is based upon our experience of language. The options of the networks are not 'universals', 'primitives' or god-given truths: they are schematic pointers to man-made meanings which can be expressed verbally. The options are presented in certain relations to each other because this is how I understand English ways of meaning; they are not there because the making of any other kind of relation is impossible. For example, in Urdu, while there seems to be a close parallel to the options [unitary] vs. [neutral] (cf. tʃunnə and dʒʌmə kʌrnə), the distinction I needed to recognize by [+vast] vs. [unmarked] does not appear necessary. The networks REPRESENT a language; they do not INVENT it. Moreover, I doubt that any grammar can invent a language, though it can make an effort to distort other people's meanings to make them appear as replicas of, say, English meanings (cf. Hasan 1984).

Lack of space does not permit a detailed discussion of the implications of turning the whole of linguistic form into grammar, but if the account of the nine lexical items presented above has appeared valid, then it certainly upholds the systemic functional view of an uninterrupted continuity between grammar and lexis. It rejects the approach wherein the bricks of lexis are joined together by the mortar of grammar. The notion of the lexicon as an inventory of items, each having its own meaning in itself, stands refuted, and the insights of Saussure 1916, Firth 1935, Hjelmslev 1961, Whorf 1956 and Halliday 1961 are confirmed. The complex relation between the signification and value of a linguistic sign is also highlighted.

The concept of reference has been a problematical one in semantics (Lyons: 1977). The interpretation of the term 'reference' as an onomastic relation to existents is a limiting one, which arbitrarily cuts the sign system into two distinct areas: there are signs such as *tree* 'referring' to TREE, a concrete object, a member of a class 'out there'; and there are signs such as *gather*, *collect* which lack referents. This leaves the question unanswered: how is it that such signs make any contact with the world of action/state, which is the only reason for their existence? Why is it that where it will to do say *the book is in that bag*, it will not do to say *the book is on that bag*?

The description offered here implies that the ways in which the reference of *book* or *bag* is achieved is essentially the same as that for *is*, *in*, *on*, *that* and *the*. Saussure created an unnecessary enigma in his account of value and signification. In part this was due to the cleavage between *langue* and *parole*. Any viable account of reference will have to take *parole* into account, and this not just so that we know that the name *John* and *the man in blue jeans* may point to the same person. But *parole* dissociated from contexts of human living is an anomaly. The reason Malinowski 1923, 1935 was able to turn Saussure's relation of value and signification upside down (Hasan 1985) was that ways of saying—*parole* within contexts—is creative of the *langue*. This is how I understand Hjelmslev's comment that process determines system; a phenomenon cannot achieve the status of a process without systematicity. Value and signification are indeed two sides of the same coin. Looked at from the point of view of the system—the *langue*—we may claim that signification depends on value; looked at from the point of view of process—the *parole*—our claim would be that value depends upon what the speakers have consistently signified by sign—how it has meshed in with their structures of action and thought. Looking for meaning in use (Wittgenstein: 1958) implies looking at both kinds of use—how a sign combines or contrasts with other signs in a string or a paradigm and how (some part of) the string applies to the world.

This line of argument needs further exploration. In most linguistic writing today, there is an uneasy amalgamation of two irreconcilable views: language as the representation of meanings that exist *sui generis*, and language as the construction of meanings, whose existence is beholden to the existence of that network of relations which, for short, we call 'language'. From the latter point of view, what is called 'world knowledge' or 'knowledge structure' is largely constructed by language itself; from the former, it is divorced from language, so that 'knowledge of the world' and 'knowledge of language' are seen as two distinct concepts. Such a view can be criticized at least on two counts: in practice it presents the advanced Western peoples' knowledge of the world as

THE knowledge of the world; if to them the shape of that world appears eminently reasonable, it is only because they are not at the receiving end of being brainwashed into someone else's ideology. Secondly, current postulates of world knowledge fail to address the fascinating question of how the information constructed by the various semiotic systems is integrated into some kind of working whole. When interest in this question arises, a delicate grammar of the type presented here would be an essential prerequisite to the enquiry. The notion of PI explicitly points out that the implicational shadows of signs are very long indeed. Such grammar has the potential of making explicit the concepts of 'semantic inheritance' (Brachman 1979) and 'conceptual dependency' (Schank 1975). At the same time, it seems likely that it will be of considerable use in explaining much of what Wilkes's preferential semantics is based on (Wilkes 1978).

The Systemic Functional model has always rejected the absurd postulate that transformations are meaning preserving—a view that can be upheld only if semantics equals the experiential meta-function and certain parts of the interpersonal meta-function selected on an *ad hoc* basis. It has also rejected the view that the only valid form a grammar can take is to trace the genealogical relationship between transformationally related strings. Once these two presuppositions are removed, transformations are transformed into the relation of agnation; and the rationale for the existence of certain transformational possibilities can be made explicit on the basis of a grammar of the type presented here (Hasan 1971).

When the grammarian's dream comes true, it will in all likelihood enable us to throw better light on the notions of synonymy, antonymy and hyponymy. It will force us to make more explicit the basis of the distinction between 'grammatical item' and 'lexical item'. Also, I believe, it will help in making more precise Firth's view of collocation (Firth: 1951a). Meanwhile, in order to translate the dream into reality much work is needed. The beginning made here represents no more than an iota of the total potential of English language for constructing meanings.

NOTE

1. Compare the discussion of marking in section 1.3 of Martin's chapter.

BIBLIOGRAPHY

Benson, J. D. and Greaves, W. S. (eds) (1985), *Systemic Perspectives in Discourse: Vol. 1 Selected Theoretical Papers from the Ninth International Systemic Workshop*, Norwood, N.J. Ablex.
Berry, Margaret (1977), *An Introduction to Systemic Linguistics, 2 Levels and Links*, London, Batsford.
Bobrow, D. and Collins, A. (eds) (1975), *Representation and Understanding: Studies in Cognitive Psychology*, New York, Academic Press.

Brachman, R. J. (1979), 'On the epitemological status of semantic networks', in Findler (ed.) (1979).
Chomsky, N. (1965), *Aspects of the Theory of Syntax*, Cambridge, Mass., MIT Press.
Collins, A. M. and Quillian, M. R. (1972), 'Experiments on semantic memory and language comprehension', in Gregg (ed.) (1972).
Dijk, T. A. van and Petöfi, S. (eds) (1977), *Grammar and Descriptions*, Berlin, de Gruyter.
Fawcett, R. P. (1980), *Cognitive Linguistics and Social Interaction*, Exeter, Julius Groos Verlag and Exeter University.
Fawcett, R. P., Halliday, M. A. K., Lamb, S. M. and Makkai, A. (eds) (1985), *The Semiotics of Culture and Language: Vol. 1 Language as Social Semiotic*, London, Frances Pinter.
Fillmore, C. J. (1977), 'Topics in Lexical Semantics', in *Current Issues in Linguistic Theory*, Cole, R. W. (ed.). Bloomington, Indiana University Press.
Findler, N. V. (ed.) (1979), *Associative Networks: Representation and Use of Knowledge by Computers*, New York, Academic Press.
Firth, J. R. (1935), 'The technique of semantics', *Transactions of the Philological Society*, reprinted in Firth 1957.
—— (1951), 'General linguistics and descriptive grammar', *Transactions of the Philogical Society*, reprinted in Firth 1957.
—— (1951a), 'Modes of meaning', in *Essays and Studies*, The English Association, reprinted in Firth 1957.
—— (1957), *Papers in Linguistics 1935–1951*, London, Oxford University Press.
Gregg, L. W. (ed.) (1972), *Cognition in Learning and Memory*, New York, Wiley.
Halliday, M. A. K. (1961), 'Categories of the theory of grammar', *Word*, 17, No. 3.
—— (1969), 'Options and functions in the English clause', *Brno Studies in English*, 8, reprinted in Halliday and Martin (eds) (1981).
—— (1970), 'Language structure and language function', Lyons (ed.) (1970).
—— (1977), 'Text as semantic choice in social contexts', van Dijk and Petöfi (eds) (1977).
—— (1985), *An Introduction to Functional Grammar*, London, Edward Arnold.
Halliday M. A. K. and Martin, J. R. (eds) (1981), *Readings in Systemic Linguistics*, London, Batsford.
Hasan, R. (1971), 'Syntax and semantics', in Morton (ed.) (1971).
—— (1984), 'Ways of saying, ways of meaning', in Fawcett *et al*. (eds) (1985).
—— (1985), 'Meaning, text and context: fifty years after Malinowski', in Benson and Greaves (eds) (1985).
Hjelmslev, L. (1961), *Prolegomena to a Theory of Language* (J. Whitfield, tr.), Madison, University of Wisconsin Press.
Leech, G. N. (1974), *Semantics*, Harmondsworth, Penguin.
Lyons, J. (ed.) (1970), *New Horizons in Linguistics*, Harmondsworth, Penguin.
—— (1977), *Semantics*, vols 1 and 2, Cambridge, Cambridge University Press.
Malinowski, B. (1923), 'The problem of meaning in primitive languages', Supplement I to Ogden and Richards (1923).
—— (1935), 'An ethnographic theory of language', in *Coral Gardens and Their Magic*, Vol. 2, London, Allen and Unwin.
Mann, W. and Matthiessen, C. M. I. M. (1983), 'Nigel: A systemic grammar for text generation (Chapter 2), ISI/RR 83–105.
Martin, J. R. (1984), 'On the analysis of exposition'. In *Discourse on Discourse* Hasan, R. (ed.). Sydney, Applied Linguistics Association of Australia, Publication No. 7. (in press).
Morton, J. (ed.) (1971), *Biological and Social Factors in Psycholinguistics*, London, Logos.

Ogden, C. K. and Richards, I. A. (1923), *The Meaning of Meaning*, London, Kegan Paul.

Saussure, F. de (1916/74), *A Course in General Linguistics*, English edn. (trs. W. Baskin), London, Fontana.

Schank, R. (1972), 'Conceptual dependency', *Cognitive Psychology*, 3.

—— (1975), 'The structure of episodes in memory', in Bobrow and Collins (eds) (1975).

Schank, R. and Abelson, R. (1977), *Scripts, Plans, Goals and Understanding*, Hillsdale, Lawrence Erlbaum Associates.

Whorf, B. L. (1956), *Language, Thought and Reality* (Carroll, J. B. ed.), Cambridge, Mass., MIT Press.

Wilkes, Y. (1978), 'Making preferences more active', *Artificial Intelligence*, 11.

Wittgenstein, L. (1958), *Philosophical Investigations*, London, Basil Blackwell.

Young, D. J. (1980), *The Structure of English Clauses*, London, Hutchinson.

8 Communicative function and semantics*

Christopher S. Butler
University of Nottingham

8.1 AIMS AND SCOPE

In this chapter I shall review critically what has been said by systemically oriented linguists (and also, at times, discussion by non-systemic linguists) about the relationship between the overall communicative function of an utterance and the semantics of the sentence uttered. After claiming that existing accounts are unsatisfactory, or at least incomplete, I shall attempt to formulate a more adequate proposal.

8.2 THREE APPROACHES TO INDIRECT SPEECH ACTS

Of crucial importance in this area are what Heringer 1972 has called 'indirect speech acts', in which the illocutionary force (see Austin 1962; Searle 1969, 1976) suggested by the surface form of a sentence is not that with which the sentence is actually uttered. The first question at issue is how much of the communicative function of utterances such as (1) and (2) below, intended and understood as attempts to get the hearer to open a window, is to be accounted for within the semantics (or, in a model which does not make a clear-cut distinction between semantics and syntax, the 'semantico-syntactic' level).

(1) Can you open the window?
(2) It's awfully stuffy in here.

Three positions on this question have been taken in the literature, and have been identified and discussed by Sadock (1974). The first of these would claim that the potential directiveness of both (1) and (2) is to be incorporated into the semantic representation. At the other extreme, we have the claim that the directiveness of both (1) and (2) is not a semantic matter at all, but that (1) is (semantically) always a question, and (2) always a statement, whatever their actual communicative function in an interaction between participants. Thirdly, there is a half-way approach, which claims that the potential

---

* I am grateful to Robin Fawcett for comments on a draft of this chapter.

directiveness of (1), but not of (2), is a semantic matter. With this taxonomy of approaches in mind, let us now turn to the proposals made by Halliday, Martin, Fawcett and Hudson.

8.3 COMMUNICATIVE FUNCTION AS SEMANTIC

Halliday (1971: 173) states that 'the relationship between, say, "question" in semantics and "interrogative" in grammar is not really different from that between a behavioural–semantic category such as "threat" and the categories by which it is realized grammatically'. This certainly suggests an approach in which communicative function is incorporated within the semantics.

A more detailed discussion of speech function is to be found in Halliday 1984, an earlier version of which was available as a mimeo version in 1977. Here, Halliday proposes a model with three levels: social–contextual, semantic and grammatical, each being interpreted as a recoding of the one next above. There are system networks at each level, as shown in Figure 8.1.

As an example of the relationships between choices from the networks, consider a request to perform some action: this would be classified at the social–contextual level as [initiating, demanding, goods-and-services]. This feature combination would be recoded at the semantic level in terms of whether the speaker's 'turn' is meant to [initiate] or to [respond], and whether it is meant to [give] ([offer] or [statement]) or to [demand] ([command] or [question]). Further recoding at the grammatical level expresses these meanings in terms of the choices from the mood network (for [major] clauses, [indicative] or [imperative], if [indicative] then either [declarative] or [interrogative], also [explicit] (full) or [inexplicit] (elliptical)). In discussing inter-level realizations, Halliday invokes the concept of 'congruence', a congruent realization being one which is typical, and selected if there is no good reason to do otherwise. The congruent realization of the feature specification [initiating, demanding, goods-and-services] would be [command], and this in turn would be congruently realized at the grammatical level as [imperative].

Typically, Halliday's account is insightful, but on closer inspection reveals a number of problems in connection with the levels and the relations between them. It is not made clear exactly what the 'social–contextual' level is, or how it relates to other levels proposed in previous work (see, for instance, the 'socio-semantic' model in Halliday 1973). Neither does Halliday show us how a 'move in discourse' is to be defined, or whether there are other units at this level, and if so what relationships they enter into. Furthermore, Halliday admits that there will be many actual speech acts which cannot easily be classified as being concerned with either [information] or [goods-and-services]. The experience of Montgomery 1979 in attempting to assign actual examples of interaction to these categories suggests that there are certain inadequacies in Halliday's formulation.

At the semantic level, Halliday does not say how the 'speech functions' of command, statement, question and offer are to be defined, or how categories such as 'exclamation' would fit in. Furthermore, it is quite unclear why the

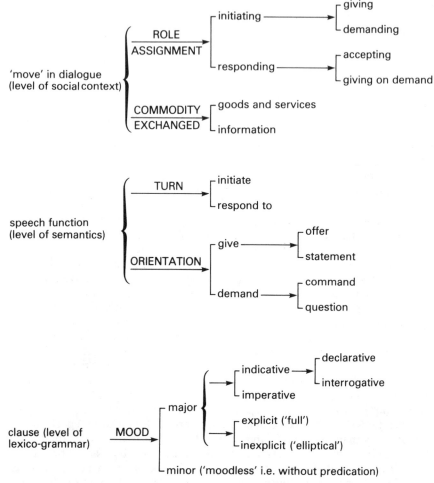

Figure 8.1 Halliday's networks (from Halliday 1984: 12, 13, 15)

[initiate]/[respond] system is regarded as part of the semantics at all: it is said to relate to the speaker's 'turn', and the terms of the system appear to be in one-to-one correspondence with the [initiating]/[responding] terms in the 'role assignment' system at the social–contextual level.

A further set of problems is concerned with inter-level realization, and in particular with the area of 'congruence'. Since Halliday does not offer definitions of the semantic 'speech functions', we do not know whether requests are to be taken as sub-classes of command, though this position is certainly in line with the spirit of the proposals. If this is so, sentences such as (1) would presumably be regarded as ambiguous as between a request and a true question interpretation, rather than as questions which can (noncongruently) realize the features [initiating, demanding, goods-and-services]. I shall argue against such an analysis in section 8.4. Meanwhile, we may note that although Halliday recognizes the importance of non-congruent realizations, he does not discuss them. It is difficult to see how, in a model of the type he proposes, Halliday could explain the restrictions on, and social properties of, the non-congruent realization of his higher-level options. For instance, I have shown elsewhere (Butler 1982) that the acceptability of some modalized sentences—but not others—as directives, and also the relative politeness of the acceptable modalized directives in a given social context, and their classification as orders, requests or suggestions, can be predicted from semantic properties (modal meanings and the semantics of mood) which are distinct from either their speech function or their syntax, and are also needed in order to account for other, non-directive interpretations.

Martin 1981 has proposed a semantic network for speech function (see Figure 8.2) which is based on revision and extension of Halliday's scheme. His account is a considerable advance over Halliday's in certain respects. One important difference is that Martin discusses criteria for the recognition of some of his categories. It is interesting, however, to note the kind of evidence adduced: Martin says, for example, that [goods-and-services] acts can be differentiated from [information] acts by their ability to be followed by *Okay* as a response, and that [offer] but not [command] acts can be responded to by *Thanks*. Martin is appealing here to the way in which utterances fit into the structure of discourse: indeed, he talks in terms of the 'adjacency pairs' recognized by the ethnomethodologists who pioneered the discourse analysis approach (see, for example, Schegloff 1968/72a, 1972b; Jefferson 1972; Sacks, Schegloff and Jefferson 1974/78). Martin is, however, unwilling to recognize a further level of organization 'above' the semantics, claiming that examples requiring three non-phonological strata are rare in texts. Even if this proved to be true, it would not be sufficient reason to ignore such cases. In fact, we do need to recognize a supra-semantic level of organization in order to capture a maximum of generalizations. For instance, there are semantic properties shown by the sentence in example (1), irrespective of whether its overall communicative function is to elicit information or to make a request: anticipating the discussion in section 8.5, we may say that in both cases it is true that the hearer knows, at least as well as the speaker does himself, whether he has the ability to open the window. Similarly, for example (2), whether used as an information-giver or as an indirect directive, it is true that the speaker believes (or is acting as if he believes) that it is stuffy in the room. Such generalizations are easily captured if (1) is taken to be, semantically, a question, and (2) a statement, each being potentially ambiguous as to its function at a higher level. Ironically, Martin criticizes Fawcett for an exactly parallel fault: amalgamating two strata, in this case semantic and grammatical, with consequent loss of generalizing power.

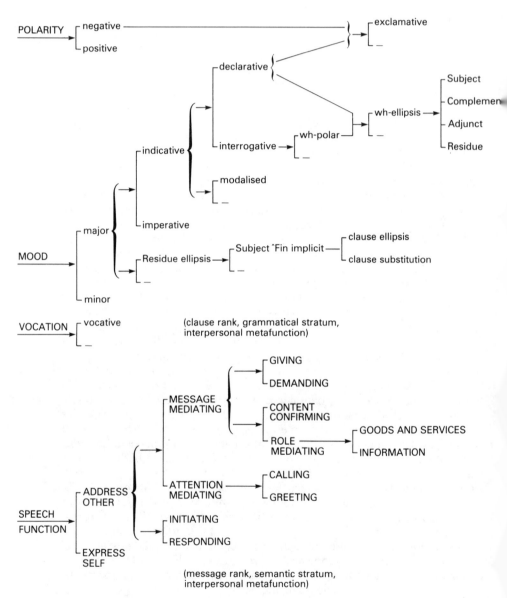

Figure 8.2 Martin's networks (from Martin 1981: 53)

8.4 THE MIDDLE PATH

Fawcett adopts the middle position, namely that although the potential directiveness of (1) is semantic, that of (2) is not. His overall model does, however, allow for the possibility that both may serve the 'socio-psychological purpose' of 'control' (Fawcett 1980: 111–2). Example (2), for Fawcett, is semantically an 'information-giver' from which the hearer may make an 'intended deduction' that he is being asked indirectly to reduce the level of stuffiness in the room. Example (1), however, is a realization of the features [request, invocation of ability, direct, anticipating ability]. Fawcett gives four reasons for rejecting the analysis of (1) as a semantic question from which a directive interpretation can be deduced; I shall argue that each of them is unconvincing.

Firstly, Fawcett argues that there are systematic semantic differences between requests such as (3) and 'information-seekers' (questions) such as (4) and (5) which are superficially identical to (3).

(3) Could you read it.
(4) Could you read it (when you finally got it)?
(5) Could you read it (if you were asked to)?

(3) and (4) are certainly different semantically: *could* in (4) has a [past time] modal, whereas this feature is not present in (3). But this does not in itself provide any evidence against the view that both (3) and (4) are semantically questions (though we must, at some point in the model, account for the fact that (4) could not function as a request). The difference between (3) and (5), however, is less clear: both have a modal which is marked as 'hypothetical', and it has been suggested (see, for example, Leech 1969: 235) that the 'tentative' meaning as in (3) can be explained in terms of an implicit conditional. Fawcett's own explanation of the semantic difference is that in (3) the addressee is actually being asked to read something, whereas in (5) he is not. This explanation, however, contravenes a criterion specified earlier by Fawcett, namely that he prefers to give an account 'patently based on criteria that are linguistic rather than on the notion of the "purpose" served by the sentence' (1980: 106).

Fawcett's second claim is that while polarity information-seekers are characteristically said with high-rising intonation (Tone 2 in Halliday's 1970 classification), requests such as (3) have a low rise (Tone 3). I find the claim of an intonational difference rather dubious, though I am willing to be convinced by experimental evidence. However, Fawcett also comments that 'there are undoubtedly occasions when the "emic" distinction between Tones 2 and 3 is lost in the "etic" fuzziness of actual usage' (111), and that 'very many polarity information seekers are uttered with a tone that is phonetically closer to Tone 3 than Tone 2, presumably following the principle of economy of effort'. If this is so, it is difficult to see how even experimental evidence could decide the issue.

Fawcett's third argument is that directives do not have truth values, while 'it is precisely the purpose of a polarity seeker to discover the truth value of the referent situation it refers to' (111). Note that once more, Fawcett is appealing to the notion of purpose, despite his earlier claims. What is more, he provides no evidence here that the directive interpretation cannot be derived from a question about truth value. Fawcett also comments on the use of adverbs such as *possibly* in requests such as (6):

(6) Could you possibly read it.

Downes (1977: 90) has pointed out that such adverbs refer to the speaker's assessment of the truth of the propositional content, and that they are therefore compatible with semantic questions, but not with commands or requests, since these cannot be true or false. Fawcett's claim is that the adverbs 'do not realize "modality" meanings, but are yet another type of "softener"' (111). Surely, however, an account such as Downes's, which needs just one meaning for the adverb (and, indeed, just one for the interrogative) is clearly preferable, on the grounds of greater generalization and economy, to one in which semantic categories are multiplied unnecessarily.

Fawcett's fourth and final argument is that if the hearer replies to a request such as (3) as if it were an ordinary question, the expectations of the speaker are felt to be frustrated, while this is not the case for a polarity information-seeker. Fawcett's comment that in the former case the hearer has 'sought to escape the task set through making a "play on words"' (112) again shows that he is invoking the notion of purposive role, and once more this seems contrary to his own recommendations. What Fawcett, like Martin, is really appealing to here is the syntagmatic relationship between acts in discourse; yet he claims that his illocutionary force network 'is part of a "sentence grammar" rather than any possible "discourse grammar"' (105, fn.).

The middle way chosen by Fawcett has also been defended, within a basically generative semantic framework, by Sadock 1974. I can do no more here than sketch in some of Sadock's arguments, and indicate why they are unconvincing (for further detail, see Butler 1982).

Sadock distinguishes between semantic requests (which he regards as a type of 'speech act idiom') and indirect speech acts in which the actual illocutionary force is not simply a semantic matter (regarded as 'speech act metaphors'). A similar distinction, between 'true impositives' and 'hints', is made by Green 1973. Sadock (1974: 99 ff.) proposes three kinds of test for recognizing the two types of speech act, based on co-occurrence, paraphrase and grammatical properties respectively.

First let us consider co-occurrence properties. Examples (7) and (8) are taken from Sadock's discussion.

(7) (=Sadock's 23) Will you close the door?
(8) (=Sadock's 24) When will you close the door?

Sadock points out that (7), but not (8), will take *please* before the main verb: this is indeed true, but can be explained in alternative ways. Leech (1977: 142), reviewing Sadock's book, has suggested that 'such syntactically peripheral elements may be more easily constrained in pragmatic than syntactic terms', and that *please* can be adequately characterized as a politeness marker, used when the speaker wants to obtain a favour from the addressee. Expanding on this suggestion, I have shown elsewhere (Butler 1982) that there is a gradient of restrictedness for *please*, such that, in general, the more transparent the speech act, the less restricted are its patterns of co-occurrence with *please*, if all possible positions in the sentence are taken into account.

Sadock also claims that only semantic requests such as (7) can occur with the indefinite vocative *someone*, and with adverbials giving a reason for the speech act. However, I find the following perfectly acceptable as an indirect request, especially if the modal is stressed:

(9) When will you close the door, someone, because I'm absolutely freezing in here.

Sadock's arguments from co-occurrence are thus very weak: indeed, we have seen that one piece of evidence, from co-occurrence with adverbs such as *possibly*, suggests that the position taken by Sadock and Fawcett is untenable.

On paraphrase relations, Sadock rightly points out that paraphrases of modalized interrogatives (his 'whimperatives') have added indirectness. Thus (11) is more indirect than (10).

(10) Can you close the door?
(11) Are you able to close the door?

Sadock argues from this that the two sentences ought to be given different semantic representations. An attractive alternative explanation has, however, been offered by Morgan 1978, who distinguishes between 'conventions of language' and 'conventions of usage', both being involved in the interpretation of some indirect speech acts. Conventions of language are concerned with the arbitrary relationships beween form and meaning: conventions of usage, on the other hand, are concerned with what sorts of things one is expected to say in certain situations in a particular culture. Morgan proposes that speakers use sentences such as (10) with the literal meaning (a matter of conventions of language), but also in the knowledge that a convention of usage exists, to the effect that the use of modalized interrogatives of the *Can you?* type is a standard way of indirectly requesting someone to do something. The request is conveyed by conversational maxims of the kind proposed by Grice 1975, 1978, but the existence of a convention of usage means that the implicature is 'short-circuited' and no longer needs to be calculated: hence the greater indirectness of (11) as compared with (10).

We are left with Sadock's arguments concerned with grammatical differences between pairs such as (7) and (8). Sadock claims that the request sense of (7), but not of (8), is lost on passivization. I find both (12) and (13) odd, even to the point of unacceptability, if the agent is present and the modal unstressed; however, (13) is no odder than (12).

(12) Will the door be closed (by you)?
(13) When will the door be closed (by you)?

But even if we agree with Sadock that these passives are acceptable, and that (12) has lost its request sense to a greater degree than (13), an explanation is available which does not involve postulating semantic requestiveness for (7) but not for (8). If *will* is volitional in (7) (and there are good arguments for saying that it is: see Butler 1982), then passivization will destroy this interpretation, since if *will* were also volitional in (12), the door would have to be the entity in which the volition resided: that is, volitional *will* is not 'voice-neutral' (see Palmer 1979: 135). For this reason, (12), like (13), can only have a 'predictive' interpretation. Thus, on passivization, (7) loses its volitional meaning and becomes merely predictive; on the other hand, (8) is (because of *when*) readily interpretable only in terms of the prediction of a future event, and so its meaning changes little on passivization.

Sadock also observes that (7), but not (8), can take the 'conditional' form *would* without the assumption of an antecedent:

(14) (=Sadock's 41) Would you close the door?
(15) (=Sadock's 42) When would you close the door?

However, as we saw earlier in discussing Fawcett's similar argument, it has been suggested that there is an implied condition even in cases such as (14). Note that if *would* is replaced by *could*, there is very little difference between sentences with and without *when*, as far as our awareness of a possible antecedent is concerned:

(16) Could you go to the shop for me?
(17) When could you go to the shop for me?

This suggests that if there are differences between (14) and (15), they are due to the properties of *would* in the two sentences, rather than to the whimperative construction itself. Again, we may invoke the volitional nature of (14), as against the predictive interpretation of (15). In connection with this and my previous argument, note that substitution of *will* by *be willing to* in (7) leads simply to added indirectness, while in (8) it leads to ungrammaticality.

(18) Are you willing to close the door?
(19) *When are you willing to close the door?[1]

8.5 THE 'SURFACE MEANING' APPROACH

During the course of the discussion so far, I have argued that an account which takes both (1) and (2) as having their literal meanings (that is, the meanings suggested by their surface form) is preferable to either the view that both are semantically directive, or the view that (1) is semantically directive but (2) is not. In the present section I shall examine briefly some important proposals made by Hudson 1975 within just such a 'surface meaning' framework.

Hudson's view is that illocutionary forces are not themselves to be treated as part of the syntax or semantics, since they are context-dependent and we do not know how many there are (this latter argument, however, is weak: we do not know precisely how many lexical items there are in any given language, but this does not mean that lexis is outside the scope of linguistics). The range of illocutionary forces which a given sentence may have can, however, be worked out from certain context-independent properties of the sentence uttered, together with general conversational maxims of a Gricean kind. These semantic properties are closely related to syntactic mood, though not in a one-to-one way, and are similar to Searle's 1969 'sincerity conditions', concerned with the speaker's beliefs or attitudes towards the propositional content. For instance, whenever the speaker utters a declarative, the hearer may infer that, provided the sentence is being used sincerely and 'normally' in relation to conversational principles, the speaker believes that the propositional content is true.

Hudson then demonstrates that the sincerity conditions attaching to a sentence cannot be associated with its syntactic structure, but must be part of the semantic representation. The form of the argument is as follows. If two sentences have the same sincerity conditions, or conditions whose differences can be predicted from other factors, they must share the same representation at some level. If it can be shown that the two sentences share no relevant syntactic properties, then the sincerity conditions cannot be syntactic, and are thus presumably semantic. The argument focuses on sentences such as (20) and (21):

(20) (=Hudson's 10a) What a pretty dress that is!
(21) (=Hudson's 10b) Isn't that a pretty dress?

Hudson shows that there are no grounds for bringing these kinds of sentence together syntactically: indeed, there are a number of syntactic differences between them. They do, however, share the sincerity condition for exclamations, namely that the speaker is impressed by the position of some point on a scale of comparison. Since there are no syntactic similarities, and since the 'degree' meaning can be expressed by any of a number of word classes, Hudson concludes that the sincerity condition is a semantic property, and proposes a semantic 'force marker', EXCLAMATION, common to the meanings of (20) and (21). He also points out that this set of arguments can be taken as evidence for the autonomy of syntax and semantics, since if the two levels are not distinguished, no way of discriminating between mood categories and force markers is available. Further arguments leading to this position can be found in Butler 1982.

Hudson goes on to demonstrate that more than one force marker can be associated simultaneously with the same sentence. For instance, (21) has not only the force marker EXCLAMATION, but also QUESTION, for which the condition is that 'the speaker believes that the hearer knows, at least as reliably as the speaker does, whether the proposition is true or false' (1975: 11).[2]

Hudson's arguments, taken together with our earlier discussion, provide a basis for the view that only those properties of sentences which are relatable, in a fairly direct though not one-to-one way, to surface mood, should be included in the semantic representation. However, if we adopt this position, how, if at all, can we account, within linguistics, for the communicative functions of sentences uttered in contexts of interaction? It is to this problem that we now turn.

8.6 BEYOND THE SEMANTICS

It is, at first, tempting simply to set up a level of speech acts on the basis of the classifications proposed by Austin 1962, Searle 1969, Ohmann 1972, Vendler 1972, or Fraser 1974—see Hancher 1979 for a useful comparison of the various proposals. However, such classifications depend crucially on the notion of the speaker's intention in performing a speech act, and this, as is obvious from the discussion in Searle (1969: 58), is not deducible simply from the form of the sentence uttered, even in the case of the most transparent illocutionary force indicating devices, namely the performative verbs. We can, however, obtain evidence for the hearer's interpretation of a speaker's utterances, and for the extent to which this corresponds to the speaker's intentions, if we look at the discourse following an utterance. Consider the following piece of (hypothetical) dialogue:

(22) A. Is that your coat on the chair over there?
      B. Oh, sorry, I'll hang it up.
      A. No, it's OK, I was just wondering if it *was* yours, because mine's very similar, and I think I left it around somewhere.

Here, B interprets A's question as an indirect request, but A really intended the remark as a straightforward information-seeker and goes on to correct B's misapprehension. If A had not followed up in this way, we could have assumed that B's interpretation was not inconsistent with A's purpose.

Speech act theorists have not, in general, sought such evidence, but have concentrated on specifying the conditions for the use of individual speech acts, considered in isolation.[3] The important consequence of this position is that speech act theory makes no predictions about the syntagmatic relations between speech acts. It is for this that the theory has been criticized by proponents of the 'discourse analysis' approach (see Sinclair and Coulthard 1975: 75). Discourse analysts themselves are concerned with precisely this kind of patterning:

... the level of language function in which we are centrally interested is neither the universal functions of language, nor the detailed function of surface formal ordering within the sentence. It is rather the level of function of a particular utterance, in a particular social situation and at a particular place in a sequence, as a specific contribution to a developing discourse. [Sinclair and Coulthard 1975: 13]

The fundamental problem of discourse analysis is to show how one utterance follows another in a rational, rule-governed manner—in other words, how we understand coherent discourse. [Labov 1970/72a: 252, page reference to the 1972 version]

Discourse analysis thus offers the possibility of accounting for the communicative function of utterances within a framework based on syntagmatic and paradigmatic relations analogous to those familiar at other levels. Because of this, discourse analysts have tended to stress the differences between their own approach and that of the speech act theorists (see, for example, Sinclair and Coulthard 1975: 14). Although they are indeed different, and although discourse analysis does offer a truly linguistic model with parallels at other levels, I shall argue below that there are important links between the two approaches.

Particularly interesting, from a systemicist's viewpoint, is the hierarchical model of discourse structure proposed for classroom interaction by Sinclair and Coulthard 1975. As is by now well known, they propose a rank scale for discourse similar to that for grammar in a 'Scale and Category' model (see Halliday 1961), and consisting, for classroom discourse, of the units lesson, transaction, exchange, move and act. At each rank, except possibly the highest, there are various classes of unit, each having a specifiable range of structural possibilities, the elements of which are realized by certain classes of the unit next below on the rank scale. Discourse units are defined in terms of the predictions they set up within the structure of the discourse: for instance, an elicitation is an act requiring a linguistic response or non-verbal surrogate such as a nod; a directive is an act whose function is to secure a non-linguistic response; an informative passes on information, and requires no response other than an indication that the addressee is still listening.

Although Sinclair and Coulthard's work is based on a very specific type of social context, studies by Pearce 1973 on radio interviews and television discussions, by Coulthard and Ashby 1973, 1975, 1976 on doctor–patient interviews, by Stubbs 1973 on committee talk, and by Burton 1978, 1980, 1981, 1982 on conversation and literary texts, have shown that many aspects of the model can be generalized to other kinds of context. There has been lively interest in the approach recently (see Berry 1979, 1981a, 1981b, 1981c; Coulthard and Brazil 1979, 1981; Coulthard, Montgomery and Brazil 1981; Stubbs 1981, a, b and Butler 1985a, b, 1986); there is no space to discuss these developments here.

An area of particular relevance to the concerns of the present chapter is the relationship between discourse acts, as defined by Sinclair and Coulthard, and illocutionary acts. It is clear from Sinclair and Coulthard's discussion that there is no one-to-one relation between discourse function and what Searle (1976: 3) calls the 'illocutionary point' of an utterance. For example, not all items whose function is to get the hearer to do something are to be classified as directives at the discourse level. Consider (23), which occurs in one of Sinclair and Coulthard's data texts:

(23) Look at the car.

This, they claim, is not a directive, but a 'clue', since its function within the discourse context is not to cause the pupils simply to look at the car, but to do so in the light of a previous elicitation:

(24) Can you think what it means?

In other words, since (23) is not an attempt to get the pupils to do something as an end in itself, but is subordinate to the main function of getting the information asked for in (24), it is not a discourse directive, although it clearly has a directive type of illocutionary point. Similar conclusions can be drawn from Sinclair and Coulthard's discussion of other acts such as 'starters' and 'cues'.

We can thus interpret Sinclair and Coulthard as claiming that utterances with the same illocutionary properties can have different discourse functions. They do recognize (29 ff.) the common properties of certain acts, by postulating what they call 'situational' categories of statement, question and command. Thus (23) would be a command although, as we have seen, it is not a directive at the discourse level. The 'situational' classification of an utterance is made from the formal properties of the sentence and the context of utterance, by means of 'interpretation rules', which I shall discuss shortly. Only after tagging with such situational features can the discourse value of an utterance be determined by considering its position in the discourse structure. It seems clear that the 'situational' categories are very closely related to the illocutionary properties of the act concerned, and that they restrict the range of discourse acts which a given utterance can perform: for instance, according to Sinclair and Coulthard (40 ff.), commands can function as directives, starters, prompts, clues, cues and asides, but not, for example, as elicitations, checks or replies.

Since there is overlap in the range of discourse functions that can be performed by acts of particular illocutionary types (for instance, questions and commands, in Sinclair and Coulthard's scheme, can both serve as starters, clues and asides), it is not the case that illocutionary acts are simply less delicate classes of discourse act. Indeed, Sinclair and Coulthard's work amply demonstrates that it is not the illocutionary acts, but the more specific discourse acts, which show, and can be recognized by, structural patterning. What I wish to suggest here is that the illocutionary properties of an utterance are important in the interpretation of the discourse function of that utterance from the meaning (and ultimately the form) of the sentence used. Sinclair and Coulthard's own interpretation rules (29 ff.) take as input the grammatical form of the sentence (mood, modalization, etc.) and aspects of the social context (characteristics of schools and classrooms in general, and of particular stages in a given lesson), and produce 'situational' categories as output. Typical of such rules is the following (32):

An interrogative clause is to be interpreted as a command to do if it fulfils all the following conditions:

   (i) it contains one of the modals *can*, *could*, *will*, *would* (and sometimes *going to*);
   (ii) if the subject of the clause is also the addressee;
   (iii) the predicate describes an action which is practically possible at the time of the utterance.

This means, for example, that in the classroom, if there is a piano in the room, (25) is to be taken as a command, but (26) and (27) are interpreted as questions, at the 'situational' level:

(25) Can you play the piano, John?
(26) Can John play the piano?
(27) Can you swim a length, John?

I would propose two amendments to the type of rule given by Sinclair and Coulthard. Firstly, as we have seen, the output can be considered in terms of illocutionary categories. Secondly, these illocutionary categories should be correlated, not with formal categories such as 'interrogative', '*will*', and so on, but with the semantic properties underlying these formal categories. For otherwise Sinclair and Coulthard have no way of explaining, for instance, why it is that *can*, *could*, *will* and *would*, but not certain other modals such as *may*, *might*, *should* or *must*, can be standardly used to signal a command to do something. As I have shown elsewhere (Butler 1982), such facts can be explained only if we take into account the meanings of the formal items and relations concerned. In this respect, the interpretation rules provided by Labov (Labov 1970/72a, 1972b; Labov and Fanshel 1977) are superior to those proposed by Sinclair and Coulthard, since they do make reference to semantic categories such as ability and willingness.

The interpretation rules of Sinclair and Coulthard and of Labov specify certain correlations between form (and/or meaning) and (illocutionary) function: they do not, however, tell us the mechanisms by which such correlations can be made. Here we need to supplement the discourse analysts' accounts with general principles of the type put forward by Grice. What I am proposing, then, is that the interpretation of utterances involves the operation of Gricean conversational principles on the meanings of the sentences used, to give as output the range of possible illocutionary forces of the utterance and an estimate of which force is most likely in the context. This is, however, not the whole story, for as we have seen, a given illocutionary act can often serve a range of discourse functions. It is also necessary to determine, by consideration of the illocutionary act and its position in discourse structure, the precise function of that act in the ongoing interaction.

Finally, let us consider how this interpretation process applies to example (1), repeated for convenience below:

(1) Can you open the window?

Semantically, this is to be taken as a question about the ability of the hearer to open the window (other semantic interpretations of the modal, such as permission and epistemic possibility, can be ruled out—see Butler 1982, section 9.3). Searle 1975 has given a detailed account of how conversational principles might operate in cases of this kind. For our example, the basic argument runs as follows. The hearer assumes that the speaker is being co-operative, and therefore that his utterance has some point to it. There are circumstances in which (1) could be taken as a straight information-seeker: as Searle points out, this would be the case if it were said by an orthopaedic specialist to a patient with an arm injury. In the absence of such a context, the hearer may be unable to find a reason for the speaker wanting to know the answer to the question, or it may be obvious that the speaker already knows the answer. In such a case, the hearer concludes that extra information is being conveyed. Since a preparatory condition on commanding and requesting is that the hearer be able to do what is being asked of him, it is likely that the speaker is making appeal, in his speech act, to a preparatory condition for an act he wishes the addressee to perform. To Searle's account we may add that since, according to Morgan 1978, there is a convention of usage to the effect that *Can you?* is a standard way of making an indirect request, once the hearer has deduced that the utterance is probably not intended as a straight question, he need not calculate the remaining implicatures.

Let us assume that the Gricean rules indicate that the utterance of (1) is to be taken as a request, as far as the illocutionary force is concerned. If the act is the only one in its move, at the discourse level, or if it is preceded by something which can serve as a preface or starter, and/or followed by something which can be interpreted as a comment or prompt, then it must be functioning as a directive, since this is the only class of act which can be the 'head' of a move and can be a request in illocutionary terms. Only if the discourse structure is not compatible with 'head' structural function is it necessary to consider alternative discourse functions for the speaker's utterance.

8.7 CONCLUSION

I hope to have shown in this chapter that a surface-oriented approach to the semantics of mood, such as that proposed by Hudson 1975, is greatly to be preferred over the positions taken by Halliday, Martin, Fawcett, Sadock and others. Such a view has the advantage of accounting for indirect speech acts, whether conventionalized (as in (1)) or not (as in (2)), by means of the same set of general principles, while also being able to explain differences in the degree of directness of various types. An account of this kind, however, still needs to be supplemented by a model of linguistic patterning above the sentence, and here I have argued that the discourse analysis approach is superior to speech act theory. Discourse structure and illocutionary force are not, however, unconnected: my suggestion is that the illocutionary properties of utterances are crucially involved in the interpretation of discourse function.

I have had no opportunity here to do full justice to the work of non-systemic linguists in this area; neither have I been able to discuss how patterning at the semantic and discourse levels might be formalized: for a full account, in terms of a model based on Hudson's 1976 'daughter dependency grammar', see Butler 1982.

NOTES

1. We may ignore the interpretation 'When are you usually willing . . .?' here.
2. Part of this condition would probably need to be changed if we wished to take into

account 'non-standard' questions such as those put by teachers and quizmasters: this is, however, beyond the scope of the present chapter.
3. There are some exceptions to this: see Green 1973 and Lee 1974.

BIBLIOGRAPHY

Austin, J. L. (1962), *How to Do Things with Words*, Oxford, Clarendon Press.
Benson, J. D. and Greaves, W. S. (eds) (1985), *Systemic Perspectives on Discourse: Selected Papers from the Ninth International Systemic Workshop*, Norwood, N.J., Ablex.
Berry, M. (1979), 'A note on Sinclair and Coulthard's classes of acts including a comment on comments', *Nottingham Linguistic Circular*, 8, No. 1, 49–59.
—— (1981a), 'Polarity, ellipticity, elicitation and propositional development: their relevance to the well-formedness of an exchange', *Nottingham Linguistic Circular*, 10, 36–63.
—— (1981b), 'Towards layers of structure for directive exchanges', *Network*, 2, 23–32.
—— (1981c), 'Systemic linguistics and discourse analysis: a multi-layered approach to exchange structure', in Coulthard and Montgomery (eds) (1981: 120–45).
Burton, D. (1978), 'Towards an analysis of casual conversation', *Nottingham Linguistic Circular*, 7, No. 2, 131–64.
—— (1980), *Dialogue and Discourse*, London, Routledge and Kegan Paul.
—— (1981), 'Analysing spoken discourse', in Coulthard and Montgomery (eds) (1981: 61–81).
—— (1982), 'Conversation pieces', in Carter and Burton (eds) (1982: 86–115).
Butler, C. S. (1982), *The Directive Function of the English Modals*, unpublished Ph.D. thesis, University of Nottingham, England.
—— (1985a), *Systemic Linguistics: Theory and Applications*, London, Batsford.
—— (1985b), 'Discourse systems and structures and their place within an overall systemic model', in Benson and Greaves (eds) (1985).
—— (1986), 'What has systemic functional linguistics contributed to our understanding of spoken text?' *Proceedings of the 1984 Working Conference on Language in Education*. Brisbane, Brisbane College of Advanced Technology.
Carter, R. A. and Burton, D. (eds) (1982), *Literary Text and Language Study*, London, Edward Arnold.
Cole, P. (ed.) (1978), *Syntax and Semantics 9: Pragmatics*, New York and London, Academic Press.
Cole, P. and Morgan, J. L. (eds) (1975), *Syntax and Semantics 3: Speech Acts*. New York and London, Academic Press.
Coulthard, M. (1975), 'Discourse analysis in English: a short review of the literature', *Language Teaching and Linguistics: Abstracts*, 8, 73–89.
Coulthard, R. M. and Ashby, M. C. (1973), *Doctor–patient interviews*, Working Papers in Discourse Analysis 1, Birmingham, English Language Research, University of Birmingham.
—— and —— (1975), 'Talking with the doctor', *Journal of Communication*, 25, No. 3, 140–7.
—— and —— (1976), 'A linguistic description of doctor–patient interviews', in Wadsworth and Robinson (eds) (1976).
Coulthard, R. M. and Brazil, D. C. (1979), *Exchange Structure*, Discourse Analysis Monographs 5, Birmingham, English Language Research, University of Birmingham.

Coulthard, R. M. and Brazil, D. C. (1981), 'Exchange structure', in Coulthard and Montgomery (eds) (1981: 82–106).

Coulthard, M. and Montgomery, M. (eds) (1981), *Studies in Discourse Analysis*, London, Boston and Henley, Routledge and Kegan Paul.

Coulthard, M., Montgomery, M. and Brazil, D. (1981), 'Developing a description of spoken discourse', in Coulthard and Montgomery (eds) (1981: 1–50).

Downes, W. (1977), 'The imperative and pragmatics', *Journal of Linguistics*, 13, 77–97.

Fawcett, R. P. (1980), *Cognitive Linguistics and Social Interaction: Towards an Integrated Model of a Systemic Functional Grammar and the Other Components of a Communicating Mind*, Heidelberg, Julius Groos Verlag and Exeter, University of Exeter.

Fawcett, R. P., Halliday, M. A. K., Lamb, S. M. and Makkai, A. (eds) (1984), *The Semiotics of Culture and Language Vol. 1: Language as Social Semiotic*, London, Frances Pinter.

Fraser, B. (1974), 'A partial analysis of vernacular performative verbs', in Shuy and Bailey (eds) (1974: 139–58).

—— (1975), 'Hedged performatives', in Cole and Morgan (eds) (1981: 187–210).

Green, G. (1973), 'How to get people to do things with words', in Shuy (ed.) (1973: 51–81).

Grice, H. P. (1975), 'Logic and conversation', Harvard William Jones Lectures, 1967, in Cole and Morgan (eds) (1975: 41–58).

—— (1978), 'Further notes on logic and conversation', in Cole (ed.) (1978: 113–27).

Gumperz, J. J. and Hymes, D. (eds) (1972), *Directions in Sociolinguistics*, New York, Holt, Rinehart and Winston.

Halliday, M. A. K. (1961), 'Categories of the theory of grammar', *Word*, 17, 241–92.

—— (1970), *A Course in Spoken English: Intonation*, London, Oxford University Press.

—— (1971), 'Language in a social perspective', *Educational Review*, 23, 165–88, University of Birmingham, reprinted in Halliday (1973: 48–71).

—— (1973), *Explorations in the Functions of Language*, London, Edward Arnold.

—— (1984), 'Language as code and language as behaviour: a systemic-functional interpretation of the nature and ontogenesis of dialogue', in Fawcett, Halliday, Lamb and Makkai (eds) (1984: 3–35).

Hancher, M. (1979), 'The classification of cooperative illocutionary acts', *Language in Society*, 8, 1–14.

Heringer, J. (1972), 'Some grammatical correlates of felicity conditions', *Working Papers in Linguistics*, Ohio State University, 1–110.

Hudson, R. A. (1975), 'The meaning of questions', *Language*, 51, 1–31.

—— (1976), *Arguments for a Non-transformational Grammar*, Chicago and London, Chicago University Press.

Jefferson, G. (1972), 'Side sequences', in Sudnow (ed.) (1972: 294–338).

Kachru, B. B. and Stahlke, H. F. W. (eds) (1972), *Current Trends in Stylistics* (Papers in Linguistics, Monographic Series 2), Edmonton, IU., Linguistic Research.

Labov, W. (1970/72a), 'The study of language in its social context', *Studium Generale*, 23, 30–87, revised version in Labov (ed.) (1972).

—— (1972b), 'Rules for ritual insults', in Sudnow (ed.) (1972: 120–69).

—— (ed.) (1972), *Sociolinguistic Patterns*, Philadelphia, University of Philadelphia Press.

Labov, W. and Fanshel, D. (1977), *Therapeutic Discourse: Psychotherapy as Conversation*, New York, San Francisco and London, Academic Press.

Lee, P. (1974), 'Perlocution and illocution', *Journal of English Linguistics*, 8: 32–40.

Leech, G. N. (1969), *Towards a Semantic Description of English*, London, Longman.

—— (1977), 'Review of Sadock 1974', *Journal of Linguistics*, 13, 133–45.

Martin, J. R. (1981), 'How many speech acts?', *UEA Papers in Linguistics*, 14/15, 52–77.

Montgomery, M. (1979), 'Modes of discourse, with particular reference to mother–child interaction', paper given at the 6th Systemic Workshop, Cardiff, September 1979.

Morgan, J. L. (1978), 'Two types of convention in indirect speech acts', in Cole (ed.) (1978: 261–80).

Ohmann, R. (1972), 'Instrumental style: notes on the theory of speech as action', in Kachru and Stahlke (eds) (1972: 115–41).

Palmer, F. R. (1979), *Modality and the English Modals*, London, Longman.

Pearce, R. D. (1973), *The Structure of Discourse in Broadcast Interviews*, unpublished M.A. thesis, University of Birmingham.

Sacks, H., Schegloff, E. A. and Jefferson, G. (1974/78), 'A simplest systematics for the organization of turn-taking for conversation', *Language*, 50, 696–735, reprinted in Schenkein (ed.) (1978: 7–55).

Sadock, J. M. (1974), *Towards a Linguistic Theory of Speech Acts*, New York, Academic Press.

Schegloff, E. A. (1968/72a), 'Sequencing in conversational openings', *American Anthropologist*, 70, 1075–95, reprinted in Gumperz and Hymes (eds) (1972: 346–80).

—— (1972b), 'Notes on conversational practice: formulating place', in Sudnow (ed.) (1972: 75–119).

Schenkein, J. (ed.) (1978), *Studies in the Organization of Conversational Interaction*, New York, Academic Press.

Searle, J. R. (1969), *Speech Acts: An Essay in the Philosophy of Language*, Cambridge, Cambridge University Press.

—— (1975), 'Indirect speech acts', in Cole and Morgan (eds) (1975: 60–82).

—— (1976), 'A classification of illocutionary acts', *Language in Society*, 5, 1–23.

Shuy, R. W. (ed.) (1973), *New Directions in Linguistics*, Washington, D.C., Georgetown University Press.

Shuy, R. and Bailey, C.-J. (eds) (1974), *Towards Tomorrow's Linguistics*, Washington, D.C., Georgetown University Press.

Sinclair, J. McH. and Coulthard, R. M. (1975), *Towards an Analysis of Discourse: The English Used by Teachers and Pupils*, London, Oxford University Press.

Stubbs, M. (1973), *Some Structural Complexities of Talk in Meetings*, Working Papers in Discourse Analysis 4, Birmingham, English Language Research, University of Birmingham.

—— (1979), 'Review of Coulthard and Brazil 1979, *Nottingham Linguistic Circular*, 8, 124–28.

—— (1981a), 'Motivating analyses of exchange structure', in Coulthard and Montgomery (eds) (1981: 107–19).

—— (1981b), 'Discourse, semantics and syntax: some notes on their relationship', *Belfast Working Papers in Language and Linguistics*, 5, 1–70.

Sudnow, D. (ed.) (1972), *Studies in Social Interaction*, New York, Free Press.

Vendler, Z. (1972), *Res Cogitans: An Essay in Rational Psychology*, Ithaca, Cornell University Press.

Wadsworth, M. and Robinson, D. (eds) (1976), *Studies in Everyday Medical Life*, London, Martin Robertson.

9 Continuative and inceptive adjuncts in English

David J. Young

University of Wales, Institute of Science and Technology, Cardiff

9.0 INTRODUCTION

This chapter is an attempt to describe an area of English syntax, namely the distribution and meanings of the items *already*, *yet*, *still* and *any longer* (synonymously *anymore*). The account given in Quirk *et al.* (1972: 376, 497–500, 504) is somewhat limited and fragmentary, and the relations of these items with grammatical aspect are not clearly brought out. The topic is also dealt with or touched upon in Traugott and Waterhouse 1969, Morrissey 1973, and Horn 1970. My account differs from these in various ways, especially in that it attempts to be more comprehensive. I do not intend to make a close comparison of my treatment with theirs, but I shall point out some of the differences in passing.

Traugott and Waterhouse, after studying the suppletive relation between *already* and *yet*, argue, I think rightly, that these adverbs are better treated as markers of aspect than as 'adverbs of time'. They then go on: '. . . we suggest that *already* should be specified as the realization of a feature or set of features associated with PERFECT.' It is, however, not very clear what the nature of the association is which they are trying to establish. Below I also question some of the steps in their argument. They further hint at the possibility of establishing an association between *still/anymore* and the progressive aspect, but regard this as outside the scope of their paper. My argument will try to show that *already/yet* and *still/any longer* are realizations of aspects in their own right— inceptive and continuative—which are dependent for their selection (though in different ways) on other aspects or aspectual characters of clauses. It seems unsatisfactory to argue an association with some particular aspect (e.g. the perfect) while leaving any association with other aspects out of account.

Morrissey refers to the Traugott and Waterhouse paper, and accepts what they say about *already/yet*, but then argues that *still/anymore* are 'related to the perfective'. Again, it is not entirely clear what the relationship is. Part of the conclusion is that *still/anymore* 'serve to establish a secondary time of reference previous to the primary time of reference (the tense of the verb) which allows the predication to be evaluated bifocally, that is, with respect to either time' (69).

Both the above-mentioned papers demonstrate that *already/yet* and *still/anymore* have something to do with aspect, but do not show how they connect with each other or with other aspects.Horn 1970 does not refer to Traugott and Waterhouse, and his concern is centrally with the suppletive relation between what are known by Quirk *et al.* (1972: 376) as non-assertive and assertive forms, and with the extent to which these are paralleled by the suppletive pair *some* and *any*. He does, however—more relevantly to my subject—draw attention to opposite features of the two suppletive pairs: *already/yet* have a forward-looking sense which makes it sensible to say of someone that he is already old, or that he is not old yet, but not that he is already young, or not young yet, while *still/anymore* have a retrospective sense allowing *He is still young* or *He isn't young anymore*, but not *He is still old* or *He isn't old anymore*. (The use of the word *anymore* in the title of Horn's paper is explained as a usage of certain dialects in which *anymore* is an assertive form, e.g. *Floyd always thinks he is right anymore*. It seems that this is fairly closely equivalent to British English *nowadays*. The point is of no importance to my argument.)

Before going any further I must point out that there are other uses of the items *yet*, *any longer* and *still* besides those that I am dealing with. I shall not dwell on the obvious ones (e.g. *This paper isn't any longer than necessary*), but I shall conclude with a short treatment of *still* as a conjunctive adjunct, partly because it is desirable to draw attention to troublesome ambiguities such as that in *We shall still have to be careful*, and partly because there are actually two conjunctive uses of *still*, one of which is more closely related to the aspectual adjunct than the other. Moreover, all of these uses of *still* may have a cohesive force and it would be of interest to examine the different types of cohesion involved.

I should also disclaim any intention of paying separate attention either to what I regard as synonyms of *any longer* and *not any longer*, namely *anymore*, *no longer* and *no more* or to sundry other items which have some relation to the same syntactic field, such as *by now*.

The main treatment falls into three sections, dealing with the meaning of the items, the suppletive relation between subsets of them (in connection with polarity and mood), and the distribution of the items in clauses of various aspects.

9.1 THE MEANING OF THE ITEMS

The meaning of these adjuncts can be explained by reference to Figure 9.1. There are two strands to the meaning: first, there is a reference point in time indicated by x placed on a line; secondly, there is a contrast with an imagined situation that is different from the actual one. This is shown by the difference between the top line of the diagram and the bottom one; the bottom one, prefixed by the word *not*, is the rejected situation. A broken line indicates a period of time during which it is not raining and a solid one represents a period when it is. Assuming present tense, as in the example chosen for

Figure 9.1 The meanings of *still* and *already*

illustration, x is the moment of utterance—but, of course, the reference point is still required in past tense or even in non-finite expressions such as *For it to be still raining* (at time x) . . . The contrastive factor in the meaning of the item *still* is that it suggests that it might have stopped raining earlier than x but has not. It would therefore not be quite an adequate explanation to say (cf. Horn 1970: 319) that the sentence presupposes that it was raining earlier than x and asserts that it is raining at x. What this explanation lacks is the notion of continuance, namely that it has not stopped when it might have done. It misses the idea that there is no break in the solid line at the top of the diagram, and it misses the idea of counter-expectation.

Turning now to *already*, *It is already raining* says that it is raining now and suggests that it might instead have started later. Again, it would not be quite sufficient to say that *It is already raining* presupposes that it will be raining later and asserts that it is raining now, since this omits to mention the essential idea of the non-delaying of the start.

Both sentences in Figure 9.1, of course, imply that it is raining now; they differ by making a contrast with different imagined situations. We might note here that the sentence with *still* has no implication about what is going to happen after x. We can say *It's still raining and it may never stop*. Similarly, we can say *It's already raining and in fact it always has been*, *already* carrying no implication about the state of affairs previous to x. Traugott and Waterhouse in their interpretation of the sense of *already* fail to point out that it suggests a contrast between the actual situation and a later inception of the state of affairs referred to. Thus they say that *She has decided to take that job* and *She has already decided to take that job* 'are little, if at all, different in meaning; if *already* has any function in these sentences, it is to emphasise the perfectiveness' (1969: 298). They then say that *He is already here* 'implies that he was not here before but has arrived'. In my interpretation, it means that he is here rather than still to arrive; and *She has already decided to take that job* means that she has not delayed taking the decision. Thus in the perfect sentence the adjunct *already* is by no means redundant, as suggested.

9.2 SUPPLETION: NEGATIVE AND INTERROGATIVE CLAUSES

9.2.1 'Straight' negatives

Figure 9.2 shows two expressions which mean it is not raining. The reference point is on the broken line instead of on the solid one. The first one, with *any longer*, means 'It has stopped raining when it might have continued until

Figure 9.2 The meanings of *any longer* and *yet*

now', and the other means 'The rain has not started instead of having begun by this time'. The top row of the positive diagrams in Figure 9.1 is the same as the bottom row of the negative ones, and vice versa. The pair of examples *It's still raining* and *It isn't raining any longer* show the well-known suppletive relation between *still* and *any longer* referring to continuity or cessation, while the other two sentences in Figures 9.1 and 9.2 show the suppletive relation between *already* and *yet* referring to inception or delayed inception. I shall say that clauses of the first type are in continuative aspect, while those of the second are in inceptive aspect.

9.2.2 'Loaded' negatives

There are still other negative expressions, however, which at first sight seem to cast doubt on the suppletiveness of the relation. These are shown in Figure 9.3.

negative	straight	loaded	inverse
continuative (*still*)	*not any longer*	*not still*	*already not*
inceptive (*already*)	*not yet*	*not already*	*still not*

Figure 9.3 Some related negative expressions

The following is a list of examples corresponding to the top row of Figure 9.3, the negations of *I can still see you*:

continuative, straight: *I can't see you any longer*
        loaded: *I can't still see you*
        inverse: *I already can't see you*

Examples corresponding to the bottom row, the negations of *I can already see you*, are:

inceptive, straight: *I can't see you yet*
        loaded: *I can't already see you*
        inverse: *I still can't see you*

Leech (1983: 156–69) analyses positive, negative and interrogative sentences which contain assertive and non-assertive items. He does not deal with the type I have called 'inverse' but he includes my 'loaded' ones. He describes both the logical form of the sentences and the pragmatic implicatures of their utterance. In his analysis of the logical form he concludes that the assertive items are always in a proposition that has a positive operator, though that proposition may be embedded in a larger proposition which has *neg* or *?* as its operator. Thus the sentence:

The train hasn't arrived yet

has the logical form:

[neg(X)]

while

The train hasn't arrived already

has the form:

[neg(TRUE[pos(X)])]
i.e. It is not true that the train has arrived already.

Leech (1983: 166) declines to provide a pragmatic analysis of this type of negative, saying that it is a 'rather different problem' (i.e. different from the problem of other negative propositions). In a footnote (172), however, he comments that 'it only allows the strictly metalinguistic interpretation which is clarified by the use of quotation marks'. Thus, presumably Leech would see the following example as typical: A says *I think you can already see me* and B replies *No I can't 'already see you'; of course not*. However, it seems that the loaded type is sometimes used when the proposition has been merely suggested rather than actually put into words. For instance, if somebody is mouthing words into a microphone from inside a soundproof but transparent cubicle, somebody outside the cubicle might say, if there suddenly developed a fault in the wiring, *I can't still hear you*. The action of the person in the cubicle is taken to suggest his belief in the proposition 'you can still hear me'.

Leech's discussion is of negation and interrogation, not aspect, so it is not surprising that he does not include examples involving *still* and *any longer*. His examples include the items *already*, *yet*, *some* and *any*. It may seem improbable that *some* would occur in denials which are merely implicit such as the one just described containing *still* (*I can't still hear you*), but I feel one cannot rule out the possibility of such a use of *already*: e.g. *He isn't already here, you know*, (*as you seem to think*).[1]

9.2.3 'Inverse' negatives

In the inverse type of negative, the assertive item, *already* or *still*, is placed outside the scope of the negation, usually before the negative particle.[2] In this type, *still* belongs to inceptive aspect and *already* to continuative; both *I can't hear you yet* and *I still can't hear you* are inceptive, suggesting delay in the start of the positive state of affairs (see p. 241 below for confirmation of this finding: continuative aspect is not compatible with the perfect, while inceptive aspect is). There is thus not a suppletive pair, but a suppletive triple to realize the inceptive aspect: *already/yet/still*. Correspondingly in the continuative there is the suppletive triple: *still/any longer/already*. The presence of *still* and *already* in both lists, though in different positions in the lists, is a result of the sense relation between these items—the relation which Leech (1974: 116–7) calls inverse opposition (cf. the relation between *necessary* and *possible*).

The difference of meaning between the plain negative (e.g. *I can't hear you yet*) and the inverse negative (e.g. *I still can't hear you*) is that the first means 'the positive state of affairs has been delayed', while the latter means 'the negative state of affairs has not ceased'. This is a difference of emphasis likely to be occasioned by the need to counter different beliefs on the part of the addressee. It does seem, however, that the continuative inverse is relatively improbable. Of the following four meanings, the last strikes one as a perverse way of expressing oneself unless the contextual pressures are very strong:

an anticipated state is delayed (*not yet*)
an actual absence of a state persists (*still not*)
an actual state is not continued (*not any longer*)
an anticipated absence of a state has begun (*already not*)

9.2.4 Interrogatives

I now want to bring into the discussion the interrogative sentence corresponding to the declaratives already treated. There are complications. It is not only that there are loaded interrogatives of the kind *Can you see me already?*, but that there are interrogatives corresponding to all the negative types in Figure 9.3. Quirk *et al.* (1972: 388–90) point out the possibility of combining *already*, realizing what they call 'positive orientation', with negation, giving 'negative orientation', as in *Hasn't the boat left already?*

Leech's analysis of the logical form of *Hasn't the train arrived yet?* is (163):

[?(TRUE[neg(X)])]
i.e. Is it true that the train has not arrived yet?

There is an implicature that 's assumes, or believes h to assume, that X is not the case', but at the same time there is the additional implicature that 's has had or believes h to have had a disposition to believe that X' (168). There is thus a conflict of expectations—an earlier, 'cancelled' expectation that the train has arrived, and a later actual expectation that the train has not arrived ('I would at first have thought it had, but something seems to indicate it hasn't'). Furthermore, in a sentence like *Hasn't the train arrived already?* there is yet a 'further degree of obliquity' arising from the additional implicature of 's or h assumes that X' ('I would at first have thought it had, something seems to indicate it hasn't, but I assume it has all the same'). The logical form of the latter is:

[?(TRUE[neg(TRUE[pos(X)])])]
i.e. Is it true that it is not true that the train has arrived already?

9.2.5 Review of the whole paradigm

The whole paradigm of forms is too complex to be shown in a table. Figure 9.4 contains a system network and a list of classified examples. Figure 9.5 is an accompanying table of realization rules for the features [inceptive] and [continuative]. The forms dealt with, in addition to those accounted for in Leech 1983, include inverse negatives, loaded negatives and all the continuative types.

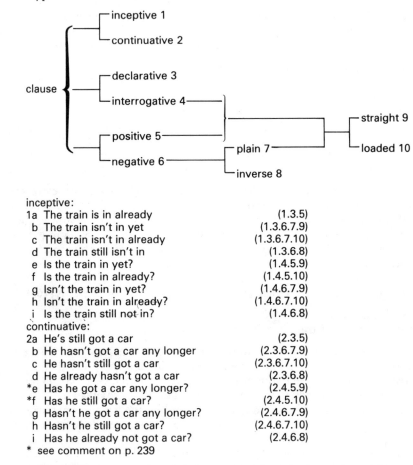

inceptive:
1a	The train is in already	(1.3.5)
b	The train isn't in yet	(1.3.6.7.9)
c	The train isn't in already	(1.3.6.7.10)
d	The train still isn't in	(1.3.6.8)
e	Is the train in yet?	(1.4.5.9)
f	Is the train in already?	(1.4.5.10)
g	Isn't the train in yet?	(1.4.6.7.9)
h	Isn't the train in already?	(1.4.6.7.10)
i	Is the train still not in?	(1.4.6.8)

continuative:
2a	He's still got a car	(2.3.5)
b	He hasn't got a car any longer	(2.3.6.7.9)
c	He hasn't still got a car	(2.3.6.7.10)
d	He already hasn't got a car	(2.3.6.8)
*e	Has he got a car any longer?	(2.4.5.9)
*f	Has he still got a car?	(2.4.5.10)
g	Hasn't he got a car any longer?	(2.4.6.7.9)
h	Hasn't he still got a car?	(2.4.6.7.10)
i	Has he already not got a car?	(2.4.6.8)

* see comment on p. 239

Figure 9.4 A system network and realizations for inceptive and
continuative adverbs in English

There follows an analysis of the meanings of the sentence types.

1a The train is already in (1.3.5)
      makes assumption that P may begin
      asserts that P has begun

FEATURE	CONDITION	ITEM USED
inceptive	declarative positive ———————— loaded	already
	straight	yet
	inverse	still
continuative	declarative positive ———————— loaded	still
	straight	any longer
	inverse	already

Figure 9.5 Realization rules for the system network in Figure 9.4

1b The train isn't in yet (1.3.6.7.9)
    makes assumption that P may begin
    asserts that P has not begun

1c The train isn't in already (1.3.6.7.10)
    makes assumption that P may begin
    remarks upon assumption that P has begun (10)
    asserts that P has not begun

1d The train still isn't in (1.3.6.8)
    makes assumption that P may begin
    remarks upon assumption that (not P) has ceased (8)
    asserts that (not P) continues

1e Is the train in yet? (1.4.5.9)
    makes assumption that P may begin
    asks whether P has begun

1f Is the train in already? (1.4.5.10)
    makes assumption that P may begin
    remarks upon assumption that P has begun (10)
    asks whether P has begun

1g Isn't the train in yet (1.4.6.7.9)
    makes assumption that P may begin
    remarks upon assumption that P has not begun
    asks whether P has begun

1h Isn't the train in already? (1.4.6.7.10)
    makes assumption that P may begin
    remarks upon assumption that P has not begun

favours assumption that P has begun (10)
asks whether P has begun

1i Is the train still not in? (1.4.6.8)
    makes assumption that P may begin
    remarks upon assumption that (not P) continues (8)
    asks whether (not P) continues (10)

2a He's still got a car (2.3.5)
    makes assumption that P may cease
    asserts that P continues

2b He hasn't got a car any longer (2.3.6.7.9)
    makes assumption that P may cease
    asserts that P has ceased

2c He hasn't still got a car (2.3.6.7.10)
    makes assumption that P may cease
    remarks upon assumption that P continues (10)
    asserts that P does not continue

2d He already hasn't got a car (2.3.6.8)
    makes assumption that P may cease
    remarks upon assumption that (not P) has been delayed (8)
    asserts that (not P) has begun

2e Has he got a car any longer? (2.4.5.9)
    favours assumption that P has ceased (see comment p. 239)
    asks whether P continues

2f Has he still got a car? (2.4.5.10)
    makes assumption that P may cease
    ? remarks upon assumption that P continues (see comment p. 239)
    asks whether P continues

2g Hasn't he got a car any longer? (2.4.6.7.9)
    makes assumption that P may cease
    remarks upon assumption that P does not continue
    asks whether P continues

2h Hasn't he still got a car? (2.4.6.7.10)
    makes assumption that P may cease
    remarks upon assumption that P does not continue
    favours assumption that P continues (10)
    asks whether P continues

2i Has he already not got a car? (2.4.6.8)
    makes assumption that P may cease
    remarks upon assumption that (not P) has begun (8)
    asks whether (not P) has begun

In these analyses P stands for the process referred to in the utterance (without the continuative or inceptive feature). Thus, for 1a to 1i, P = the process of the train being in, and for 2a to 2i, P = the process of his having a car. The wording 'remarks upon the assumption that . . .' means that the speaker is casting doubt upon or expressing surprise at the supposition indicated. This implies two attitudes to the proposition—an earlier one in favour of it and a later one that doubts or disfavours it. In negative interrogatives the speaker is reflecting on the unlikelihood of the negation ('Surely it is so').

Types 1e and 1f are commented on by Leech (1983: 163). These are the positive interrogatives of the inceptive type. 1e is a disinterested question, while 1f is prompted by some assumption or suggestion that is in the air—the speaker not only asks the question but perhaps remarks on the unexpectedness of the assumption that the train is in ('Surely not!' or 'You astonish me!'). Leech's analysis of the logical form of 1f would be:

[?(TRUE[pos(X)])]
i.e. Is it true that the train is in already?

And his pragmatic analysis contains the implicature (167) 'speaker assumes, or believes hearer to assume, that X'. This seems straightforward. But it would be interesting to know how Leech would have analysed the syntactically equivalent types 2e and 2f in the continuative series. With these a problem arises, and I have given them an interpretation that does not follow the pattern set by the other types. For some reason 2e *Has he got a car any longer?* is an unusual form of question. It seems negatively loaded, while 2f *has he still got a car?* is neutral. This is in contrast to 1e *Is the train in yet?*—which is neutral—and 1f *Is the train in already?*—which is positively loaded.

9.3 ASPECT

Clauses in which the adjuncts under investigation occur must have a feature of continuousness. The meanings which I have outlined above (Figure 9.1) have the continuance of a process (either an event or a state) as an essential component: stopping and starting imply lastingness up to or after a point in time. Therefore a clause which presents an event as momentary cannot take adjuncts of the type in question. The following is a list of examples that are unacceptable in this way. (The sets of four examples in this section are confined to continuative positive, continuative straight negative, inceptive positive and inceptive straight negative.)

He still broke his leg yesterday
The postman didn't call this morning any longer
McEnroe already hits it into the net
He didn't catch the first train yet

The feature of continuousness can be manifested in a clause in one or more of several ways; the clause may be stative, habitual or progressive. All of the examples listed above are non-stative, non-habitual and non-progressive. (If the last two are considered ambiguous, being open to habitual interpretation, it is only the non-habitual interpretation that is here being characterized as unacceptable. This kind of ambiguity is dealt with below.)

I will first illustrate and comment upon these kinds of continuousness; but there is also a kind that is associated with the perfect aspect and I will look into this rather different case afterwards.

Clauses that name a stative process are continuous by virtue of their aspectual character (for *aspectual character* see Lyons (1977: 706), where, however, it is verbs rather than clauses which are said to have an aspectual character). States are necessarily extended in time. The following examples are of stative clauses in continuative or inceptive aspect:

Bill still likes sugar in his coffee
He doesn't live in London any longer
He's already a member
He doesn't know the job very well yet

Habitual aspect is not necessarily overtly realized and in that case can only be inferred from the context. Thus, *Bill went to town on the bus* might be referring to one occasion or to a characteristically repeated series of occasions. Habitual aspect is overt if the quasi-modal verb *used* (*to*) is used: *Bill used to go to town on the bus*. It is also overt if there is a frequentative adjunct present such as *always*, *normally*, *usually*, *never*, *sometimes*: e.g. *Bill normally went to town on the bus*. Finally, habitual aspect is overt if there is a continuative or inceptive adjunct present: *Bill still went to town on the bus*. In the present tense the non-habitual interpretation of a clause such as *Bill goes to town on the bus* tends to be confined to special kinds of discourse such as recountings of the plots of novels. Nevertheless, taken out of context, such a clause is strictly ambiguous, but, as with the past tense, the ambiguity disappears if a continuative or inceptive adjunct is inserted: *Bill still goes to town on the bus*. The following examples illustrate continuative and inceptive aspect in habitual clauses:

Bill still goes to town on the bus
He doesn't buy Lyons's tea any longer
He already hits the ball firmly
He doesn't clean his own shoes yet

Progressive aspect is always overtly realized in ways that are perfectly familiar. The following examples illustrate this:

He's still coming downstairs
He isn't cutting the hedge any longer
He's already writing his second novel
He isn't having dinner yet

In general a clause cannot be both progressive and stative, but there is nothing to stop it being both progressive and habitual. In the following examples a frequentative adjunct is included in order to make the habitual interpretation inevitable:

He's still sometimes going to town on the bus
He isn't normally buying Lyons's tea any longer

He's already usually hitting the ball firmly
He isn't often cleaning his own shoes yet

Another combination of aspects is habitual with stative. In these examples I have included a little more context in order to make the habituality of the process easier to accept:

In most schools the headmaster usually still has total authority
The tickets aren't often for sale at the box office any longer
Whenever I ask anybody to join, he's almost always already a member
When the milkman comes, I'm sometimes not awake yet

Perfect aspect is a special case in the present connection since it is incompatible with continuative adjuncts, although inceptive adjuncts combine with it without trouble. This means that in a positive perfect clause *already* can occur but not *still*: *He's already passed the finishing line*, but not *He has still passed the finishing line*. The latter would imply that what's done might be undone. Earlier I drew attention to Horn's remark (1970: 324) that some lexical items (e.g. *old*, *dead*, *mother*) have a semantic feature denoting on inalienable characteristic. One cannot sensibly say *He isn't dead any longer* without a special reinterpretation of the adjective *dead*. It appears that this meaning of inalienability is 'grammaticalized' by the English perfect. The state of having passed the finishing line, once achieved, can never be repudiated. In the negative, *not yet* is in order but not *not any longer*:

* He has still passed the finishing line
* He hasn't brought your newspaper any longer
  I have already spoken to him
  I haven't spoken to him yet

Figure 9.6 displays the distribution of the adverbs in perfect clauses. It can be seen that if the restriction is viewed as a restriction on continuative aspect, we have to regard the inverse negative *already not* as a realization of continuative and the inverse negative *still not* as a realization of inceptive (this is a confirmation of the finding stated above in section 9.2.3 about suppletive triples—see p. 234:

* He already hasn't passed the finishing line
  I still haven't spoken to him

perfect	positive	negative		
		straight	inverse	loaded
continuative	*still	*not any longer	*already not	*not still
inceptive	already	not yet	still not	not already

Figure 9.6 The distribution of continuative and inceptive adverbs in perfect clauses

The incidence of continuative and inceptive aspect in the clause is shown in the network in Figure 9.7. The features [continuative] and [inceptive] are realized by insertion of the adverbs under discussion. Which adverb is used depends on other feature selections in mood, polarity and 'loading' (or 'orientation'), as indicated in Figure 9.5.

A further question that arises is how this network is situated in the functional components of the grammar. In terms of the functional components proposed by Fawcett (1980: 95 and 156), the place for these systems would be in the 'time' department of the experiential component. Note the dependence of continuativeness and inceptiveness on aspectual features of the clause. Fawcett makes a distinction between 'time' and 'time specification'. The adjuncts in question are not time specifications: they do not answer questions expressible with *when*, *how often*, *how long*, etc.

However, it is not entirely clear that there is no affinity with another functional component. We have seen that an essential feature of the meaning is one of counter-expectation. From the point of view purely of experiential meaning, we could argue that *He is still hungry* and *He is already hungry* express the same proposition—that he is hungry. The implied contrasts with other situations than that which actually prevails, introduced by *still* and *already*, are reminiscent of the meaning of polarity (see interpretations of the utterances on pp. 231–2 above). Fawcett (1980: 110) writes: '. . . every negated clause carries the assumption that the affirmative equivalent is "in the air"', and later (173):

> If the denial of a proposition . . . carries the inference that the addressee may have made a FALSE ASSUMPTION that the denied proposition was in fact the case, the knowledge of the universe drawn on in this component depends, as in the last, on the performer's estimate of what is in the addressee's mind.
> . . . often, indeed, it is the aim of a negative speech act to ANTICIPATE a referent situation that the addressee MIGHT be about to formulate, and so FORESTALL the establishment of that proposition . . .

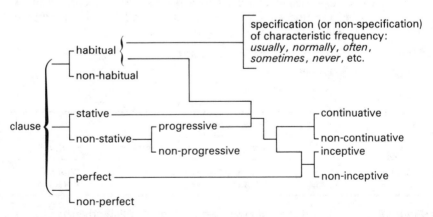

Figure 9.7 Aspectual features of the clause

There are therefore clear parallels with negativity. On p. 33, however, Fawcett writes (concerning the possible addition of an 'inferential component' to handle such 'purely inferential' items as *even*, *only* and *just*): 'Inferential meanings of a similar type are also built into other components, e.g. in temporal items (which belong in the experiential component) such as *already* and *yet*.' The following discussion on the cohesive *still* may suggest further difficulties in confining it to the experiential component.

Even if these questions were settled, the network offered in Figure 9.7 is still only an approximation to a final statement since there is the possibility of having more than one of these adjuncts in a single clause. Consider, for example, *He's still always already waiting, whenever I arrive, just as in the old days*; or (speaking of somebody undergoing a cure for addiction to a drug which taken in large doses deprives him of the power to speak) *He has already sometimes still been able to speak*. There is obviously a need for recursive selection of the features when more than one of the entry conditions is met.

9.4 CONJUNCTIVE ADJUNCTS

Finally I shall consider the conjunctive use of the adverb *still* and the cohesive force of the conjunctive and aspectual adjuncts.

The conjunctive *still* which is paraphrasable with *nevertheless* makes explicit the internal organization of the discourse. I use the term *internal* here in the sense of Halliday and Hasan (1976: 239–41). It is opposed to external conjunctive cohesion, which is external to the organization of the discourse and makes use of a connection in the thesis. An example of the internal *still* is to be found in:

He has still achieved a great deal

Here *still* has to be taken as conjunctive since it would not make sense as a continuative ('He has not ceased to have achieved a great deal'). It is interesting to note that there is still a factor of continuance in the conjunctive meaning; it can be paraphrased 'despite this, it remains true that . . .'. The *Oxford English Dictionary* explains this usage (*still* adv., 6,b) as a variety of usage (6,a) developed from the sense 'indicating continuance of a previous action or condition'. Goldsmith's line *For e'en though vanquished he could argue still* is quoted to illustrate 6,a, and this neatly shows how the historical development is feasible. It is remarkable, considering how distinct these two senses of *still* usually appear in context, how difficult it is to construct an example of the internal conjunction which, taken out of context, is not ambiguous (e.g. *He can still afford a short holiday*—'despite what has happened' vs. 'as against what I have just said'.) There is no ambiguity, however, in examples like *He is still old* (where ceasing to be old is not possible) or *Joan was still burned at the stake* (where the process is presented as an entire event).

The conjunctive adjunct is necessarily cohesive since it reflects the logic of discourse structure. The aspectual adjunct may be cohesive, but is not necessarily so. *Jack still works for ICI* might be making appeal to the addressee's general knowledge of Jack's circumstances (e.g. that he has worked for the firm for a long period, or that he has been talking of leaving) rather than to the fact that circumstances such as these have just been talked about, though the latter possibility is, of course, quite likely. Thus, if aspectual *still* is cohesive, it is cohesive in a way resembling reference rather than conjunction.

There is still another conjunctive use of *still*, and this is, in the terms of Halliday and Hasan 1976, the 'external' one. It can be illustrated as follows: *Jack climbed the ladder several times. The first time it slipped, and he fell down. The second time a rung broke, and he fell again. Then he tried a third time, but he still fell.* The paraphrase for this sense of *still* is 'again on this occasion as before'. It shows clearly as a distinct use from aspectual *still* when, as here, it is attached to a process that is not presented in continuous aspect. Further examples would be: *When she made a fair copy, she still spelled the word wrongly*, and *Even at his fourth attempt, he still didn't hit the target*. This *still* realizes a conjunctive relation in the text depending on identification of an occasion just mentioned, and an earlier series of occasions; it compares with *This time he succeeded*. It is external conjunction in that it refers to 'thesis time' rather than to the sequence of presentation in discourse. In Halliday and Hasan's classification of conjunctive relations it seems to belong to the category *complex temporal external repetitive* (1976: 266), though they do not list the word *still* under this or any other heading. The items they list for this category include *next time* and *this time*.

It is characteristic of conjunctive adjuncts that they cannot come within the scope of a negation (though this may not be true of those containing a reference item such as *on this occasion*). Hence a negative clause containing conjunctive *still* has no corresponding form with *yet*: *He still didn't hit the target*; **He didn't hit the target yet*. By contrast, the aspectual *still* easily translates into the straight negative with *yet*: *he still hasn't hit the target*; *He hasn't hit the target yet*. (NB *He didn't hit the target yet* is interpretable, but only in a habitual sense.)

To summarize, it seems we can distinguish (among many others) three senses of *still*:

a. aspectual: e.g. *He is still hungry* ('He has not ceased to be hungry')
b. conjunctive, external: e.g. *He still failed to convince me* (even now as before)
c. conjunctive, internal: e.g. *He has still achieved a great deal* (nevertheless)

Whether there is a corresponding set of meanings for the inceptive is an interesting question which I shall not pursue, but it is at least clear that *already* has no conjunctive uses:

a. aspectual: *He is already hungry*
b. conjunctive, external: ? *He soon convinced me*
c. conjunctive, internal: ? *In fact he has achieved a great deal*

NOTES

1. While working on a late revision of this section of my chapter, I came across the following in a book on discourse analysis: 'A student has joined two workmen in a pub, and they have bought him a drink, although they do not already know him' (Stubbs 1983: 59). The assumption is made that the workmen may get to know him (they have met in a pub). An assumption could be made that they already know him (they have bought him a drink). This assumption is denied.
2. Taglicht (1984: 122) sets up three classes of adverbial: nuclear—'items that must always be inside the domain of sentence negation'; intermediate—'items that may be inside or outside the domain of sentence negation'; and peripheral—'items that must always be outside the domain of sentence negation'. Our items *still* and *already* are obviously intermediate adverbials, while *yet* and *any longer* are nuclear. There is unfortunately no discussion of our aspectual adverbials, since the topic of Taglicht's book is focusing devices.

BIBLIOGRAPHY

Fawcett, R. P. (1980), *Cognitive Linguistics and Social Interaction: Towards an Integrated Mode of a Systemic Functional Grammar and the Other Components of an Interacting Mind*, Heidelberg, Juilis Groos Verlag and Exeter University.
Halliday, M. A. K. and Hasan, R. (1976), *Cohesion in English*, London, Longman.
Horn, L. R. (1970), 'Ain't it hard anymore', in *Papers from the 6th Regional Meeting of Chicago Linguistic Society*, 318–27.
Leech, G. N. (1974), *Semantics*, Harmondsworth, Penguin.
—— (1983), *Principles of Pragmatics*, London, Longman.
Lyons, J. (1977), *Semantics*, Cambridge, Cambridge University Press.
Morrissey, M. D. (1973), 'The English perfective and *still/anymore*', in *Journal of Linguistics*, 9, 65–9.
Quirk, R., Greenbaum, S., Leech, G. N. and Svartvik, J. (1972), *A Grammar of Contemporary English*, London, Longman.
Stubbs, M. (1983), *Discourse Analysis*, Oxford, Blackwell.
Taglicht, J. (1984), *Message and Emphasis, on Focus and Scope in English*, London, Longman.
Traugott, E. C. and Waterhouse, J. (1969), 'Already and yet: a suppletive set of aspect-markers', *Journal of Linguistics*, 5, 287–304.

Part V
The daughter dependency grammar version of the theory

10 Daughter dependency theory and systemic grammar

R. A. Hudson
University College London

In *Arguments for a Non-transformational Grammar* (1976) (henceforward *Arguments*) I have advocated a theory called Daughter dependency theory (henceforward DDT), and this chapter is an attempt to justify the ways in which DDT differs from systemic grammar.[1] *Arguments* is mainly about the differences between DDT and transformational grammar, so I felt it would be more appropriate to keep the discussion of its relation to systemic grammar for a separate occasion, on the assumption that many potential readers of *Arguments* would not be sufficiently familiar with systemic grammar to follow the discussion. The present volume seems an ideal place for it, and I hope that what I say below will go some way to making up for the fact that up till now I have made relatively few attempts to explain to my 'systemic' colleagues why I have found it necessary to abandon some of the fairly basic principles of systemic grammar. To start with, however, we can consider the respects in which DDT is similar to systemic grammar.

10.1 SIMILARITIES BETWEEN DDT AND SYSTEMIC GRAMMAR

The most important characteristic shared by DDT and systemic grammar, but in effect by no other theory of syntax, is the use of 'features on higher nodes'—in other words, the fact that in both theories clauses and phrases may be cross-classified and sub-classified, by means of systems or their equivalent in DDT. It is hard to overstate the importance of this characteristic, since it has so many ramifications throughout the rest of the grammar. For instance, it means that in both theories the rules which introduce immediate constituents ('realization rules', in one sense of the term) can be sensitive to quite specific sub-classifications of clauses and phrases, and only introduce immediate constituents of the right kind to fit the particular sub-class in question. Thus, assuming that the class of 'gerund clauses' will be identified by means of features of the clause we can formulate the realization rules in such a way that the first verb in such clauses will be an -ing form (like *playing* in *Playing squash is tiring*); whereas in a main clause, the first verb can be specified by the realization rules as finite. Largely as a result of this facility in both theories, it is never necessary to change features of constituents or to delete constituents. Moreover, different sub-classes of clause or phrase often allow different ranges of immediate constituent, so in both theories immediate constituents tend to get introduced one at a time, each one by a rule sensitive to a different feature of the clause or phrase concerned. Because constituents are introduced one at a time in this way, the rules which *introduce* them can easily be separated from the rules which *order* them, so there is no need, as in other theories, to introduce them in some kind of 'normal' order, and then reorder them.

In both theories the consequence of having features on higher nodes (plus a certain amount of other apparatus, such as function labels) is that structures can be generated correctly first time—there is no need for any rules for reordering, for changing features, for deleting items, or for in any other way undoing the effects of earlier rules. In other words, there are no transformations in either theory, and for each unambiguous sentence only one syntactic structure need be generated, rather than a series of structures including a deep structure, a surface structure, and a number of other intermediate structures. This characteristic of the two theories seems to me to be perhaps their greatest attraction, virtually irrespective of the aims of the user of the theory. For the generative grammarian, the analyser of texts, the language teacher, or the student of 'artificial intelligence', there seems to be nothing but gain in reducing the number of syntactic structures to one per sentence, provided, first, that this single structure contains all the syntax of the sentence (both the 'deep' relations and also the 'surface' relations, so that the syntactic structure can be related directly to both the semantic and the phonological structures); and, second, that it can be generated in a revealing and natural way. In both theories these two conditions seem to be satisfied, though I believe that DDT generates structures in a rather more revealing and natural way than does systemic grammar (e.g. Hudson 1971).

There are a number of other similarities between DDT and systemic grammar: for instance, they both tend to encourage relatively 'flat' structures, rather than 'tall' ones with many rank-steps and few immediate constituents per structure. However, none is as significant as the use of features on higher nodes, either in terms of their ramifications, or in terms of their uniqueness to these two theories. It is worth pointing out, in this connection, that this is also one of the most significant properties of Firth's theory of 'prosodic analysis', where 'prosodies', which are formally the same as features, are assigned to larger units than segments—syllables and words, or 'feet' and tone-groups, according to the type of phenomenon in question.

10.2 THE ROLE OF FEATURES

We turn now to the first of the main differences between DDT and systemic grammar: in DDT, features reflect similarities between items ONLY with respect to syntactic distribution and with respect to internal structure to the extent that this can be related to syntactic distribution. In particular, there is no place in DDT for syntactic features which reflect either semantic similarities or structural similarities but no distributional similarities. For instance, if it turns out that there is no difference in distribution between positive and negative clauses, or between clauses with and without an object, no features will be attached to clause nodes to distinguish these types. This principle has some surprisingly radical consequences for the analyses one produces. It means, for instance, that virtually all the clause-features associated with Halliday's transitivity and theme are no longer needed, and neither is the distinction between wh- questions and 'polarity' questions, since these distinctions appear to have nothing to do with syntactic distribution: wherever a wh- question can appear, syntactically speaking, so can a polarity question, and vice versa.

From the point of view of a generative grammar, at least, it is simply common sense to apply the principles we have just stated, since otherwise the grammar is unnecessarily complex. It reduces, in effect, to the principle 'Only postulate a syntactic feature when you need it in the grammar'. Of course, what you 'need' in a grammar depends on what theoretical assumptions one makes—in this case, in particular, on the assumptions one makes about the relations of syntax to semantics. If one assumes, for instance, that syntax and semantics are separate levels and that the rules which relate the syntactic structure to the semantic structure cannot take account of syntagmatic relations in the syntactic structure, then clearly it will be necessary to summarize all the semantically relevant aspects of the (syntagmatic) structure of a clause in the features of the clause as a whole. However, I see no reason for making this assumption, so I believe the rules relating syntax to semantics will be able to 'read' the syntactic structure of a clause and work out from that what its meaning must be. This being so, there is no need for features of the clause to group clauses together on the basis of semantic similarities.

Similarly, if one assumes that the features of a clause should completely determine its internal structure, then it follows that every difference in internal structure between two clauses must be reflected by differences in their features, whether these features have anything to do with the clause's distribution or not. For instance, there will have to be clause-features distinguishing between the main clauses in 'For John to be late is unusual' and 'It's unusual for John to be late'. However, again I see no reason for making this assumption—though I thought there were reasons when I wrote *English Complex Sentences* (1971)—so DDT allows the rules relating clause features to their internal structures to be optional (or determined by features of the verb, as we shall see below). For example, extraposition (as in the example just quoted) is optional, as is the rule for moving a wh- item to the front of a question. Indeed, the latter rule is optional in two senses: first, it simply allows the possibility that in any interrogative clause some wh- item is at the front (since there is no feature difference between wh- interrogatives and polar interrogatives, as we have already seen); and, second, it allows ANY wh- item to be moved foward, regardless of its function as subject, object or whatever. In this way, DDT avoids the problem of ensuring that the features that determine which function the wh- item must have are compatible with the functions that are needed in its structure for other reasons (for instance, if there is a feature 'indirect object as wh- item', then the clause must also have the features that require it to contain an indirect object).

The principle that syntactic features should be postulated only when they are needed in the grammar has another, quite far-reaching consequence: the sub-classification of items in syntax is not open-ended and variable in delicacy, but is completely determined by the rules of the grammar in question. Every distinction which is presupposed by the rules must be made in the classification rules (alias systems), and no other distinctions must be made. Of course, this has nothing to do with the practical interpretation of 'delicacy', whereby in textual analysis you can pick and choose among the features you choose to specify in classifying clauses in a text. But what it does mean is that the lexicon cannot be considered to be 'most delicate grammar', by simply extending the classification of, say, words until every class has just one member, a lexical item—with *apple* in one class and *pear* in another class, for example. So far as I know, there is no difference between *apple* and *pear* in the syntactic rules that apply to them, and the only differences between them are in their meanings and their pronunciations. Assuming this to be so, we can conclude that there is no syntactic difference, as such, at all between pairs of sentences like 'He was eating an apple' and 'He was eating a pear', and the syntactic features in the structure of one will be exactly the same as those in the structure of the other; the only differences will be in their semantic and phonological structures.

In conclusion, a DDT grammar will contain far fewer syntactic features, and generate sentence structures with far fewer features per node, than a systemic grammar for the same language. From this point of view, DDT occupies a midway position between systemic grammar, where features proliferate, and transformational grammar, where there are none at all on higher nodes (though they can proliferate wildly on terminal nodes).

10.3 SISTER DEPENDENCIES

Systemic grammar belongs clearly to the group of grammars called 'constituency grammars', which also includes all the American schools derived from the structuralist movement (transformational grammar, stratificational grammar and tagmemics). This means that in the structures generated the only relations which are shown explicitly (other than sequence relations) are part/whole relations—that is, all the lines in a structure show relations between constituents and their immediate constituents (or, in the terminology I tend to use, between 'mothers' and their 'daughters'). In contrast with this group of grammars, there are 'dependency grammars', in which the only relations that are shown in a structure are those between parts, between 'sisters'. In most such grammars the nodes of a structure represent words or morphemes, and the lines between them show dependency relations. To take an easy example, a constituency grammar will generate a structure for 'Cows moo' with a node for the whole clause and another for each of the words, and lines connecting the latter to the former, with the latter lower on the page than the former. On the other hand, a dependency grammar will generate a structure containing just two nodes, one for each word, and a line pointing from *moo* to *cows* to show that *moo* depends on *cows*.

The accepted notation of dependency theory is confusing, from our point of view, since it also uses the vertical dimension on the page, but this time to show the direction of the dependency relation, with the 'modifier' always lower than the 'head'. It would be confusing for the reader if I used the vertical dimension in both of these ways, since there is a big difference between 'A is part of B' and 'A depends on B'—between saying '*cows* is part of *cows moo*' and saying '*cows* depends on *moo*'. To avoid this confusion, I shall reserve the vertical dimension for the part/whole relation, and use arrows to show the direction of the dependency between parts (with the arrow pointing from the head towards the modifier). A pure constituency-type structure for 'Cows moo' would therefore be like (a) below, and a pure dependency-type structure would be like (b):

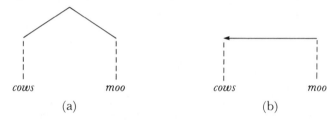

cows   moo   cows   moo

(a)   (b)

The trouble with choosing between these two approaches is that each of them has virtues which the other lacks. The constituency approach has the virtue of identifying items larger than words—clauses and phrases—so that the grammar can make generalizations about these items; for instance, this allows us to distinguish between interrogative and declarative clauses, or between relative and adverbial clauses, without having to pretend that these properties were properties of some particular word, such as the verb. Moreover, systemic grammars depend crucially on being able to assign features to higher nodes, as we have already seen, so it is essential to have higher nodes, as in the constituency approach; and the same is true, of course, of DDT grammars.

On the other hand, the dependency approach has the virtue of being able easily to capture dependency relations between parts—between verbs and their complements, between auxiliary verbs and the verbs they 'take', between prepositions and their complements, between noun and antecedents and relative clauses, between main clauses and subordinate clauses (in those constructions where the latter are not embedded in the former). These are all constructions which have traditionally been described in terms of dependency relations between parts, but the constituency approach cannot capture this relationship directly: the best it can do is to show both the parts as being dependent on the same feature of the mother—the systemic approach. For instance, the dependency of the object nominal on the verb is shown by classifying clauses in such a way that one class will consist of clauses which contain a transitive verb and an object; then verbs have to be classified as transitive or not, and realization rules say that clauses belonging to the class concerned contain BOTH a transitive verb and an object nominal. In other words, the dependency of the nominal on the verb is shown in making BOTH of them depend on the same clause feature. (I have deliberately simplified the analysis—I realize that all the current analyses of transitivity are very much more sophisticated than the simple transitive/intransitive distinction I am implying here, but I do not think the general point I am making is affected by this.)

One disadvantage of the systemic approach, which it shares with the transformational approach and all other constituency-based approaches, is that there is nothing in the structure of the sentence, as such, to show that it is the class of the verb that determines whether the object is allowed, rather than the other way round (or rather than neither of them being relevant to the other, as with the various auxiliary verbs in English). This information can only be deduced by studying the grammar. This is a disadvantage not only because native speakers presumably have at least as much awareness of this relationship as they do of constituency relationships, but also because there are a number of rules in the grammar which need to refer to these dependency relations between parts. For instance, there is a very simple generalization which seems to come quite close to being true in English and many other languages: that the dependent element follows the element on which it depends. (By contrast, there are languages such as Japanese in which they are the other way round.)

Another disadvantage of the systemic approach is that it means that the grammar has to include a very much larger number of features on higher nodes than are needed in DDT grammars, and most of these features will have nothing to do with the distribution of the clause or phrase concerned, but will have the job simply of showing dependencies among its parts. Moreover, alongside all these extra features on higher nodes we still need exactly the same range of features for classifying the 'head' words (verbs, prepositions, and so on) as we need if we are allowed to show the dependencies directly between the parts, as in dependency theory.

I have tried to show the virtues that each of the two competing approaches has: constituency grammars are good because they have part/whole relations; dependency grammars are good because they have part/part relations. The obvious question is whether it is not possible to have the best of both worlds, and the answer, not surprisingly, is that in DDT it is possible: DDT grammars generate structures which show BOTH part/whole relations AND part/part relations. In the case of 'Cows moo', there is a part/whole relation between each of the words and the whole clause, but there is also a part/part relation between the two words, so the structure generated would be a combination of (a) and (b) above:

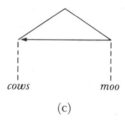

(c)

However, DDT departs even more radically than this from the constituency approach of systemic grammar: there are some part/whole relations which it DOES NOT show explicitly in the structure, or at least not by means of a line connecting the part directly to the whole. Instead, it only connects the whole to those of its parts which depend, for their presence or their features, on the features of the whole, rather than on features of one of its parts. In 'Cows moo', this is true of both words, since the features of the clause require on the one hand that it contain a finite verb (*moo*) and on the other hand that it contain a subject (*cows*). However, if we change the example to 'Cows eat grass', we find that *grass* depends on the features of the verb *eat*: if the latter had been intransitive, the former could not have been present. Therefore, in the structure which a DDT grammar generates for this sentence, there is no direct link between the node representing *grass* and the one representing the whole clause. On the other hand, the structure still shows that *grass* is a part of the clause because it is in a part/part relation to an item (*eat*) which is shown as being in a part/whole relation to the whole clause. The structure would include the following lines:

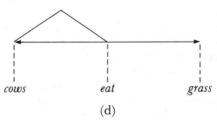

(d)

In other words, the lines in a DDT structure ALL show dependencies: the horizontal lines (with arrow-heads) show part/part dependencies ('sister dependencies'), while the vertical or diagonal ones show dependencies between parts and wholes ('daughter dependencies').

It might be objected, against this approach, that the systemic approach allows greater flexibility in describing transitivity patterns, since the pattern of verb complements in a clause (subjects, objects and the like) can be described without tying the distinctions rigidly to verb classes—the point being that many verbs can occur in more than one pattern. However, this objection loses its point when one separates the lexicon from the syntax, as in DDT, since it is possible simply to leave many verbs UNSPECIFIED in the lexicon for the systems concerned. To continue with our simplified analysis of transitivity, in terms of a two-way classification of verbs as either transitive or intransitive, it is easy to show that many verbs in English can occur either with or without an object, simply by leaving them unspecified in the lexicon for the distinction between transitive and intransitive. This allows them to be used either with the feature transitive or with the feature intransitive—in particular sentence structures—without complicating either the rules of syntax or the lexicon in any way.

How does a DDT grammar actually generate structures like (c) and (d)? A simple answer is possible, although the details are complex (particularly in the 'sequence rules'). One set of rules ('daughter dependency rules') defines dependency relations between features of wholes and features of those parts which depend on these features; these rules are simply the 'realizational rules' of some versions of systemic grammar (such as my version in 'English Complex Sentences'), but under a different name. Another set of rules ('sister dependency rules') defines the dependency relations between parts. Between them, these two sets of rules are responsible for the PRESENCE of all the constituents of a sentence. Finally, there is a third set of rules, called 'sequence rules', which are responsible for the ORDER of constituents within the sentence, taking account, among other things, of the dependency relations already established.

Taking the structure for 'Cows eat grass' as an example, the daughter dependency rules specify that the features of the clause require two daughters: one with the features for a finite verb (like *eat*), and the other with those for a nominal (like *cows*). The sister dependency rules specify that a verb with features such as those for *moo* (which include not only 'finite' but also others such as 'verb' and 'transitive') needs two sisters: both nominals, but one depending on the feature 'verb' and the other depending on the feature 'transitive'. Finally, the sequence rules say that a nominal depending on the feature 'verb' precedes the verb, and is to be identified with the nominal that depends as a daughter on the clause, and that any other nominal must follow the verb. This completes the syntactic structure for 'Cows eat grass', except that each of the nodes has to be fully labelled with features, supplied by the classification rules, alias systems. In order to add phonological and semantic details about the words, the lexicon has to be consulted, but this takes us out of the strictly syntactic part of the analysis.

10.4 FUNCTION LABELS

In systemic grammar a distinction is made between 'elements of structure' or 'functions' and 'classes' or 'features'; for instance, Subject, Predicate, Complement and Adjunct are the names of functions, while Nominal group and Verbal group are the names of classes. Functions are needed as well as classes, it is claimed, because we sometimes need to refer to items in 'functional' terms, that is, with reference to their role in the sentence containing them. Thus it is necessary in some rules to refer to the subject of a clause, but there is no CLASS that one can use for this purpose, since the class of items which can occur as subject can also occur with other functions.

While agreeing that a distinction has to be made between 'functional' and 'classificatory' definitions, I do not agree that this need be shown in this way, by having two sets of labels on each node, one showing the item's function and the other showing the classes to which it belongs. The reason is that the functional information is already available, in a DDT structure, in the dependency lines. For example, the structure for 'Cows eat grass' shows that *grass* is the object by showing that it is the nominal which depends on the feature 'transitive' of the verb; whereas *cows* depends simply on the feature 'verb' (and also on features of the clause, of course). Thus any item can be identified functionally simply by referring both to its own class and to the feature (of another item) on which it depends. The notation for making such reference is very simple: it is simply the notation used in stucture diagrams. For example, the object of a clause can be defined as 'nominal ⟵ transitive', which can be translated into a noun + relative clause construction, as 'the nominal which depends (as a sister) on the feature transitive'.

One immediate gain from eliminating function labels in this way is that the features of the whole can be related DIRECTLY to the features of the parts, rather than having to be related indirectly, via the parts' functions, as in systemic grammar. Consequently, instead of having two types of rule, one corresponding to the 'feature realization rules' of systemic grammar and one to 'function realization rules', we need in DDT only the one type, corresponding to 'feature realization rules' (our daughter dependency rules). This represents a considerable simplification with very little extra cost elsewhere in the grammar.

However, I have to admit that there is SOME cost, in that we cannot get away entirely with just features labelling the nodes. In particular, there is no way that I know of in which we can define notions such as Halliday's 'theme' simply in terms of features, precisely because the items covered by such terms can have a very wide range of features, and can depend, moreover, on an equally wide range of other features. Taking the example of 'theme' (for which I have used the label TOPIC, perhaps not very appropriately), there seem to be good reasons for thinking of some kind of 'positional slot' existing at the front of a clause, which we might call its theme, and which may be 'filled' by a variety of classes of item—by a front-shifted object for instance, or a wh- item in an interrogative clause (as in 'People like that I can't stand' and 'Who did you see?' respectively). The reasons for postulating such a slot are syntactic rather than semantic (so far as I know, these two classes of item are OPPOSITE in meaning to each other: for instance, front-shifted objects are usually anaphoric and often definite, whereas wh- items are by definition indefinite). The two classes are mutually exclusive (a clause cannot contain both a front-shifted object and also a front-shifted wh- item), and in both cases the item concerned may be 'raised' out of an embedded clause inside the clause in question (as in 'People like that I should think she'ld say we ought to avoid inviting to the party at all costs' and 'What does he say we ought to tell her to get?'). Moreover, the sequence rules for positioning the items in such functional slots seem rather different from those needed for other items—functional slots are all up at the beginning of the clause, and rules thar refer to functional slots take priority over most other types of rule.

Consequently, in DDT structures a FEW nodes in each clause (and possibly in each nominal group too) bear specifically functional labels which are introduced by special rules, called 'function assignment rules'. As their name implies, these rules are unlike any rules in systemic grammar, since they assign functions to bundles of features which are present for other reasons— i.e. they apply to the features introduced by the dependency rules—rather than introducing new items, defined functionally, as with systemic feature realization rules. Even with this extra apparatus, DDT grammars are much simpler than they would have been if they had to assign function labels to all nodes as in systemic grammar.

10.5 SYSTEM NETWORKS AND CLASSIFICATION RULES

In section 10.1 we saw that the most important similarity between DDT and systemic grammar was in their ability to classify items, particularly clauses and phrases, in terms of features, thereby allowing for both cross-classification and sub-classification. This is done in systemic grammar by means of systems, organized in system networks, and in DDT it is done by classification rules, which can also be organized as a network. Moreover, from a formal point of view systems and classification rules are the same. However, alongside these fundamental similarities between DDT and systemic grammar there are a number of differences which need to be explained.

First, in my work on DDT I have not yet found any cases where it is essential, or even advantageous, to have a DISJUNCTION of features as the input to a classification rule. In other words, I have not found any cases where I would need to use a left-facing square bracket if I were using a network notation. This being so, it seems reasonable to treat it as a matter of principle that the input to a classification should be either a single feature or a conjunction of features, but never a disjunction (until we find a case where a disjunction really is necessary). In this way we restrict the power of the theory considerably, by ruling out any grammar containing disjunctions as input to classification rules. However, we can go further than this: we can rule out any grammar containing disjunctions in ANY syntactic rules (other than function assignment rules, interestingly enough—again justifying the inclusion of such rules as a completely separate type) on the grounds that, so far as I know, there are no such rules. That is, again I know of no rules in syntax which would benefit from being allowed to include a disjunction of features. This is a big claim to make, on the basis of an obviously limited range of experience, but it is always best to make one's hypotheses as big as possible, since they can always be pared down in the light of further experience (by adding caveats such as the one about function assignment rules). If this claim turns out to be true, it amounts to the principle that all syntactic classes should be 'natural classes', in the sense in which this term is used in Generative phonology: any class of items referred to in any rule must be definable in terms of less features than any of its sub-classes (which means, in effect, that it must not include any disjunctions).

Another difference between DDT and systemic grammar is that in DDT all the classification rules for syntax can be grouped together into one (enormous!) network, whereas in at least some versions of systemic grammar different system networks are postulated for different environments and/or for different ranks. The reason for rejecting the 'polysystemic' approach in DDT is that it misses generalizations: it prevents us from generalizing across environments or ranks, as the case may be. Of course, the reason for adopting a polysystemic approach in the first place is precisely because there are differences between environments or ranks in the ranges of options they allow, and it is claimed that it would be misleading to identify elements occurring in different environments.

However, there are other ways, even in systemic grammar, in which one can express such differences between environments or ranks: within the system network itself one can decide to which larger classes any given system should apply, and the realization rules can specify which features are obligatory in any environments which do impose restrictions. Consequently, there seems to be no advantage in postulating different system networks in the grammar, to outweigh the considerable disadvantage of missing generalizations on a large scale and, as I have said, a DDT grammar contains a single integrated set of classification rules, corresponding to a single system network with the term 'item' (for 'syntactic item') at the extreme left.

One last difference remains to be explained: the name of the theory. The reason for abandoning the term 'systemic' is that I had already abandoned the name 'system', which I found completely unhelpful in explaining the theory to the uninitiated: outside certain circles in Britain, 'system' scarcely exists as a technical linguistic term. 'Classification rule' seemed a much more revealing name for these rules. Having made this change, there was no point in continuing to call the theory 'systemic', so I had to look round for an alternative. I cannot claim that the name 'daughter dependency theory' is one of the strong points of the theory, but at least it reflects the emphasis on dependency relations and on part/whole (mother/daughter) relations. I hope a better name will be found: one promising candidate, suggested by Michael McCord, is 'unistructure syntax', which I should probably have adopted. However, there are many other weak points in the theory I am calling daughter dependency theory at present, as there are in every other theory, so maybe it would be wise to reserve the better name for the theory that will supersede it.

NOTE

1. This chapter was written as a paper in 1977, since when my position on several of the issues mentioned in it has changed radically—though I think that only one of these changes has represented a move towards the systemic position. Some of the developments in my thinking are the following:

(a) I now believe that no constituent structure is needed, so there is no need for any higher nodes, or for features of higher nodes, or for daughter dependency relations.

(b) I think features are a poor mechanism for showing 'valency' of verbs (and other governing items); I now prefer to show the types of syntactic Complements (objects, etc.) that a verb takes more directly, by a syntagmatic representation in the lexicon; consequently, there is no longer any need for sister dependency rules (though sister dependency relations are of course still needed in syntactic structures), nor is there any need for more than a small number of syntactic features, reflecting basic part-of-speech classification and inflectional categories.

(c) I have reverted to the use of explicit function labels for notions like 'subject' and 'object', though unlike Systemic Grammar these now relate one word to another word.

(d) Although I still believe syntactic and semantic structures are distinct, I no longer believe that it is possible to generate a complete sentence structure at the syntactic level without referring to the semantics; for example, the grammar refers to 'circumstantial' elements in terms of their semantic properties, rather than their syntactic characteristics, so a 'purely syntactic' grammar could not allow circumstantial elements in sentence structures.

I have discussed these changes, along with others, in a series of working papers, a number of which have been published (Hudson 1980a, b, c), and I have developed the ideas more fully in Hudson 1984.

BIBLIOGRAPHY

Hudson, R. A. (1971), *English Complex Sentences: An Introduction to Systemic Grammar*, Amsterdam, North Holland.
—— (1976), *Arguments for a Non-Transformational Grammar*, Chicago, University of Chicago Press.
—— (1980a), 'Daughter dependency grammar', in Lieb (ed.) (1980: 32–50, 106–7).
—— (1980b). 'Constituency and dependency', *Linguistics*, **18**, 179–98.
—— (1980c), 'A second attack on constituency: a reply to Dahl', *Linguistics*, **18**, 489–504.
—— (1984), *Word Grammar*, Oxford, Blackwell.
Lieb, H.-H. (ed.) (1980), *Oberflächensyntax und Semantik*, Tübingen, Niemeyer.

11 Voice neutrality and functional roles in the English clause: a contribution to daughter dependency grammar

J. Taglicht
The Hebrew University of Jerusalem

11.0 INTRODUCTION

This chapter suggests a way of accounting for the phenomenon of 'voice neutrality' in a variant of Hudson's daughter dependency grammar. It is claimed that two changes are required for this purpose: (1) the addition of the classification rule [+predicate:±personal], and (2) the addition of COMPLE-MENT to the set of labelled functions.

11.1 FUNCTIONAL ROLES IN DAUGHTER DEPENDENCY GRAMMAR

All grammars distinguish in some way between classes of items, such as nouns, pronouns, or adjectives, and syntactic functions, such as subject, object, or complement; but the way this distinction is made depends on the theory.[1] We have 'labelled' functions, which are atomic concepts, and 'configurational' functions, which are analytical expressions specifying a class of linguistic items and a place in a structure. For example, in most TG grammars, 'subject' = the noun phrase that is an IC of a sentence, and 'object' = the noun phrase that is an IC of a verb phrase. One of the questions that every theory of grammar must answer is: how much 'labelling' of functions is necessary? Daughter dependency grammar, as expounded in Hudson 1976, uses a very small set of functions, which includes SUBJECT (i.e. 'mood subject') and TOPIC (alias 'theme'). In addition, there are configurational functions, but these differ from the configurational functions of 'standard' TG grammar in two respects:

(a) The places are defined not in relation to labels for major categories (e.g. S, VP) but in relation to specific features, e.g. 'object of verb' depends on the feature +transitive.
(b) The places may be defined
   (i) in relation to 'mothers', e.g. +noun ← +nominal for 'head of nominal

phrase' (with the lowered arrow marking daughter–mother dependency);

(ii) in relation to '(elder) sisters', e.g. +nominal ← +transitive for 'object of verb' (with the raised arrow marking sister–sister dependency.

Just as objects are sister-dependent on transitive verbs, so past participles can be sister-dependent on auxiliary *have*, or the infinitive marker *to* and the -*ing* form on different classes of catenative verbs. In this way DDG (unlike 'orthodox' systemic grammar) gives direct expression to the idea that transitive verbs 'govern' objects, that the perfect auxiliary governs a past participle, and so on.

11.2 VOICE NEUTRALITY IN ENGLISH

The term 'voice neutral' has been used by Huddleston (1969: 258) and by Palmer (1974: 87) to characterize verbs that resemble *seem* and *may*, as used in the examples below, in permitting the passivization of a following verb without the truth value of the sentence being affected (the examples are Huddleston's).

(1a) His remarks seem to have offended her
(1b) She seems to have been offended by his remarks
(2a) His remarks may have offended her
(2b) She may have been offended by his remarks

This property is not shared by verbs like *intend*, or *will* in its volitional sense, as appears from (3) and (4) below:

(3a) He did not intend to offend her
(3b) She did not intend to be offended by him
(4a) He wouldn't take her home
(4b) She wouldn't be taken home by him

The phenomenon of voice neutrality, in this sense, was previously examined by Svartvik 1966 and by Rosenbaum 1967. Here I shall extend the use of the term so as to cover also the behaviour of verbs like *believe*, or verbs like *want*, which permit the passivization of a following nominal phrase + active infinitive construction without change in the truth value of the sentence:

(5a) We wanted the doctor to examine him
(5b) We wanted him to be examined by the doctor

Contrast verbs like *persuade*:

(6a) We persuaded the doctor to examine him
(6b) We persuaded him to be examined by the doctor

These constructions have of course been extensively treated by transformationalists (Chomsky 1965); Rosenbaum 1967, etc.).

Voice neutrality in the narrower sense, as in (1) and (2) above, can only be accounted for by setting up a class or classes of verbs which do not contract transitivity relations with nominal phrases, that is, which do not have NPs as subjects or objects. This is done in Huddleston 1969 (where the approach is transformational) by a combination of two devices: (a) Jespersen's split-subject analysis, for voice-neutral catenative verbs, and (b) the exclusion of auxiliaries from transitivity relations, with items like volitional *will* represented as main verbs in deep structure.

In systemic grammar, there has been no explanatory account, so far, of voice neutrality in either of the senses specified above. It is the object of the remainder of this chapter to give an account of voice neutrality in the wider sense within the general framework of daughter dependency grammar.

11.3 THE FEATURE [−PERSONAL] AS A KEY TO VOICE NEUTRALITY

The analysis of verbs in Hudson 1976 seems to me to be the most successful attempt to date to do justice both to the resemblances and to the differences between the various classes of English verbs, auxiliary and non-auxiliary. It lacks one very important distinction, however, which is crucial in the present context: the distinction between +personal and −personal.[2] The notion of [−personal] (or 'impersonal') verbs, that is, of verbs without subjects, is familiar in the grammar of Latin, Old English and other languages.It is also required in the grammar of present-day English for such sentences as:

(7) It's raining
(8) It's blowing a gale
(9) It's dark outside
(10) It's awful when they yell like that
(11) It says in this book that there are no snakes in Iceland
(12) It's time we faced the facts

I shall endeavour to show that [−personal] verbs also provide the most satisfactory explanation for voice neutrality in the first of the two senses distinguished above. The structural diagrams for (13) and (14) below will make this clear:

(13a) They had to appoint John
(13b) John had to be appointed
(14a) They hoped to appoint John
(14b) John hoped to be appointed

In Figure 11.1, all dependency relations are indicated by arrows. These point either from mothers to daughters (higher level to lower level) or from governing sisters to dependent sisters (same level of structure). The names of the features of predicate words have been made as transparent as possible; for the places of these features in the system network, see the Appendix.[3]

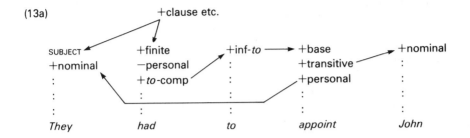

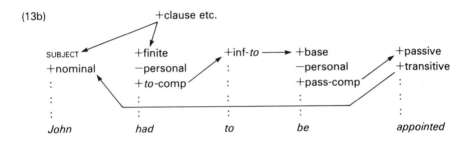

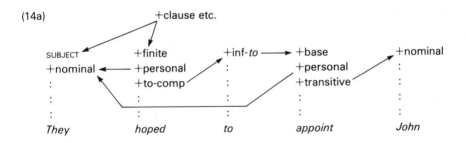

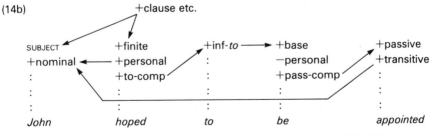

Figure 11.1 Structural diagrams for sentences (13a, b) and (14a, b)

In this analysis the verb *hope* has a subject, by virtue of possessing the feature [+personal], whereas the verbs *have* and *be*, being [−personal], have no subjects. Consequently, the constituent with the mood function SUBJECT is simultaneously involved in (14) in two distinct transitivity relations, as shown by the two arrows to [+nominal] in the SUBJECT constituent, which derive in (14a) from two distinct [+personal] verbs, and in (14b) from the feature [+personal] in the first verb and the feature [+transitive] in the last. In (13), on the other hand, the SUBJECT is involved in transitivity relations with one verb only, deriving in (13a) from [+personal] and in (13b) from [+transitive]. This is of course exactly what happens in the simplest pairs of active and passive clauses, as exemplified in

(15a) They appointed John
(15b) John was appointed

where *John* is in both cases the +nominal item depending on the feature [+transitive], that is the object, of *appoint*. The object of the verb *appoint* is also the subject of the passive participle *appointed*: so in (15b), as in (15a), *John* is subject of the main verb (see Appendix, (c), Identity Rules).

From the point of view of accounting for voice neutrality, it makes no difference whether we regard the complementation of the governing verb as verbal, with a single clause accommodating two or more verbs in a chain of verb–verb dependences, or as clausal, with as many clauses in the structure as there are verbs. Hence, where no other considerations intervene, the concept of verb complementation will naturally be preferred, by virtue of its greater economy (minimal embedding). This economy is one of the attractions of the notion of 'phase' as used in Halliday's original scale-and-category model, or in Sinclair 1972. The concept of phase, together with that of the verbal group, enables one to account for strings of verbs, both auxiliary and non-auxiliary, within a single clausal structure. It is one of the advantages of daughter dependency grammar that it can use a single feature [+verb-comp] (see Appendix, (a)) to account for what is common to dependence on auxiliaries and dependence on catenatives, but is accounted for in different ways in other versions of systemic grammar.

The option for the feature [+verb-comp] and the choice between [+personal] and [−personal] are not limited to verbs but exist also for non-verbal predicate words, both adjectives and adverbs, as will appear from (16)–(19) below:

(16a)   They were quick to notice the difference
(16b)   *The difference was quick to be noticed
(17a)   They were liable to notice the difference
(17b)   The difference was liable to be noticed
(18a)   They were out to impress their neighbours
(18b)   Their neighbours were out to be impressed
(19a)   They were about to close the gate
(19b)   The gate was about to be closed

Here *quick* and *out* are seen to be [+personal], whereas *liable* and *about*[4] are [−personal] in these constructions. Hence active and passive are equivalent in (17)and (19), but not in (16) and (18).

So far, the examples of [−personal] predicate words that we have discussed have all had the feature [+verb-comp] or the feature [+attributive] in addition. In such cases, as the examples show, the SUBJECT of the clause is supplied by an item that depends directly or indirectly on the [−personal] predicate—the subject of *appoint* in (15a), of *notice* in (17a), of *close* in (19a);and the objects of these verbs in the corresponding (b) sentences. The chain of dependence can be quite long, as in (20):

(20) They may seem to have been liable to get angry

Here the words *may*, *seem*, *have*, *been*, *liable*, and *get* are all [−personal], and the subject of *angry* is SUBJECT of the clause. But [−personal] predicates need not be [+verb-comp] or [+attributive]; and if they are not, they govern a 'dummy subject' *it* (see Appendix, (c)), which receives the mood function SUBJECT:

(21) It's snowing
(22) It's dark in this room

When [−personal] predicates govern *that* clauses or infinitive clauses, the sentences have the same superficial appearance as sentences with 'extraposed' clausal subjects, but the clauses that depend on [−personal] predicates cannot be front-shifted:

(23a)   It's time we started/(for us) to start
(23b)   *That we started/(for us) to start is time
(24a)   It seems that he's right
(24b)   *That he's right seems

Contrast:

(25a)   It seems clear that he's right
(25b)   That he's right seems clear

Here the *that* clause is subject, but of *clear*, not of *seem*. The combination of [−personal] with [+verb-comp] enables us to provide a single explanation for all instances of voice neutrality in the narrower sense, without the split-subject anaysis and the pyramids of embedded clauses which would otherwise be necessary. It meets the two demands that must be made on any explanation of the phenomenon: (1) that it be unified, accounting in the same way for the identical behaviour of auxiliaries and catenatives in this respect, and (2) that it be integrated in a general account of transitivity and active–passive correspondences.

11.4 'RAISING' AND VOICE NEUTRALITY

The notion of 'split' embedded clauses, though unnecessary (as we have seen) for the first kind of voice neutrality, is still required for the second kind. In sentences like

(26) I want there to be no mistake

or

(27) I want it to be understood that the decision is final

we have no reason for denying the existential *there* or the anticipatory *it* the function that they always have in independent clauses, i.e. SUBJECT. But since SUBJECT (as opposed to 'subject of the verb') depends on the future [+clause], it follows that there must be a dependent clause, not merely a dependent verb with its dependent sisters, both in (26) and in (27). We therefore assign the feature [+clause-obj] to the verb *want* in (26) and (27). It is also possible, of course, for the clause that is the object of *want* to have an ordinary nominal phrase as SUBJECT, e.g.:

(28a) I wanted you to examine the boy
(28b) I wanted the boy to be examined

Here the item that is SUBJECT of the infinite clause clearly does contract transitivity relations, but only with the verb in its own clause, as is shown by the entailment relationship between (28a) and (28b). Contrast (29), where (a) does not entail (b):

(29a) I advise you to examine the boy
(29b) I advised the boy to be examined

In sentences of the type represented by (29), the NP that follows the top verb must be its object (note that neither existential *there* nor anticipatory *it* is possible in this position), and in addition this same NP must be the subject (active or passive) of the first of the following predicate words that has a subject. The transitivity relations contracted by the inter-verbal NP will predict the difference between (29a) and (29b), if we posit the features [+transitive] and [+verb-comp] for *advise*, and the features [+personal] and [+transitive] for *examine*, together with a rule that will cause the object of the higher verb to conflate with the subject of the lower verb.[5]

So far we have emphasized the differences between (28) and (29), but there are also important resemblances, which have long been recognized both by transformationalists (Rosenbaum 1967; Stockwell, Schachter and Partee 1968, rev. 1973; Postal 1974) and in systemic grammar (Hudson 1971). Postal 1974 gives many strong arguments to support the view that in (28), as in (29), the inter-verbal NP is an IC of the matrix clause. In a transformational framework, this obliges one to write a rule that will extract the NP from the embedded clause and implant it in the matrix. In a systemic grammar, it is possible to regard an item as being simultaneously an IC in a matrix and in an embedded clause (see Hudson 1971 and 1976). I shall here follow Hudson 1976 in applying to this phenomenon the term 'raising' (which is familiar from transformational writings on the subject and derives ultimately from Kiparsky and Kiparsky 1970, and also in dispensing with embedded clauses in sentences like (29a, b).[6] Figure 11.2 illustrates the structures for (28a, b) and (29a, b).

In this analysis, raising depends on the feature [+split-obj] in the governing verb. In (28a, b) in Figure 11.2, the SUBJECT of the embedded clause is shown to be simultaneously a separate constituent (nameless so far) of the matrix clause.[7] If the governing verb is also [+passive], as is the case with *believed* in (30) below, the splitting of the embedded clause is more obvious, since its SUBJECT (*There*) is simultaneously SUBJECT of the matrix clause:

(30) There was believed to be life on Mars

The split clause *There to be life on Mars* is object of *believe* and hence also subject of the passive participle *believed*. It is in this sense only that the present analysis retains the notion of 'split subject'.

11.5 THE FUNCTIONS OF RAISED ELEMENTS IN THE MATRIX CLAUSE

We now come to our last major problem: what status does the SUBJECT of the object clause have in the matrix? According to Hudson 1976, the SUBJECT item is 'raised' to be a sister to the clause in which it is a constituent (or, to be more precise, in which it is a dependent sister to a daughter of the clause),and its status in the matrix is further specified by its conflation there with [+nom ⬅ + transitive], or in other words with the object of the superordinate verb. It seems to me that although there is a good case for raising to 'derived object' in a transformational grammar (see Postal 1974), we cannot justify the corresponding 'conflation with object' in a daughter dependency grammar. The argument against such an analysis runs as follows: firstly, all the reasons that have been given for 'raising to derived object' are totally unconnected with transitivity functions in the systemic sense and relate only to constituency and left-to-right ordering. Secondly, the raised item in the embedded clause may be one that cannot function as object anywhere else in daughter dependency grammar (existential *there*, anticipatory *it*). Thirdly, the attribution of object function to the raised item destroys the possibility of giving a coherent account of active–passive equivalence in daughter dependency grammar, based on transitivity relations in the way proposed above.

The conclusion, it seems, must be that the status of the raised item will have to be provided for in terms of mood functions: SUBJECT if the superordinate verb is passive, COMPLEMENT if it is active. SUBJECT-TO-SUBJECT raising (as in (30) above) is uncontroversial; but SUBJECT-TO-COMPLEMENT raising encounters the difficulty that COMPLEMENT has so far not been considered to have any place at all in daughter dependency grammar. If it were shown that COMPLEMENT is indeed unnecessary in the rest of the grammar, we would not

(28a)

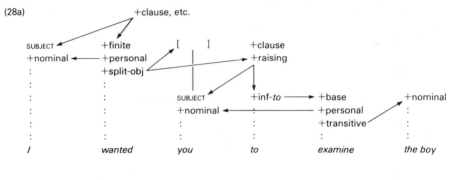

(28b)

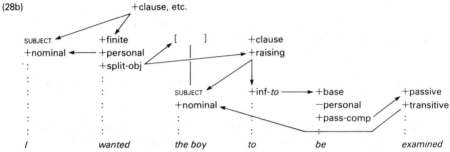

(29a)

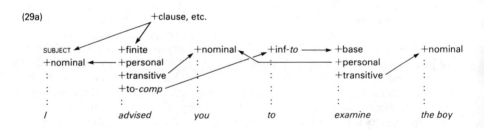

(29b)

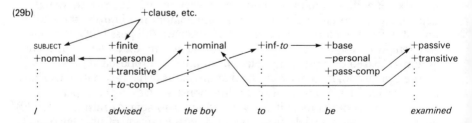

Figure 11.2 Structural diagrams for sentences (28a, b) and (29a, b)

be justified in setting up such a function merely in order to provide for raised items; but in eliminating COMPLEMENT, Hudson 1976 relies on 'peripherality assignment rules' which are still 'regrettably undeveloped' (97). So far, there seem to be no good grounds for supposing that such rules will handle the ordering of clause constituents more efficiently than the mood functions familiar to systemic theory. The facts to be accounted for are now set out.

The unmarked position of a nominal phrase which is the object of an active verb is immediately after the verb. This position it does not have merely by virtue of being a nominal phrase, since nominal phrases may also function adverbially, in which case they have different place options:

(31a)   I saw your brother the other day
(31b)   *I saw the other day your brother

Nor can the object be said to have this position by virtue of being dependent on [+transitive], for the subject of existential *be*, which is [+nominal $\leftarrow$ +personal] has the same position in unmarked order, as in (32a), not as in (32b):

(32a)   There was a meeting the other day
(32b)   *There was the other day a meeting

And the dummy element *it*, which also does not depend on [+transitive] (see Appendix, (c)), has the post-verb position assigned to it nevertheless:

(33a)   He resented it, I think, that you did not support him
(33b)   *He resented, I think, it that you did not support him

Such facts can be dealt with in a grammar which assigns the function COMPLEMENT to [+nominal, +phrase] $\leftarrow$ [+transitive], to the subject of existential *be*, and to the dummy object *it* in those contexts in which it occurs.

Now the raised item, as Postal shows (1974: 134 ff.) is subject to ordering constraints that correspond to those on the nominal phrase as object:

(34a)   He preferred his friends, of course, to be there
(34b)   *He preferred, of course, his friends to be there
(35a)   He advised his friends, of course, to be there
(35b)   *He advised, of course, his friends to be there

In *for . . . to . . .* clauses there is no raising; hence

(36) He preferred, of course, for his friends to be there

We conclude, therefore, that the 'raised' SUBJECT is COMPLEMENT in the matrix clause if the governing verb is active.

11.6 CONCLUSION

We have seen that it is possible for daughter dependency theory to account satisfactorily for the two kinds of voice neutrality distinguished in section 11.2 above, provided that we introduce certain modifications: firstly, that we add the system [+predicate: ±personal] (some predicate words govern subjects and some do not); and, secondly, that we add the function COMPLEMENT to those already recognized by the theory.

Each of the two kinds of voice neutrality is given a unitary explanation: the first is dealt with by positing [−personal] predicate words which govern verbs, and the second by positing clause-embedding and the 'raising' of the SUBJECT of the embedded clause—to matrix SUBJECT if the governing verb is passive, and to matrix COMPLEMENT if the governing verb is active.

NOTES

1. The original version of this chapter (1976) dealt also with structures and functional roles in other models of systemic grammar. A shortened version was read at a meeting of the Linguistics Association of Great Britain in 1978. I am grateful to Dick Hudson, Anita Mittwoch and Yael Ziv for their helpful comments.
2. The system [+predicate: ±personal] had a place in an earlier version of Hudson's daughter dependency theory, but was abandoned because it complicated the 'peripherality assignment rules' (Hudson, personal communication). On peripherality, see section 11.5 and Hudson (1976: 97).
3. The system network in the Appendix is different from that in Hudson 1976, which necessitates corresponding adjustments in other rules. But the essential characteristics of DDG are unaffected.
4. The [−personal] use of *about to* in (19) is to be distinguished from the use of *not about to* in the sense of 'having no intention to' which now seems to be fairly widespread in American English. This latter use is [+personal]. A few [−personal, +verb-comp] adjectives (e.g. *likely*) have related homophonous forms which are [+clause-subj]: *It is likely that he . . .*
5. Compare the conflation of subject with subject in (14) above. Such conflation rules can be dispensed with if we make the generation of a (configurational) subject conditional on the availability of a (labelled) SUBJECT and leave the identification of the corresponding arguments to the semantics. Whatever we decide, we must provide also for the conflation or identification of prepositional objects (e.g. with *appeal to*, *call upon*) and we must make an exception for the beneficiary object (with *promise*).
6. The decision to do without clause-embedding in (29), like the same decision for (14) above, is not forced on us by the theory. Should it turn out that clause-embedding is needed here after all, the adjustments are easily made.
7. The representation of the 'raised' item at more than one level in the diagram serves to make the relationships clearer to the eye than they are in Hudson 1976. Dependency relations can also be indicated without arrows, by means of indexing, thus:

	+clause, etc. (1)	
(1) SUBJECT	(1) +finite	(2) +nominal
(3) +nominal	+transitive (2)	
	+personal (3)	
They	*appointed*	*John*

Here the relations are shown by making the numeral to the right of the governing feature identical with the numeral to the left of the corresponding dependent feature.

Appendix

(a) THE CLASSIFICATION OF PREDICATE WORDS

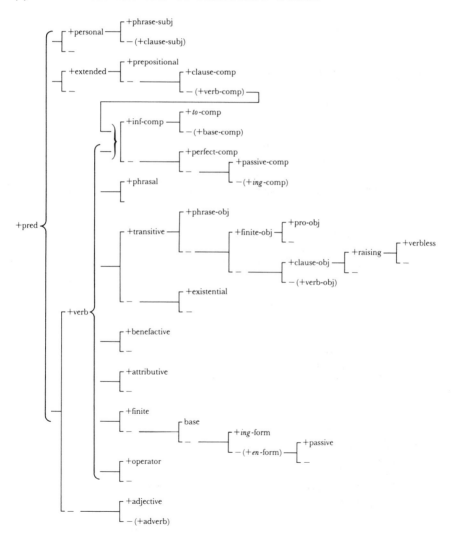

(b) SAMPLE LEXICON

be +op, −trans,
    (1) −pers, +attrib (Is it ready?);
    (2) −pers, +pass-comp (Was it found?);
    (3) +pers, +exist (Was there trouble?); etc.
have
    (1) −op, +pers, +trans (Did you have lunch?);
    (2) ±op, +pers, +trans (Has he (/Does he have) any money?);
    (3) ±op, −pers, −trans, + *to*-comp (. . has to go);
    (4) +op, −pers, −trans, +perf-comp (. . has gone); etc.
hope −op, +pers, −trans,
    (1) +prep (. . hope for rain);
    (2) + *to*-comp (. . hope to succeed); etc.
likely
    +adj, −pers, + *to*-comp (. . likely to go); etc.
persuade
    −op, +pers, +trans, + *to*-comp (. . persuaded him to go); etc.
resent −op, +pers, +trans
    (1) +phrase-obj (. . resents interference);
    (2) +pro-obj (. . resents it that . . .); etc.
seem −op, −pers, −trans
    (1) +attrib, ±prep (. . seems odd (to me));
    (2) + *to*-comp (. . seems to like it);
    (3) +clause-comp (It seems that . . .); etc.
want −op, +pers, +trans,
    (1) +phrase-obj (. . wanted them);
    (2) +verb-obj (. . wanted to leave);
    (3) +split-obj (. . wanted them to leave); etc.

(c) SOME ADDITIONAL RULES

Sister dependency:
+personal → +nominal /NOT +passive (non-passive subject)
+passive → +nominal (passive subject)
−personal → *it* / NOT (+verb-comp OR +attributive) (impersonal *it*)
+existential → *there*
+clause-subj
+pro-obj
+finite obj, +passive
+ *to*-comp, +passive   } → *it* / NOT (sister clause = TOPIC)
+transitive → +nominal ('direct' object)
+benefactive → +nominal, +phrase ('indirect' object)
+prepositional → +preposition

Identity
+nominal ⬅ +passive = +nominal ⬅ +transitive, OR
                    = +nominal ⬅ +benefacive, OR
                    = +nominal ⬅ [preposition ⬅ +prepositional]

(The passive subject may be direct, indirect, or prepositional object of the verb.)

BIBLIOGRAPHY

Bierwisch, M.and Heidolph, K. E. (eds) (1970), *Recent Advances in Linguistics*, The Hague, Mouton.
Chomsky, N. A. (1965), *Aspects of the Theory of Syntax*, Cambridge, Mass., MIT Press.
Huddleston, R. D. (1969), 'Predicate complement construction in English', *Lingua*, 23, 241–73.
Hudson, R. A. (1971), *English Complex Sentences*, Amsterdam, North Holland.
—— (1976), *Arguments for a Non-Transformational Grammar*, Chicago, University of Chicago Press.
Kiparsky, P. and Kiparsky, C. (1970), 'Fact', in Bierwisch and Heidolph (eds) (1970).
Palmer, F. R. (1974), *The English Verb*, London, Longman.
Postal, P. M. (1974), *On Raising*, Cambridge, Mass.; MIT Press.
Rosenbaum, P. S. (1967), *The Grammar of English Predicate Complement Constructions*, Cambridge, Mass.; MIT Press.
Sinclair, J. McH. (1972), *A Course in Spoken English: Grammar*, London, Oxford University Press.
Stockwell, R. P., Schachter, P. and Partee, B. H. (1973), *The Major Syntactic Structure of English*, New York, Holt, Rinehart and Winston.
Svartvik, J. (1966), *On Voice in the English Verb*, The Hague, Mouton.

Part VI
Phonology

12 Aspects of word phonology

V. Prakasam
Punjabi University, Patiala

12.0 INTRODUCTION

A phonological description of a language can be characterized in terms of three components: the higher (combinational) component, the basic component, and the Sandhi component. The higher component deals with what is called 'sentence phonology', while the basic component deals with 'word phonology'. The Sandhi component deals with the 'linking' between the two components. Here I shall try to deal with different theoretical aspects of word phonology, and also of that part of morphology which is linked to 'phonology'. For a detailed study of the theoretical aspects of sentence phonology, see Prakasam 1979, and for the study of the Sandhi component Prakasam 1976a.

12.1 PHONETIC FEATURES

Before going into the details of word phonology, let us briefly describe what we can call 'parametrical phonetics' (Prakasam 1985: 1–7). We can set up a general set of phonetic features chosen on the basis of the following criteria (cf. Schane 1973: 25, 33):

(1) the features must be adequate to characterize the phonic quality of all the possible sounds of human languages
(2) they must be adequate for characterizing important phonetic differences between languages.

Let us call such phonetic features 'prime features', and accept Ladefoged's definition of such features: 'A prime feature is a measurable property that can be used to classify the sounds of a language' (1975: 238). The prime features will ideally be of three classes: physiological, acoustic and auditory. The conflation of these classes is not the ideal situation. The reasoning is simple: a sound has its physiological 'origin', acoustic 'travel' and auditory 'reception' ('perception') (cf. Ladefoged 1980; Fudge 1973: 174).

The prime features are established with reference to certain parameters.

For the purpose of illustration we shall talk about a tentative set of parameters to describe the prime features of the physiological stage:

(1) air-stream mechanism (e.g. pulmonic, glottalic, velaric);
(2) air-stream direction (e.g. ingressive, egressive);
(3) the state of glottis (e.g. voiced, voiceless);
(4) the position of velum (e.g. nasal, oral);
(5) articulator/approximator (e.g. apical, laminal, dorsal);
(6) place of articulation/approximation (e.g. dental, palatal, velar);
(7) manner of articulation/approximation (e.g. obstruent, sibilant, close, open);
(8) the position of lips (e.g. labialized, neutral);
(9) air-stream force (e.g. aspirated, non-aspirated);
(10) vocal-fold vibration frequency (e.g. rising tone, falling tone).

By 'approximation' we refer to the vocalic type of articulation where the active and passive articulators come close but do not touch each other. On the other hand, 'articulation' refers to consonantal type of articulation where the organs of speech involved touch each other. This distinction between 'approximation' and 'articulation' is slightly different from Ladefoged's distinction.

The following procedure needs to be adopted in the description of the sound system of a given language (for details see Prakasam 1985: 1–7):

(1) describe a sound in terms of the relevant parameters;
(2) identify the 'decisive' parameters and the correlative parameters;
(3) distinguish between 'dynamic' and 'static' parameters;
(4) to achieve this, we have to observe the functional behaviour of the segments in Sandhi contexts.

12.2 THE BASIC COMPONENT

The basic component deals with the phonological units of the following types:

Unit		Structural formula
Foot	:	Formatives + foot prosodies
Formative	:	Syllables + Formative prosodies
Syllable	:	Phonemata + syllable prosodies

The foot prosodies will be actually part of the Sandhi component. We will see, however, that the other prosodies of the basic component will influence the 'trend' of the Sandhi prosodies.

12.2.1 The phonological prime

Let us start with the concept of the phonological prime (different from 'phonetic prime feature'). The phonological prime for American structuralist phonemic theory was the phoneme. For the Generative Phonologists the phonological prime is the distinctive feature. For the Prosodists, the phone-matic unit and prosody are the primes. The approach to Systemic Phonology taken here adopts the prosodic viewpoint, with certain modifica-tions.

12.2.2 Abstract vs. concrete layers

To explain the systemic concept of phonological prime, let us first bring in the difference between the phonetic layer and the phonological layer, and the relationship between the two. Phonologically relevant information within each unit is bi-dimensionally present—paradigmatically (units) and syntag-matically (prosodies). On the other hand, phonetic structures are the concrete manifestations of the abstract phonology and the relevant phonic information is to be specified uni-dimensionally. The abstract representation is predic-tably related to the concrete representation. The predictability exists in two directions: (1) in terms of placement (locational) and (2) in terms of exponence (exponential). Prosodies of the abstract structure are reflected in the RELEVANT successive units of phonetic representation.

12.2.2.1 *Segmentality condition rejected*

The abstract phonological structure of the kind envisaged here not only rejects the conditions of linearity, invariance and bi-uniqueness (see Chomsky 1964), but also the 'segmental' condition (see below). By 'segmental condition' we mean that (1) a bundle of features found as one unit at the phonological level should be related to only one unit at the phonetic level and vice versa, and (2) all the associative features should be given equal value. This condition seems to be implicit in Postal's statement that a phonological feature is a purely segmental property (1968: 122). To illustrate our point:

(1)

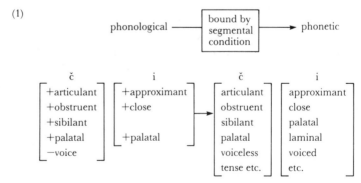

The only difference we can see in these two layers is this: the feature matrix on the left is non-redundant and classificatory, and the one on right is specificatory. But the 'segmental' character of units is maintained intact. The features in 'č' and 'i' are not indexed as to their functional importance in the phonic behaviour of the language. In other words, all the five features stated for 'č' in the left matrix are of equal values, as are the features stated for 'i'.

12.2.2.2 *The 'elevation' of features*

Let us take the case of the 'affricates' of Telugu to explain the transition between phonetic and phonological strata. In Telugu, affricates have two phonetic variants, one 'palatal' and the other 'prealveolar' (dental). The palatal exponent co-occurs with 'front' vowels and the prealveolar one with 'back' and 'central' vowels. The terms 'palatal', 'dental', 'back', 'front' and 'central' only tell us about the phonetic character of the sounds concerned. But this description does not show any 'naturalness' in the environmentally conditioned variation. Consider the following feature statement:

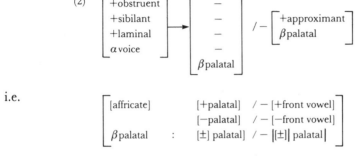

i.e.

$$\begin{bmatrix} [\text{affricate}] \\ \beta\text{palatal} \end{bmatrix} \quad : \quad \begin{bmatrix} [+\text{palatal}] \quad / - [+\text{front vowel}] \\ [-\text{palatal}] \quad / - [-\text{front vowel}] \\ [\pm] \text{ palatal}] \quad / - |[\pm]| \text{ palatal} \end{bmatrix}$$

In other words, a laminal obstruent–sibilant (=affricate, cf. Prakasam 1972: 106) acquires palatality (č/ǰ) while occurring with a palatal vowel and non-palatal (c̣/j̣) character with a non-palatal vowel. The features of PALATAL and NON-PALATAL are classificatory but not specificatory. To translate the latter phonological category into a phonetic feature (positive integer), we need to add the following 'specificatory' statements:

(3)   (a) $[-\text{palatal}] \longrightarrow [\text{dental}] \quad / \quad \begin{bmatrix} +\text{obstruent} \\ +\text{sibilant} \end{bmatrix}$

(b) $[-\text{palatal}] \longrightarrow [\text{velar}] \quad / \quad \begin{bmatrix} +\text{approximant} \end{bmatrix}$

'Velarity' and 'palatality' are two phonetic features which specify the place of approximation in the case of vowels—u, o, a (velar) and i, e, æ (palatal). Of these two phonetic features 'palatality'—but not 'velarity'—has been found 'decisive', and so is abstracted and 'elevated' to phonological status, taking into consideration the consonant-vowel co-occurrence relationship. This view, though functional, does not transcend 'segmental' condition.

12.2.3 Syntagmaticity vs. paradigmaticity

It has been mentioned above that phonological information is characterized as either of syntagmatic value or of paradigmatic value. Before bringing in the terms 'prosodies' and 'phonematic units' for these categories in 1948, Firth captured the distinction by distinguishing between 'correlations' and 'articulations' in 1935 (see Firth 1957: 22, 23). This distinction is carried over into Systemic Phonology (Barnwell 1970; Mock 1970; Prakasam 1972). The syntagmatic value of a phonological category is judged in two (in fact three, see below) ways:

(1) a feature may be spread or realized phonetically over a structure such as a syllable or a formative as a whole;
(2) a feature, though not phonetically realized over the whole structure, may be relevant to a structure by marking its boundaries.

The former is 'distributively syntagmatic' and the latter is 'demarcatively syntagmatic'. Some features may have both functions. For example, 'stress' in English is predominantly of the former type whereas in Telugu 'stress' is predominantly of the latter type (see Prakasam 1972: 15, 91). If we consider stress in English as a property which can be distributively stated for the whole of the syllable, it has the following phonetic exponents: (1) acute pronunciation of the vowel, and (2) aspiration of the voiceless onset or lengthening (slight) of the voiced onset of the syllable. Thus the phonetic exponence of the phonological category of 'stress' is found on both 'peak' and 'onset' (for some comments on stress in English, see Firth 1957: 24, 45).

12.2.3.1 'Static' vs. 'dynamic' value of features

A paradigmatic feature is one whose significance can be attributed to one segment. There are some features which are neither 'distributive' nor 'demarcative' in character. These are not, however, simply paradigmatic in character, because they influence the phonic character of the adjacent sounds in derivational alternation and Sandhi contexts—i.e., when sounds occur in close juncture, where the transition from one sound to another occurs without distinctive pause. This significance is the 'dynamic' quality of a feature as distinct from the 'static' quality of another feature, which does not have any influence on an adjacent sound in a Sandhi context.

Thus there are three syntagmatic aspects distributive, demarcative and dynamic. Let us consider the following:

(4) omi*t* — omi*ss*ion
    permi*t* — permi*ss*ion
    admi*t* — admi*ss*ion
    divi*de* — divi*s*ion
    colli*de* — colli*s*ion
    deri*de* — deri*s*ion
i.e. /t/   /ʃ/
     /d/   /ʒ/

'Replacement of an alveolar obstruent by a palatal sibilant' is apparent here. The more significant point is the retention of the phonatory quality of the final consonant of the verb. Any functionally significant phonological treatment should account for the difference between the [+voice] correlation and other features of articulation, like apicality and obstruence. (This particular statement is valid only for the data given here.)

A comprehensive treatment of English phonology will have to distinguish between dynamic features and static features. (For a detailed account of such features in Telugu, see Prakasam 1976.) This is a theoretical decision which one has to make, keeping the empirical evidence in view. Failing to distinguish on this functional basis amounts to ignoring linguistic facts. Once we have made the right theoretical decision we can abstract 'dynamic' features as consonant-centring or vowel-centring syllable-part prosodies (cf. Henderson 1966) and keep them off 'static' features which will constitute paradigmatically relevant phonemata. As a methodological alternative one may prefer to state the 'dynamic' and 'static' features as constituting one phonological segment without, however, losing their functional distinctness (cf. Prakasam 1976a). These two alternatives can be presented as follows (here the distinction is based on the data given in (4)):

(5)

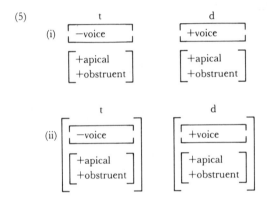

The features in the horizontal box are 'dynamic' (prosodic) and the features in the vertical box are 'static' (phonematic). In (5) (i) the dynamic elements are represented as independent prosodic categories. In (5) (ii) the 'dynamic' and the 'static' elements together constitute a single phonological segment. The need to recognize such phonological segments is convincingly presented in Smith and Wilson (1979: 139–40).

To recapitulate, a feature has syntagmatic value if it is non-unisegmental: (1) distributively, (2) demarcatively, and finally (3) dynamically.

12.3 EFFICACY OF THE FUNCTIONALIST APPROACH

We shall illustrate the efficacy of the functionalist approach by taking a very interesting phenomenon of Telugu phonology: 'length' (for details see Prakasam 1976b, 1982, 1985: 82–6). This has a demarcative function with reference to the phonological unit 'formative' parallel to the grammatical unit 'morpheme'. The following items of length are found in Telugu:

(1) vocalic length (:)   — e.g. ka:pu   (yield of fruit)
(2) consonantal length (c)   — e.g. kappu (roof)

(3) (pre-consonantal) (N)   — e.g. kampu (bad smell)
    nasal length
(4) y-diphthongal length (y) — e.g. kaypu (intoxication)
(5) w-diphthongal length
    (w)   — e.g. kawlu (lease)

The five features of length constitute the 'prosodic system of length' operative at the rank of 'formative' in the phonological hierarchy of Telugu (for '+native' words) (for details see Prakasam 1972: 97–102). They are terms in a system for they are mutually exclusive and operate at the same structural 'point'. They are considered formative prosodies because they demarcate formative boundaries and their exponential location in the structural realization at the phonetic level is predictable: the exponents of these prosodies occur after the first phonetic syllable:

PHONOLOGICAL	PHONETIC	
: ka lu	ka:lu	(leg)
c ka lu	kallu	(palmyra wine)
N pa ṭa	paṇṭa	(crop)
N ka pa	kampa	(thorny bush)
N ka da	kanda	(an edible root)

As the examples show, vocalic length (:) lengthens the vowel of the first syllable, 'c' lengthens the consonant of the second syllable, and 'N' gives nasal initiation to the consonant of the second syllable. Similarly, 'diphthongal' length (y/w) gives a glidal coda to the first syllable. This sytemicization is not a linguist's artefact (cf. Praksam 1976b); it is a synchronic fact of language with diachronic implications.

In the earlier stages of Telugu, vocalic length was not a term in this system and could co-occur with 'nasal' length. The syntagmatic relation has yielded to paradigmatization. One of the most important aspects of language change is the revision of system membership. The Telugu case is exemplified by the following:

Earlier Telugu   Modern Telugu
i:nga   (flea)   i:ga
va:ṇḍu   (he)   va:ḍu

Different dialects of Telugu seem to have retained different length features while implementing the system-revision in the structure of words:

Old form	Telagana Dialect	— Circar dialect
ku:ŋkuḍu (soapnuts)	ku:kuḍu	— kuŋkuḍu
pe:ṇḍa (dung)	peṇḍa	— pe:ḍa

12.3.1 Polysystemicity

It is this kind of functional view which made Prosodic Analysis and thence Systemic Phonology adopt a polysystemic approach to language. Prosodic Analysis follows the practice of setting up different systems based on 'etymological' (e.g.'+native', '−native'), 'morphological' (e.g. verbal piece, nominal piece), and 'structural' criteria. The last aspect refers to the practice of setting up different C-systems and V-systems for initial, medial and final syllables of words (strictly speaking, 'formatives'). Here we modify the practice, taking into consideration Halliday's view that such a completely divorced polysystemic statement might amount to 'neglecting likeness' in an attempt to 'recognizing unlikeness' (1967: 11). We will therefore theoretically accept the concept of proposing 'general' systems to cover the common features of a language and then several 'specific' systems to cover the difference in some areas of the language. For example, in the structure of a 'formative' in Telugu, we find that the initial syllables fall under a 'general' system and non-initial syllables under 'specific' systems (see Prakasam 1972: 103–18, 136–40). The distinction between 'general' and 'specific' systems has to be made with reference to a unit at a particular rank.

The 'mid' vowels (e, o) besides the other non-mid vowels (a, i, u) occur only in the initial syllables of a formative, whereas in the non-initial syllables only a, i, u occur. The only exception to this is the case of a few nominals where in the non-initial syllables we find 'e' (but not 'o'). Interestingly, these 'e-syllables' have 'i/a-substitutes' in the so-called non-standard dialects, and sometimes also as informal or free variants, even in the standard dialect:

peṭṭe	— peṭṭi	(box)
palle	— palli	(village)
vadine	— { vadini / vadina }	(sister-in-law) (elder brother's wife)

If the phonological description of a language can automatically (even if partially) delimit morpheme boundaries, it would naturally be a more appropriate description of language than one which cannot do the same (cf. Firth 1957: 42).

12.3.2. The redundancy phenomena

Redundancies are the phenomena whose occurrence is conditioned by, and so predictable from, other features. These redundancies can be either syntagmatic or paradigmatic. The former are also called 'morpheme structure conditions' (m.s.c.) because they are concerned with the co-occurrence of segments in the structure of a morpheme (Stanley 1967). For example, in Telugu, once we specify that there is a consonant cluster in a syllable (in native lexical items), we automatically imply that the second consonant is 'r'. Generally in non-prosodic literature redundancy of location seems to be ignored. In Systemic Phonology this kind of m.s.c. will be accounted for by assigning 'r' to a prosodic category. Its occurrence, as opposed to its absence, is posited in the phonological representation, its placement and its feature specifications on the phonetic layer being stated by 'phonetic experience' statements. The paradigmatic redundancy is concerned with the specification of features within a segment. For example, if we specify a segment for 'nasality', it is redundant to specify it for 'voice' too. In English and Telugu, 'voicing' of the nasals is not dynamic, as voicing of obstruents is. We cannot have '+voice' segment clustering with '−voice' segment, e.g. * vs, fz, zt, sd. But the nasals cluster with voiceless sounds:

plinth	/plɪnθ/
mint	/mɪnt/
camp	/kæmp/

This is possible because 'voicing' is a co-exponent of the 'nasality' category. This phonetic feature of 'voice' is different from the 'voice' feature of [+voice] prosody. In this theory, therefore, we do not state redundancy phenomena separately, and they are accounted for in terms of the differences between prosodic and phonematic values of features.

Let us take also the case of the 'aspirated' allophones of /p/, /t/ and /k/ in English. In this matrix the aspirated exponent figures in as a cumulative exponent of the dynamic and static features of the phonological segment, and also the syllable prosody of 'stress'. (It might be possible to establish 'stress' as a formative prosody in English.) If this is accepted, the concept of allophone and the phenomenon of redundant feature of aspiration in this case will become unnecessary. Instead we shall speak of phonetic units as cumulative exponents of phonological segments and other prosodies. This has become possible because this theory rejects the 'segmentality' condition.

12.3.2.1 *Phonetic redundancies*

Phonetic redundancies are concerned with feature specifications which are determined by phonic environment. For example, to specify 'k' as '+front' before i (as in 'quay' /kiː/) is phonetically redundant. In a Prosodic Analysis matrix the frontness of 'k' is considered as an exponent of 'Y-prosody' (palatality) which affects the vowel as well as the consonant. In the methodological alternative proposed here, 'palatality' of the vocalic segment will be considered a 'dynamic' feature which influences the exponence of the preceding consonant. Here too the 'redundancy' concept seems to be redundant.

12.3.3 'Markedness' and its systemic significance

The notion of 'markedness' is primarily a Praguian notion which has been brought into systemic grammar (Halliday 1967: 21, 33–5; Elmenoufy 1969; see also Martin in this volume). In Praguian linguistics, 'markedness' (+) stood for the 'presence' of a feature and 'unmarkedness' (−) for the 'absence' of a feature. In Systemic Phonology, however, it has different implications in different contexts. 'Unmarked' in many cases means 'neutrality' with reference to another system of options (see Prakasam 1979). In the case of 'phonemata' as well as other units in this theory, markedness is used with prosodic implications. If we say that obstruents and fricatives in English are 'marked' for the system of 'voice', what we mean is that obstruents and fricatives co-occur with either of the voice prosodies '+voice' (v), or '−voice' (v̄). In the alternative representation, it means that 'voicing' in obstruents and fricatives is dynamic in character. On the other hand, when we say vowels and nasals are 'unmarked' for voice, it means that the 'voice' phenomenon is not dynamic in the case of these sounds. Instead, it is an inherent feature. In Telugu, 's' is unmarked for the voice system. The voicelessness here is an inherent feature. Systemically, the system of VOICE could be presented as follows:

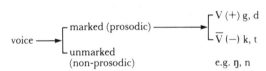

As has been mentioned above, 'voicing' and 'nasality' are co-exponents of a single prosody. In other words, we do not treat the phonetic features of '±voice' as exponents of the same phonological categories in all the segments. Instead we treat them as exponents of different categories with different functional values (cf. Firth 1957: 22–3). This will help us avoid having two representations in abstract phonology: one non-redundant and another redundant (for a similar attempt in Natural Phonology, see Wojcik 1976). To sum up, 'markedness' tells us of a 'dynamic' choice and 'unmarkedness' tells us of an inherent 'static' specification.

We have so far discussed the following points:

(1) 'elevation' of certain features as phonological categories;
(2) abstractness of phonology, concreteness of phonetics and the rejection of 'segmentality' condition;
(3) syntagmaticity of features; dynamism as a syntagmatic function;
(4) markedness in phonology.

12.4 LEXICAL REGISTRATION

Let us now look at the problem of lexical registration in terms of systemic phonology. In Prosodic Analysis, Allen talks of the desirability of abstracting the structure of a lexical item and explaining the environmentally conditioned variation in terms of junctional statements (Allen 1956: 144; Palmer 1970: 32, 43, 134, 249; Firth 1962: 106). Postulating a specific structure for each morpheme and then deriving certain variants from the basic structure is the common practice among the Ancient Indian linguists too. This becomes an important issue in view of the differences between what I call the 'static' morphological view and the 'process' morphological view (see Prakasam 1975). Some of the American Structuralists held the static view, positing the concept of 'allomorph' where different alternants are given equal value. Interestingly, Bloomfield held the 'process' view of positing a basic form and deriving other alternants from it (1933: 212).

The distributional criteria and sameness of 'semantic distinctiveness' have been treated by some linguists to be more important than phonological structure. For example, the English morpheme of plurality has been said to have allomorphs like z, ɪz, s, ən, {ʊ → iː}, Ø (exemplified by *dogs*, *horses*, *cats*, *oxen*, *feet* and *sheep*).

A distinction is made, no doubt, between phonologically conditioned allomorphs and lexically conditioned allomorphs. Let us examine the problems involved in this static approach. It is of course a fact that all six items termed allomorphs of a morpheme do express the same 'sememe'. If we take a morpheme as a formal unit expressing one or more sememes, the phonological commonness cannot be sacrificed at the altar of complementary distribution. We can speak of the lexically conditioned allomorphs as synonymous morphological exponents (Vachek 1966: 332) (see below). We can treat the phonologically conditioned allomorphs morphonemically (cf. Firth 1957: 2).

12.4.1 The 'allomorph' redefined

If we take this stand, the concept of 'allomorph', as it is usually understood, does not stand up. We can retain the concept of 'allomorph' as a sort of 'allied morpheme', and bring together lexically conditioned morphemes expressing the same sememe. Another use for this concept could be purely formal–functional: when we use a particular morpheme to function, for example, both as a verb and as a noun (e.g. *love*, *water*), we can say the nominal and verbal uses of 'love' are allomorphic (see below). Similarly if an adjective or a verb is used with two different structural functions, say as a modifier and as a predicate, we might term them as allomorphs (e.g. *tall* in *the girl is tall* and *the tall girl*).

12.4.2 The morpheme of plurality in English

Let us discuss in detail the phonologically conditioned allomorphs of the morpheme of plurality in English—*z*, *iz*, *s* (cf. Zwicky 1975; Prakasam 1975). First let us look at the static view which treats the three 'allomorphs' as of equal quality.

(1) *iz* after sibilant and affricate (obstruent–sibilant) consonants;
(2) *s* after voiceless consonants;
(3) *z* elsewhere (after voiced sounds).

In examples like *bananas* and *umbrellas*, where the plural form is /z/, the shape is predicted on the basis of the fact that the preceding vowel is voiced in a way that is similar to voiced consonants like b, d, g and v. Functionally this similarity is dubious. The voicing of the vowels is an 'inherent' feature, but not a 'marked' feature. Moreover, the morpheme structure conditions in English do allow the vowels to co-occur with voiceless as well as with voiced consonants. But this is not possible with consonants where voicing is a marked feature. One might say that the co-occurrence of a vowel with a voiceless consonant is an intra-morphemic property that need not be brought into inter-morphemic problems. But that would amount to the fact that the intermorphemic conditions do not (have to) agree with the morphemic conditions. A convincing attempt has been made by Gillian Brown (1970: 8.9) to show that (intra-) morpheme structure conditions apply across morpheme boundaries. Sandhi alternation is always an attempt to achieve vowel and consonant harmony, in line with morpheme structure conditions. If this is accepted, we do not find any natural motivation for the plural suffix to be a voiced sibilant after vowels.

If we want to take into consideration the m.s.cs so as to motivate phonological processes (and thence statements), we may have to take a particular form as the basic form and the other forms as derived. In this case the form which occurs in the unmotivated contexts is sure to take precedence over others to be chosen as the basic shape. In the case of plural morpheme, the voiced sibilant offers itself as the unpredictable basic form. It is more convenient to take the non-syllabic /z/ as basic rather than the syllabic /ɪz/, which was chosen by Bloomfield. The syllabicity is predictable, not its reduction. Then we can say that the sememe of plurality is expressed by a formal unit (i.e. a morpheme) which has the phonological shape of /z/ which undergoes certain changes (i.e. Sandhi processes) before being phoneticized.

12.4.3 Perceptual plausibility

We might now say a few words about the ability of a given solution to convince. This 'convincingness' takes the strongest form when it is shown to be what people speak of as 'psychological reality.' But there is a less strong position which can be called 'perceptual plausibility' (Prakasam 1976b). The concept can be attributed to Robins's stand (1957, in Palmer 1970: 193): 'It is not of course implied that linguistic analysis can or should be based on the

... *sentiment linguistique* of native speakers: it is desirable that the analysis should not be in violent disagreement with it.'

To illustrate the incompatibility of allomorphic solutions and plausibility, let us look at the morpheme of plurality in Telugu. If one follows the allomorphic solution, plurality is expressed by two allomorphs /lu/ and /ḷu/.

(1) /ḷu/ occurs after words ending in a
    syllable with a 'retroflex' consonant: e.g.   baḍi   baḷḷu
                                                     (school)   (schools)
(2) /lu/ elsewhere: e.g.   āku   āku*lu*
                                                     (leaf)   (leaves)

I asked several Telugu speakers whether they could identify /ḷu/ to be a meaningful expression in Telugu and the answer was in the negative. On the other hand, they very easily recognized /lu/ as the pluralizer, and they said that /ḷu/ did not exist independent of the whole expression and that it was a variant of /lu/ conditioned by the preceding word. The native speaker's perception therefore prefers the 'process' solution of taking /lu/ as the basic shape and /ḷu/ as post-Sandhi form. This argumentation applies not only to the bound morphemes but also to the free morphemes, where a specific lexical registration has to be made and from which other forms are derived as post-Sandhi forms.

12.5 MORPHOLOGICAL FUNCTION OF 'SOUNDS'

There is another related problem in the area of phonological representation of morphemes. This concerns what Firth calls morphological function of 'sounds' (1957: 37). Look at the following:

Noun	Verb
breath	breathe
bath	bathe

Let us also look at the following examples from Telugu:

Verb		Noun	
(cook)	vanḍu	vanṭa	(cuisine)
(swarm)	mu:gu	mu:ka	(crowd)
(bend)	vangu	vanka	(bend/crescent)
(swim)	i:du	ɪːta	(swimming)
(resound)	mo:du	mo:ta	(resound)
(play)	a:ḍu	a:ṭa	(play)
(sing)	pa:ḍu	pa:ṭa	(song)

The relationship between the verbal and nominal forms can be stated in three ways, and a 'correct' choice of the solution depends on further semantic, syntactic and phonological research (Prakasam 1972: 135). We can take the verb form as basic and derive the nominal form by devoicing the final consonant and replacing the vowel. As an alternative we can take the noun as basic and derive the verbal. But the interesting question one has to consider is to have a neutral base with a broad semantic range, and state both nominal and verbal as derived, in which case the voicedness and voicelessness become significant for word-class distinction. One might even speculate that a morpheme has only two features—phonological and semantic—and the syntactic aspect need not be considered as part of the raw material. (Hockett 1966: 4) refers to a similar situation in Nootka.)

12.6 SUMMARY

I have discussed in the course of this chapter several aspects of theoretical importance for phonology. It has been stated that a set of prime features should not be a 'conflation' of categories of the three phonetic stages: physiological, acoustic and auditory. For each of the stages a distinct set of (phonetic) prime features has to be postulated. At this stage the scientist could restrict himself to 'narrow and abstract phonetics', in the way Firth meant it (1957: 34–5): 'Abstract, because being "panglossic", it can only place sounds such as universal categories and attach symbols to them. It is purely descriptive and non-linguistic, since it ignores phonological structure and function.' One should not miss here the semantic 'fate' of the word 'abstract'—the way it means 'more physical and less functional', as in 'abstract phonetics', and the way it means 'less physical and more functional' as in 'abstract phonology.'

The moment we transcend the 'uni-dimensional threshold' of phonetics and move over to phonology or 'systemic phonetics', as Firth termed it (1957: 35), we are on the path of 'integrative studies, more pragmatic, more functional, more "linguistic"' (1957: 34). Here we cannot be as 'panglossic' as at the 'narrow phonetic' stage.

The condition of 'segmentality' has been explicitly rejected, while establishing the relationship between 'phonological' and 'phonetic' layers of phonic study. It has been suggested that we should try to have the same parameters for the study of vowels and consonants. This was the common practice among the Ancient Indian linguists too. The distinctions of 'decisive' vs. 'correlative' parameters and 'static' vs. 'dynamic' features have been established, bringing in the functional value of the features (for details, see Prakasam 1976a).

A case has been presented for 'process morphology' while discussing the concept of lexical registration. In this connection the problem of 'perceptual plausibility' has been brought in which is neither the 'nominalist stand' nor the 'mentalist stand'. This is in line with the 'behavioural' standpoint of Halliday.

A suggestion has been made towards the end about the possibility of establishing syntactically neutral morphemes. Further research is warranted in this area.

For a detailed and comprehensive phonic study of Telugu in the systemic framework, see Prakasam 1972. The need for a similar serious systemic study of the English sound system is clear.

BIBLIOGRAPHY

Allen, W. S. (1956), 'Structure and system in the Abaza verbal complex', *Transactions of the Philological Society*, 127–76.
Barnwell, K. G. L. (1970), *A Grammatical Description of Mbembe (Adun Dialect): A Cross River Language*, unpublished Ph.D. thesis, University of London.
Bazell, C. E., Catford, J. C. and Halliday, M. A. K. (eds) (1966), *In Memory of J. R. Firth*, London, Longman.
Bloomfield, L. (1933), *Language*, New York, Holt, Reinhart and Winston.
Brown, G. (1970), 'Syllables and redundancy rules in phonology', *Journal of Linguistics*, 6, 1–17.
Chomsky, N. (1964), *Current Issues in Linguistic Theory*, The Hague, Mouton.
Cohen, D. and Wirth, J. R. (1975), *Testing Linguistic Hypotheses*, Washington, D.C., Hemisphere Publishing Corporation.
Elmenoufy, A. M. E. S. (1969), *A Study of the Role of Intonation in the Grammar of English*, unpublished Ph.D. thesis, University of London.
Firth, J. R. (1957), *Papers in Linguistics 1934–51*, London, Oxford University Press.
—— (1962), *Studies in Linguistic Analysis*, Oxford, Blackwell.
Fudge, E. (ed.) (1973), *Phonology*, Harmondsworth, Penguin.
Greenberg, J. H. (ed.) (1966), *Universals of Language*, 2nd edn., Cambridge, Mass., MIT Press.
Halliday, M. A. K. (1967), *Intonation and Grammar in British English*, The Hague, Mouton.
Henderson, E. J. A. (1966), 'Towards a prosodic statement of Vietnamese syllable structure', in Bazell *et al.* (eds) (1966: 163–97).
Hockett, C. F. (1966), 'The problem of universals in language', in Greenberg (ed.) (1966: 1–29).
Ladefoged, P. (1975), *A Course in Phonetics*, New York, Harcourt Brace Jovanovich.
—— (1980), 'What are linguistic sounds made of?', *Language*, 56, No. 3, 485–902.
Mock, C. C. (1970), *The Grammatical Units of the Nzema Language: A Systemic Analysis*, unpublished Ph.D. thesis, University of London.
Palmer, F. R. (ed.) (1970), *Prosodic Analysis*, London, Oxford University Press.
Postal, P. (1968), *Aspects of Phonological Theory*, New York, Harper and Row.
Prakasam, V. (1972), *A Systemic Treatment of Certain Aspects of Telugu Phonology*, unpublished D. Phil. thesis, University of York.
—— (1975), 'Morpheme revisited', *Indian Linguistics*, 36, 308–12.
—— (1976a), 'A functional view of phonological features', in *Acta Linguistica Hungaricae*, 26, Nos 1–2, 77–88.
—— (1976b), 'Perceptual plausibility and a language game', *Anthropological Linguistics*, 323–7.
—— (1977), 'An outline of the theory of systemic phonology', *International Journal of Dravidian Linguistics*, VI, 24–42.
—— (1979), 'Aspects of sentence phonology', *Archivum Linguisticum*, X (New Series). 57–82.
—— (1982), 'The system of length in Telugu', *Pakha Sanjam*, XV, 349–56.
—— (1985), *The Linguistic Spectrum*, Patalia, India, Punjabi University.

Robins, R. H. (1957), 'Aspects of Prosodic Analysis', in Palmer (ed.) (1970: 188–200).

Schane, S. (1973), *Generative Phonology*, Englewood Cliffs, N.J., Prentice Hall.

Smith, N. and Wilson, D. (1979), *Modern Linguistics*, Harmondsworth: Penguin.

Stanley, R. (1967), 'Redundancy Rules in Phonology', *Language*, **43**, 393–436.

Vachek, J. (1966), *The Linguistic School of Prague*, Bloomington; Indiana University Press.

Wojcik, R. (1976), 'Remarks on natural phonology', *CUWPL*, **3** 47–58.

Zwicky, A. M. (1975), 'Settling on an underlying form: the English inflectional endings', in Cohen and Wirth (eds) (1975: 129–85).

Index

Note: entries in square brackets e.g. [complex], indicate features in systems.

Abelson, R. 187
abstract vs. concrete (layers of phonology) 274–5
access (system) 188
accompanier 155
accordion gambit 25
[acquisition] 190
act (as a discourse unit) 74, 81, 223
  informative-elicitation 82, 86
action clause *see* material clause/process
active function 95
actor
  primary 77, 79, 82, 83
  secondary 77, 79, 82, 83
adjacency pair 45, 77, 215
adjectival group 137
adjunct 135, 230
  conjunctive 230
  frequentative 240
  inceptive 230
adverb/adverbial 218
  intermediate class 245
  nuclear class 245
  peripheral class 245
affected
  affected-carrier 144, 151
  affected-centred process 155
  re-expression test for 142
affective (functional component) 100
agent 131, 135, 154, 187
  agent-carrier 144
  agent-oriented 205
  re-expression test for 142
  third party agent 144
agnation 209
air-stream
  direction 273
  force 273
  mechanism 273
alienable object 188
Allen, W. S. 282
Allerton, D. J. 180

allomorph 282
anaphora/anaphoric 116, 117
Anderson, J. 24, 158
[anticipating ability] 217
approximation/approximator 273
articulation/articulator 273, 276
ascriptive clauses 131
Ashby, M. 45, 46, 61, 223
aside 75
aspect 230, 239–44
  aspectual character 244
assertive/non-assertive forms 231
assigner 154
attributive (clause/process) 136, 137, 151–5, 169–170
  attribute/attribuant 137
  [attributive] 263
  attributive complement 135
  re-expression test for attribute 142
Austin, J. L. 212

Barnwell K. G. L. 276
Bendix, E. H. 180
behalf 148
benefaction (system) 188, 190
  [benefactive] 190
  benefactive circumstance 199
  [beneficile] 190
  benefiter 191, 204
beneficiary 131, 145, 146–50, 155
Bennett, D. C. 180
Benson, J. D. 104
Bernstein, B. 69, 70, 71, 73
Berry, M. 41, 42, 45, 49, 51, 52, 53, 62, 67, 68, 69, 76, 77, 78–88, 89, 103, 104, 158, 180, 187, 223
  text by 41–63
Biggs, C. 109
Birmingham discourse analysis/analysts 41, 53, 61, 64, 71
Boadi, L. 123, 180
Brachman, R. J. 187, 209

bracketing
    in the representation of structure 90
    'ordered and' brackets 26
    'ordered or' brackets 26
    square brackets 16
Brazil, D. C. 43, 223
Brown, G. 283
Bühler, K. 95
Burton, D. 66, 69, 77, 89, 223
Butler, C. S. 66, 71, 77, 90, 97, 132, 135, 137,
        151, 215, 221, 223, 225, 226
    text by 212–29

calculus (predicate and propositional) 108, 114
carrier 140
    re-expression test for 142
    simple carrier 144
Carroll, S. 100, 101, 102, 103
cataphora/cataphoric 116
causation 143, 144
[change] 160, 178
character (system) 188
characterizing (process) 152
Chomsky, N. 14, 259, 274
circumstance 139, 140, 192
class 74, 78, 253
    class-inclusive relationship 137, 151
    natural class 255
classification rules 249, 255, 256
classificatory/classified/classifier 137
classroom discourse/interaction 42, 223
clause 68, 134
    [clause] 264
    clause complexes 110, 112
    [clause-object] 264
    embedded clause 265
    matrix clause 264, 265
client 147, 148, 192
    re-expression rule for 147
clue 75, 78, 223
cognate range 163
cognizant 171
cohesion 121
cohesive function of intonation 122
Collins, A. M. 187
collocation 209
    collocational restrictions 151
command (as situational category) 213
comment 76, 78
communication linguistics 104
communicative function 212–27
compound role 143
compound location 172
complement 36, 166
[complex] 190
conative function 95
conceptual dependency 187

conditional realization 168
conflate (realization statement) 185
congruence 213
    congruence network 167, 170
conjunctive 114
    conjunctive environment 19
    conjunctive relations 244
consolidated system network 159, 162, 179
    for relational processes 159
constituency grammar 259
[constrained] 190
context 101
    social 41
[continuative] 242
    continuative adjunct 230
    continuative aspect 234
    continuousness 239
continuity of grammar and lexis 206
conventions of language and usage 219
conversational maxim 219
Cook-Gumperz, J. 71
cooperant 203
    [cooperative] 203
correlation 275
    correlative parameter 273
Coulthard, M. 41–9 passim, 61, 64, 66–70
        passim, 73, 74–8, 86, 89, 120, 121, 222, 223,
        225
covert (participant roles) 134, 162, 165
created 142
    re-expression test for 142
Cruse, D. A. 141, 174
cue 224

daughter (dependency) 249
daughter dependency grammar 67, 226, 246–
        57, 260
    rules, 16, 253
Davies, E. C. 45
Davies, H. M. P. 122, 125
decisive parameter 253
[declarative] 18, 213
deep grammar 114, 115
deep relations 247
deixis network 30–1, 37
delicacy 16, 185
demand for information (polar, WH-) 36
dependency relations 250, 260
    dependancy theory notation 250
deprivation 202
    [deprivation] 190
[determinate] 200
Di Pietro, R. J. 45
[direct] 217
directive 74, 75, 78, 80, 217, 223
    indirect 215
    modalized 215

discourse
analysis 223
categories 70
functions 65
grammar 218
structure 41, 45, 64–90, 124, 223
units 223
discourse organizational functional component 100
[discrete] 205
disjunction (of features) 255
disjunctive environment 19
displayed system network 159, 162
for relational purposes 159
[disposal] 187
distinctive feature 274
Downes, W. 218
Dressler, W. U. 64, 115, 118, 120, 121, 122
duality 110
dynamic parameter 273
dynamic value of features 276

Edmonson, W. 71, 76
[effective] 185
elegance 134, 179
element of structure 17, 253
elicitation (discourse act) 223
Ellis, J. 107, 109–17, 119–26
text by 107–29
Elmenoufy, A. M. E. S. 281
embedding
clause embedding 268
embedded clause 265
Enkvist, N. B. 126
entailment relationship 264
equative clause/process 131, 136, 137
esphoric 116
event 187
exchange 42, 46, 47, 48, 55, 68, 78, 80, 223
action-oriented 80, 81
information-oriented 80
proposition-oriented 85
exclamation 213
as semantic force marker 221
existential clause 156
experiential function 97, 100, 107, 184
[explicit] 213
exposition structure 124
expressive function 95, 97
extraposition 248

Fanshel, D. 225
Fawcett, R. P. 16, 19, 24, 28, 65, 69, 90, 97, 99, 100, 101, 104, 107–12 passim, 114, 122, 125, 131–5 passim, 141, 151, 152, 156, 158, 159, 162, 167, 171, 174, 178, 179, 180, 187,

207, 217, 218, 226, 242, 243
text by 130–83
features 14–38, 132, 144, 247, 253, see also semantic features
for social roles 45
feature realization rule 254
non-terminal feature 16, 141
prime feature 272
socio-semantic features 34
terminal features 16, 24
Fel'dman, N. I. 126
[feminine] 15
field (of discourse) 96, 121, 122
Fillmore, C. J. 130, 140, 174, 180, 187
finite 36, 134
Firbas, J. 95
[first] 15
Firth, J. R. 16, 94, 132, 185, 208, 209, 275, 276, 279, 281, 284, 285
foot 273
formative (unit of phonology) 273, 277
frames 43, 46, 48
Fraser, B. 222
[free] 190
French 44
Fudge, E. 272
function 253
assignment rules 17, 255
configurational 258
configuration of functions 84
insertion rules 17
labelled function 258
realization rules 254
functional component, meta-function 26, 94–104, 107–26
functional grammar 133
functional slot 79, 80
functional role 258
functional sentence perspective 95
[fused] 205
[future] 15
[future transaction] 62

gates 28–9
gender 15
genre 89, 121
generic situation 103
generic structure 89, 121, 123, 124
[give] 213
given (in information structure) 118
glottis 273
[goal] 172
goal structure 82, 90
Goffman, E. 44, 45, 77
[goods-and-service] 213
grammar/grammatical
constituency grammar 259

grammar/grammatical (*cont.*)
  grammatical functions 17, 36
  grammatical item 209
  grammatical level (of language) 213
  grammatical subject 95
  sentence-grammar 115
  text-grammar 115
Greaves, W. S. 104
Green, G. 218, 227
Gregory, M. 67, 99, 100, 101, 102, 103, 104, 126, 133
  text by 94–106
Grice, H. P. 219, 225
group complex 113

habitual aspect 240
Halliday, M. A. K. 17, 20, 21, 28, 30–7, 41, 60, 64–71, 86, 88, 89, 95–125, 131–49, 152–60, 166, 169, 173, 176, 180, 181, 184, 185, 188, 191, 207, 208, 213, 226, 244, 281
Hancher, M. 222
Harman, G. 111, 125
Harris, S. Z. 14
Hartmann, R. 115, 119
Hasan R. 45, 62, 89, 96, 99, 100, 115, 117, 121, 122, 124, 125, 126, 133, 150, 161, 180, 184, 207, 208, 240
  text by 184–211
Hawkins J. A. 117
Heasley, B. 118
Henderson, E. J. A. 277
Henrici, A. 16
Heringer, J. 212
heuristic function 96
heuristic test 188
hierarchical structuring 81, 82
[higher] 48
Hjelmslev, L. 185, 208
Hockett, C. F. 14, 285
holonym/paraholonym/quasi-paraholonym 118
homophoric 116
Horne, L. R. 230, 231, 232, 240
Huddleston, R. D. 16, 20, 137, 147, 180, 259, 260
Hudson, R. A. 17, 18, 19, 22, 23, 25, 33, 37, 67, 97, 100, 107, 109, 180, 220, 226, 258, 260, 264, 265, 267, 268, 246, 247, 257
  text by 246–57
Hurford, J. R. 118
hyperonym 117–18
hyponym/parahyponym/quasi-parahyponym 117, 118
hypotactic relations 112

ideational (meaning/function) 67, 78, 79, 80, 84, 87, 90, 96, 107

identifying (clauses/processes) 136, 137, 151, 170
  identified/identifier 176
Ikegami, Y. 158
illocutionary force 34, 73, 74, 212, 220
  illocutionary force indicating device 222
  illocutionary category 225
  illocutionary type 224
imaginative function 96
[imperative] 213
[imperfective] 178
implicature 219, 235
[implicit] 213
implicit conditional 217
inalienability 241
inception 233
  delayed inception 233
  [inceptive] 236, 242
  inceptive adjunct 230
  inceptive aspect 234
[independent] 202
indefinite vocative 219
[indeterminate] 200
[indicative] 213
indirect directive 215
indirect object 249
inferential functional component 100
inferential meaning 243
information
  focus 139, 166
  [information] 213
  structure 124
  system 196, 197
informational function 97, 100
information-giver 215
informative 223
[inherent] 190
inherent roles 134
[initiating] 213
inner (circumstance) 158
inquiries 131
insert (realization statement) 185
instrument 174
instrumental function 96
intended deduction 215
intensive (process) 137
interactional function 96, 100
interpersonal (function/meaning) 65, 67, 78, 80, 84, 87, 90, 96, 97, 107, 184
interpretation rules 224
[interrogative] 16, 213
  interrogative clause 224
  positive and negative interrogatives 239
[interrupt] 73
intonation
  cohesive function of 122
  high/low rising 217

inverse negatives 233, 234–5
item 132, 256
  and arrangement approach 14
  and paradigm 14
  and process 14
I/T (if/then) notation 21, 22
[iterative]/[non-iterative] 190
[invocation of ability] 217

Jefferson, G. 45, 215
Jesperson, O. 180
Johnson Laird, P. N. 179
Jones, K. 119, 120–1

key 43, 47
Kiparsky, C. 265
Kiparsky, P. 265
Kleene, S. C. 108, 125
Kneale, W. 108, 110, 125, 126
knower
  primary knower 68, 79, 82, 86
  [primary knower] 49
  secondary knower 68, 79, 82, 86
knowledge
  of the universe 168
  of the world 208
Kress, G. 30, 99

Ladefoged, P. 272
Lamb, S. M. 14, 26
language 208
  functions see function and meta-function
  in use 125
Labov, W. 222, 225
Lee, P. 227
Leech, G. N. 180, 187, 217, 233, 235, 239
length (in phonology) 277, 278
lesson (discourse unit) 223
levels of analysis 70
Levinson, S. C. 82, 85
lexicon 208, 252
lexis 184–209
  lexical item 185, 187, 209
  lexical registration 282
  lexical typology 118
  lexical unity 161
linguistic structure 123
[liquid] 203
loaded negative 233
localist hypothesis 158
location 140
  re-expression test for 142
  locational process 136, 137, 139, 155, 172–4
logic 108, 113
logical function 95, 100, 107–26, 184
logical linguistic structure 124
logical subject 95
Lyons, J. 136, 138, 152, 153, 180, 187, 240

MacLure, M. 44
magical function 95
[maintain] 160, 178
main verb 134, 166
  main verb-completing complement 156
[major] 185
Malinowski, B. 94, 95, 208
Mann, W. C. 28, 131, 207
manner 139
markedness 281
marking
  conditional 20, 22, 26
  negative and positive 20, 21, 26
  derivational 22, 28
Martin, J. R. 100, 101, 102, 103, 104, 116, 169, 178, 209, 214, 226, 281
  text by 14–40
Martinet, A. 94
[masculine] 15
[material] 187
material clause/process 130, 153
  material network 141
Mates, B. 125
Mathesius, V. 95
mathetic function 96
matrix clause 264, 265
matter 139
Matthiessen, C. M. I. M. 28, 131, 209
[maximum social distance] 62
McIntosh A. 96
meaning
  formal meaning 26, 37
  immediate meaning 138
  inferred meaning 138
  non-formal meaning 30, 31, 36, 37
  meaning potential 70
medium 140, 187
  medium-oriented 205
mental processes 130, 171
meronym/parameronym/quasi-parameronym 118
meta-function see also functional component 95–104
metalingual functional component 100
metaphor
  complex 188
  grammatical 188
  metaphoric likeness 68
metonymic likeness 68
minimal labelling 134
Mock, C. C. 276
modality 218
  modalized interrogative 219
  modalized sentences 215
  modalized directives 215
mode (of discourse) 96, 121, 122
Mohan, B. 112, 125, 180

Montgomery, M. 47, 48, 49, 69, 213, 223
mood 18, 31, 35–7
Morgan, J. L. 219, 226
morpheme 277
    morpheme structure conditions 280
    morphological function of sounds 284
Morrissey, M. D. 230
mother (dependency) 249, 258
move 42, 83, 223
    answering 66, 75–6, 78
    challenging move structure 77, 78
    comment 42
    evaluate 42, 46, 48
    feedback 42
    follow-up move structure 76
    greeting 73
    initial 73
    initiation 42
    opening move structure 74
    response 42

narrative function 95
nasality 20
natural phonology 281
negation 108, 109
negative orientation 234
network *see* system network
[neutral] 178, 192
new (in information structure) 118
[nominal] 262
    nominal group 151
nomination 75
[non-count] 194
non-primary choice 176
non-verbal action 81, 83
number 15

object 258
object-complement 155
objectivization 188
[offer] 213, 215
Ohmann, R. 222
options 80
    behavioural semantic options 70
    network of options 184
order (realization statement) 185
organization of utterance 95
outclassify (realization statement) 185
overt (participant role) 162, 165

palatal/palatality 275
Palmer, F. R. 220, 259, 282, 283
paradigm 185
    paradigmatic 184
    paradigmaticity 275
parametric phonetics 272

paratactic relations 112
parole 208
part/part relations 251
part/whole relations 251
Partee, B. H. 264
participant roles 130, 134, 135
    in English relational processes 175
particularization 108
particulate structures 98
passive (system) 166
    [passive] 265
passivization 220, 259
passivizability criterion 139, 176
[past] 15
[path] 173
Pearce, R. D. 223
perceptual plausibility 283
perfect (aspect) 230, 241
    [perfective] 178
    perfectiveness 232
peripherality 268
    assignment rules 268
person 15
[personal] 260
Petöfi, J. 64
phase 262
phenomenon 170
phonatory quality 276
phonology 184
    phonological prime 273
    phonological unit 273
phora 116
[phrase] 267
Pike, E. G. 94, 99
Pike, K. L. 94, 98, 99
pleasee 148
    re-expression test for 148
place 139, 140
[planned] 200
plosive phonemes (in English) 20–1
[plural] 15, 194
plurality 110, 283
polarity 110, 111, 114
    polarity information-seeker 217
Poldauf, I. 95
[polite] 73
polysystemicity 256, 279
positive operator (of proposition) 234
positive orientation 235
possessed 142
    re-expression test for possessed 142, 163
[possessive] 30
possessive (clauses) 136, 137, 140, 143, 163–6
possessive process network 144, 164, 165
Postal, P. M. 264, 267, 274
[potential] 190
pragmatic function 95, 96

Prakasam, V. 272, 273, 275, 276, 277, 278, 279, 282, 283, 284, 286
  text by 272–88
predicate 36
  [predicate] 267
  predicate words classification 269
preferential semantics 209
pre-invitation 82
pre-select (realization statement) 185
pre-sequence types 82
[primary knower] 49
procedural felicity conditions 131
process 114, 131, 187
  lexically productive process types 136
  lexically restricted process 152
  process-range 149
process morphology 285
progressive aspect 230, 240
prompt 75
proposition 80, 108
propositional completion 80, 87
prosodic analysis 246
pseudo-cleft transformation 153
purpose 139
purposive role 102

quantity-quality group 151 *see also* adjectival group
quality 139
quality of thing 151
quantifier 108
question
  as situational category 224
  as semantic force marker 221
  polarity question 248
  [question] 213
  WH-question 248
Quillian, M. R. 187
Quine, W. V. 125, 126
Quirk, R. 134, 180, 230, 231, 235

raising 254, 264–5
  subject-to-complement raising 265
  subject-to-subject raising 265
[random] 198
range 149
  range-like constructions 156
rank 16, 26, 66, 89
react 75
reactance 185
reason 139
realization 184
realization rule/statement 16, 80, 132, 185
  for give-type clauses 168
  for inceptive and continuative adverbs 236, 242
  for possessive relational processes 167

recipient 192
recursion 110
  in clause, sentence, group 112
  in word, morpheme 113
  recursive systems 28, 112
redundancy 280
re-entry (to a semantic system) 135, 139, 170
re-expression tests (for roles) 141–2, 143
reference
  referent situation 65, 108
  referent thing 65, 108
  referential expression 110
reflex in form 16
[reflexive]/[non-reflexive] 190
register 96, 103, 121, 133
  field-determined register 102
regulatory function 96
Reiser, H. 64
relation
  hypotactic 112
  paratactic 112
  part/part 251
  part/whole 251
  semantic 112
relational network grammar 26
relational processes 130–81
  relational process network 141
replacement 148, 149
  re-expression test for 150
  representational function 95, 96
request 79
  [request] 217
  semantic request 218
restrictions
  co-occurrence and sequencing 79, 85
resultative (participant role) 153
reversibility criterion 139, 176
rheme, 119
Rochester, S. 116
role 132, 136, 144
  functional role 258
  role (sub-category of circumstance) 139
  role assignment (system) 214
role-switching 55
Rosenbaum, P. S. 259, 264

Sacks, H. 45, 56, 215
Sadock, J. M. 212, 218, 226
Sampson, G. 99
Sandhi 272, 273, 276, 283
Sandulescu, C. 64
Saussure, F. de 132, 178, 185, 208
Schachter, P. 264
Schane, S. 272
Schank, R. 187, 209
Schegloff, E. A. 45, 56, 215

Searle, J. R. 212, 221, 226
[second] 15
segmental condition 274
selection expression 168
semantics 101, 184
semantic distinctiveness 282
semantic feature 132 *see also* feature
semantic inheritance 187, 209
semantic level of language 213
semantico-syntactic level of language 212
semantic relations 112
semantic stratum 184
semantic structure 64
  of sentence 95
sememe 282
semiotics 101
sentence 119
  grammar 218
  phonology 272
sequencing rules 17, 253
Seuren, P. A. M. 109
signification 208
[simple] 190
sincerity condition 221
Sinclair, J. McH. 41–5, 64, 66–9, 70, 73, 74–8,
  86, 89, 119, 120, 180, 222, 223, 262
singularity 110
sister (dependency) 249, 252, 259
  sister dependency rules 17, 253, 270
  sister-sister dependency 259
situation 101
  situational categories 70
Smith, N. 277
social activity 102
social contextual level of language 213
social control strategies 71
social control theory (of Bernstein) 70
social roles 44, 48, 56
socialization 34, 35
socio-semantic model of language 213
socio-semantic approach (to discourse analysis) 64, 69
softener 218
  [softener] 74
[solid] 203
[source] 173
speech act 71, 79, 90
  speech act theory 222
  indirect speech act 212, 218
speech function 35–7, 65, 213
split embedded clause 264
[split-object] 265
split-subject analysis 260
Stanley, R. 280
starter 75, 78
statement (as situational category) 224
states of knowledge 131

stative parameter 273
Stockwell, R. P. 264
straight negative 232
stratification 32, 33
Stratificational grammar/linguistics 14, 26,
  132, 249
stratum 16
Strevens, P. 96
structure
  deep 114
  elements of 17;
  of situation 124
  surface 114
Stubbs, M. 44, 45, 46, 47, 55, 71, 89, 223, 245
stylistic infelicity 194
sub-catogorize (realization statement) 185, 188
  sub-categorization rules 25
sub-classification of items 249
subject 18, 36, 135, 166, 258
  subject-complement 155
suppletion 232
  suppletive relation 231
surface relations 247
Svartvik, J. 259
Sweet, H. 95
syllable 273
synonym 117
syntagm 185
  demarcatively syntagmatic 276
  distributively syntagmatic 276
  syntagmatic 114
  syntagmaticity 276
system 84, 95, 111, 125
  primary systems 136
  system membership 278
systemic functional grammar/model 133, 185,
  209
systemic grammar 132
system network 15, 17, 25, 97, 130–81, 214, 216
  for circumstantial roles of client, pleasee and
    replacement 150
  for deixis 30–1, 37
  for differentiating roles 52
  for inceptive and continuative adverbs 236,
    242
  for locational processes 172
  for relational processes 159, 160, 161
  for threat 34, 72,
  first level networks 37
  illocutionary force network 218
  lexico-grammatical network 184
  mediated network 37
  second level network 37
  semantic network 36, 178
  sociosemantic network 34–5, 64, 65, 72, 74,
    133, 178
systemic path inheritance 187

Taglicht, J. 245
  text by 258–71
tagmemics 249
Taylor, N. M. 111
Telugu 275, 279, 280
tenor (of discourse) 96, 101, 102, 121, 122
  functional tenor 100, 101, 102, 103
  personal tenor 100, 101, 102
tense 15, 28
  secondary tense 111–12
text 89, 96
  analysis, 64
  demarcation 115, 121
  linguistics 114
  structure of 116, 119
  textual cohesion 121
  textual units and classes 120
  textual (meaning/function) 67, 78, 80, 81, 82,
    88, 96, 98, 107–26, 184
  textual linguistic structure 124
  textualness 116
  texture 89, 121
thematic function 97
thematic build up 156
theme 119, 139, 166, 176, 248, 254
thesis time 244
thing 151, 187
[third] 15
threat 74
  network for 34, 72
time 139
  time and time specification 242
Tittensor, D. 113
token 176
topic 90, 254, 258
[total] 30
transaction (as discourse unit) 223
[transaction initial] 73
transformational grammar 249
[transitive] 262
transitivity 31, 134, 185, 248
  entry conditions for 187
  transitivity types 180
Traugott, E. C. 230, 232
truth value 217, 259
turn 81, 90
Turner, G. J. 33, 34, 35, 37, 64, 69, 70, 72, 82,
    86, 87, 88, 112, 125, 133, 180
  text by 64–93
type 188, 189

ultimate client 192
unistructure syntax 256
unit complex 112
[unitary] 192
univariate structure 112
universe of discourse 117
universe of interpretation 110
[unmarked] 194
Ure, J. N. 125
Uren, O. 20

Vachek, J. 95, 282
value 176
Van Dijk, T. E. 115, 117, 119, 120, 121, 122
[vast] 194
velum 273
  velarity 275
[verb-bond] 263
[verb-comp] 262, 268
verb valency 257
verbal group (English) 28, 262
vocal fold vibration frequency 273
voice 20, 139, 166, 185
  non-primary status 176
  voice neutrality 220, 258–71
voice onset 276
volition 220
Von Wright, G. H. 108, 110, 113, 125, 126

Ward, D. 113
Waterhouse, J. 230, 232
whimperative 219, 220
Whorf, B. L. 185, 188, 200, 208
Widdowson, H. 115
Wilks, Y. 209
Wilson, D. 276
Winograd, T. 29
wiring 26–9, 38
  terminal wire 28
Wittgenstein. L. 208
word
  complexes 111
  phonology 272–86
  morphology 112
word and paradigm model 14

Young, D. J. 135–207
  text by 230–45